THE ARCHAEOLOGY OF
MEDIEVAL ENGLAND
AND WALES

THE ARCHAEOLOGY OF
medieval england
and wales

John Steane

THE UNIVERSITY OF GEORGIA PRESS
Athens

CONTENTS

LIST OF FIGURES

LIST OF PLATES

PREFACE

My intentions in writing this book were to examine the kind of evidence which recent developments in archaeology have to offer in furthering the study of medieval English and Welsh history. This evidence has accumulated over the last 25 years during an unprecedentedly extensive burst of archaeological activity. It is of three main kinds: below-ground deposits, above-ground structures and artefacts. During the boom of the late 1960s and 1970s which led to so much central town redevelopment it was the first of these, buried remains, which yielded the most dramatic information. Now that recession has given British archaeologists a breathing space it is being realised that a new look at upstanding remains can yield great profits. The objects too are being submitted to ever more sophisticated study techniques and a comparative approach based on quantified statements is beginning to appear.

The material evidence is, however, only one source for reconstructing the past and many medieval historians would argue that it is not the most valuable or illuminating. There is a danger in their regarding archaeological evidence simply as a source of background or illustrative material used to confirm historical statements which have already been inferred from the documents. This in Sawyer's words reduces archaeology to 'an expensive way of telling us what we know already'. In fact, of course, there are myriad aspects which archaeology can illumine from the pre-literate origins of medieval society, the many gaps in the documentary record and in particular the interests of the non record-making classes.

The structure of this book is to take a series of important themes such as Government,

Religion, the Countryside, and so on, which are then approached in a roughly chronological way. I have included in the Middle Ages everything from the ninth to the mid-sixteenth century, from the Danish invasions to the Reformation. I was brought up on a battered copy of F.P. Barnard's *Companion to English History* (*Middle Ages*) (Oxford, 1902), and much well beaten ground which was traversed then I have not attempted to cover again. For information about heraldry, costume, armour, parish church architecture and coinage I would refer readers to Barnard and to A.L. Pooles' revision: *Medieval England* (Oxford, 1958). My approach is that of the field archaeologist, more concerned with the impact of man on the urban and rural landscape. The thread which runs through the book is a technological one — how structures were built, how objects were made. My own digging experience is limited largely to rural and industrial sites. Inevitably a good number of my examples of field work are drawn from the areas I know best, the central and southern Midlands. However, I have made rapid forays into East Anglia, the north and the west of the country, and rather longer explorations into Wales.

The people who have helped me most can be divided into four groups: my teachers, fellow archaeologists, the librarians and the typists. My allegiance to the subject of history I owe to the genial influence of 'Guts' Gayford (as we used to call him), Senior History Master at Dulwich. This was reinforced by a powerful dose of medievalism at Magdalen from Bruce McFarlane and Karl Leyser. William Hoskins introduced me to the historical evolution of the English landscape. Max Hooper's lectures on hedgerows and Oliver

Rackham's work on woodland made a deep impression on me and I have derived much benefit from the informal gatherings of the Historical Ecology group. An interest in building materials I owe to the geologising of my brother Christopher. Since joining the Oxfordshire Museum Service I have benefited from the friendly encouragement of two directors, Richard Foster and Jim Bateman, and the critical expertise of James Bond, John Rhodes, Ival Hornbrook and Elizabeth Leggatt. My fortnightly discussions with Tom Hassall have been invaluable in providing me with insights into urban archaeology. I am grateful to Philip Page, Richard Chambers, Brian Durham and Maureen Mellor of the Oxford Archaeological Unit for their expenditure of time on my queries. I have also relied heavily on the work of other excavators. Brian Davison of London, Evelyn Baker of Bedford, Brian Dix of Northamptonshire, Martin Petchey, Robert Croft and Paul Woodfield of Buckinghamshire have all put me in touch with developments in their areas. L.S. Colchester has conducted me up the west front and over the high roofs of Wells Cathedral. Among the archaeologists whose books have recently contributed most to my understanding I number Warwick Rodwell, Martin Biddle and Colin Platt. Platt's masterly synthesis of archaeological investigation and social history, *Medieval England* (London, 1978) has been a particular inspiration.

I have visited a number of museums in search of illustrative material and have been made welcome by the staff of the British Museum, the Winchester Research Unit, the Museum of London (Brian Spencer), City of Birmingham (David Symons), Bedford (Penny Spencer), Buckinghamshire (Mike Farley), Northampton (Robert Moore), Ashmolean Museum (Arthur McGregor), Museum of Oxford (Dan Chadwick), Winchester (Elizabeth Lewis), Exeter and Dorchester (Dorset). I acknowledge the courtesy and ready provision of a stream of books and articles from the staff of the libraries of the Ashmolean Museum, the Bodleian and Society of Antiquaries, London.

Cynthia Bradford's photographic talents have enhanced the illustrations. I have received generous help with other illustrations from John Williams, John Hurst, Brian Hindle, Evelyn Baker, Paul Woodfield, Brian Dix, Robert Croft, Laurence Butler, Jonathan Coade, Mrs Beard and Carol Morris. I am grateful to Mike Raines who drew Figures 1.11, 2.6, 4.6 and 4.7. Professor J.K. St Joseph kindly provided comments on his aerial photo, Plate 2.12. I acknowledge the kind permission to visit buildings and property from the Bishop of Winchester, the Bishop of Bath and Wells, and Mr Christie Miller of Clarendon (Wilts.). I am glad to record the ready co-operation of the clerk of works of Salisbury Cathedral, the Bursars of New College, Magdalen College and Lincoln College, Oxford and the Steward of Christ Church College, Oxford who enabled me to visit buildings in their charge.

I am particularly indebted to the learning and infectious enthusiasm of Dr John Blair, Fellow and Tutor in Modern History at the Queens College, Oxford who read through an earlier draft and suggested many improvements. My mother and my wife Nina have saved me from many stylistic infelicities. I acknowledge my daughter Katy's help in compiling the index. The bulk of typing the earlier drafts of the manuscript was undertaken cheerfully by Lisa Toogood, helped in the later stages by Clarissa Pigott and Elsebeth Wulff. One final reason why writing has been a pleasure is the unfailing encouragement and support of the editor, Leslie Alcock.

1

THE ARCHAEOLOGY
OF MEDIEVAL
GOVERNMENT

It might be thought that archaeology, which has been described as 'the study of the physical evidence — structures and artefacts, both visible and buried — of the history of mankind',[1] has little to offer to the study of medieval government. Certainly, far more emphasis has been given in the recent past to the publication, analysis and explanation of the voluminous administrative records of the Middle Ages. In fact, the surviving remains of buildings and objects left by the rulers of medieval England are important evidence in understanding their exercise of power. At the risk of gross simplification of a complex subject, three main power centres of medieval England will be looked at: kings, bishops and boroughs. First, a brief survey will be made of the structural evidence of royal power and the mystique surrounding it: coronations, crown wearings, funerals and tombs. The buildings used for royal residence, administration and protection will be described. Secondly, the architectural expression of episcopal and municipal authority will be reviewed. Thirdly, the archaeology of medieval justice will be considered. Finally, we will look at the artifactual side of medieval government, the crowns, plate, crosiers and seals which gave tangible expression to authority.

1. The Coronation

One of the most graphic scenes in the Bayeux tapestry is the sight of a man climbing onto the roof of Westminster Abbey, intent on placing the weathercock at the highest point. This act symbolised the completion of the rebuilding of the Benedictine abbey by Edward the Confessor. He wore his crown here on Christmas Day, 1065, only a few days before his death. The tapestry shows the funeral cortège wending its way to Westminster where Edward was buried. The Norman Kings, claiming to be the legitimate successors of the Anglo-Saxon dynasty, wished to emphasise these links by being crowned in the abbey. The reputation of the royal church was consolidated in 1181 when Edward the Confessor was canonised. King Henry III (1216-72), who had been crowned in haste at Gloucester on his accession, underwent a second coronation at Westminster 'so strong was the Abbey's claim to authenticate the king's title in this way.'[2] Henry decided to rebuild the choir of the Confessor's church and gave a special prominence, as we shall see, to the provision of a magnificent shrine for his predecessor, the royal saint.[3]

Henry III had exalted ideas of kingship which he was unable to carry out in real life because of baronial opposition and the unstable nature of his own character. The rebuilding of Westminster Abbey enabled him to sublimate these political ambitions in architecture. The resulting building contains a number of exceptional features, parallelled in Louis IX's coronation church at Rheims, which distinguishes it as a place where coronations were carried out. In the first place the main entrance front was not (as now) at the west where King Edward's Norman-style church as yet remained intact, but at the north.[4] Here was the state entrance, on the side nearest to the Palace of Westminster and to Whitehall, the road connecting Westminster to London. The three steeply gabled portals were copied from the main front of Amiens Cathedral.

The second unusual feature is the crossing under the central tower. Here, at the intersection of the two vistas of the church, was a space for setting up the throne for the coronation. It was visible from all parts of the abbey because it was placed high up on a stage covered with tapestry gleaming with cloth of gold. Furthermore, the architecture was adapted for the accommodation of large numbers of spectators. Not only did they fill the ground floor but they were found in their hundreds in the great spaces specially constructed above the arcades in the triforiums.[5]

The long queue of visitors to see the crown jewels in the Tower shows the eternal fascination to the public of the glittering panoply of royalty. Unfortunately the crown jewels used by medieval kings have now disappeared.[6] A number of them were broken up at the time of the Civil War of Cromwell's time when it was thought that the monarchy had been dispensed with forever. A new set, in fact, had to be made for the coronation of Charles II in 1661. The liturgy still used at coronations, however, has hardly changed. At the coronation the new king or queen entered Westminster Abbey preceded by the Great Sword of State and by the Swords of Justice and Mercy. This last had a broken point and perhaps originated as the Sword of Tristan, part of the regalia brought back to England by Matilda, the widow of the Emperor Henry V and King John's grandmother. The robes of the monarch were laid aside for the anointing which was done when the holy oil was applied by the officiating bishop or archbishop to the new sovereign's head, breast and palms. The spoon, which is still used, is the oldest object among the regalia; it dates from the twelfth century. The monarch then donned certain ancient robes and ornaments which were derived from St Edward's body when it was transferred by Henry III to a new and splendid shrine.

He was also crowned with St Edward's crown, 'of gould wyerworke sett with slight stones and two little bells'. This Saxon crown was broken up during the Commonwealth but it was apparently never made into coin, and it is even possible that the new crown made for Charles II after the Restoration was made with the same gold. At any rate, 'St Edward's crown' is the name still given to the coronation crown of the monarchs of England. Medieval kings had more than one crown: Edward II had no less than ten in 1324. One, which Edward I had, 'the golden crown, adorned with divers stones', was notoriously heavy: he remarked humorously that the English crown did not so much 'honour' as 'onerate' the king!

The medieval crown jewels have been replaced. The coronation chair, new-made by Edward I in 1300-1, still stands in St Edward's Chapel, battered by souvenir hunters and defaced by graffiti. It was originally designed to be made of bronze but the king changed his mind and substituted oak planks. These were gorgeously covered with glass mosaic and gold leaf which was impressed into designs of animals, birds and leaves. On the back is the figure of a king, his feet on a lion.[7] The most famous feature lies under the seat. This is a rough block of sandstone with iron staples and rings fitted at each end to allow a carrying pole to be passed through them. This was the stone of Scone on which Scottish kings used to be crowned and which was captured by Edward I in 1296 and brought back as a spoil of war.

2. Royal Tombs

If Westminster Abbey was planned by Henry III to be a scene of crowning triumphs, it was also to become a royal mausoleum. His predecessors, the Angevins, Henry II and Richard I, had been buried deep in Angevin territory at Fontrevault. John, his father, had been interred at Worcester. Henry adopted Edward the Confessor as his patron Saint and caused his relics to be translated into a magnificent shrine in the centre of the rebuilt choir.[8] This was decorated with marble, porphyry and glittering gilt tesserae in writhing columns and had body-sized niches whereby the stream of pilgrims might come into close proximity to the Saint. Nearby, and at the same time, he designed his own tomb. Edward I, his son, commissioned lifesize bronze effigies, the first to be cast on this scale in England, to be placed on the tombs of his father, and his beloved wife, Eleanor of Castile. Just as Henry III had initiated the coronation church of the French king, Louis

IX, so Edward began to copy the idea of filling a church with monuments of his ancestors.[9] In their turn, nearly all his successors on the throne of England, and quite a few of their consorts, chose to be sepultured around his shrine.

The royal tombs enable one to grasp something of the charisma surrounding medieval kingship. Considered as the largest artifacts cast in bronze in England, remaining to us from the Middle Ages, the effigies at Westminster also give an insight into contemporary metallurgical techniques. At the outbreak of World War II the royal effigies were removed from their positions and stored in safety. This occasion provided an opportunity for the study of methods employed in England for casting and gilding on this large scale. The two earliest, Henry III and his daughter-in-law, Queen Eleanor, thought to be the work of William Torel, goldsmith of London, are of unusual weight: their thickness varies from 5 to 10 cm. Torel apparently first modelled the figures in clay or wax and made, in each case, a separate mould for the right hand. The left hand was cast as part of the figure. A mould was then formed over the whole of the rest of the work. The clay model was then turned over and a recess 1.52 m long, 30 cm wide and 10 cm deep was cut to reduce the weight. It is possible that bell founders were called in to advise; the underside of the model was provided with suitable runners and vents and a mould made over it. The casting was done by the *cire perdue* process and the gilding was applied with an amalgam of gold and mercury.

Contrasting with the magnificence of these tombs raised to his father and his wife's memories, Edward I's own tomb is quite plain, of five massive Purbeck marble slabs with a sixteenth century inscription which baldly states in Latin 'Here lies Edward the first, hammer of the Scots ('Malleus Scotorum'), keep the faith' and gives the wrong date, 1308 (it should have been 1307!). Edward's is the only royal grave to have been opened. When this was done in 1774 'The face . . . was of a dark brown or chocolate colour, approaching to black and so were the hands and fingers'. The body was clothed in a rich red silk damask decorated with what sounds like theatrical jewellery, very showy and studded with stones of glass or paste. Over these was a royal mantle of rich crimson satin fastened by a magnificent fibula of metal. The body was measured as being 6 ft 2 in (1.88 m) but it was not deemed appropriate to investigate the limbs, sheathed in cloth of gold so, 'how far the appellation of long shanks, usually given to him was properly applicable cannot be ascertained'.[10]

Within 50 years, the Confessor's Chapel was ringed around with a series of grandiose royal funeral monuments which are today without parallel in Europe. A number of these effigies, it is thought, are accurate portraits of their royal subjects. Eleanor of Castile, for instance, has the high forehead, straight nose and long flowing hair which we can recognise from a picture of her on her seal. The head of the effigy of Edward III shows an uncanny resemblance to his death mask also preserved in the Abbey.[11] Only the mouth has been straightened out; Edward had suffered from a stroke which deprived him of speech at the end of his life.

Technically some improvement is noticeable from the earlier tombs. The thickness of Edward III's effigy has been reduced down to between $\frac{1}{2}$ to $\frac{3}{4}$ in (1.3 to 1.9 cm). The hands were cast separately. The face, hands and large areas of the drapery were carefully chased, filed and scraped. The thickness of the gilding was from five to fifteen thousandths of an inch (0.00508 mm–0.001693 mm).

Edward III's wife, Philippa of Hainault, is shown as 'an unkindly if faithful representation of the heavy body of an old woman in her fifties'.[12] The effigies of Richard II and his wife, Anne of Bohemia, lie side by side next to Edward III's tomb. Unfortunately their tomb has been stripped of many of its attendant angels and weepers, little figures standing in niches mourning the royal pair. Even the arms of the effigies are missing but the draperies which cover the form of the king are richly chased with the king's personal heraldic insignia of the white hart and the broom (the Plantagenet botanical emblem). The haunting face with its narrow lidded eyes and oval face gives some impression of the weakness but at the same time emphasises the artistic sensibility of this ill-fated king.

There is a considerable difference in technical quality between these two effigies. Anne of Bohemia evidently caused the founder great difficulty. He found it necessary to recast a substantial part of the front of the body by running fresh metal into the mould; there were many blow-holes in different parts of the figure necessitating patches where he wished to build up the thickness of the metal. Richard II's effigy on the other hand is an excellent example of skilful casting, with an average thickness of 9.44 mm.

Henry V, the conqueror of France, wished to be buried at the east end of the abbey but there was no room so a stone platform was built to enclose the tomb, and above it was erected a chantry chapel reached by two spiral staircases and covered with tier upon tier of statues.[13] The timber effigy of the king was encased with a suit of silver gilt but, unfortunately, successive robberies have reduced it to a headless trunk of blackened wood which has only recently had a new crowned head and hands made of resin attached to it.

During the Wars of the Roses it is not surprising that there was a break in the succession of royal burials at Westminster. Henry VI certainly wanted to be buried here and had actually marked out a chosen spot, but his unhappy death in the Tower was followed by his burial at Chertsey Abbey and ultimately he found a resting place at St George's Chapel, Windsor. Edward IV was interred at Windsor as well. Henry VII, the victor over Richard III at Bosworth, saw to it that his opponent had an obscure funeral at Leicester but planned a return to Westminster for his own dynasty. He built a special royal chapel at the east end of the Abbey designed to be a witness to the hereditary legitimacy and solid power of the new Tudor monarchy. Here under panelled fan vaulting with its magnificent drooping pendants — supported on serrated transverse arches, below a frieze of angels and walls and windows studded with Tudor badges of rose and portcullis in infinite profusion, lie the great bronze open-work grilles which surround the Tudor tombs.[14] The effigies of Margaret Beaufort (his mother), Henry VII and Elizabeth of York lie on tombs of pure Renaissance design and executed by an Italian, Torrigiani; but the apostles, saints and prophets in stone which are ranged round the chapel are medieval English, and reflect very well the religious beliefs of the chapel's founder. There are even one or two local Breton Saints to whom Henry apparently had appealed, during his years of exile before the battle of Bosworth.

Torrigiani was apparently a highly competent master in metal. Not only are the castings of an average thickness of 1.3 cm or less, the quality of detail is remarkably fine. The sculptor worked on touching up the modelling and sharpening the drawing and correcting the surfaces of the wax model before the metal was cast. Such lifelike and large size effigies were in fact a severe test of skill. The Tudor dynasty was forced to call upon the resources of Renaissance Italy to supply this need.

3. The Palace of Westminster

The principal residence of the kings of England from the reign of Edward the Confessor (1042-66) until that of Henry VIII (1509–47) was at Westminster (Figure 1.1). Here, lapped by the waters of the River Thames, a vital line of communications, and close by the Abbey, there arose a veritable royal suburb. It was linked with London by King Street (now called Whitehall) and Strand, and along these thoroughfares grew up the houses of the nobles and bishops. But, close as it was to London, it was within the jurisdiction of the Abbot of Westminster and outside the control of the mayor and aldermen of the City. To begin with it was simply a royal residence; the permanent treasury, for instance, remained at Winchester. At a time when royal authority was exercised with a minimum use of written record, the seat of government was where the king happened to be. Gradually, however, the king's court gave birth to the various departments of royal government and the Palace of Westminster became a great complex of buildings containing almost every aspect of English government. Today its site is largely occupied by the Houses of Parliament and indeed their official

Figure 1.1: Ground Plan of Royal Palace of Westminster (after Allen Brown *et al.*, 1963)

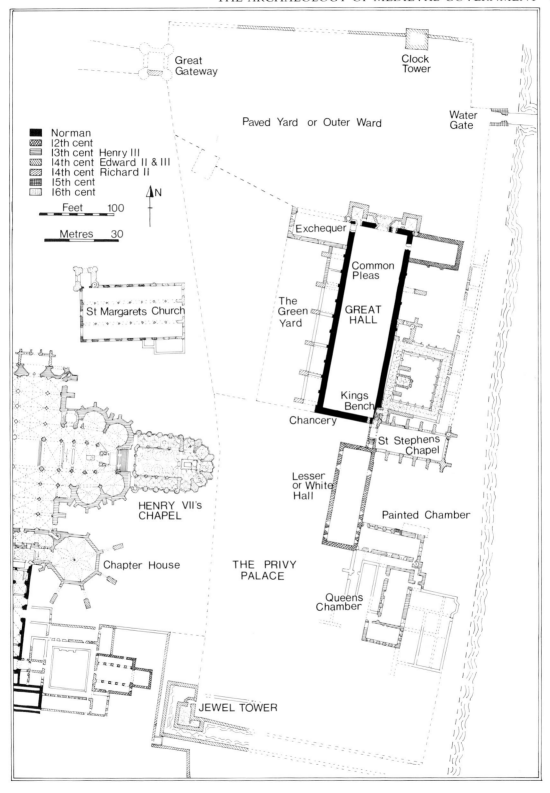

Norman
12th cent
13th cent Henry III
14th cent Edward II & III
14th cent Richard II
15th cent
16th cent

Feet   100

Metres   30

N

name is still the Palace of Westminster.[15] Several disastrous fires in 1298, 1512 and 1834 have destroyed a number of these buildings but much remains, although embedded in later rebuilding, especially Barry's great scheme of the 1850s. Archaeology, combined with a study of the documentary record, building accounts and numerous illustrations made from time to time, enables us to reconstruct substantial parts of the former palace (see Figure 8.5).

The greatest and most famous of these is Westminster Hall, built by King William Rufus 1087-9. The scale of this hall, the largest Norman hall known, is astounding. It measures nearly 73 m × 21 m in area. The Norman walls, in spite of much refacing, can still be traced below the level of the string course. Some of this stonework has been uncovered at the south end of the long east wall and an idea of the richness of the sculptured decoration can be gained from looking at the carved capitals now preserved in the Jewel Tower. It seemed less spacious than its successor because the interior was obstructed by two lines of stone pillars or wooden posts to hold up the roof.

Rufus' hall lasted unchanged until 1394 when Richard II began to rebuild the walls and replace the crude Romanesque openings with traceried windows in the new Perpendicular style. To span the great space he employed the master carpenter, Hugh Herland, to build the largest timber roof in medieval Europe. Six hundred tons of oak are incorporated in two principles of construction, the arch brace and the hammer beams — so-called from the horizontal baulks nearly 60 cm by 90 cm thick and ending in carved angels. The tremendous thrust of this dynamically designed roof was taken by the strong buttresses outside, such a notable part of the scene from Parliament Square.[16]

Within Rufus' hall was the ceremonial centre of the Anglo-Norman kingdom. William I made a practice of holding three great feasts a year at which he wore his crown. He invited his bishops, abbots, earls and barons with their retinues, to these occasions. They spent Whitsuntide at Westminster: then moved to Gloucester at Christmas and to Winchester, the old capital of Wessex and seat of the treasury, for Easter. Westminster Hall

was also sometimes used in the twelfth and thirteenth centuries for meetings of royal councils.

The Exchequer came to be housed in a building adjoining, and by 1178 the hall had become the principal home of the courts of justice. From the fourteenth to the nineteenth century the court of Chancery sat in the south-west corner, King's Bench in the south-east corner, and Common Pleas near the middle of the west wall (see Figure 1.1). Herein were enacted some of the most dramatic events in the history of the medieval kingdom of England. Sir William Wallace, the Scots national hero, was tried here for treason in 1305. Richard II was ceremonially deposed here in 1399. His usurping cousin, Henry IV, held his coronation banquet in the same building. When one walks south across Parliament Square and along St Margaret Street this sense of drama may be lacking but one can sense something of the higgledy piggledy development of the Palace of Westminster. To the north of Westminster Hall is the railed enclosure known as New Palace Yard. Around this courtyard in the Middle Ages clustered the offices of the government servants. Here was the treasury of the English Exchequer, here lawyers congregated. This was the official or public part of the palace. Southwards the modern road, St Margaret Street, cuts across what was the main courtyard of Edward the Confessor's palace. Around Old Palace Yard, as it was called, were the private residences of kings. On the site of Richard I's equestrian statue was the White Hall. Further south lay the Painted Chamber. This was an impressive room decorated in the thirteenth century with six bands of painting including warlike scenes from the Old Testament, the coronation of St Edward the Confessor and 2 m-high figures of the virtues — Truth, Bounty and Meekness — triumphing over the vices. Although these were all destroyed in the fire of 1834 we have a good idea of what they looked like because careful coloured engravings were made by an artist, Charles Stothard.[17]

We have seen that Henry III successfully emulated the examples of Louis IX of France in creating a great coronation church at Westminster. The three Edwards attempted to rival Louis' magnificent royal chapel of St Chapelle by building St Stephen's Chapel in the palace.[18] St Stephen's Chapel was two-storied in design. The servants in the palace used the lower chapel; this still survives as the vaulted undercroft of St Mary's, now a nondenominational chapel for MPs. For the exclusive use of the royal family was the upper part. This, although comparatively small in size, was 50 years in building and a further 20 in furnishing. The progress of the building was an indication of the fluctuating fortunes of the Crown's internal and overseas commitments. When money was not being spent on foreign adventures it could be spent on prestigious buildings. It was also incomparably richly decorated with sculpture, mouldings and paintings; some portions of this painted decoration can be seen in the British Museum. St Stephen's Chapel, in fact, was a key building in the development of the Perpendicular style. It became a college in 1348, and cloisters and houses were built for its dean, 12 canons and 13 vicars. When the college was dissolved in 1548, the chapel became the meeting place for the House of Commons. This was the building in which Chatham, Burke and Fox held Members of Parliament under the spell of their oratory. Gradually the medieval features were obliterated or obscured as panelling and galleries were inserted. Finally, the chapel was reduced to ruins by the fire of 1834. We can, however, reconstruct its appearance both before and after by studying the valuable drawings made under great difficulty by John Carter and Frederick Mackenzie.

The surviving fragment of the Palace of Westminster which is perhaps least changed is the little fourteenth-century Jewel Tower which stands in the shadow of the Victoria Tower. Since Edward III did not wish to encroach on his own garden he built on land seized from the monks of Westminster. It was protected from fire and burglary by a moat. The monks recorded delightedly that William de Husseborne, the Keeper of the Privy Palace, died eating a pike caught in the forbidden waters of the moat! In the L-shaped tower were stored the king's own valuables as distinct from the coronation regalia and the exchequer treasure. These included rich apparel, plate and jewels and were known as the royal 'wardrobe'. The Jewel Tower went on serving an important function in the eighteenth century, when it was used as a repository for the records of Parliament. While it was being restored recently, excavation revealed that the battered ashlar face of the structure was supported on an oak wall plate and elm piles.[19] The piles can be seen inside the building which has now become a museum.

4. *The Exchequer*

When William the Conqueror took over the old English state he found it had quite an effective financial system. His revenue was derived in the main from Crown lands, customary payments from the shires and boroughs and the profits of justice. In the eleventh century the treasury had been fixed at Winchester, the ancient capital of the kingdom of Wessex. As far as ready money was concerned, however, Edward the Confessor had kept it in a box under his bed! The officials who administered the finances of the kingdom followed the king around on his travels. At least as early as 1110, the sheriffs, the royal officials in every shire, were attending twice yearly at an office already known as the Exchequer to render their accounts to the king's ministers of money previously paid to the treasury. From an account written by the author of a book known as *The Dialogue of the Exchequer* we know that these proceedings were taking place in buildings on the east side of the Palace of Westminster. It was in the Lower Exchequer or Receipt that the money was received, weighed and put away in sealed chests. In the Upper or Greater Exchequer the accounts were gone through on the chequered table cloth (where calculations similar to those performed on an abacus were made).

It was perfectly possible for the officials to continue to follow the king round on his itineraries but, from Henry III's time, it does seem that the Exchequer was the first department of government to detach itself from the ever-moving court. By 1244 it came to occupy the site at the north end of the west side of Westminster Hall, a site it was to retain until the reign of George IV. Archaeology has revealed the foundations of the Receipt Building. When they were exposed in 1913 their architectural characteristics showed that the building was originally constructed in the twelfth century.[20]

Tangible remains of these early financial transactions have also survived in the form of exchequer tallies.[21] These were strips of notched hazelwood issued by the Exchequer as receipts for payments made to the king: they were also preserved as records of loans and similar transactions. The sum of money was marked in a series of notches along the stick which was then split lengthwise. The creditor retained one half and the debtor the other. When the money was due for payment the halves were put together; in this way it could be proved that neither record had been tampered with. A hoard of several hundred of these tallies, dating from the thirteenth century, was found in repairs to the Chapel of the Pyx at Westminster Abbey.

This vaulted Norman undercroft next to the chapter house was used by early medieval kings as one of their store places for coin, plate and jewels. Here was kept the pyx or box containing specimens of the current coinage in gold and silver which were periodically tested by comparison with certain standard trial pieces of gold and silver. Despite the fact that its immensely thick walls and low vault give the impression of the strength of bank vaults, there was a celebrated burglary there in 1303 which involved a bankrupt known as Robert de Pudlicote. Apparently the whole community of 40 monks was under suspicion.

Archaeology provides vivid evidence for the steps taken against the miscreants. The approach to the Pyx Chamber on the northern side was walled off and the area of the treasury was thus reduced by one-third. Nailed to the inside and outside of the door by which this passage was entered have been found the remains of the skin of a fair-haired, ruddy-complexioned man. The same grim lining was fastened to the sacristy door in the south transept. A more important result was that the king decided to shift his storehouse valuables to the safer enclosure of the Tower.[22]

5. The Tower of London

The Tower of London, to a greater degree than the buildings we have been discussing at Westminster, still has the capacity for recreating in the imagination the reality of power which medieval kings exercised.[23] It was first and foremost a royal stronghold, built on the eastern edge of the city deliberately to overawe the turbulent Londoners. Not surprisingly it was continually adapted and its defences brought up to date according to latest military thinking throughout the Middle Ages. Like many other castles it was meant to house as well as to protect its lord. The Tower surrounded a royal palace and centre of administration. It provided a safe repository for bullion, jewels and records; within its cells state prisoners were accommodated. Coins were minted here, and in the Later Middle Ages it became an arsenal for war supplies. The core of medieval buildings which performed these functions has been somewhat masked until recently by continuing additions and sweeping restorations particularly in the mid-Victorian period. Archaeological excavation which began just before World War II has been able to give valuable insights as to how the Tower contributed to the power of medieval kingship.

In Tudor times it was commonly thought that the Tower had originated with the Romans and the White Tower was called 'Caesar's Tower'. It was in fact built by William the Conqueror together with two other castles, one to become Baynard's Castle close to the site of Blackfriars station and the other, 'Montfichet Castle' to the north. All three were 'strongholds made against the fickleness of the vast and fierce populace'. William chose the site for his hastily-built campaign fort where Roman walls gave protection on two sides; the Normans actually repaired the Roman wall on the river front. To begin with a ditch was dug protecting the fortress from the west and enclosing an area 107 m by 46 m.[24] It was only in 1078 that work was begun on the stone great tower, later to be called the White Tower. In plan it was evidently designed to be a fortified palace rather than a residential fortress. The fortified palaces of France and Germany in the ninth and tenth centuries had hall, chambers and chapel as separate buildings arranged around a courtyard. In the Tower these are compressed vertically into one structure for greater security. The normal rectangular plan of the keep was modified at the Tower (and at Colchester) by the addition of semicircular-ended chapels which project from the end walls. Moreover, despite the immense thickness of the walls, 4.6 m thick at the base, and 3.4 m at the top, they are pierced with sizeable windows. These were admittedly enlarged by Sir Christopher Wren. The main materials were Kentish ragstone shipped up the River Thames and, in addition, some stone was brought from Caen in Normandy. A few other Norman details remain, two fireplaces are inserted in the thickness of the walls of the entrance floor and are on the upper floor. Garderobes or lavatories are sited next to the staircase walls.

The arrangement of living space within the walls of the White Tower was of a basement under two residential floors, not three as now; the third and topmost was an insertion and was originally only the second stage of the second floor. The basement had two store-rooms; one with a well 12 m deep. The entrance or first floor was presumably occupied by the constable and other officers of the garrison. The hall was used as a great room for meals and also as sleeping quarters for the servants. Above, the second floor contained the principal royal residential suite. Here was 'the inner sanctum, the seat of majesty, the *arx palatina* of William fitz Stephens' phrase'.[25] It alone has access to the austere splendour of St John's chapel. Such a second-floor hall, provided with the additional light and air of a mural gallery, doubtless influenced the builders of twelfth-century tower-keeps such as Castle Hedingham, Dover and Rochester.

The accommodation, despite its ingenuity of plan layout, proved too cramped and spartan and few occasions of royal residence at the Tower were recorded for the next hundred years. Repairs were carried out in Henry II's time to the White Tower and to 'the king's houses in the bailey', so presumably these had replaced the royal apartments in the upper part of the White Tower. Steps were now taken to

bring the fortress up to date. At the end of the twelfth century, while Richard I was away on crusade, William Longchamp, Bishop of Ely and Justiciar, strengthened the Tower by extending the bailey to the west and by encircling it with a curtain wall flanked by towers at each corner. One of these towers, the so-called Bell-Tower, remains of this work. Excavations at its foot have revealed the plinth of the polygonal tower built about 1190; its faceted sides were more effective at removing blind spots from the defenders' point of view and provided a curved surface which could deflect missiles.[26] It also formed part of the original river front and reminds us that not very effective measures were taken to provide the tower at this time with a wet moat.

During the reign of Henry III (1216-72) the Tower was vastly strengthened by the completion of the circuit of walls and eight new towers, surrounded by a wide wet moat kept permanently under water by the use of sluice gates. One of these towers, the Wakefield Tower, was the largest mural tower in the castle and it has recently been restored after archaeological excavation both inside and out (Figure 1.2). Several metres of the infilling were removed from the base and its full height has been exposed. It served as a guard chamber and its arrow loops commanded the river approach. The clearance of the upper chamber revealed the presence of the slots of the thirteenth-century floor beams. These radiated out to support the circular floor and have been restored. The great chamber was heated by a large hooded fireplace and near it, and facing the lancet windows, was a recess where it was likely that the royal chair of estate was placed.

It seems that under Henry III and Edward I the palace within the castle of the Tower equalled in splendour the royal residences of Windsor and Winchester. Henry III lavishly rebuilt and redecorated the great hall which lay between the Wakefield and Lanthorn Towers. Archaeological excavation has discovered the footings of the west wall of the great hall and it can be assumed that this would have been aisled with stone columns, lit by tall windows and covered by a steeply pitched roof. The great hall at Winchester Castle was rebuilt for Henry III at the same time and no doubt on similar lines. We also know that the king's

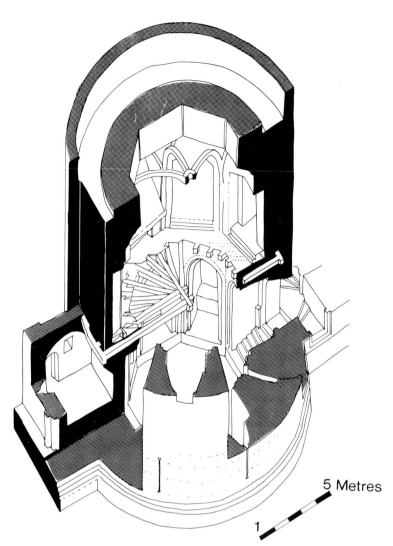

Figure 1.2: Wakefield Tower, Tower of London (after Hammond, 1978)

5 Metres

chamber and the queen's chamber were rebuilt; walls were whitewashed inside and out and five shiploads of Purbeck marble from Dorset were brought in to decorate the interiors. A final touch was provided by the art-loving king, Henry III; he ordered the outside of the tower itself to be whitewashed and drainpipes were led down to the ground to avoid the walls being stained by water running off the roof.

Edward I, a great warrior who had first-hand experience of the latest developments in war and fortification in the continent and Holy Land, next made radical alterations to the Tower. He provided the whole circuit of walls with a second lower outer curtain to give the castle a double defence. This enabled soldiers stationed on the inner one to shoot over defenders on the outer walls. Also if the outer wall fell besiegers would still have an even loftier barrier facing them. On the river side, Henry III's watergate had been on the site of the Wakefield Tower. Edward I, probably copying from the King of France's palace at the Louvre, built out a new entrance, St Thomas' Tower. This had a great arched gate opening onto the water (later known as Traitor's Gate) and over it were palatial royal apartments. Finally he constructed an ingenious and complex principal landward entrance, consisting of three double gates with drawbridges and portcullises connected by causeways. The outermost of these, the Lion gate, has disappeared but the causeway, joining the gate and the Barbican, has been exposed including the drawbridge pit. This causeway which runs parallel to the main walls was exposed to flanking fire from the battlements. At the barbican the entrance causeway makes a right-angled turn before going through two sets of twin gate-towers, each with its drawbridge pit. It is not surprising that with such developments costing within ten years twice what Henry III had spent in 50 years, Edward I felt able to challenge the traditional liberties of the Londoners.

The Tower seems to have been used as a state prison even before any record exists of its being employed as a royal residence. The great enlargement during the reigns of Henry II and Edward I made it possible to imprison large numbers of the captured Welsh and Scots nobility. In Edward I's reign as many as 600 Jews were thrown into the sub-crypt of the White Tower. The advantages of the Tower as a state prison were, first, its situation. High-ranking prisoners were frequently tried at Westminster and brought to the Tower by river; they could easily be interrogated by government officials because of its proximity to the centre of government. Secondly, there was plenty of space for confining prisoners, either individually or in batches in the 20 or so towers and gatehouses. Finally, the Tower was (often mistakenly) thought to be secure; in fact prisoners quite often communicated with their friends and escapes were not unknown. The evil reputation of the Tower as having a warren of secret dungeons beneath it is largely mythical. One only survives and has been recently restored — it is a windowless niche leading off the crypt of the chapel of St John.

Since Edward I's reign the Crown increasingly used the Tower as a centre of administration. It became one of the major royal treasuries and here was a safe repository for jewels and plate as well as legal and financial records. Here also Edward I established what became the largest mint in the country and the only one where gold was coined. To begin with the mint was in the barbican, the Lion Tower, but soon it was housed in a building in the western outer ward which it occupied until 1811. The place is still called 'Mint Street'.

During the reign of Edward III (1327-77) England became increasingly enmeshed in wars with France. Enormous quantities of war supplies were brought from every county and stored in the Tower. The devastating firepower of the English archers which secured such impressive victories over the French at Crecy and Poitiers was made possible by the huge quantities of bow staves and arrows collected here. The Tower, moreover, specialised in the manufacture of siege engines and the earliest guns issued to English soldiers.

6. The Rural Palaces and Houses of the English Medieval Kings

The Norman and Angevin kings were constantly on the move, riding from one manor to another, crossing the Channel frequently, visiting every corner of their widespread lands, in order to satisfy the demands of government, to supply the needs of a voracious court, or to indulge in the pleasure of the chase. We have already noticed that the ceremonial occasions, when they appeared in state surrounded by their barons, required the use of three great halls — at Westminster, Gloucester and Winchester. Their less formal needs were satisfied by accommodation provided in castles and hunting lodges. Royal itineraries can be followed by examining the charters which kings issued as they went round the country.

Most of these royal residences were only slightly fortified and of a somewhat improvised character (Plate 1.1). Their geographical distribution is revealing: they stood in good hunting country and in the twelfth-thirteenth centuries are found in a band stretching from Yorkshire to Somerset, from Essex to the New Forest wherever there were large areas of royal forest. The hunting lodge built by Richard I at Kinver in Staffordshire may be

Plate 1.1: Grove Priory, Bedfordshire. An alien priory of Fontrevault (Normandy) used by the Crown as a royal residence during the thirteenth and fourteenth centuries. The large rectangular building in the centre is the chapel. To the right is a vestibule flanked by porch and vestry. On the far right is the hall. Excavations began in 1973 (Photo: Bedfordshire County Council)

Figure 1.3: Ground Plan of Royal Hunting Lodge, Writtle, Essex (after Allen Brown *et al.*, 1963)

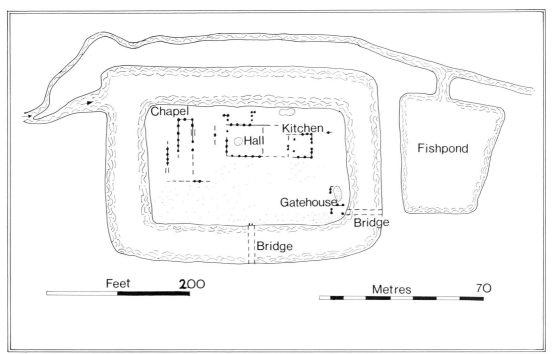

regarded as typical of the smaller royal houses: from exchequer accounts it appears to have consisted of a hall with adjacent offices (buttery and pantry), a kitchen, a chamber and a gaol for the imprisonment of forest offenders. It was surrounded by a palisade and entered through a gateway defended by a brattice.* Carp and bream were provided from

* A temporary wooden palisade or tower, used in sieges.

a fishpond. At Writtle in Essex the layout of King John's hunting lodge has been recovered by excavation (Figure 1.3). A rudimentary defence was provided by an enclosing ditch which would have discouraged wild animals and vagrants, and controlled entry and exit by two bridges. It would have also provided upcast to make up the levels of the site and would have helped to confine the course of the stream, and provide a source of water to the fishponds. The main buildings at Writtle were one range of chapel, hall and kitchen built of timber, cob and thatch, occupying just under one half of the enclosed area. The rest was a large courtyard approached from either of two bridges. Vivid evidence for the documented visits of Edward I in the period 1277-1305 is found by the presence of French polychrome wares.

In addition, the Angevin kings had three residences which we can describe as palatial but the royal records more accurately refer to them in the plural 'domus regis' — the houses of the king — which brings out their rather incoherent planning resulting from the medieval habit of adding one apartment to another.

None of these early medieval palaces has survived in anything like its original form. Westminster was almost completely reconstructed as it became the seat of government in the Later Middle Ages. Woodstock survived as a picturesque congery of buildings into the eighteenth century when it was demolished at the order of the Duchess of Marlborough. Clarendon was never built over and excavations in the 1930s, though in some ways not undertaken under ideal conditions, have revealed a great deal.[27]

Clarendon gave its name to a forest of considerable size which lies immediately to the east of Salisbury. Its attraction to the Angevin kings is doubtless connected with its proximity to good hunting country and it was near Winchester, the ancient capital of Wessex. Henry II was perhaps the last king of England who thought of Winchester as his chief town. He greatly enlarged and embellished the palace and his expenditure for work at Clarendon reached its climax of £268 17s 9d in 1176-7. Henry III continued to decorate and build; the Liberate Rolls are full of detailed instructions,

involving paintings, sculptures, stained glass, metalwork and tiles.[28] It seems, however, that the roofs of the buildings were ruinous at the beginning of Edward I's reign and many repairs had to be carried out. Edward III continued to extend and rebuild; the great hall, gates, well and park all received attention. The palace went out of favour during the Tudor period and began to be used as a quarry like nearby Stonehenge and Avebury. William Stukeley visited the site of the palace in 1723 and described it: 'Part of the building is still left, tho they have been pulling it down many years. Tis chiefly of flint and was a large place upon the side of a hill, but no way fortifyd.'

The remains of the palace can still be traced along a thickly wooded scarp 3.2 km east of Salisbury. Among creepers and hazel coppice stand sizeable chunks of flint walls; pier bases mark the floors of halls; heaps of broken green glazed tiles show that they once glowed with colour. A flight of stairs in ashlar lead down into the cavernous wine cellar.

The Palace at Clarendon was not systematically planned (Figure 1.4). The nucleus consisted of a great hall, 25.3 m × 15.5 m, with two arcades of four bays, which was surrounded by kitchens and other offices and stood on the edge of a steep northerly slope with a large courtyard to the south. The great hall was entered by a porch erected in 1244 and three doorways in the screens led into butteries and a cloister round which there were two kitchens. One was for royal use and one for normal domestic use. Such a separation of food processing activities is characteristic of hierarchically-conscious medieval society. It is found in greater monasteries where the abbot's food was prepared in a different kitchen to that of the monks. Further to the east were large suites of rooms, often independent structures, but joined together by long pentices.★ They were laid out round gardens or grass plots. Here were the kings' and queens' separate accommodation. The walls of Clarendon Palace were built of flint with ashlar quoins; tiles were used in profusion often in herringbone fashion. Thick plaster covered them and the external faces were whitewashed. The roofs were apparently covered with shingles

★ A covered walk connecting buildings.

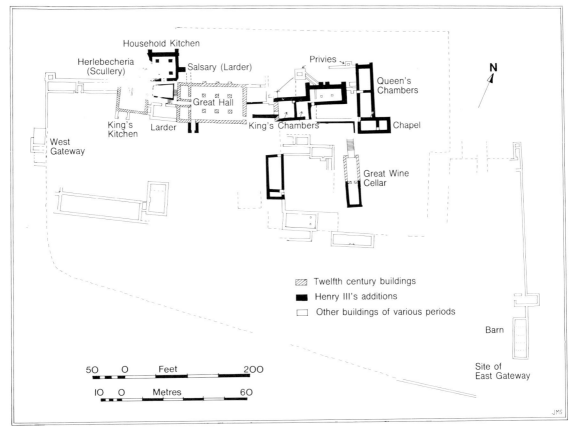

Figure 1.4: Ground Plan of Royal Palace, Clarendon, Wiltshire (after Allen Brown *et al.*, 1963)

which decayed rapidly, bringing multiple problems of maintenance, but they were capped with serrated ridgetiles. From the architectural fragments which have been picked up it appears that there was rich sculptured decoration (Figure 1.5). Particular care was lavished by Henry III on the painted decoration. The sheriff was commanded (32nd year of Henry III) 'to make a new mantel before the chimney in the king's chamber . . . and cause to be painted the wheel of Fortune and Jesse and to cover the king's pictures in the same chamber with canvas lest they should be injured'. Further 'we command you to wain-scot our chamber under our chapel and remove the wall which is across that chamber and to cause the history of Antioch and the combat of King Richard to be painted in the same chamber and to paint that wainscot of a green colour with golden stars'. When Professor Borenius was excavating in the

1930s his workmen picked up a number of little lead stars and crescents which were doubtless part of one of these rich decorative schemes (Figure 1.5).

Everything suggests that in the thirteenth century Clarendon was one of the finest of the king's country houses and the fragments preserved in the Salisbury Museum still bear witness to its vanished glories.

7. *Episcopal Palaces*

Medieval kings were conscious of the far-reaching importance of the church in every aspect of the life of their kingdom. Strong rulers like William I and Henry II were determined to control it through their choice of archbishops, bishops and abbots. The king's right-hand advisers were the Archbishops of Canterbury and York: a man such as Lanfranc

Figure 1.5: Clarendon Palace, Wiltshire. Architectural fragments in Salisbury Museum: carved head of a young man, lead ornaments, tiles

or Stephen Langton had many of the powers of a modern Prime Minister. The centre and fount of authority within each diocese was the bishop. He was pastor, judge and disciplinarian of his flock but he was also a great landowner and feudal lord owing counsel to the King and performing administrative duties, such as collecting taxes and carrying out the law. Such an energetic programme required the bishop to travel perpetually through his diocese, visiting one or another of his estates, just as the king moved through his kingdom. Inevitably archbishops and bishops needed buildings located at strategic places or on their estates throughout their sees. Hence arose episcopal palaces, manor houses and castles.

This development can be followed in the diocese of Winchester. It was one of the wealthiest sees of medieval England, centred on the ancient capital of the Anglo-Saxon kingdom of Wessex and covering the counties of Hampshire and Surrey. The twelfth-century bishops planted a network of palaces and castles which included a town house at Southwark on the south bank of the Thames

Plate 1.2: Bishops Waltham, Hampshire. The palace of the bishops of Winchester was begun *c.* 1135 by Henry de Blois, brother of King Stephen. The castle-like palace was dismantled by Henry II on restoring order after Stephen's 'anarchy'. It was rebuilt on a grand and spacious scale in the late Norman period, much of the west and south ranges remaining, including a massive corner tower (in the centre of the aerial photo). Extensive remodelling took place in the fifteenth century under Bishop William of Wykeham, Cardinal Beaufort and Bishop Langton. The palace was surrounded by a moat and this in turn was only part of a vast quadrilateral earthwork which spreads far beyond the ruins. The town developed alongside the palace with a grid-like plan (Photo: Cambridge University Committee for Aerial Photography, taken 6.7.72)

used when they were in London. Bishop Henry de Blois (1129-71) added or reconstructed six more.[29] He was one of the greatest magnates of the age; the grandson of the Conqueror, son of the Count of Blois and Chartres and brother to Stephen, King of England and Theobald IV, Count of Blois. He was a man possessing supreme administrative skills and, in addition, was a patron of letters and the arts of jewellery, illumination, enamelling and goldwork. He was prodigiously wealthy, receiving the combined revenues of the see of Winchester and Glastonbury, one of the richest abbacies, a total of about 40 manors. With these resources he was able to undertake a major building programme; he rebuilt the abbot's quarters at Glastonbury; he erected three castles in Wiltshire and Hampshire where most of his estates lay, as well as two more on outlying manors at Taunton in the west and Farnham in the east.

The most impressive archaeological remains of Bishop Henry's career, however, were found by Biddle's excavations at the episcopal palace and castle at Wolvesey (Figure 1.6). This stands in the south-east quarter of Winchester within the walls of the Roman and medieval city, a fact of interest because there is little doubt that the diocesan organisation of the medieval church stemmed from Roman administrative traditions. Biddle's excavations revealed that during the early twelfth century the Norman palace consisted of two isolated blocks facing each other across an open courtyard. The earlier of the two the 'west hall' was probably built *c.* 1110 by Bishop Walter Giffard and was a self-contained residence containing one of the largest Norman halls ever built. It was 53 m in length with the main block 26 m wide and a cross-block 11 m in width and 44.5 m long. The T-shaped plan is paralleled by the eleventh-century *'Palatium Tau'* of the archbishops' palace at Reims. Across the courtyard, Bishop Henry de Blois constructed an 'east hall' in superb ashlar

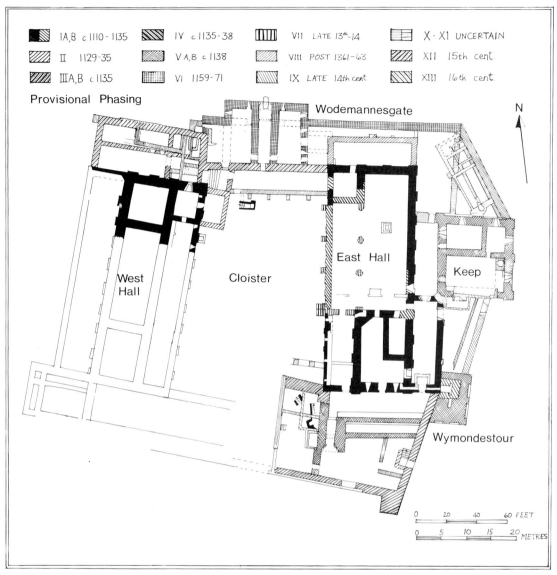

Figure 1.6: Ground Plan of Bishop's Palace, Wolvesey, Winchester (after Biddle, 1971 and Biddle, 1975)

masonry. This consisted of a hall and principal chambers towering above an aisle which ran the whole length on the west and a shorter aisle on the south-east. It seems likely that the 'west hall' formed the bishop's private apartments throughout the rest of the Middle Ages and that the addition of Bishop Henry was the great hall of the palace, perhaps a hall of audience. The uncertain security of Stephen's reign doubtless accounts for the attempts at fortifying Wolvesey Castle, which included

furnishing it with a keep with rather thin walls (subsequently used as the palace kitchen), a strong curtain wall and two turreted gateways. Defence seems to have been the paramount consideration at one of the bishop's other castles at Farnham. Here a massive tower with a deep well was buried in an earthen motte and probably served as the foundation for an elaborate timber superstructure. Accommodation for the Bishop's retinue was provided in a great timber-aisled hall of which one pillar,

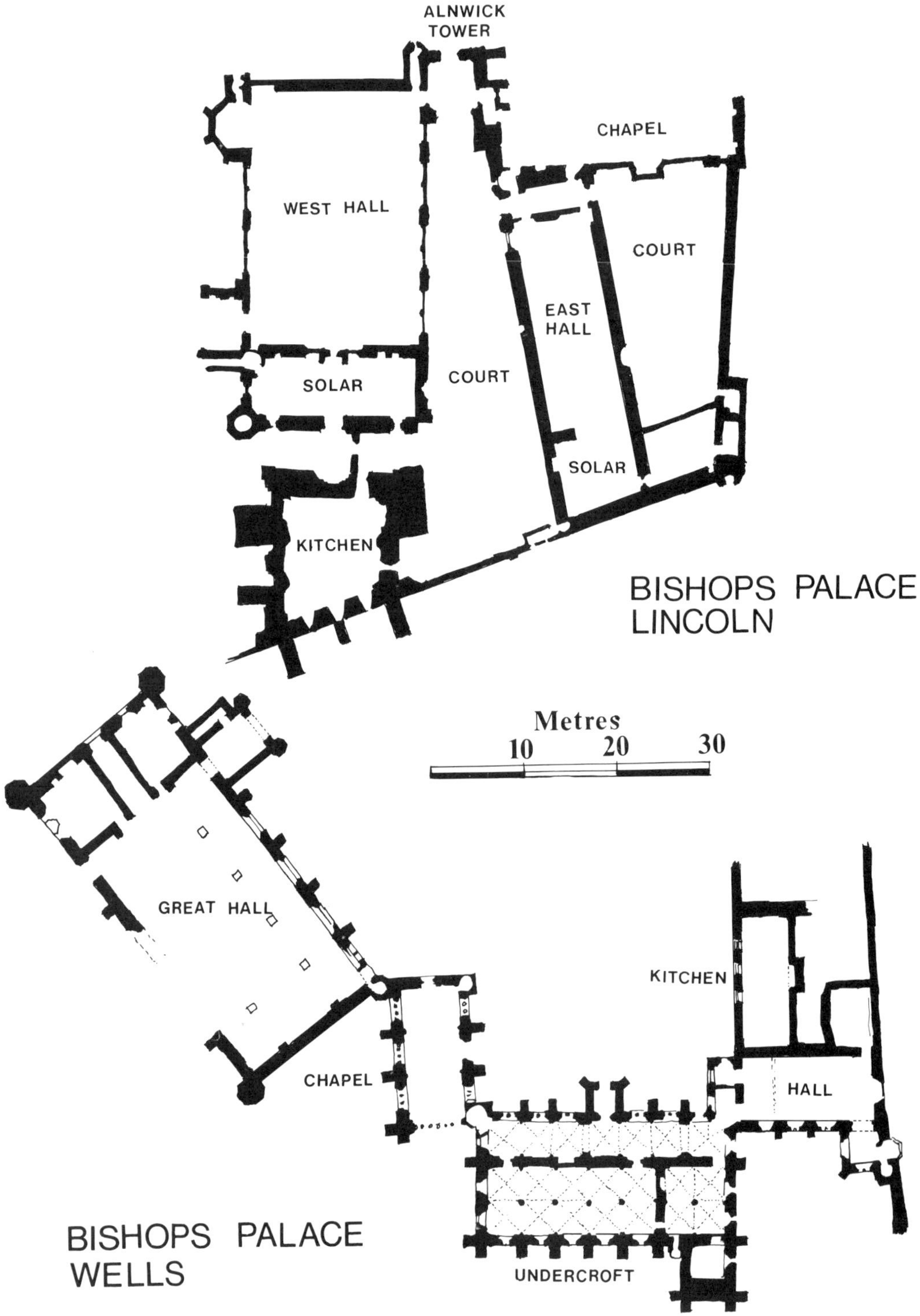

Figure 1.7: Ground Plans of Bishop's Palaces at Lincoln (after Chapman *et al.*, 1975) and Wells (after Wood, 1968)

with a scalloped capital, remains.[30]

A somewhat similar process can be followed if we turn northwards to the diocese of Lincoln.[31] The see was a Norman creation since the cathedral had originally been at Dorchester-on-Thames. Bishop Remigius, one of William I's nominees, founded a new cathedral on the top of the ridge overlooking the River Witham within the circuit of the Roman fortress. Security and once again the Roman administrative connection obviously counted for a good deal. Robert Bloet, the second Norman bishop, was licensed by Henry I to make a gate in the Bail and Bishop Alexander was granted 'the *Porta* of Eastgate with all the lands that are beyond it, for his dwelling'. Robert de Chesney probably laid the foundations of a palace here between 1155-68. He was allowed to perforate the wall of the Bail 'for his entrance and exit, towards the church and so to build that his buildings might extend from one wall to the other'.

The plan of the Bishop's Palace at Lincoln (Figure 1.7) illustrates very well the three prime functions of an episcopal palace: the provision of a large meeting place, the hall, for ceremonial occasions; the addition of a chapel where the spiritual life of the bishop could be conducted amidst suitable pomp; and, thirdly, the private apartments, sufficiently stately for the bishop and his retinue.[32] We have noticed that there were two halls at Wolvesey; there were also two at Lincoln, an east hall built by Bishop de Chesney and a west hall built by St Hugh, bishop 1185-1200. This latter was a four bay aisled ground-floor hall designed in the grand manner with marble-shafted columns and windows entered on the south-west through a two-storeyed vaulted porch. At the southern end is a chamber-block with two ground-floor rooms separated by a central passage connecting the hall to the kitchen. Above was a large and imposing chamber heated by a fire in the gable end and with the additional amenity of a garderobe in the south-eastern tower. These were evidently the bishop's private apartments and a certain amount of seclusion was possible. They overlook a courtyard which has recently been excavated, producing interesting bone and ceramic evidence of the high standard of living of the medieval bishops of Lincoln. Finally, a

new chapel was added by Bishop Alnwick (1436-49) and he also linked the east and west halls with an inner entrance tower.

The enormous see of Lincoln stretched from the Humber to the Thames. It was divided by Remigius into seven archdeaconries each corresponding roughly to the shire which composed it. Another archdeaconry, that of 'Lindsey', was founded in the twelfth century, centred on Stow. We have noticed how the bishops of Winchester built a network of castles and palaces from which they could control and administer their see. The bishops of Lincoln similarly took steps to safeguard their interests. When the last eastward extension of the Cathedral broke through the city wall the authorities obtained from the Crown the right to enclose and crenellate their whole area, in effect creating a city within a city. Castles were also built by Bishop Alexander (1123-47) at strategic points at Sleaford (Lincs.), Newark (Notts.) and Banbury (Oxon.). In the Later Middle Ages comfortable semi-fortified houses took the place of the castles. A fine palace with a great tower of brick was built at Buckden (Hunts.) and the late medieval bishops preferred to reside here rather than in the out-of-date and cramped quarters of the old palace at Lincoln.[33] A splendid fragment of another palace of the bishops of Lincoln has recently been restored by the Department of the Environment at Lyddington (Leics.) (Figure 1.8).[34]

When we turn south-westwards to look at the Bishops' Palace, Wells (Somerset),[35] we meet with some remarkably similar features to the palace at Lincoln though on an even more magnificent scale (Plates 1.3, 1.4, Figure 1.7). In the first place there is the same hint that times were becoming more violent in the fourteenth century; the palace is surrounded by a moat and a curtain wall with bastions, the work of Bishop Ralph of Shrewsbury (1329-63). Inside there is a splendid pair of halls separated by about 50 years. Bishop Jocelyn's building of *c.* 1230-40 has a vaulted cellar which supports a first-floor hall, 21 m × 8.5 m with a smaller chamber to the north flanked by a garderobe giving it an L-shaped plan. Bishop Burnell's hall-block was much larger, with a ground-floor hall 35 m × 18 m aisled in five bays. There is a two-storeyed chamber-block

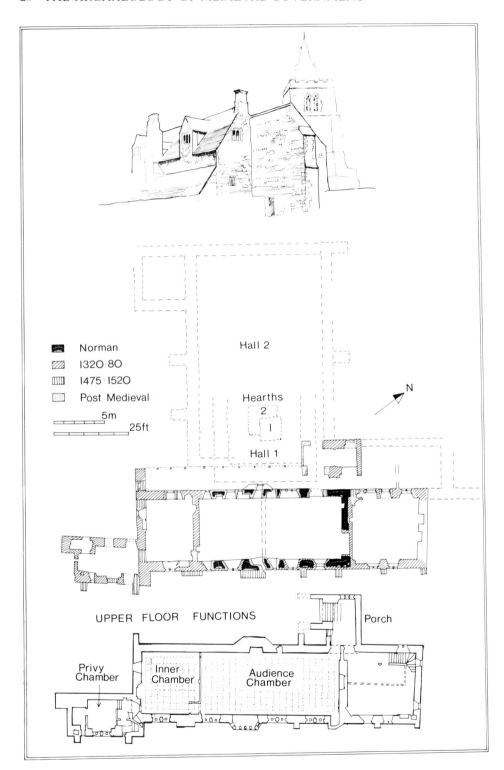

Figure 1.8: Ground Plan of Bishop's Palace at Lyddington, Leicestershire (after Woodfield and Woodfield)

Plates 1.3/1.4: Wells, Somerset. The Bishop's Palace, moated and walled by the mid-fourteenth century, had two halls, those of Bishop Jocelyn *c.* 1230 (Plate 1.3, above) and Bishop Burnell *c.* 1280-90 (Plate 1.4, below). The latter was 35 m long and nearly 18.3 m wide. It contains one of the earliest examples of what became the standard layout: porch, screens and passage leading into the kitchen. We face the kitchens; fireplaces remain in gable-end. Fine room above (Photos: J.M. Steane)

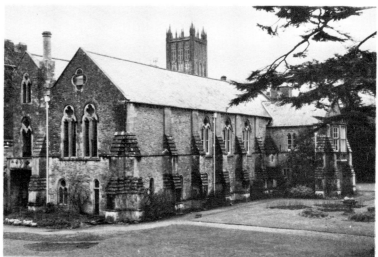

of the same width at the west end. It seems likely that these rooms were used for guests if the bishops continued to use the earlier apartments reached through the chapel at the other end.

Perhaps the finest remains of a medieval bishop's palace and the city surrounding it can be seen at St David's (Pembrokeshire).[36] Here the cathedral, bishop's palace and medieval canons' houses all stood within a walled enclosure referred to as the new close (*novam clausam*) in a document of 1334. The most impressive entrance is from the city through a great gatehouse which also served as bell tower, prison and guard chamber. Below, almost hidden from the sea in a deep valley, lies the little cathedral. Beyond are the walls and crenellations of the bishop's palace. This occupies three ranges round a courtyard. The first dates from the twelfth century and fragments of two apartments can be traced over a vaulted undercroft. The gatehouse on the north, connected to the bishop's chapel and the bishop's private apartments down the eastern side, are the work of Bishop Thomas Bek (1230-93). Again, as we have noticed at Wolvesey, Lincoln and Wells, a second range was constructed complete with chapel, chamber and hall. These are all on the first floor above vaulted undercrofts and are the work of Bishop Henry de Gower (1327-47). The great hall was linked to the private apartments by means of a covered passage which also connects with the contemporary kitchen.

The characteristic of medieval episcopal palaces which emerges from these examples is the peculiar provision of two halls. This implies a separation of the bishop's private apartments from the buildings in which his public or ceremonial acts are performed. The same tendency is seen in monasteries where separate accommodation was built for the abbot apart from the common life of the monks. In secular life it went with an increasing growth of caste feeling; the nobility and aristocracy were becoming more conscious of their breeding. In architectural terms this led to the provision of high tables and dais set aside for the lord's meals in the hall; in great houses antechambers and audience chambers were built where suitors were siphoned off before reaching the noble lord who was to be found holed up in the privacy of his closet. At Lyddington there was a hall for great festive occasions (now demolished) as well as a suite of three rooms, audience, inner and privy, which could be used to filter pressing petitioners from the bishop (Figure 1.8).

An excellent example of the pains to which a great episcopal administrator would go to achieve privacy is seen at Acton Burnell (Shropshire).[37] Robert Burnell, Chancellor of England and Bishop of Bath and Wells, was instrumental in shaping the passing of a long series of statutes, modernising the administration and strengthening the royal power in the reign of Edward I. At Wells, as we have seen, he built a magnificent aisled hall which illustrates the splendour in which he lived. At Acton Burnell, his birthplace, he erected a crenellated manor house. The rectangular building with towers at each corner is divided into two main stories with constables' accommodation below and a fine first-floor hall above. In an adjoining outer chamber would assemble the gentlemen and courtiers in attendance on the chancellor or seeking personal audience of him: 'in the hierarchical society of the Middle Ages it was unthinkable

that they should be left to jostle with the lowlier visitors in the antechamber on the ground floor'.[38] Above the hall was the bishop's camera, his suite of private chambers with its bedchamber and adjacent garderobe, and small rooms above allotted to the chaplains and secretaries. Here then, if the visitor was allowed to penetrate so far, could be found the great man. Acton Burnell is topped by crenellations — the fact that the wall walk is only accessible through the bishop's rooms indicates, if proof were needed, that they were designed for show rather than for military use.

8. Cities, Boroughs and Guildhalls

So far in our survey of the tangible remains of medieval government we have only looked at royal and episcopal power. We should, however, misunderstand the nature of medieval society if we imagined that all power resided with the king, barons and the bishops. The towns were one area upon which power to some degree devolved. Before the Norman Conquest, London was already a formidable city; it had a more elaborate organisation than other towns which included a folkmoot, attended by all Londoners who were summoned to its open-air meetings three times a year by the great bell of St Pauls.[39] The detailed legal business was conducted by a bench of experts, the aldermen who met at the Hustings every Monday at the Guildhall. During the twelfth century further progress was made towards self-government. By a charter of 1130 the men of London obtained control of their own taxation; they were also able to choose the justiciar who tried the pleas of the Crown. By the beginning of the thirteenth century they were electing their own mayor. Power, however, was strictly monopolised by the merchant companies who supplied all but nine of the 260 aldermen known to have been elected in the fourteenth century.

The seat of government in London from the second quarter of the twelfth century was the Guildhall.[40] Henry of Cornhill summoned the citizens in the reign of Henry II 'in aula publica'. In the thirteenth and fourteenth centuries there are references to the 'great hall or great

Guildhall' where the 'immense commonalty' gathered to elect the mayor or to take other important decisions. At the west end the floor was raised on a stone vault and on the dais thus formed the Hustings Courts were held. Under the hall was an undercroft where stone and timber were stored; this crypt was probably built *c.* 1270-90 and part still remains under the western half of the present building. There are also references to the chamber of the Guildhall where the City's records and cash were kept, accounts were rendered and more secret business was transacted. The mayor's and sheriffs' courts were also sometimes held there. South of the Guildhall was a courtyard which resembled a cathedral close. Here was a chapel and a gateway.

The soaring medieval town halls of Belgium and Northern Italy, Ypres, Bruges, Ghent and Bologna are architectural embodiments of the social and economic aspirations of their rich mercantile corporations. In 1411 the City of London decided to rebuild their Guildhall on a more magnificent scale. They employed John Croxton to design a new Guildhall about double the size of the old; it was to have a new and extended crypt, a porch, a mayor's court and kitchens. Despite being burned down in 1666, cut about by the insertion of monuments in the eighteenth century, and ruined by German bombs in 1940, sufficient of the medieval masonry still survives to impress. The old undercroft was kept to serve as the hall to be used while the rest of the building was under construction. A second crypt, with Purbeck marble columns and a complex lierne vault, was added with a stately entrance to the east. The great hall itself which rested on these two crypts was clearly built in emulation of Westminster Hall. It measures 46.2 m × 14.6 m and was the second largest open span covered in England in medieval times. There is still debate about the mode of roof covering. Croxton apparently planned to vault the hall in stone, judging from the tall clustered piers, but in fact the money probably ran out. It may have had a hammer-beam roof which accounts for the strange blocking of sections of the west window. We know at any rate that in 1491 two wooden louvres were inserted in the roof to let in the light and let out the smoke. The

most remarkable internal feature were great screens of tracery running along the lateral walls, in front of the windows. These were, unfortunately, removed by the insertion of monuments and doorways in the eighteenth and nineteenth centuries. Part of the highly ornate porch which was thickly encrusted with arcading, niches and statues survives. Croxton also designed a new mayor's court building which lasted until the 1880s. From careful drawings made before its demolition, it seems as if it was as well designed as the rest of the building. Here was the meeting place for the court of aldermen where cases concerning the law merchant were heard; the book room housed the City's administrative and judicial records.

York, the capital of the north, was similarly equipped with a capacious civic building in the fifteenth century.[41] The City and Guilds of St Christopher and St George jointly built a Guildhall on the east bank of the River Ouse in *c.* 1449-59. The main hall was reduced to a shell in the bombing of 1942 but has been faithfully restored. It followed the usual medieval pattern in having a screens-passage* across the east end and a dais at the west end with an open fireplace in the middle. Here plays were performed; the Crown Court sat at the west end and the Court of Nisi Prius at the east end. Around the hall were service buildings including a kitchen, a buttery, pantry and stores and rooms used for the custody of prisoners and ammunition.

Earlier than the guildhalls of London and York is the twelfth-century hall of St Mary's gild at Lincoln, now (1983) undergoing restoration.[42] It is sited on the east side of High Street, Wigford, below the ridge crowned by the castle and cathedral. Entrance was through an elaborate gateway into a basement heated by a splendid fireplace. Most of the upper structure has been removed but enough remains to show that the gild enjoyed its assemblies in a first floor hall, 19 m long and 5 m wide, lit by four two-light windows and decorated at the north gable end by arcading. In the L-shaped extension was further accommodation for what must have been one of medieval Lincoln's most prestigious institutions (Figure 1.9).

* A cross passage in a medieval house between the hall and the service end.

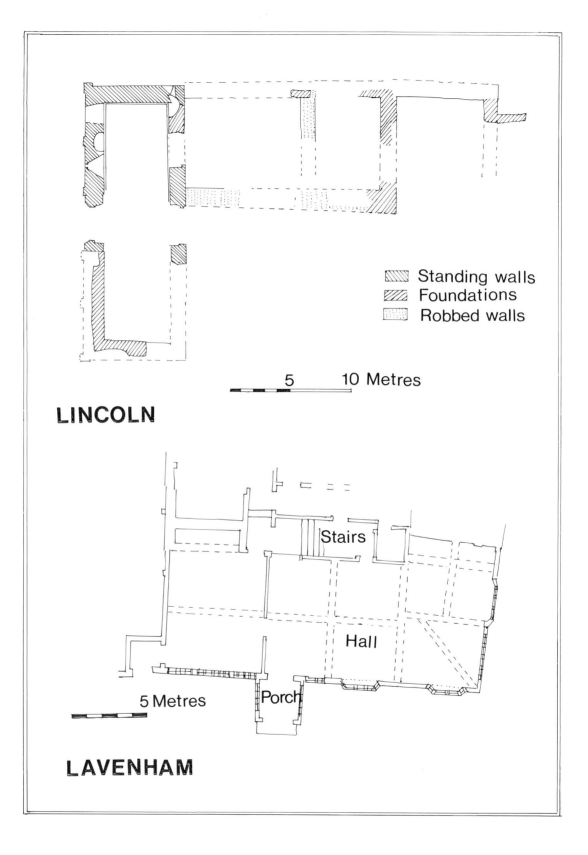

Standing walls
Foundations
Robbed walls

5   10 Metres

LINCOLN

Stairs

Hall

5 Metres

Porch

LAVENHAM

Despite these unusually grand examples, English medieval public halls have been dismissed by S.E. Rigold as 'a poor lot'.[43] Only in East Anglia, in his view, do they come within hailing distance of the glories of the Netherlands and north Germany. He points out that they can be divided into two main classes (Figure 1.9). The first are mutations of the typical late medieval dwelling house — and consist of a ground-floor hall, usually a high hall with a storeyed chamber at either end. Examples are at Canterbury, Leicester and St Mary's Hall, Coventry. Lavenham (Suffolk), on the south side of Market Place, built in 1528-9 is a particularly well preserved example with a main hall measuring 9.7 m × 5.2 m; from here the wool trade was regulated by the gild of Corpus Christi and religious feasts were held.[44] Subsequently it was used as a town hall and prison, ending up as a workhouse, an almshouse and a wool store. At Bury St Edmunds as early as the thirteenth century the townspeople built themselves a civic hall.[45] In 1304 the monks accused them of holding 'illicit conventicles' in the Guildhall. They rebuilt their ground-floor hall towards the end of the fifteenth century with a splendid ten bay king-post roof, a fine porch and a kitchen which in addition to the roasting of aldermanic venison, was used to bake rye bread for distribution as doles to the poor.

The second type was derived from the early medieval 'first floor hall'. The oldest examples at Ipswich and Great Yarmouth toll house had strong undercrofts and external staircases. At King's Lynn there were three public halls, all located beside the market places, the natural foci for the economic life of the town and for much of its social and political life.[46] These were the Steward's Hall in the Tuesday market, the Monday Hall and Sparrow Hall in the Saturday market. There is no trace above ground of these buildings but two of the Guildhalls survive, Trinity Guildhall in Saturday market and St George's Hall in King Street.

Trinity Guildhall was burned down in 1421; its replacement cost £220 and took 16 years to

Figure 1.9: Ground Plans of Medieval Guildhalls at Lincoln (after Magilton, 1982) and Lavenham (after Purcell *et al.*, 1983)

build. It was on a long and narrow plot and was planned at right angles to the street with an entry passage retained down the left side. The hall was raised on a vaulted undercroft and access was by an external staircase. Such a building gave the gild maximum flexibility in their use of the building. They kept their wine and mill stones in the undercroft and subsequently it was used as the town gaol: the hall was a single space internally with a stone flagged floor and roofed by massive tie beams with scissors-braced rafters. A flamboyant front was added by the decorative facing of chalk and flint in the fifteenth century. St George's Guildhall, built after 1406, occupies a long narrow plot between King Street and the River Ouse and though smaller and less elaborate offers similar accommodation — i.e. a two-storeyed hall with its gable end fronting the street. The cooking was done in a separate kitchen.

These buildings were multi-purpose secular meeting places, they housed gilds and fraternities, they were also used as court rooms, toll booths, theatres, gaols, storehouses and places where merchants gathered. Their successors were the typical English townhalls of the sixteenth to the eighteenth centuries with the hall carried on pillars, an open market space beneath, an internal staircase and a small store or lock up.

9. The Archaeology of Justice

Justice, like every other aspect of medieval life, was impregnated with religion. One of the most popular subjects for wall paintings in medieval churches was the Last Judgement — with Our Lord sitting on a throne dispensing dooms like a feudal lord. Proof in lawsuits or criminal cases was not sought for in human evidence but depended on the judgement of God which could be ascertained by the processes of ordeal or trial by combat. In the former the alleged criminal was trussed and lowered into a pool of consecrated water; if he sank he was oddly adjudged innocent: if the water refused to receive his sinful body he was thought to be guilty. In theory such ordeal pits ought to be locatable. A fifteenth-century Canterbury rental applies the name 'Hosdelpette' to a riverside meadow outside the city walls in St Mildred's parish which may well refer to the town ordeal pit.[47]

An alternative mode of establishing right by an appeal to divine judgement was trial by battle. In the little Gloucestershire village church of Stowell are painted two diminutive figures equipped with the special gear for champions engaged in a trial by combat — wearing tunics, carrying square shields, and banging away at one another with double-headed picks.[48] Their position under a painting of the Last Judgement symbolised a link between earthly and heavenly justice.

In 1355, Bishop Robert Wyville of Salisbury challenged the right of William Montacute, Earl of Salisbury, to the castle of Sherborne. The dispute might well have led to a trial by battle and the bishop (a small man) prepared his champion to fight on his behalf. The issue never came to a fight but the bishop's rights were upheld and his executors could not resist in commemorating the bishop's walkover by engraving on his brass his champion complete with shield and pick below the triumphant bishop shown seated in his castle.[49]

This case seems to have been settled out of court, but the places where medieval courts and moots were held often went back to antiquity and at times had sacred connotations. Many meeting places of the administrative units of Saxon England known as hundreds (they were called wapentakes in the Danelaw) are pinpointed by place-names.[50] They are found on hilltops, road junctions and near isolated trees and stones. In Leicestershire the men of Framlands met on a high clay ridge 3.2 km north of Melton Mowbray. The men of Gartree wapentake met at Gartree Bush ('tree with a barked and subsequently overgrown gash on its stem'). In other places prominent stones marked the moot meeting place. Gascote was centred on 'a large stone at a place at the top of Syston field'. An ancient burial mound might be chosen as at Guthlaxton where 'Guthlac's stone' stood by an old tumulus. In neighbouring Northamptonshire the hundred meeting places were invariably sited in the middle of the countryside. The hundred of the Nesse of Borough, for instance, met where two ancient roads inter-

sected at the junction of the three parishes of Helpston, Upton annd Ufford.[51] The Abbot of Peterborough had the right of holding this court and all the hamlets and villages of the Soke came to Nassaborough.

Occasionally, moot mounds seem to have been constructed especially for the purpose. Bledisloe Tump (Glos.), formed by digging a ditch across a natural spur overlooking the Severn, was dated to the twelfth century and is regarded as the hundred meeting place. The shire moot of Berkshire used to meet at Cuckhamsley Hill (alias Scutchamer Knob) on the Berkshire Ridgeway.

Shire meeting places originated in the open air but tended to move to county towns. It is not known where the original meeting place for the shire court in Leicestershire was located. A possibility is Shericles Farm in Peckleton parish and when Sparkenhoe hundred was carved out of Guthlaxton wapentake it is likely that the ancient shire moot site was taken over by the hundred between c. 1086 and 1130. The shire court was moved to Leicester where it may well have been housed in 'Le Motehalle' mentioned in documents of 1300. The county court was rebuilt by Edward III between 1332 and 1344.

The sheer size and impressiveness of a medieval county court hall has been recently established by a study of the Duchy Palace at Lostwithiel in Cornwall.[52] Here Earl Edmund built a great hall in the closing decades of the thirteenth century. A few fragments of the building survive and these, with an engraving by Buck in the early eighteenth century, enable us to reconstruct it as a great hall of eight bays with two-light decorated gothic windows set in each gable and a rose window set high in the northern gable. It was of great size, about 33.6 m in length and 7.3 m wide; this places it in the same class as Winchester and Eltham. The hall was only one of a complex of buildings including convocation hall, stannary ★ 'blowing house' and 'weighing house' and gaol. The function of this group was certainly not to provide living accommodation for the earls. In the first place the

★ The districts, tin mines and smelting works of Cornwall and Devon, formerly under the jurisdiction of Stannary courts.

'palace' was the administrative centre of the Duchy: here were to be found the Steward, who exercised the duties of Sheriff on the Earl's and Duke's behalf. Here were the Receiver and Feodary who collected the revenue and supervised the feudal rights. The palace was also the venue of the county court, the perquisites of which were among the duke's rights. Thirdly, Lostwithiel was a coinage town where much of the tin mined within the county was assayed, stamped and weighed for export. The 'corner' (coin) of the tin ingot was melted and assayed in the weighing house and blowing house to the west of the great hall.

The subject of medieval crime and punishment is clouded with lurid overtones. If one accepts the chroniclers who give us a *News of the World* view it seems that society was violent and punishments severe if not savage. The Anglo-Saxon Chronicle tells us, for instance, that in the year 1124 Ralph Bassett held a moot of the king's thegns at Hundehage in Leicestershire. Here he hanged 43 thieves and six men were castrated and had their eyes put out.

Archaeological evidence for medieval modes of punishment is of two kinds; the sites of gallows and the remains of prisons. Many of the medieval gallows in Wales were sited on a hill outside the liberties★ of towns.[53] The place name element 'wearg' (from which was derived Middle English — Waritre — meaning gallows-tree, where felons were hanged) often pinpoints the place. Hence 'Warren Tree Hill', 3.2 km north-east of the town of Cardigan at the borders of Cardigan and Llangoedinan parishes. The gallows of Rhuthun town was at Gall tegfa, 1.6 km south-west of Rhuthun. Local tradition says that this name is a corruption of Gallt-y-dagfa which means 'Strangulation Hill'. Clearly gallows' sites were deliberately chosen to make a maximum impression on the onlooker. Combe gibbet is situated on a long barrow on the ridge between Walbury Hill and Inkpen Hill, the highest elevation in Berkshire. The bodies of executed criminals were buried near the sites of gallows. At Stockbridge (Hants.), 41 skeletons were found buried in shallow graves with little or

★ Area of jurisdiction.

no attempt at orientation.[54] A number showed clear evidence of decapitation and at least 16 had their wrists crossed behind their back. It was possible to date the group because one of the men had been insufficiently searched and the remains of a purse were found under his armpit containing coins of the time of William the Conqueror.

The horrors of medieval imprisonment have at times been the subject of romantic exaggeration, but in fact imprisonment was so expensive a procedure that it was used only comparatively rarely during the Middle Ages. It was certainly employed to keep prisoners in custody awaiting trial. Tremendous delays of justice meant that prisoners often died before their cases came to trial. Amercement as a punishment was preferred to imprisonment. If a man could pay for his offences this was more profitable to the lord holding the court — *Justitia est magnum emolumentum.*

Most county gaols were built within the protective shell of a castle's walls and accommodation for the ordinary run of prisoners was found by building small wooden huts or 'cages' in the castle yard.[55] More eminent prisoners were housed in the gatehouses or turrets of castles. Sometimes there were specially constructed prisons. At Conwy Castle a prison tower, including a dungeon, was built *c.* 1285. Similarly the gatehouse of Chester Castle was designed to include a prison. The basement of Caesar's Tower in Warwick Castle was built as a prison in the fourteenth century.

The materials used for constructing medieval prisons followed a similar pattern to that of urban housing. Timber was the universal mode of building until the thirteenth century. The sources of supply for the gaols of Aylesbury, Oxford and Wallingford were the forests of Bernwood and Shotover. Stone was used increasingly thereafter. Because escapes had occurred at the prison of the Prior of Dunstable the chronicler proudly recorded that it was rebuilt of stone and mortar. In the sixteenth century brick began to supplement stone.

Some attempt was made to segregate serious offenders from petty trespassers. In 1360 at York Castle, for instance, it was taken for granted that felons should be kept underground and there were many prisons where the basement storey was the place of dishonour. Such places from the fourteenth century were called 'dungeons' or pits, since at times they were excavated or were in the lower parts of towers. Trap doors bolted on the outside sealed these basements. At Conwy visitors to the castle can inspect the dungeon where felons were imprisoned which lies below a chamber, in which the debtors were lodged. Bigger prisons might have several chambers; at Oxford in 1420, 19 doors were mended suggesting a complex of rooms or cells.

Separate quarters were prepared for Scotsmen at Carlisle and for women in the borough gaol at Oxford. This latter was intended for prostitutes and was nicknamed 'the maidens' chamber'. It has been suggested that the Chancellor was more anxious to protect the morals of the academical clerks than the women! Such prisons acquired names which recall their appalling living conditions. The Bishop of Wells' prison was known as the 'Cowhouse': the king's prison at Clarendon Palace was called the 'Bullpit'. An inn at Thame (Oxon.) believed to have been the Bishop of Lincoln's prison was nicknamed 'The Bird Cage'. Together with the term 'gaol bird' they all imply the herding of animals in a foetid atmosphere. Perhaps the most unpleasant was 'Little Ease' in the Tower of London, so constructed that the prisoner could not stand, nor sit but only crouch.

There are very few buildings which can claim to retain substantial portions of purpose-built medieval prisons. These include the 'Manor Office' at Hexham, Lydford Castle (Devon) and the former gaol of the liberty of Ely. The first is a stone building with walls 2.7 m thick, 24.4 m long by 10 m broad and 15.2 m high, dating from the fourteenth-fifteenth centuries. On the ground floor there are no windows in the long side except slits to light the stair; in the upper floors, the original windows are confined to the east and west walls. The ground floor at Lydford seems to represent the 'stronghouse' for the stannary or forest prisoners.[56] At Ely are the remains of a building with a medieval plan with the gaoler surrounded at close quarters by his charges and sharing with them a common yard.

Such medieval prisons contained further equipment for restraining the inmates. Several pairs of stocks were commonly found. The gaoler of Salisbury Castle was charged with the death of prisoners from exposure in the stocks in 1383 which suggests an out-of-door location. 'Irons', *ferramenta* consisting of chains, rings, collars, fetters, bolts, shackles and manacles, were also used to attach the limbs of prisoners. Such objects did not wear out and many have been preserved. Anvils, and mallets for the fixing and removing of irons, are often mentioned. Halters were used when prisoners were taken away from prisons to be tried. There are few mentions of domestic utensils. At Battle in 1520-1 an earthenware pot and a pair of wooden bowls were bought for the use of the prison.

On the other hand they were not without water which was supplied from wells, and fireplaces are recorded. Coldness is at times reported as a cause of death in coroner's inquisitions despite the fact that doubtless much lower temperatures were tolerated in the Middle Ages than at present. It was a charitable act on the part of a Bury St Edmunds' woman who provided under the terms of her will in 1492 for seven faggots to be supplied each week to the borough gaol from All Saints to Easter.

10. Emblems of Power

The Early Middle Ages in England saw a hierarchical society emerge, composed of classes each of which performed set functions in human affairs which were considered to be ordained by God. Kings were regarded as quasi-sacerdotal persons, leaders in war, founts of justice, the source of honours. Barons were great feudal lords, administering congeries of estates, bound by their allegiance to give their lords good counsel and to serve them in war. Bishops were pastors and judges and also often great civil servants. Peasants were expected by their labour to support the upper stages of the structure of church and state. The relationships between the classes were expressed formally in symbolic acts; royal authority was displayed in crown wearings and constant progresses through the country. Privileges such as land tenures were confirmed in the ceremonies of homage and fealty. Military service was consecrated in the honour of knighthood. Episcopal power was invested by the king when he handed over to the bishop elect the insignia of his office. Such events were not empty play-acting. To an illiterate age, such symbolism rendered in pageantry was more meaningful than the written word.

Archaeology is concerned with the tangible expression of these emblems of power. Kingship, as we have seen, was vested in cult objects which served as a link tying the rulers into the two worlds, terrestrial and transcendental.[57] Pagan Anglo-Saxon kingship, as represented by the Sutton Hoo ship burial, was peculiarly associated with the cult of certain animals such as the boar, the dragon and the stag. The helmet for instance, is covered with representations of the boar. There were other royal insignia which became more important as Christianity sanctified the institution; the helmet dropped out and was replaced by the crown. It is significant that a crown was buried with Edward the Confessor, not a helmet. Kings were always prompt to absorb charisma from respectable but obsolescent institutions such as the Roman Empire. Several of the Sutton Hoo cult objects have been paralleled with symbols of authority in the later Roman period. William I modelled his own *corona* after the continental imperial diadem.

The later medieval kings were also adept at fortifying their position by adding from time to time to their symbols of authority. Edward III, for instance, skilfully seized upon the propaganda advantages for the monarchy when he founded the Order of the Garter.[58] The blue garter became the symbol of the exclusive order, originally confined to only 26 knights, but which included some of the greatest names in the land. Garters and robes were issued and a great state banquet was held in the tower of Windsor Castle, then in process of reconstruction. Inside the Castle, the collegiate chapel of St Edward was enlarged and re-dedicated as the chapel of St Edward and St George.[59] The cross of St George was embroidered on the garter robes. Each member of the 'Society, Fellowship, College of Knights' had a superbly carved

stall. Soon the order had its own herald. In this way Edward III channelled the enthusiasms of the age of chivalry to support the Crown. It is significant that Edward IV consolidated his own very shaky hold over the throne by injecting new life into the order 130 years later. He began to rebuild the collegiate chapel of St George and furnish its sumptuous interior with fittings of a cathedral-like splendour. The stalls are particularly relevant to our theme.[60] They consist of three tiers: the topmost is reserved for the knights of the Garter and the dean and canons; the middle one for the military knights, the minor canons and the choirmen; the lowest for the choirboys. The garter stall plates were described by St John Hope, the historian of Windsor Castle, as an 'heraldic storehouse of the highest artistic excellence' unequalled in Europe. There are no less than 87 surviving from before 1485. They are of copper or brass; on their gilded or silvered surfaces the arms of the knights have been richly enamelled or painted.

Heraldry was a system of devices, attached to the helmets and painted on the shields of knights, which made them instantly recognisable when they rode into the tournament field clad in full armour. The twelfth-century coats or arms were simple and clear but gradually the system became more elaborate and increasingly formal. Families linked by kinship or dependant tenure with a dominant line adopted the same arms but with a 'difference', some modification of the original design.[61] Gradually heraldry was forged into an instrument which helped to rivet a caste system onto society in the Later Middle Ages. Noble tombs of the fourteenth and fifteenth centuries are encrusted with innumerable shields all proclaiming name-dropping connections. They are useful again for identification purposes when inscriptions have been defaced.

Political affiliations could be displayed by the use of badges, which might well be heraldic in origin. During the Later Middle Ages magnates collected around them groups of men who, for the time being, recognised their lordship, enjoyed their protection, gave them support in the courts and might fight for them in continental wars or civil strife. Badges acted as heraldic labelling devices; they had to be simple, easily remembered and instantly recognisable. Yorkist supporters wore the white rose or the sun; the Bourchiers used a common man-made object like the knot. Some badges incorporated rebuses or visual puns. Abbot Kirkton, one of the last prelates of Peterborough, left his badge, a church with a barrel or tun under it on the gate leading to the deanery. Political badges are found carved round the necks of alabaster effigies of ambitious noblemen; they were distributed as jewels to supporters. At times they were painted *ad nauseam* over schemes of interior decoration. Sir Richard Clement, a minor Tudor courtier who bought Ightham Mote in Kent in 1521, made a remarkable declaration of political allegiance by powdering over his new possession red roses, fleur-de-lis and pomegranates.[62] These were the symbols of the three kingdoms linked by Henry VIII's first marriage, England, France and the united crowns of Aragon and Castile. Here the choice of heraldic badge was dictated by Clement's hopes of political advancement by his royal patron. Other families, more sure of themselves, used their own insignia to display their power and connections.

The fortunes of one such great family can be followed by studying their tombs. The de la Pole family rose in three generations from being fishmongers of Hull to producing a Lord Chancellor of England. The effigy of William de la Pole can be seen in Holy Trinity Church, Hull. The de la Pole leopards' heads appear on the fonts of the church there and at Hedon (Yorks.). In the south chancel aisle can be seen the old de la Pole arms: two bars nebulv and their later coat: azure, a fess between three leopards faces or. It was by William's mercantile transactions that he made a fortune enabling him to finance the wars of Edward III. His son, Sir Michael, was created Earl of Suffolk and married the daughter of the Earl of Stafford. The arch above his tomb is studded with the de la Pole leopard badge and the Stafford knot, and the arms of the two families appear on the font. The widow of the fourth Earl and first Duke lies in a magnificent tomb at Ewelme (Oxon.) where she and her husband built a palace, almshouses and restored the church. Her husband was blamed for the English loss of France and was assassinated. John de la Pole, second Duke,

seemed to retrieve the family fortunes and married Elizabeth Plantagenet, sister of Edward IV. This, however, sealed the fate of the family. The Tudors set out to exterminate all descendants of the Plantagenets.

Occasionally these carved and painted replicas of arms are supplemented by a display of the actual helms, swords and coats of arms carried in the funeral processions and afterwards hoisted up over the tomb (Figure 1.10). Such achievements are very vulnerable to robbery, vandalism and decay but there is an outstandingly important one hanging high over the tomb of the Black Prince in Canterbury Cathedral. The helm with its crest and cap of maintenance, jupon, targe, gauntlets and scabbard are there; sword, dagger and spurs have been lost.[63]

These were the cult objects of chivalry: less ostentatious because they were buried deep in the tomb, but equally powerful emblems of ecclesiastical authority have been found (Figure 1.11). The effigy of Walter de Gray,[64] Archbishop of York (1216-55), in the south transept of York Minster is made of Purbeck marble and shows a figure vested in the full regalia of an archbishop — amice, chasuble, dalmatic, tunicle, alb, stole and maniple. The hands are gloved and the effigy has a ring on its middle finger. The feet are shown trampling on a dragon, the symbol of evil: the pastoral staff is thrust into its throat. What is more remarkable is that when the tomb was opened the remains were found accompanied by the instruments of the mass, a silver parcel-gilt chalice and paten and the symbols of episcopal power, a gold ring with a large cabochon sapphire, a small ruby and emerald (attributed with magical powers) and a pastoral staff or crosier with a splendidly carved walrus-ivory head. Bishop Bitton of Exeter, who died in 1307 and was buried at the foot of the steps leading to the high altar, was exhumed in 1763. His bones were not recorded but his gold and sapphire episcopal ring and a silver-gilt chalice and paten bearing the remains of a wafer — covered by a cloth — were all recovered.[65]

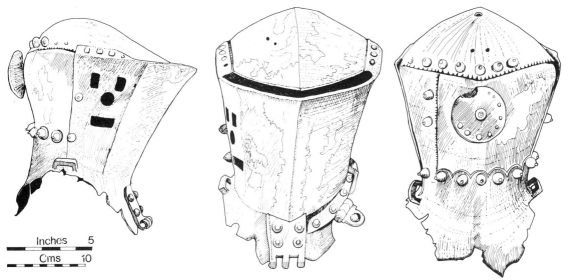

Figure 1.10: Tilting Helm from Melbury Sampford Church, Dorset. Placed there in memory of William Browning, Lord of the Manor, d. 1472. Weighs nearly 18½ lb; originally brightly burnished and surmounted by owner's crest in carved wood. Dorchester Museum

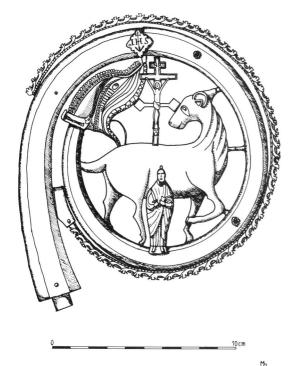

Figure 1.11: Bishop's Crosier, Ashmolean Museum, Oxford, twelfth century

11. Seals

In the Early Middle Ages English society was groping its way out of an era of violence by constructing a more ordered community. One sign of this was that it was no longer considered good enough to hold land and rights, one had to have documentary confirmation that one was the rightful owner. Authentication of such documents was provided by seal impressions. Seals are a potent symbol of authority. This is shown by the care with which they were originally made; they are triumphs of the diecutters' art.[66] Their value increased in almost direct proportion to their age and they were invested with an almost magical significance. For these reasons medieval seals have survived in great numbers in archives, museums and guildhalls.

Anglo-Saxon charters did not have seals attached to them, simply the names of witnesses, accompanied by the sign of the cross. From the time of Edward the Confessor onwards there is a continuous series of royal seals attached to documents.[67] Barons had their own personal seals. Boroughs celebrated their liberties by acquiring them. Practically all ecclesiastical institutions, monasteries, peculiar jurisdictions, guilds, chantries, fraternities and military orders had their distinguishing seals.

The earliest seals are frankly crude in conception and execution. By the thirteenth century a more assured style is noticeable. The device is skilfully designed to fit into the confined space and the dies are accurately and deeply cut. Gradually towards the end of the Middle Ages this simplicity is succeeded by greater elaboration. Canopies, tabernacles and heraldic opulence tend to obscure the design with meaningless intricacies. The main shapes are circular and pointed-oval; others such as lozenge and shield shape are possible but rare. Royal and official seals tended to favour the circular shape. The pointed oval is found in many ecclesiastical and monastic seals because it was well suited to standing figures and persons (or saints) appearing under arched canopies. Usually the seal was provided with a handle which was a flange at right angles to the back of the die; pierced for suspension and providing a grip for the user. Where seals and counter-seals were used (as with the important series for the delivery of wool and hides and the customs' seal of York in the time of Edward I), one die was provided with projecting little pegs, which fitted snugly into loops on the other die. The device was usually placed centrally surrounded by the inscription: this was nearly always in Latin though French and English are occasionally used. Roman capitals were used between 1072 and 1174: rude Lombardic 1174-1215, good Lombardic 1206-1345; bold Black letter 1345-1425 and fine close Black letter 1425-1500. The Renaissance saw Roman capitals back in vogue.

The value of seals to the archaeologist is threefold. They provide evidence for the former physical presence of the owner or official holder. They reflect governmental, municipal or ecclesiastical policy and they supply us with incidental information about architecture, costume and shipping (Figure 4.8). A man's seal was a valued personal possession; it was not unreasonable for the excavators of Southampton to identify the owner of a house site with Richard of Southwick when they found his seal in a pit in the back of the property. Occasionally seals seem to have been 'bought off the peg'. One found at Penhallam Manor (Cornwall) bears stock religious devices and cannot be connected with any individual.

The designs on local seals of towns are particularly informative. Those of inland towns usually display a building of some kind. At Exeter and Worcester there is a guildhall, at Canterbury, Winchester and Rochester there is a castle or tower, isolated or encircled by a wall. One of the Oxford seals shows a representation of the east gate of the town's fortifications. Bridges, being impressive achievements of civil engineering, also figure as subjects. Rochester's seal shows a bridge of seven pointed arches with the River Medway flowing through them, like a child's eye view of a hydro-electric scheme. The splendid series from the port towns of Poole and Weymouth (Dorset) show medieval ships from the thirteenth century onwards (see Figure 4.8).[68]

The importance of the wool and cloth trade in the economy of medieval England is symbolised in the numerous official seals produced (see Figure 7.9). There were seals for subsidies on cloth, and for the delivery of wool and hides for various localities. These had the arms of England on one side on a shield, and on the other, without a shield. There is a fine royal silver seal for the port of London and one for the collector of the royal subsidy for the port of Southampton. The official aulnager or ell-measurer at Winchester, which was the chief seat of the cloth trade in the country, had a seal as befitted his duty to regulate the quality and measure in cloth. The series of the admirals' seals of the fifteenth century have a naval device, a ship, its mainsail emblazoned with the owner's arms, a lantern at the stern and a pennon flying from the masthead.

Local seals were carefully kept in guildhalls. Here also were the other civic insignia which have in general survived much less well. Maces and civic plate were more vulnerable to being melted down, or simply being replaced with more elaborate successors. While the Dorset towns of Poole, Dorchester, Corfe Castle and Weymouth have all retained their medieval seals, none of the other civic insignia of these towns are older than the sixteenth century and most are post-Restoration in date.

References

1. Quoted by Fowler, P.J., *Approaches to Archaeology*, London, 1977, 176.
2. Harvey, B., *Westminster Abbey and its Estates in the Middle Ages*, Oxford, 1977, 25.
3. Lethaby, W.R., *Westminster Abbey and the King's Craftsmen*, London, 1906, 9.
4. Scott, G.G., *Gleanings from Westminster Abbey*, London, 1863, 36.
5. Ibid., 25.
6. Butler, Sir T., *The Crown Jewels and Coronation Ritual*, London, 1970.
7. Scott, *Gleanings from Westminster Abbey*, 124, plate XXVI.
8. Lethaby, *Westminster Abbey and the King's Craftsmen*, 319; and Lethaby, W.R., *Westminster Abbey Re-examined*, London, 1925, 226.
9. Stone, L., *Sculpture in Britain. The Middle Ages*, Harmondsworth, 1955, 142.
10. Ayloffe, Sir Joseph, 'An account of the body of King Edward the First as it appeared on opening his tomb in the year 1774', *Archaeologia*, III, 1775, 376.
11. Hargrave Graham, R.P., 'The earlier royal funeral effigies. New light on portraiture in Westminster Abbey', *Archaeologia*, XCVIII, 1959, 160-9.
12. Stone, *Sculpture in Britain*, 192.
13. Lethaby, *Westminster Abbey and the King's Craftsmen*, 281-2.
14. Royal Commission on Historical Monuments (England), *Inventory of Historical Monuments in London, Vol. I, Westminster Abbey*, London, 1925, 65.
15. Allen Brown, R., Colvin, H.M. and Taylor, A.J., *The History of the King's Works*, London, 1963, 491-552.
16. Ibid., 527-33.
17. *Vetusta Monumenta*, vol. VI, 'A memoir on the painted chamber in the palace of Westminster' by Tokewode, J.G., chiefly in illustration of Mr Charles Stothard's series of drawings from painting upon the walls of the chamber, 1842.
18. Topham, J., *Some Account of the Collegiate Chapel of St. Stephen, Westminster*, no date; and Smith, J.T., *Antiquities of Westminster, The Old Palace, St. Stephen's Chapel*, London, 1807.
19. *Med. Arch.*, IX, 1965, 200-1.
20. Allen Brown, *et al.*, *The History of the King's Works*, 541.
21. Jenkinson, H., 'Exchequer tallies', *Archaeologia*, LXII, 1911, 367.
22. *Archaeologia*, XLIV, 377.
23. Allen Brown, *et al.*, *The History of the King's Works*, 706-29.
24. *Med. Arch.*, VIII, 1964, 255-6.
25. Allen Brown, R., 'Some observations on the Tower of London', *Arch. J.*, 136, 1979, 99-108.
26. Hammond, P., *'Royal Fortress', The Tower of London, Through Nine Centuries*, London, 1978, 19.
27. Borenius, T. and Charlton, J., 'Clarendon Palace. An interim report', *Antiq. J.*, XVI, 1936, 55-85.
28. Pettigrew, T.J., 'Notes on the Ancient Royal Palace of Clarendon', *J.B.A.A.*, XV, 1859, 246-64.
29. Biddle, M., 'Wolvesey: the *domus quasi palatium* of Henry de Blois in Winchester', *Chateau Gaillard, European Castle Studies*, III, Chichester, 1966, 28-36.
30. Ex inf. W.J. Blair.
31. Owen, D.M., *Church and Society in Medieval Lincolnshire*, Lincoln, 1971, 20-1.
32. Chapman, H., Coppack, G. and Drewett, P., *Excavations at the Bishop's Palace Lincoln, 1968-72*, Sleaford, 1975, 6.
33. Royal Commission on Historical Monuments (England), *An Inventory of the Historical Monuments of Huntingdonshire*, 1926, 35.
34. Thompson, M.W., *The Bedehouse, Lyddington, Leicestershire*, DoE Guide Book, undated.
35. Wood, M.E., 'Thirteenth century domestic architecture in England', *Arch. J.*, CV, Supplement, London, 1950.
36. Ralegh Radford, C.A., 'The Bishop's Palace and ecclesiastical city of St. David's', *Arch. J.*, CXIX, 1962, 333-5.
37. Ralegh Radford, C.A., 'Acton Burnell Castle' in Jope, E.M. (ed.), *Studies in Building History*, London, 1961, 94-104.
38. Ibid., 103.
39. Stenton, D.M., *English Society in the Early Middle Ages*, London, 1965, 177-9.
40. Barron, C.M., *The Medieval Guildhall of London*, London, 1974.
41. Royal Commission for Historical Monuments (England), *City of York, V, Central area*, 1981, 76-81.
42. Hill, Sir F., *Medieval Lincoln*, Cambridge, 1965, 162-3; and Lincoln Archaeological Trust, *Tenth Annual Report*, Lincoln, 1982, 8-7.
43. Rigold, S.E., 'Two types of court hall', *Arch. Cant.*, LXXXIII, 1968, 1-22.
44. The National Trust, *The Guildhall*, Lavenham, no date.
45. Statham, M., 'The Guildhall, Bury St. Edmunds', *Procs. of Suffolk Inst. of Arch.*, 1968, XXXI, part 2, 1969, 117-57.
46. Parker, V., *The Making of King's Lynn*, Chichester, 1971, 140-1.
47. Urry, W., *Canterbury under the Angevin Kings*, London, 1967, 198.

48. Tristram, E.W., *English Medieval Wall Painting, the Twelfth Century*, Oxford, 1944, 45.

49. Rogers, H.W., *Bishop Robert Wyville, the 14th Century Memorial Brass*, Salisbury, no date.

50. Cox, B.H., 'Leicestershire moot sites, the place-name evidence', *Transactions of the Leicestershire Archaeological and Historical Society*, XLVII, 1971-2, 14-21. I am grateful to M. Petchev for allowing me to read his essay on Hundred moot sites in advance of publication.

51. Beresford, M.W. and St Joseph, J.K.S., *Medieval England, An Aerial Survey*, Cambridge, 1958, 260-1.

52. Pounds, N.J.G., 'The Duchy Palace at Lostwithiel, Cornwall', *Arch. J.*, 136, 1979, 203-17.

53. Melville Richards, G., 'The sites of some medieval gallows', *Arch. Cambrensis*, CXIII, 1964, 159-65.

54. Gray Hill, N., 'Excavations on Stockbridge Down 1935-6', *Proceedings of Hampshire Field Club and Archaeological Society*, XIII, 1937, 247.

55. Pugh, R.B., *Imprisonment in Medieval England*, Cambridge, 1968, especially Chapter XVII which deals with the structure and contents of prison buildings.

56. Saunders, A.D., 'Lydford Castle, Devon', *Med. Arch.*, XXIV, 1980, 123-86.

57. Chaney, W.A., *The Cult of Kingship in Anglo Saxon England*, Manchester, 1970, 121-56.

58. McKisack, M., *The Fourteenth Century*, Oxford, 1959, 251-4.

59. Allen Brown *et al.*, *The History of the King's Works*, 874-81.

60. Pevsner, N., *Buildings of England, Berkshire*, London, 1966, 275.

61. Collins, S.M., 'Differencing in English medieval heraldry', *Antiq. J.*, XXVI, 1946, 172-5.

62. Starkey, D., 'Ightham Mote: politics and architecture in early Tudor England', *Archaeologia*, CVII, 1982, 153-63.

63. Borg, A., *Arms and Armour in Britain*, HMSO, 1979, 12.

64. Ramm, H.G., *et al.*, 'The tombs of Archbishops Walter de Gray and Godfrey de Ludham in York Minster and their contents', *Archaeologia*, CIII, 1971, 101-47.

65. Beacham, P. *et al.*, *Archaeology of the Devon Landscape*, Exeter, 1980, 93.

66. Tonnochy, A.B., *Catalogue of British Seal Dies in the British Museum*, London, 1952.

67. Heslop, T.A., 'English seals from the mid ninth century to 1100', *J. Brit. Arch. Assoc.*, CXXXIII, 1980, p. 16.

68. For Dorset borough seals, see Royal Commission on Historical Monuments (England), *County of Dorset 2, South East*, IV, 115a, Plate 36, 339a, Plate 35.

FORTIFICATIONS

1. The Origins of Castles

The origins of communal defensive systems in medieval England can be traced at least as far back as the eighth century in Mercia. Here it is possible that two successful rulers, Aethelbald and Offa, took the first steps towards strengthening their realm with public works by building fortified planned-towns sometimes connected with bridges. At Hereford, excavation has proved a town with a Saxon core composed of a rectilinear layout, surrounded by an intramural street and a defensive ditch, focusing upon a fortified bridge.[1] All these are attributed to the late eighth/early ninth century. It has recently been suggested on topographical grounds that Bedford may also have been the subject of Mercian defensive forethought, possibly designed to act as a bulwark against Viking raiders.[2] Certainly the present street pattern suggests a burh to the north of the bridge, with a rectilinear layout; to the south a fortified bridgehead. If this is true it means that the inspiration for the burghal defence system, until recently attributed to Wessex under Alfred, is much earlier and to be found in Central England.[3] The Anglo-Saxons of the Kingdom of Wessex applied such lessons in defensive skills when in turn they suffered repeated Viking attacks. To begin with, Scandinavian marauders had the advantages of surprise and mobility when approaching the long, exposed coasts of southern England, indented with river estuaries leading deep into the country. To counter this threat a web of fortresses was stretched over the Wessex heartland; in particular the borders, the fords, the estuaries and the road junctions were guarded. King Alfred is now

credited with garrisoning these burhs rather than creating their grand strategic design. Their construction, at places like Lydford (Devon), Wareham (Dorset), Wallingford and Oxford (Oxon.) and Cricklade (Wilts.), meant that everyone in Wessex was within 40 km of a place of refuge where he could take his family and property, and where the local armed levies could rally when a Viking raiding party was sighted in the area.

Such fortifications were centres of resistance designed 'to shelter all the folk'. A good deal more controversial is the question: did the Saxons have private fortresses? Ordericus Vitalis, the chronicler, was quite clear in his own mind on this one. He described how King William traversed the country 'for the fortresses which the Gauls call castella (castles) had been very few in the English provinces' and he attributed the failure of the English in withstanding the Normans to their lack of castles.

It may well be that private fortresses were not widespread in late Saxon England but excavations at Sulgrave (Northants.),[4] and Goltho (Lincs.) have shown that Ordericus' generalisation was too sweeping. At Sulgrave there was a defensive element in the form of a ditch and bank surrounding the pre-Conquest timber hall. A tower-like substructure of stone and timber, embedded in the later Norman ringwork, was at first claimed by the excavator to be a thegnly towered gatehouse, subsequently interpreted as a freestanding tower, but ultimately it has emerged as a domestic building which served as the basement for a small tower in the Norman set-up. The ringwork at Goltho surrounding the egg-shaped enclosure of the Saxon manor was less

Plate 2.1: Lilbourne, Northamptonshire. This motte and double-bailey castle lies immediately to the east of the manorial church and controls the crossing of the River Avon. Green lanes converge across open fields towards it. This part of the Northamptonshire uplands is masked with boulder clay and the ridge-and-furrow of medieval furlong blocks show up well as shadow marks in the winter sunshine. The village nucleus now is found 0.8 km to the south of the castle and church (Photo: Cambridge University Committee for Aerial Photography, taken 27.1.69)

ambiguous;[5] it was a bank 6.7 m at its base with an outer ditch 2.7 m wide. The construction date was *c*. 1000 AD. Thegnly defences, in fact, scarcely distinguishable from early Norman castles, are to be found in the late Saxon period.

It remains true that the castle was not intensively exploited as an instrument of government at both a local and a national level until the arrival of the Normans. Recent research has established that so-called 'Norman' motte and bailey castles are in fact the result of a complex series of influences from a number of continental sources interacting in some areas on a local tradition.[6] It seems that the division between citadel and forecourt is likely to be Rhenish in origins: the emphasis on the height of the motte and its crowning tower may prove to have originated in Normandy or Anjou, where towers of stone and timber are found from the tenth century onwards. The Anglo-Saxons may have contributed the timber gatehouse and certainly the idea of the ringwork. There is little evidence for the presence of large numbers of pre-Conquest motte and bailey castles in Normandy. In fact the Conquest itself, by bringing together men from diverse surroundings such as Normandy, Brittany, Maine, Anjou, Flanders and southern Italy may have acted as the catalyst for a rapid development of early types of fortification.

The majority of these early earthwork castles were simple enclosures which in many cases have been modified afterwards by the addition of a motte (Plate 2.1).[7] The three castles founded in Herefordshire by Norman adventurers during the reign of Edward the Confessor, at Ewyas Harold, Richard's Castle and at Hereford Castle, all had acquired mottes by the end of the twelfth century, but this feature was not necessarily there in their primary form. In fact the excavation of the eleventh-century defences at the Tower of London illustrates a similarly early type of campaign fort which, to begin with, was merely a fortified enclosure.[8] The area at the Tower was 100 m × 50 m wide defended on the east side by the Old City Wall of Roman London (repaired by Alfred the Great), on the south side by the river, and on the north and west sides by a new ditch and presumably by a rampart. It may well be that the White Tower, built in the 1080s, was erected within the cramped quarters of this earlier bailey.

The reason for William's fortifications of the Tower was obvious. In the chronicler's words he wished to overawe 'the fickleness of the vast and fierce populace' of London. On his return to England in 1067 to face a revolt in the south-west, we are told that he constructed a castle at Exeter, and once again this seems to have been a garrison-type fort of the enclosure type, this time with a stone gatehouse. Excavations at Castle Neroche in south Somerset show a similar design (Figure 2.1).[9] This castle is strategically placed on the north-east scarp of the Blackdown Hills, commanding the approaches to Devon and Cornwall. It is likely that it served as a base for suppressing the disturbances of 1067-9 and that Robert, Count

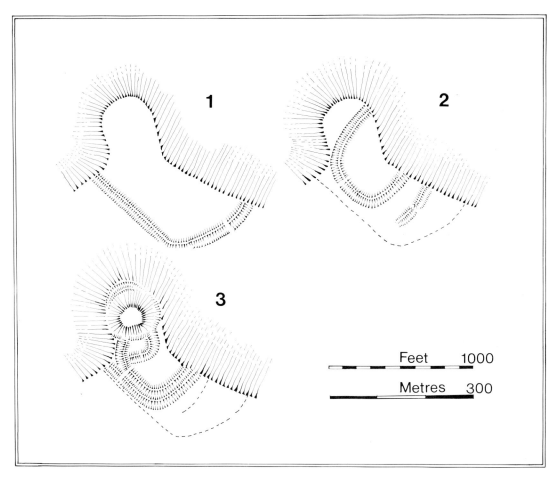

Figure 2.1: Ground Plan of Castle Neroche, Somerset. Period 1: Undated defence. Period 2: 1067-9. Enclosure strengthened. Period 3: Motte added to Period 2 enclosure and one corner subdivided to act as a barbican (after Davison, 1967)

of Mortain, ordered the strengthening of the Period 2 fortification here. A smaller enclosure was thrown up within an earlier and undated defence and in the excavator's words 'a troop of horse based on Neroche could effectively "bottle up" the whole of the south west'. Some 230 cooking pots, with rim forms characteristic of northern France, were found in the excavations. The site was converted to a motte and bailey castle in Period 3. The mound was heaped astride the Period 2 enclosure, one corner of which was subdivided to act as a barbican. Davison had calculated that the motte took approximately 13,780 man days (of 12 hours per day) to build, a period of from four to six months. This can be com-

pared with the time taken by Sir Arthur Evans, an experienced archaeological excavator, to build the Jarn Mound on Boars Hill, overlooking Oxford in the 1930s. This motte, with a summit 9 m in diameter, was erected by 20 men using small railway trucks and a tower crane. It took three years!

Along the Welsh border, ringworks and mottes were thrown up within a few years of the Conquest of England (Plate 2.1). In 1070 William I gave Roger de Montgomery, his kinsman and close friend, the honour of Shrewsbury. Near the edge of this territory, on a ridge of boulder clay overlooking the river and ancient ford of Rhyd-Whiman, Roger built a castle which became known as

'Hen Domen' — 'the old mound'.[10] The meticulous excavation of Hen Domen by Barker has greatly enriched our knowledge of the range and nature of the structures to be found within early Norman castles. Around the bailey perimeter was a timber fighting platform. The earliest buildings included a stake fence, a chapel, a series of rectangular structures, a timber tower and a group of lean-to constructions, next to the platform. These would have served the fighting garrison which doubtless used Hen Domen as a base for launching attacks on Central Wales. In phase 2 (1175-1200) it seems that the centre of the bailey was a cobbled open space. A three-bay, apsidal-ended chapel, with possibly a detached bell tower, replaced the earlier building. Hints of the violent life on this border castle were given by a burned-down timber tower and a deep cess pit which had been filled in with clay, cut for latrine pits, and may well have been used for housing prisoners. During the last phase of occupation, the castle is likely to have been used as an early warning station to fit in with the strategy of the new stone castle at Montgomery nearby. The motte was a primary feature of the earthworks at Hen Domen and was made by cutting a circular outer ditch, then piling the turf and the clay from the outside edge towards the centre. The remains of a succession of five bridges were found — the earlier ones were 3-3.7 m wide but the last one was of a gang-plank type, familiar from that depicted at Dinan in the Bayeux tapestry. The finds were those which one would expect to be associated with a frontier garrison — arrowheads, lanceheads, knives, an axehead, spindle whorls (evincing the presence of women) and bone draughts-men (for whiling away time off duty). We are also given graphic reminder of the dangers of life by the discovery of two great toe bones, a humerus, horse bones, and half a leather ankle boot! Hen Domen was abandoned in the first half of the thirteenth century.

Despite the fact that Hen Domen seems to have been a textbook example of a 'motte and bailey' castle, there was no blueprint for these early Norman castles. In fact excavation is beginning to show that they were the results of innumerable experiments, each adapted to its surroundings — some more or less success-ful. Another category, less well known, but also numerous, is the 'ringwork' (Plate 2.1).[11] King cites 198 examples as compared with 723 mottes and 141 other castles known to have existed before 1215. It was 'a version of the familiar embanked enclosure of northern Europe contracted to form an enclosure of a single lord's dwelling'. The size of Norman ringworks varies from Old Sarum which is one of the most intimidating of all earthworks, 110 m × 95 m from rim to rim — with a scarp 17 m high, to the tiny earthworks at Dol Aeron at Llanlleonfel (Brecknock) which in area measures only 16.5 m × 14.5 m from rim to rim. In distribution, ringworks are common in a wide band along the English Channel and along the Bristol Channel coast of Wales. They are scarce and scattered in north Wales, West Midlands and around London. Three concentrations correspond with compact baronial holdings in Cornwall (Count of Mortain), in Gower (where the peninsula has only ringworks) and Glamorgan. It seems that these dense groups were the result of local castle builders imitating some successful earthwork in the neighbourhood.

Excavation at Castle Tower, Penmaen, has given a good indication of the entrance and interior structures to be expected lying under the turf covering of these earthworks.[12] In the first phase there was an elaborate timber gatetower of post-hole and sill construction, which in reconstruction is shown as being half-timbered with doors each of two leaves, some 2.75 m wide hung on opposite posts. The doors were probably flanked by narrow guard chambers, walled with wooden parti-tions jointed into sole plates which, resting directly on the ground, would not have left any archaeological record. They would also have provided support for the upper works of the gatehouse which might have taken the form of a bridge or possibly 37 sq m of accommodation. The pitched roof would have rested on the fighting platform. The weakness of such a tower is (as we have seen with Hen Domen) its vulnerability to fire. It was in fact burned down, and replaced by a narrower entrance lined with dry stone. The buildings within Castle Tower, Penmaen, consisted of a small two-bay timber hall with detached kitchen, which was succeeded by a very

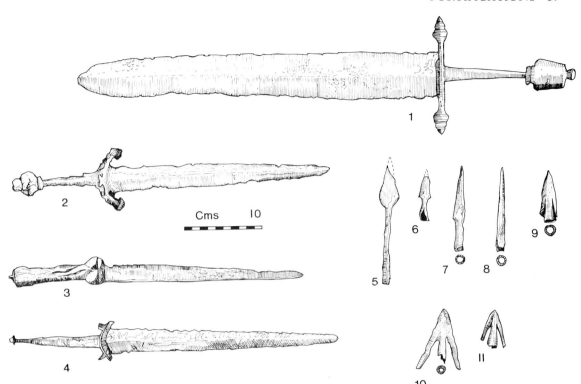

Figure 2.2: Sword, Daggers and Arrowheads, Northampton Museum. 1. Sword with heavy pommel and quillons. 2. Late fourteenth-century dagger, a two-edged military weapon with pommel and quillons. 3. A fourteenth/ fifteenth-century kidney dagger. Pommel is brass, wooden handle. Single-edged blade. 4. Late medieval dagger. 5-6-7-8. Twelfth/thirteenth-century military arrowheads. 9. Late medieval armour-piercing arrowhead. 10-11. Barbed hunting arrowheads

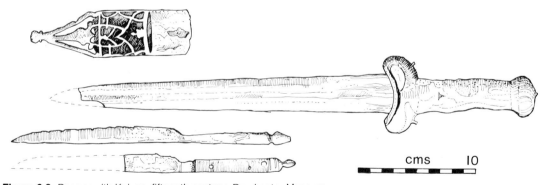

Figure 2.3: Dagger with Knives, fifteenth century, Dorchester Museum

crudely built hall with rounded corners, an irregular layout and a sloping floor. If this was the manor hall of Penmaen in the thirteenth century it illustrates well the squalor resulting from unsettled conditions on this part of the Anglo-Welsh border.

Precursors of gatehouse towers such as that at Penmaen have been traced back to Carolingian and even to Roman prototypes. Other fortifications in early Norman England seem to have been authentically original in design. Such is the extraordinary construction excavated by Kent at South Mimms (Herts.).[13] Here the castle built by Geoffrey de

Mandeville was crowned by a massive tapered timber-framed tower which had the motte piled up around its base. The mound itself was revetted by a circular palisade so that in fact no earth was visible externally: the tower appeared to rise from a solid wall of wood. Footings for a timber tower of another design were excavated by Hope-Taylor at Abinger in Surrey.[14] Here, around the edge on the top of the motte, were found the sockets for the stockade and its bracing supports. Within the centre were the post-holes dug to take the vertical timbers of the watchtower. It seems that Abinger's castle was crowned with a tower on stilts very similar to that shown in the Bayeux tapestry at Dinan. This building had replaced a previous structure which had collapsed. Abinger for a time was the *caput* of a little group of Surrey manors held below tenant-in-chief level.[15] It was a baronial castle, and had only a short life before it was abandoned, the site never being refortified. One last eccentrically designed castle may be cited. Michael le Fleming received Aldingham (Lancs.) and the land around on the coast of Furness from Henry I between 1107 and 1111.[16] His first defence was a ringwork, 35 m in diameter, defined by a rampart 2.5 m high. This was filled in and replaced by a motte on which were built timber structures. In the thirteenth century the mound was heightened by a further 2 m and a revetment of timber set in a foundation trench 2 m deep was built against the mound. This was never finished and the castle was abandoned to the eroding sea.

Abinger and Aldingham are both reminders that such fortifications were built in lowland and highland Britain as a rapid and temporary solution to a pressing political danger. Both the king and his barons were land-hungry aliens in an unfriendly land, determined to hold onto what they had won by force of arms. Such earthen fortifications seem simple enough but they were a sufficient answer to the cavalry of mailed knights, which were the main threat in eleventh-century warfare. With their deep ditches, steep banks and stout stockades, they made a sudden and impetuous attack by foot soldiers a dangerous operation. From the king's point of view they were political necessities, deliberately sited to over-awe towns, and to keep vital areas in subjection. William I, in his journey north to put down the rebellion in Yorkshire in 1067-8, caused castles to be constructed at Warwick and Nottingham, two at York, one on either side of the River Ouse (see Plate 2.11), others at Lincoln, Huntingdon and Cambridge. Whole quarters of towns might be flattened to make way for them. At Northampton and Wallingford earthen castles covered quadrants of the Saxon walled towns. At Oxford an enormous motte was heaped on top of Saxon streets and houses (see Figure 4.6). At Lincoln Domesday Book records that 166 houses were destroyed to make room for the castle. A similarly dramatic example of the conquerors' arrogance and aggression is the siting of the motte and bailey earthworks of Mileham in Norfolk, straddling the main road which is diverted round them.

As the king and baronage tightened their grip on the country, their resources increased and they were able to expend more in constructing permanent buildings in stone which could offer a greater degree of comfort and security. Furthermore, the improvements in the firepower of medieval siege engines demanded a response in greater sophistication in the arts of fortification. What happened was that, over a period of time, certain elements of the motte and bailey castles were replaced by stone. Practically all castles were built and rebuilt gradually and in a piecemeal fashion.

2. The Evolution of Castles

The three main elements which underwent improvement in the twelfth century were the walls enclosing the bailey, the gateway and the keep. To begin with, timber palisades along the rest of the ramparts surrounding the bailey tended to rot away and they were replaced by crenellated stone walls, with a platform or rampart walk on the inside, to enable the garrison to man the walls when the castle was under attack. Such early curtain walls simply acted as an advanced screen; they were not, to begin with, punctuated with bastions. Eynsford Castle in Kent, for instance, was surrounded by an oval curtain of forbidding height. Corfe (Dorset), similarly, had its crowning hilltop surrounded by a massive encircling wall (see Plate 4.7). Secondly, the gateway which was potentially a weak point, and an obvious target for attack by besiegers, was strengthened by adding a stone gatehouse. At Bramber in Sussex, although there was a central motte, the focus of defence appears to have shifted in the twelfth century to the curtain wall and a gatehouse, which was made into a tower or keep by the addition of two upper storeys. This type of conversion also happened at Richmond in Yorkshire; here an early gatehouse was transformed into a tower keep by the blocking of the entrance passage and the addition of storeys.

At Porchester (Hants.), the Roman walls of the Saxon shore-fort were refaced by the Normans who also added a new Landgate and Watergate. These were plain utilitarian structures with thick walls and semicircular arches; they did not add anything to the offensive potential of the castle because they were not projecting in front of the walls. They simply made it more difficult for an enemy to get in.

It was not until the thirteenth century that the principal entrance was strengthened by building stone towers, one on either side. Skipton (Yorks.) and Rockingham (Northants.) furnish good examples. The most usual and most impressive way in which a motte and bailey castle was brought up to date was to build a new square or rectangular stone keep (Plate 2.3). Undoubtedly the Crown led the way. William the Conqueror himself, in building two mighty palace keeps at the White Tower, London and at Colchester, had shown how it was possible to combine fortress, administrative centre, apsidal-ended chapel, barracks and military storehouse, all in one. They represent 'a brilliant compression of the Carolingian palace' but they were not typical of the generation which experienced the Conquest, because they were far too expensive to repeat (see pp. 9-10).

Reconstruction, involving the provision of a keep, was carried through in dozens of other castles during the twelfth century on a less palatial scale than these two great royal works. There were two main types: the shell keep and the tower keep. In the former, which was relatively inexpensive to add, the stockade on the earthern rampart surrounding the flat summit of the motte was simply replaced by stone. This stone wall provided a tough shell against which timber and stone-walled buildings were set. Windsor (Berks.) is an excellent example of a long-lived shell keep. Although its familiar crenellated upper works are largely nineteenth century in form, the tower part preserves the plan of the Norman original. The best idea can perhaps be obtained by looking at an aerial view of Carisbrooke (Isle of Wight). Here the polygonal wall on the top of the mound was connected to the bailey by a link wall which climbs steeply up the motte. At Restormel (Cornwall) the shell keep encloses the mini-bailey and in both there are series of stone buildings against the inner face of the keep (Plate 2.2). At Berkeley (Gloucs.) and Totnes (Devon) the motte itself is encased in a shell keep. At Castle Acre (Norfolk) the unfortified manor house was surrounded by an enlarged and heightened shell keep (Plate 2.3).

The other main type, the tower keep, was dedicated to defence.[17] Among its characteristics were immensely thick walls which might be (as at Dover) between 6.4 m and 7.3 m thick. At Bungay (Suffolk) excavations have revealed foundations of a keep about 21.3 m square sunk into gravel as an anti-mine base. A splayed or battered base also helped to resist the picks, battering rams and mines of attackers. The walls of such keeps were made of a skin of ashlar or masoned stone encasing a core of rubble and mortar. The entrance was usually at first-floor level, approached by an external staircase at right angles to it, and sometimes covered by a forebuilding which frequently was added as an afterthought. At Bungay the forebuilding was very large, 9.7 m × 6.1 m; its lower chamber probably served as a prison.

Within tower keeps, despite the fact that many of them are now ruinous, it is possible to make out the original arrangement of the chambers by looking at the walls. There are five main features to look for. The most obvious are the windows: non-existent in the ground floor — any openings would have weakened its defensive capabilities; heavily splayed slits in the first floor; gradually widening towards the top of the tower. The positioning of the chapel can frequently be recognised by the more generous provision of

42 FORTIFICATIONS

Plate 2.2: Restormel, Cornwall. Originally a ringwork (with faint traces of a bailey) raised by Baldwin Fitz Turstin in the twelfth century, the shell-keep castle of slate and Pentewan stone was erected *c.* 1200. The original entrance, a square gate tower, may predate the keep. Apartments of timber and stone including kitchen, hall, solar and barrack room ringed round the interior and a barbican was added in the thirteenth century. A square tower on the left containing a chapel was attached to the shell *c.* 1280. These accretions were made during the lordship of Richard, Earl of Cornwall, son of Henry III, and Edmund, Earl of Cornwall (Photo: Cambridge University Committee for Aerial Photography)

Plate 2.3: Castle Acre Castle, Norfolk. The cellars and foundations of the great 'Norman country house' are buried in the mighty ringwork crowned with a shell keep of the later twelfth-century castle of the De Warenne family. The country house was converted into a keep before the end of the twelfth century. (Photo: J.M. Steane, taken 1983)

windows. Their splaying enabled arrows to be shot although the range of fire was distinctly limited. Seats were constructed in the thickness of the wall in the upper levels. Secondly, the floors can be reconstructed in the mind's eye by noting the slots and corbels used to take the beams and joists carrying the floors. Fireplaces and chimneys are arches and vents in the thickness of the wall often with majestic stone hoods supported on little columns. Lavers or piscinas are to be seen at hand-height in some chambers. Garderobes or stone-lined lavatories are often situated in towers connected to the living accommodation by mercifully dog-legged passages. They debouched their ill-smelling contents down pipes or the outside walls. Communication between various floors was provided by one or more staircases. These, with their wedge-shaped stone steps spiralling around a centre column, are skilful pieces of masons' work. Finally, no keep was complete without its well, stone-lined or rock-hewn, and at times plummeting hundreds of feet to the water supply below.

There were certain military weaknesses in the typical keep-and-bailey castle of the twelfth century. The keep, despite its strength, was a largely passive mode of defence. The tower keep of Orford Castle (Suffolk) hardly has a single effective arrow-loop. If the bailey of such a castle was taken, the defenders would retire into the keep, but once there they could do little to annoy their attackers. The arrow slits gave a very limited field of fire; the single entrance could be bottled up. Even the corners of an immensely thick-walled square keep could be knocked off or undermined, as happened when King John besieged Rochester Castle in 1216. Starvation might well reduce the defenders in the end. What was required was a more aggressive strategy of defence which would keep up with improvements in siege artillery. In fact military engineers turned to improve the bailey defences and when these had been perfected, the keep was obsolescent. The new theory of design which emerged redistributed and multiplied the strong points by constructing towers along the circuit of the curtain walls (Figure 2.4). To begin with these towers were rectangular, but ultimately they were made drum-shaped or circular, and were thus less vulnerable to mining and tended to deflect missiles. In addition they rose from battered plinths, and missiles dropped from the battlements ricocheted with splintering force against an enemy approaching the foot. Arrow slits, skilfully sited in the towers, covered every foot of the curtain by crossfire. Each tower moreover was a self-contained unit, a defensible cell when the adjoining stretch of wall had been breached.

Published descriptions of castles tend to concentrate on stylistic features and the every-day functions of separate buildings, over-looking the fact that the whole complex was primarily grouped for defence.

An imaginative analysis of the defences of Framlingham (Suffolk) shows how the castle worked in war.[18] Here the defences, erected in the last quarter of the twelfth century, are concentrated on an oval circuit with 13 square towers, open-backed with removable floors, projecting at intervals ranging 10-20 m along the curtain wall. Small mobile groups of men would have defended the northern half of the circuit from the wall-head. Fifty-six men are named in the Bigod garrison of 1216, and this works out at four men per tower and length of wall. Along the southern circuit there was a much greater concentration of firepower. There were pairs of arrow slits at low level, with two longbowmen accommodated in one embrasure firing through separate slits. They each had a full 45° of traverse with a depression arc of 35° to 60° standing, or 0° to 45° kneeling. Their field covered the slopes of the ditch and the bailey. Above were slits at parapet level: there were also further slits on the tower tops, and at the angle of the tower projecting at the south-east corner and the curtain. Fire diagrams at the three levels demonstrate that every inch of the southern front of Framlingham Castle could have been swept with withering arrow power if the garrison had been fully manned.

A convincing series of experiments was carried out at White Castle (Monmouthshire) when actual long bows were used to shoot real arrows through slits in projecting towers.[19] Experience showed that the fields at the base of the walls were adequately covered by the enfilading arrow slits and that there was only one dead zone. However, it was also demonstrated that the besiegers could place arrows through the slits from *outside* the castle a significant proportion of times! Defenders standing behind the slit in fact were in a surprisingly vulnerable position.

Another way of transferring the centre of power from one concentrated strong point, the keep, to the perimeter, was to strengthen and multiply the entrances by means of gatehouses (Figure 2.4; Plate 2.4).[20] Massive double-towered entrances were further provided with outer defences or barbicans. These entrances were rendered more formidable by the drawbridges, which have now vanished, but the slits through which chains went to winches and counterpoise mechanisms can be detected above the archways. Immediately above the archway are stones corbelled out, known as machicolations or murder holes. Down these the defenders could rain rocks, and beams, but probably not boiling oil, on those attempting to force an entrance. Slits above the gateway housed great spiked doors or portcullises which could be slammed down. The gates themselves were heavy, with several layers of timber planks studded with hand-forged nails, and fortified behind with drawbars. The guard chambers were sited in either side of the gateway towers. Castles were also provided with a second main entrance, and additional small, but easily defended, lesser or postern gates. The enemy now was forced to invest the whole perimeter to guard all exits while the besieged, having more opportunities, could stage sallies and counterattacks. These developments in fact began to turn the balance of power decisively in favour of beleaguered

garrisons and an important stage in the road towards impregnability of fortresses was reached.

The excavations at Sandal Castle (West Yorks.), 1963-73, produced from underneath 2.4 ha of accumulated earth and scrub, a dramatic example of these kinds of development (Figure 2.4; Plate 2.4).[21] Here a timber castle on a motte and horseshoe-shaped bailey was replaced by stone fortifications during the early thirteenth century. Most remarkable was the D-shaped barbican whose ditch was cut out of the centre of the earlier bailey. It was connected by a drawbridge to the projecting double gatehouse towers. Both barbican and towers were revetted around their bases with cut and finely shaped ashlar masonry. The gatehouse in turn was linked by wing walls up the steep sides of the motte to the great stone tower ringed round with turrets on the summit. Such a formidable pile was the work of the Warennes, Earls of Surrey, and subsequently Hamelin Plantaganet, bastard half brother of Henry II, who began the rebuilding

Plate 2.4: Sandal Castle, West Yorkshire. Motte with double-towered gatehouse behind barbican (Photo: City of Wakefield Metropolitan District Council)

in stone. It must still have been impressive in the 1480s because Richard III initiated a number of grandiose additions to what he planned was to be the centre of his power in the north of England.

3. Castle Building in Wales

The most spectacular programme of castle building in medieval Britain, which incorporated the latest engineering improvements, was launched by Edward I when he planned the conquest of Wales.[22] It was accomplished in two stages. He decided in 1277 to build a group of five new castles to secure and consolidate English power and to contain the

Welsh ruler of Gwynedd within the limits of his northern lands. In the north the chosen sites were Flint on the Dee estuary, Rhuddlan near the mouth of the Clwyd and Rhuthun in the valley of the Clwyd; in the south at Builth, on the upper Wye, and Aberystwyth on Cardigan Bay. The second phase in 1282 was to attempt the conquest of Snowdonia by ringing the mountainous massif round with coastal castles, striking by their very situation at the roots of native independence. The siting of all these castles was masterly. Each is planned to control either a routeway (Caernarfon in this way controls the southern entry to the Menai Straits), the exit of a valley (Conwy is on the estuary of the River Conwy) or an area of rich cornland (Beaumaris controls

Figure 2.4: Ground Plan of Sandal Castle, West Yorkshire (after Butler and Mayes, 1983)

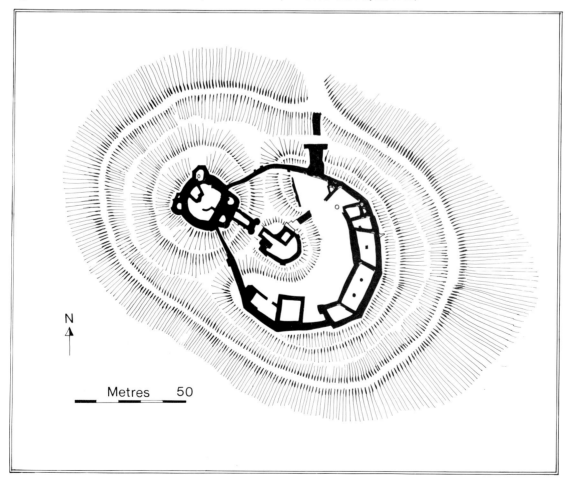

Anglesey, the granary of north Wales). Further, they were more than strong points because they protected towns of English colonists whose control of the newly conquered north Wales was meant to be economic as well as military.

Caernarfon and Conwy are the two finest examples of the new type of castle where the whole focus of defensive power has been placed in the single circuit of towered walls. Both have exploited highly irregular sites; in both the mural towers are so positioned that there is no point in the circuit of the walls which cannot be exposed to crossfire. On the south side at Caernarfon, in particular, medieval fire power was skilfully concentrated. Below the crenellated ramparts, upper and lower shooting galleries were contrived in the thickness of the walls. Arrow slits were so devised that one archer could fire at three different angles or three men could let fly in different directions. It is said that only forty men were required as a garrison.

Both castles are provided with cross walls so that should one half be taken the other can continue the struggle; both castles have two main gates, defended at Caernarfon by great gatehouses, at Conwy by huge drum towers. The chief external difference between the two is that the towers at Conwy are rounded; those at Conwy polygonal. They were remarkable for their costliness. Caernarfon called for an outlay of £19,000. Conwy was even more expensive, the bill here came to £20,000. A comparable figure for today is gained by multiplying by a hundred, making 2 million pounds.

For all their impressiveness, neither of these two castles represents the peak of scientific engineering, which is found in the so-called concentric castle. Here the main enclosure or inner ward is surrounded by lofty towers which overlook a second and outer wall encircling the castle. This also has flanking towers, lower and slighter. Both circuits can be defended by two distinct parties shooting at the same time. Beaumaris (Anglesey), built between 1295 and 1298 for £7,000, is the culmination of the concentric plan. The towers are very cunningly arranged to give a maximum field of fire upon an approaching enemy. The outer gateways north and south are out of

alignment with their corresponding gatehouse. An enemy carrying the first gates of the castle and penetrating into the 'lists' (as the area between the two wall circuits is called), is forced to approach the main gates at an angle thus exposing his shieldless flank to the raking crossfire of the defenders.

From acute structural observation and methodical site excavation much has been learned about the building of the great Edwardian Welsh castles. To unravel their history, to consider the administrative planning, the organisation of labour and the supply of materials, it is necessary to study the very full documentary record, Pipe Rolls, and other detailed accounts related to their construction.

Early in 1278 it seems that the professional direction of these castle projects had been entrusted to a military engineer-architect, Master James of St George, 'ingeniator' who came from Savoy where he had been involved in building a group of castles in the Viennois for the king's uncle, Count Philip of Savoy. Master James was well rewarded by Edward I and received, among other grants, the unprecedented award in 1284 of 3s a day for life, and 1s 6d a day to his wife, Ambrosia. This was a job the responsibilities of which were comparable in scale to those of one of the top executives today, say the Chairman of ICI or the British Steel Corporation. They included, first of all, the collection of an enormous labour force by scouring the whole country from not only Wales and the Marches, but from Northumberland to Somerset. Freemasons, roughmasons, quarriers, carpenters, smiths, carters and boatmen gathered together, sometimes under duress, to engage in the king's works. The numbers of men involved in the building of Beaumaris Castle, for instance, included 400 masons, 2,000 labourers, and there were jobs for 30 smiths and carpenters. Numerous orders went out to supply this labour-force. 'The keepers of the (vacant) See of Winchester are ordered to have 1,000 quarters of wheat, 600 quarters of oats and 200 quarters of barley carted to Chester.' The roads were full of marching workmen accompanied by mounted sergeants and guides and wagons carrying their tools. The carpenters were particularly busy in the early stages of building a castle like Conwy. The first works were the putting up of a timber *bretagium* (brattice) to enclose the site. Great quantities of timber had to be felled and cut for building work-huts, for raising a variety of buildings to house the wardrobe★ and for making barrows, bayards, scaffolding and cranes. The *fossatores* hewed out rock-cut ditches and moats, and cut rock platforms and foundation trenches for the walls and towns. At this stage the masons came in: we find a mason called John Flauner at Conwy, cutting the rock, building walls and a turret near the water gate, battlementing a stretch of the northern part of the town walls, making 142 arches in different parts of the castle and walls, making chimneys at the mill gate and for a chamber at Sir Otto de Grandison's Hall, and working 250 stones for voussoirs for various doors and windows in the castle, and so on.

Such works needed regular injections of money and if this ran out the construction came to a standstill . . . '*et tunc cessavit opus pro defectu pecunie*'. The money all had to be transported from either England or Ireland. In less than six months in 1295 as much as £6,500 was issued for Beaumaris Castle alone; this represents over one-and-a-half million silver pennies. Stone, lime and sand also needed to be stockpiled. The building stone was obtained from quarries close to the site but freestone was often brought long distances. At Harlech freestone was brought by land and sea from Egryn, 11.3 km to the south; lime and limestone had to come by sea from Caernarfon and Anglesey, a distance of 96.6 to 112.7 km. Four sources of building materials were used for Rhuddlan. Some stone came by water from Cheshire, and some from a quarry on the Elwy, a distance of 6.4 km. One hundred carts, 60 wagons and 30 boats were used to bring stone and sea coal (for burning lime) for Beaumaris. Coal was shipped to all the northern castles from Whelston, near Holywell, in Flintshire. Timber mainly came from the forests on either sides of the Mersey estuary, and later from the wooded sides of the valley of the River Conwy. Lead was brought in from Shropshire and some was shipped from the Mendips via Bristol. Iron for making

tools, and steel for hardening and sharpening tools was used in quantities by the smiths, especially for repairing the chisels of the quarriers and stone dressers.

A careful study of the castle walls and towers themselves reveals a number of fascinating details. There are various horizontal breaks and changes in material or alignment; it was common masons' practice to cap an uncompleted stretch of work with a thin spread of mortar at the end of a season. A temporary coping of thatch was provided during the winter months, to prevent frost damage. The joint is likely to be of a double thickness of mortar here. It was also common practice to erect a scaffold of vertical poles and horizontal putlogs, all tied together with rope. The lower ends of the poles were set in post-holes in the ground and are frequently found in archaeological excavations. Since medieval walls were normally built on both sides simultaneously, the putlogs were passed right through at times. Spiralling lines of small round holes at Conwy Castle reveal that loads of stone were wheeled or dragged up scaffolding fixed at an incline, not horizontally. Other large square holes are to be seen at a uniform level below the crenellations: into these were fixed timber beams, which supported overhanging screens to shelter archers along the wall tops.

Those parts of the castle, constructed of timber, have to be recreated largely in the imagination of the visitor. Wood rots away quite quickly. We know for instance that the timbers in eight major towers of Beaumaris Castle which were never completed had already perished by the middle of the fourteenth century. Timber was used for ladders, shuttering, centring, for the floors and roofs, doors and gates, partitions and window shutters of stone-built structures, for timber-framed structures, and for bridges.

Most timber components of castles have disappeared altogether and can only be reconstructed from beam holes, putlog holes and slots. In waterlogged conditions, however, at the bottoms of moats, are found the remains of bridges by which the castles were approached.[23] Moats, in a number of ways, provide ideal conditions for the preservation of timber bridges. The bottom was usually level

----

★ Office or department of royal or noble household charged with care of wearing apparel.

and the natural scour slight; where a bridge has been dismantled or reconstructed on another plan often the plates were reused or just abandoned as not worth salvaging. Finally, anaerobic conditions favour the preservation of timbers complete with joints. Hence at Eynsford (Kent) or Caerlaverock (Dumfries) a succession of bridges has been found side by side or in close stratigraphic relation.

Castle bridges were of three types. A few were supported on rigid piles or sharpened stakes driven straight into the bed of the moat. Far more frequently, however, the timber uprights were trestles slotting into crosswise beams known as sole plates. These were shored by supporting struts also embedded in sole plates. The rigidity was given to the structure by the timbers bearing the walkway. This was the 'transverse trestle'. A third and more stable structure still was provided by sole plates running in both directions. This was the 'self stable' type. A gap in the walkway was left in the bay nearest to the entrance to the castle and this was of course spanned by the drawbridge. Of 40 surviving bridge structures, 28 are of the 'transverse trestle' type and at least ten, probably two or three more, are 'self stable'.

By the end of the Middle Ages the science of defence had so far outstripped the developments of attacking weapons available to besieging forces that castles tended to be bypassed. Military activity during the Wars of the Roses was virtually confined to marches, countermarches, skirmishes and battles in the field. In the past, the introduction of gunpowder into warfare as another reason for the decline of castles, has been exaggerated. By the time that artillery of sufficient power had been developed to threaten contemporary methods of fortification the castle had already seriously declined in importance. In one area, however, in the far north of England, near the Scottish border, local conditions forced great and lesser landlords to defend themselves as best they could from the numerous incursions of the Scots. 'Pele towers', as they were called, were rectangular towers standing within a small simple walled courtyard or 'barmkiln'. They were in effect simplified and usually smaller rectangular tower keeps. Their owners could not afford the vastly expensive structure of a

major castle incorporating the latest features of advanced fortification.

4. Castles as Residences

So far we have emphasised, quite rightly, the primary role of the castle as fortress. It had, however, a secondary purpose, that of residence. This has received less attention partly because it is a less exciting topic than the eternal dialogue between defence and offence, and partly for the simple archaeological reason that living accommodation is built less robustly and therefore survives less completely than more massively built walls and towers. There are close parallels with residences provided on undefended sites although castles are more compressed in their plan-layout. Towers, for instance, encouraged multi-storey accommodation. The Bishop of St Davids, who had only the one castle in his diocese at Llanwhaden, could offer his guests what in effect were luxury flats in the range adjoining the south curtain wall. Also as defences became thinner, more windowed, or were lowered in the Later Middle Ages, residential suites abandoned their spartan austerity and flowered luxuriously. The results included Edward III's princely restructurings of the upper ward of Windsor Castle, rivalled by the Ducal magnificence of John of Gaunts' Kenilworth.

Until recently the accounts of the internal buildings in castles have relied heavily on the terse reference to building in such sources as Henry II's Pipe Rolls or the detailed instructions for decorations in the Liberate Rolls of Henry III. Archaeological examination of levels inside castles is providing a wealth of information about the buildings and the life style of their occupants. Weoley Castle now occupies a most unlikely spot among the semidetached houses of a Birmingham suburb (Plates 2.5, 2.6). It is characteristic in that the earlier building phases c. 1100-1200 of this baronial fortification were mostly of timber construction. A hall in stone was built c. 1200-60 connected by a covered corridor to a wooden kitchen whose floor was renewed six times. This evidence for heavy use emphasises a feature common in castles. Large numbers of

Plates 2.5/2.6: Weoley Castle, Birmingham. Two views under snow of the layout of this site, after excavation. Plate 2.5 (above) shows the great hall with central fireplace, looking towards the kitchen area. Plate 2.6 (below) shows the defences and the moat. The great hall is in the distance beyond brew and bakehouse (Photos: J.M. Steane)

people gathered together here during peace-time for administrative or judicial reasons, they paid their rents or attended courts and were entertained as a result. A complete rebuild followed at Weoley in the late four-teenth century when a new gatehouse, guest-house, chapel and replacement stone hall were added. A further two ranges of stables, brewhouse, bakehouse and laundry were added along the south and western sides. There was also evidence in the form of quantities of manure and straw that part of the moated area was being used as a farmyard at this time. Discoveries at Stamford Castle, 1971-6, reinforce this last point. Here there were corn-drying kilns, bake-ovens and a wine cellar, reminding us that the castle community was an economically self-sufficient unit, the castle a food-processing plant as well as a fortress.

5. Henry VIII's Coastal Defences

In 1538-9, Henry VIII was faced by the possible combined threat of invasion from France and Spain. His coffers were, for the time being, full of spoils from the Dissolution of the Monasteries and he undertook a pro-gramme of castle building which was the first coastal defence on a national scale since the Romans had built the Saxon shore-forts (Plate 2.7).[24] His intention was to protect the landing places, harbours and anchorages along the Channel. 'His Majesty in his own person', said the Tudor historian Lambarde, 'without any delay, took very laborious and painful journies towards the sea coasts . . . and in all such doubtful places His Highness caused divers and many bulwarks and fortifications to be made'. Henry seems to have been influenced by recent advances in fortifications made on the continent, particularly in Germany and the hand of a master engineer, Stefan von Haschenperg, is evident here.

The siting of these fortifications is inter-esting. The Thames estuary was made safer by the building of a fort at Tilbury. The Downs anchorage in the narrow waters between the Kentish and French coasts was probably Henry's priority. Here he built castles at Sandown, Deal, Walmer, Sandgate and Camber (Figure 2.5). Dover was given improved harbour works and gun batteries were plugged into the cliffs, see p. 52. Further down the Channel, the passage of the Solent between the Needles and the mainland was protected by Hurst Castle. Calshot Castle commanded the entrance to Southampton water and was backed up by Netley Castle across the estuary to the north.

The entrance to the River Medina on the Isle of Wight was controlled by two block-houses at East and West Cowes. Furthermore, Portsmouth's defences were strengthened, and Weymouth Bay dominated by two forts (Plate 2.7). And so it continued all the way down to the south-western peninsula, including castles at such places as Falmouth and Dartmouth.

These 'artillery castles', as they have been called, were specifically designed for mounting cannon but militarily speaking were out of date almost as soon as they were built.[25] They all show the same characteristics of design, being centrally planned and concentrically defended, their round walls, bastions and parapets being designed to deflect gunshot.

Camber Castle (Sussex) stands, squat and menacing, on a shingle ridge above salt marshes 1.6 km to the south-west of the former Cinque Port of Rye (Figure 2.5).[26] It was built to command the entrance to a large natural harbour, an ideal landing place for a French invasion. Intensive archaeological and documentary investigation has established three main bursts of building. Sir Edward Guldeford began the low round gun tower in 1512-14. Henry VIII commissioned Stefan von Haschenperg to remodel it in 1539-40, despite worries about the incipient silting-up of the haven. The result was an elaborate concentric structure; four bastions backed by stirrup-shaped towers were linked to each other by an eight-sided curtain. Vaulted tunnels joined the bastions to a passage ringing round the central tower which was progres-sively raised and strengthened to take great guns. A third defensive skin was supplied by massive semicircular bastions added to four sides of an octagonal enclosure of ponderous strength. These works required a specially built bridge by which wagonloads of stone could be brought from the local quarries at Fairlight, Hastings and Playden. Caen stone

Plate 2.7: Portland Castle, Dorset. This fort was built by Henry VIII as part of his coastal defence system against the threat of invasion by Francis I of France. It was ready for use in 1540. It formed with Sandsfoot Castle a pair of fortresses facing one another across Weymouth Bay. It was designed for heavy artillery. The outer defences protecting it from landward attack have largely gone but were apparently shot-proof banks and ditches (Photo: J.M. Steane)

(paradoxically provided by the potential foe, the French) came in by sea and was exchanged for billets. Timber for the floors and scaffolding was prepared in the woods of Udimore, Beckley and Appledore. Bricks and lime, on the other hand, were manufactured on site, with clay, straw and chalk brought from Dover. All this material was topped up with second-hand stone and hard-core plundered from one of the religious houses of Winchelsea. Like many modern armaments, Henry's efforts were immensely costly and quickly obsolescent. Camber's guns were never fired in anger. The fears of the military Cassandras proved justified; the haven silted up and Camber Castle was abandoned.

In this, the most extensive (and expensive) scheme of work of its kind undertaken in England until the present century, the State had directly concerned itself with defensive measures almost for the first time. It is the end of the story as far as the castle as a joint residence and fortification is concerned. In the future, as artillery became more powerful, fortifications sank lower and were buried in earthen ramparts. Houses for the nobility went their own separate way.

6. Town Defences[27]

We have noticed that during the period of Danish invasions back in the ninth and tenth centuries AD, fortified towns or 'burhs' were bases to which the army could rally and thence make sorties; they were places of refuge for people from the surrounding countryside; they were bases which might discourage attack owing to their strength. To begin with, these fortified places were south of the Thames; as the English began to take the offensive and carry the war into the Danelaw, the Danes themselves were forced to fortify their conquests. This was the origin of such Danish burhs as Derby, Nottingham, Leicester, Stamford and Lincoln. From the period of the Norman Conquest until the thirteenth century one gains the impression that while castles were important, fortified towns were not. Towards the end of the twelfth century there is increasing political and commercial activity in towns and the chronicler, Richard of Devizes, remarked that during the absence of King Richard I (on crusade) 'castles were strengthened, towns were fortified, and moats were dug'. Moreover, between 1204 and 1220 England was faced with a serious double threat of invasion from both France and Wales and this led to a renewed interest in building fortifications round towns.

We hear about this in the documents in three ways. First, the towns themselves were granted the right to levy a tax on goods coming into the town called a 'murage' grant (from the Latin *murus* — wall). This tax was to be spent on walling the town. Secondly, the government might make grants of timber to help build defences. In 1215, for instance, Winchester and York received baulks of timber for use in making 'the turrets of the

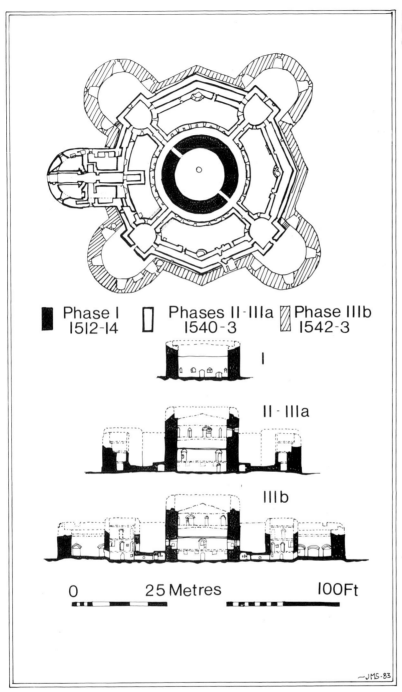

Figure 2.5: Evolution of Ground Plan of Chamber Castle, Sussex (after Biddle, 1982)

city and to make the wall walks'. Thirdly, cash grants were made by the government, or dues were reduced from towns which were expected to apply the proceeds towards defences. When towns were fortified from the start like the planned towns of Beaumaris,

Conwy, Caernarfon, Denbigh, Flint and Rhuddlan, their walls were paid for by direct royal subsidy.

The development of town defences shows a fairly close parallel progress with that of private castles. To begin with, burhs were walled with ditches and earthen ramparts, sometimes crowned with a palisade, sometimes fronted by a slight stone wall. From the thirteenth century stronger walls with formidable towers and heavily defended gateways began to appear. It is usual for the castle (if there was one within the town) to have some connection with the town defences. Usually the castle occupied the highest point in the town and the town defences joined up with it. This happens at Arundel (Sussex) and Totnes (Devon). The castles at Carlisle (Cumberland) and Shrewsbury (Shropshire) project beyond the wall but at Ludlow (Shropshire), Canterbury (Kent) and Southampton (Hants.) they stood within the circuit. The plan of the outline of the walls around the town was almost always either rectangular or circular and attempts were made to fit them into the lie of the ground. There are often cases where the stone walls have been linked to earlier defences. At York, Lincoln, Chester and London they have been attached to Roman fortresses and the line of the Roman fort has been simply extended (see Figure 2.6). Where Saxon timber defences were replaced, again the stone fortification represents an extension; this happened at Hereford, Worcester, Nottingham and Oxford (see Figure 4.6). These extensions were meant to include built-up areas which had occurred since the original circuit. To enable supplies and troops to reach the wall quickly a road called a *pomerium* was built and this can still be traced in many towns even though stretches of the wall have now disappeared. Oak Lane, Norwich, Cuckoo Lane, Southampton and Behind the Walls, Shrewsbury, are examples. Outside the wall was usually a ditch which prevented archers and, later, gunners from approaching too close to the vulnerable base of the walls and towers where there were blind spots in the defences. These ditches frequently had to be cleansed or scoured and occasionally we find townsfolk actually building houses in them!

As in castles the earth banks and ditches were little more than passive measures of defence. Stone-walled towns soon acquired other features which enabled townsmen to defend themselves more aggressively. They added mural towers or turrets from which they could discharge a crossfire of missiles to control the areas along the walls. These at first were shallow half-round projections; later D-shaped towers were found extending further from the wall. They exposed a smaller area to attacking fire, were better positioned to give flanking fire and could turn the wall through an obtuse angle more easily. In the fifteenth century more square towers were built than round; they may have been easier to mount and operate artillery. The finest examples of town defences in Great Britain are again those of Conwy and Caernarfon. The plan here was to create a masonry barrier difficult to breach and sectioned within so as automatically to isolate any scaling party which might have gained an entrance to the wall top. Each of the flanking towers was designed to act as a kind of circuit breaker between one section and the next. Only in one place, at Oxford, was an attempt made to defend the town by means of two circuits of walls — the inner overlooking an outer as was done in the concentric castles (see Figure 4.6).[28]

The wall-walks themselves were useful in maintaining communication between the towers, which frequently had no staircases themselves. But they were also used as a base from which volleys of arrows could be fired. Additional protection was provided by crenellation, and sometimes wooden frameworks or *bretasches* were erected to enable archers to command the dead ground below the walls. Occasionally there were two levels of arrow slits; the upper row was used from the wall-walk and the lower from ground level. Towards the end of the Middle Ages gunports were inserted, circular holes topped by a vertical slit. The earliest example is in the west walls of Southampton, dated to *c.* 1360, and measuring 12.7-15.2 cm in diameter, and the length of the slit about 1.12 m. One can trace the increase in size of the vertical hole to accommodate larger guns. By 1418 at Southampton, when the Catchcold tower was built, the hole had increased to a diameter of 27.9 cm. Guns had certain disadvantages in

Plate 2.8: London Wall. The north-western bastion of London Wall overshadowed to the north by the tower of St Giles Cripplegate and to the south by a concrete bridge leading to the modern development of the Barbican. (Photo: J.M. Steane)

Plate 2.9: Oxford. Former line of city wall incised on paving stones between Clarendon building and Bodleian Library. The building with the pyramidal roof is the Chapel of St Mary at Smith's Gate which stood immediately to the north-east of the town-gate of that name. It was built 1520-1 and is now part of Hertford College (Photo: Oxfordshire County Council Department of Museum Services)

use; they were less manoeuvrable than bows and were slower to bring into action; their line of fire was limited to a straight line, and their range was not so great, nor were they as accurate for a long time as a well-trained bowman. They did, however, have a certain psychological value and their noise no doubt boosted the morale of the defenders!

Again, as in castles, more trouble was taken over gateways than any other part of town defences. Their importance is indicated by the fact that in a number of towns the gates were built in stone before any other part of the defences. The early examples were rectangular structures, a single passageway going between two guard chambers. Projecting semicircular

towers were added onto the front face and by the mid-fourteenth century two circular towers flanking a passageway had become normal. The chambers above the arch housed the winding gear of the portcullis, and at times they were used for other purposes such as a Guildhall, at Southampton, or the Exchequer, as at Caernarfon. Towards the end of the Middle Ages with a relaxation of military requirements they became rectangular again. They were now simply civic status symbols, decked with the trappings of fortification, but displaying as well (as at York with coats of arms and statues), the wealth and prestige of the town. For these reasons the walls and gates of towns were shown on the seals of cities;

Plate 2.10: Oxford. Former line of city wall has determined the alignments of the Sheldonian (right) and the old Bodleian (left) (Photo: Oxfordshire County Council Department of Museum Services)

that of the barons of London shows part of the city over the wall. Colchester, Oxford and Shrewsbury also depicted the town wall on their seals, the symbol of civic pride. The town wall in fact had other purposes than a means of defence against attack. It could help to police people coming in and going out of the town. It was obviously easier to collect tolls when all merchants had to come through the gates. The degree of safety acquired by the walled town attracted traders to markets. Finally the wall itself, its towers and gatehouse, might be a source of profit. Mural towers were leased out to private individuals, and this helped in their upkeep. On London's wall as many as four of the towers were inhabited by hermits! Gateways might serve as gaols or chapels. The fact that no less than 108 out of the 249 towns which were in possession of charters by 1520 were walled, shows that fortification was highly regarded as a badge of freedom from seignorial interference. Only eight out of the 46 towns owned by the church

were walled and many of the other unwalled towns had been deliberately founded by lords who wished to keep them under their control.

7. A Medieval Walled-town: York

The most complete set of medieval town walls in England, and among the finest in Europe, are those of York (Plate 2.11; Figure 2.6).[29] With a perimeter of just over 3.2 km and enclosing an area of 106.4 ha they are not as long as the former fortifications of Bristol, Coventry, London, Newcastle and Norwich. York is divided into three parts by the River Ouse which flows from north-west to south-east and by its tributary the River Foss, running north-south to a confluence below the old city. The largest of these parts is the central area of York which includes the site of the Roman fortress; on the opposite bank of the Ouse is the Micklegate area; a third and smaller lozenge-shaped area is east of the Foss

Plate 2.11: York. Looking north-west. Practically the whole of the core of the historic city is seen in this photograph. The Minster straddles the rectilinear legionary fortress. The Viking and medieval city with numerous church towers and spires is contained between the two rivers; Ouse on the left and Fosse on the right. In the foreground are William I's two castles, the Old Baile under the blob of trees left foreground and on the opposite bank the motte with Clifford's tower on the top and the Castle in the shield-shaped area below it. The bastioned town walls are visible bottom left, bottom right and top right but are less noticeable from the air than the flowing traffic streams of the renewed road systems which contrast with the narrow thoroughfares of the medieval city. (Photo: Cambridge University Committee for Aerial Photography, taken 11.7.70)

with Walmgate as its axis.

Three periods of urban defences can be seen at York. The Roman defences of the playing-card shaped legionary fortress were sited on the north-east bank of the River Ouse; on the opposite bank was the civil town. The Danes took the city in 867 and covered the former defences with a broad earth bank crowned with a palisade. They extended the enclosure outside the Roman wall to the marshy banks of the two rivers. In 1068-9 William I built two castles to the south-east of the city, one on each bank of the Ouse, the Old Baile and Clifford Castle. The Danish earth bank was strengthened by the Normans and an extension was built to enclose the Walmgate suburb. Stone gates were erected at Micklegate Bar, Victoria Bar, Bootham Bar, north-west of the present March Bar, at Walmgate Bar,

and perhaps elsewhere. In the middle of the thirteenth century the walls, built of white magnesian limestone from Tadcaster, were erected on top of the earth rampart. Henry III, in the meantime, rebuilt York Castle and, in 1266, St Mary's Abbey started to enclose its precinct with a similar wall to that of the city. The Walmgate sector of the wall was built after 1345, and the Red Tower and Fishergate postern tower were not built until the reign of Henry VII.

The most unusual feature of the walls of York is that they top an earthen bank. This strange position is largely due to the covering of the ruined Roman walls by the massive bank when the city became the Viking capital. When the defences were extended to other suburbs, ramparts of a similar scale were dug. Their size led to the building of stone walls on

Figure 2.6: Viking and Medieval York (after RCHM, 1972)

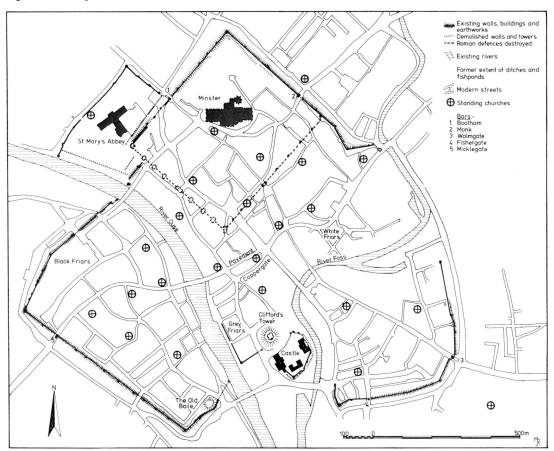

the top rather than in front of them. The walls are consequently low in comparison with those of Oxford and Southampton. They are equipped with numerous towers averaging 70 m apart. There are three basic forms. The oldest are semicircular; rectangular towers are next in sequence; and the demi-hexagonal towers occur in all parts of the city walls. Nearly all the towers had a stone rear wall. The towers were provided with arrow slits, the most usual type being a simple vertical slit but often they have elaborate terminals with splayed recesses behind it. Altogether there are 168 arrow slits in the defences.

The four main gates or Bars have passages 3-3.7 m wide which could be blocked by an inner and an outer gate with a portcullis in front. Barbicans were added with gates at their entrances but only one still projects at Walmgate. Portcullises survive at the four main bars but only one, Monks Bar, is in working order. The grate is 4.3 m high and 3.7 m wide with 12 metal shod spikes at the foot. A horizontal windlass, turned by wooden handspikes, operates it from the second floor of the gatehouse. They fit into sockets and there is an iron ratchet and pawl at one end which prevents the windlass from slipping back but allows the portcullis to be lowered in a hurry by a flick of the hand. There is only one ancient gate left, mounted on the inner arch of Walmgate Bar. The carpentry has an outer face of vertical oak boards; the inner face boards are horizontal. Broad headed nails stud the outer face. There is a small wicket 1.2 m high and 60 cm broad. Some attempt was made to bring the defences up to date by adding two gunports on the third floor of each gate. Two guns were supplied to each bar in 1511. It is possible that the gallery across the front of the gatehouse was used for loading or cooling cannon set in fixed beds trained on these apertures. Further gunports were inserted in other places in the walls.

8. Moated Sites

Castles provided a measure of security, a sense of magnificence and an illusion of power for the nobility and the Crown. Town defences protected burghers or impressed their business rivals. There was a third type of fortification which is only just beginning to be better known — the moated site (Plate 2.12; Figure 2.7).[30] This has been defined as 'an area of ground, often occupied by a dwelling or associated structure, bounded or partly bounded by a wide ditch which in most cases was intended to be filled with water'. They are very numerous; some 5,300 moats are listed in the records of the Moated Sites Research group. Their general distribution demonstrates an obvious link with the lowland areas underlain by clay in northern, central and eastern England. Large numbers are found in those parts of the country which are potentially ill-drained — where chalk, limestone, sand or gravel are absent. Particular concentrations occur in three areas. The first is near Chelmsford and Harlow in Essex and Bishop's Stortford in Hertfordshire where there are 61 sites in the 100 km^2 TL51 of the National Grid. A second sizeable concentration (47 sites) in the 100 km^2 north of Framlingham (TM 27) is located in an area extending from Suffolk into Essex. A third area is around Birmingham — where there are 36 sites per km^2. One feature is common — they are found in greater densities in areas of woodland where colonisation occurred during the Later Middle Ages. Such landscapes are characterised by small fields, hedged and fenced, held in severalty, surrounding small hamlets and single farms.

The classification of moats by types of siting has been attempted. Since the basic idea behind the moat was to keep it filled with water, this is the chief clue to understanding the site. There are four main types: (1) those deriving their water supply directly from streams or rivers. Here the inlet and outlet channel will need to be recognised — there may be an enlarged outer bank on the down-slope side damming back the water; (2) moats dug on low-lying ground, deriving their water from natural seepage or by channelling from nearby streams; (3) those set on permanently damp ground which might even be on a hillside where there are springs; (4) a few sites are on hilltops or slopes and were never meant to be filled with water.

As for the shape of moats they defy straightforward analysis. They can in fact be of

Plate 2.12: Bassingbourne, Cambridgeshire. These moats lie near the junction of the chalk slopes and clay vale in the basin of the upper Cam 14.5 km south-west of Cambridge. They show up in this aerial photo taken in the drought summer of 1976 by reason of the contrast in colour between the crop ripening in the field and over filled-up ditches. In the foreground there is a contrast in tone between the black soil filling the ditches and the whitish chalk marl surrounding them. The earthworks seem to represent at least three constructional phases. The rectangular central moat is probably twelfth century in date. The elaborate outer moat with bastions perhaps dates from a licence to crenellate in 1266. The third narrower enclosure is likely to be later. Other medieval features are an entrance causeway and a black rectangle on the right probably a fishpond. Further disturbances in the foreground are filled-in coprolite diggings made in the nineteenth century. (Photo: Cambridge University Committee for Aerial Photography)

almost any shape. (Plate 2.12; Figure 2.7). Perhaps the classic site is where the enclosure or island is roughly rectangular, but they can be circular or D-shaped. Many were only moated on three sides; a show of defence might be maintained by only moating two sides of an enclosure. It is often difficult to tell what the original form of the earthwork was because they have so often been tampered with. Some are partially filled, a wet ditch choked with vegetation may be all that is recognisable. In others stream action may have resulted in the widening of one side; many were undoubtedly adapted for fishponds. Cattle scrapes may reveal the former presence of stone revetments or clay linings. Traces of abutments betray the existence of former bridges. More often access was provided by causeways but where there are two or three, they probably date from the period after the moat was abandoned.

Most moats were designed to enclose a house and associated structures such as barns and stables; others appear to have been empty of buildings and probably surrounded orchards or gardens. It is not completely clear that their principal function was military. They appear during the period 1200–1325, and may have served as a defence against the violence of plundering troops and local undesirables. Although moats were not formidable defences

they were valuable psychological barriers; their water was a necessary insurance against the ubiquitous risk of fire. Their social significance is that they were constructed by all seignorial sections of medieval society; the majority enclosed structures which might be termed 'manor houses'. Others encircled messuages attached to freehold estates which did not have manorial rights; the partially moated state of many sites suggests that the moat was to some extent a status symbol, a fashion originating among the aristocracy and extending downward through society, to the lesser knights and freemen. The phenomenon of the moated site underlined the separateness and exclusive character of the lord's share of the wealth in the community. It has even been suggested that they might have been used to protect the lord from his own peasantry. It must have been common knowledge among the nobility and gentry of later medieval England that their compeers across the channel had been savaged by frequent and bloody risings of the Jacquerie.

In Wales a somewhat different story emerges. Most moated sites so far recorded are found in the east and south.[31] These were in the areas on the edge of the territory conquered and dominated by Llywelyn ap Iorwerth and his grandson, Llywelyn ap Gruffydd, in the thirteenth century. Edward

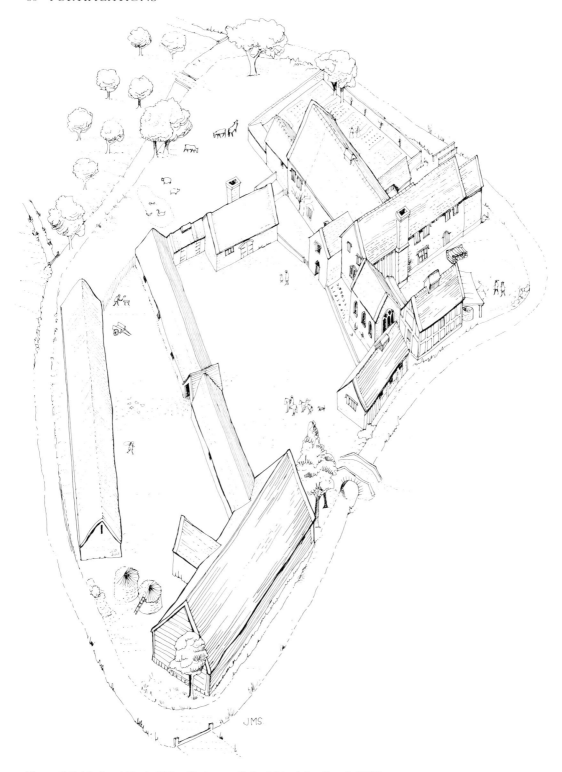

Figure 2.7: Medieval Moated Site, Chalgrove, Oxfordshire (after Beard, 1983)

I's final solution of the Welsh problem, as we have seen, was to create the Principality of Wales, riveted by eight new royal fortresses. Most of the moated-sites are found in the rest of the country where the anarchy of the autonomous marcher lordships flourished until 1536. They were largely associated with English names, such as de la Roche in Carmarthenshire, and Norris, de Cardiff, and de Sully in Glamorganshire. These were the heavily manorialised areas. In the absence of tower-houses,[32] such as were built in large numbers in the border zone between Scotland and England, moats would have provided some protection from petty brigandage and feuding along the unsettled march.

A chronology based on very scattered and imperfect information suggests that there were five main phases in the history of medieval moated sites. In the mid-twelfth century they tended to appear adjacent to clayland villages but during the thirteenth century manor houses migrated to the periphery of villages as settlements grew in size and lords grew more ambitious in planning their establishments. Phase II saw a great leap forward of the construction of moated sites in the period 1150-1200. In the Forest of Arden it has been noticed that the moat builders included freemen, franklyns, small landowners and even men from the upper ranks of the peasantry. Phase III, 1200-1325, saw the idea diffusing throughout rural society with about 44 per cent of the 5,000 or so sites being built. The uncertain and occasionally violent tenor of society encouraged the process, further stimulus being given by the expanding seignorial prosperity of this period; it fuelled the social aspirations of a wider group of people. The period 1325-1500 saw a pronounced falling off in numbers of moats constructed; this reflected the general depression of economic conditions but disorders such as the Peasant's Revolt and the Wars of the Roses at times injected new interest. The period after 1500 saw the abandonment of large numbers of previously moated homesteads with rising standards of comfort and a greater sense of domestic security; many older sites were abandoned or remodelled. A legacy of 'old hall sites was left and the moats began to be filled in all over the country'.

References

1. Sandford, A., *Hereford, Archaeology in the City*, Hereford, no date, 5-6.
2. Baker, D. *et al.*, 'Excavations in Bedford 1967-77', *Bedford Arch. J.*, 13, 1979, 296-8.
3. Hinton, D.A., *Alfred's Kingdom: Wessex and the South 800-1500*, London, 1977, has a detailed discussion of the burghal defence system, 30-41.
4. Davison, B., 'Sulgrave', *Current Archaeology*, 12, Jan. 1969, 22; *Med. Arch.*, XVII, 147, XVIII, 98f, XX, 39.
5. Beresford, G., 'The excavation of the deserted medieval village of Goltho, Lincolnshire', *Chateau Gaillard Studies*, VIII, Caen, 1977, 55.
6. Davison, B.K., 'Early earthwork castles: a new model' in Taylor, A.J. (ed.), *Chateau Gaillard Studies*, III, Chichester, 1969, 37-47.
7. Davison, 'Sulgrave', 38-9.
8. Davison, B.K., 'Three eleventh century earthworks in England, their excavation and implications', *Chateau Gaillard Studies*, II, Cologne, 1967, 40-3.
9. Davison, B.K., 'Castle Neroche: an abandoned Norman fortress in South Somerset', *Somerset Arch. & Nat. Hist. Soc.*, 116, 1972, 16-58.
10. Barker, P., 'Hen Domen, Montgomery: excavations 1960-7' in Taylor, A.J. (ed.), *Chateau Gaillard Studies*, III, Chichester, 1969, 15-28.
11. Cathcart King, D.J. and Alcock, L., 'Ringworks of England and Wales' in Taylor, ibid., 90-127.
12. Alcock, L., 'Castle Tower, Penmaen, a Norman ringwork in Glamorgan', *Antiq. J.*, XLVI, 1966, 178-210.
13. Barker, P., *Techniques of Archaeological Excavation*, London, 1977, 252-3.
14. Hope-Taylor, B., 'The Norman motte at Abinger, Surrey, and its wooden castle' in Bruce Mitford, R.L.S. (ed.), *Recent Archaeological Excavations in Britain*, London, 1956, 223-49.
15. Blair, J., 'William Fitz Ansculf and the Abinger motte', *Archaeol. J.*, 138, 1981, 146-8.
16. Davison, B., 'Aldingham', *Current Archaeology*, 12, Jan. 1969, 23-4.
17. Renn, D.F., 'The Anglo-Norman keep 1066-1138', *Journal of Brit. Arch. Assoc.*, 3rd ser., XXIII, 1960, 1-24 offers the best general account of keeps. Also Braun, H., 'Bungay Castle, report on the excavations', *Procs. of Suffolk Inst. of Arch.*, XXII, 201-23; Renn, D.F., 'The keep of Wareham Castle', *Med. Arch.*, IV, 1960, 56-68; Allen Brown, R., *Orford Castle Suffolk*, DoE Guide, London, 1978.

At Bungay is an excavated mine shaft and tunnel made by besiegers under one corner of the keep and the forecourt. Strangely it does not appear to have caused a collapse.

18. Renn, D., 'Defending Framlingham Castle', *Procs. of Suffolk Inst. of Arch.*, XXXIII, 1976, 58-67.

19. Jones, P.N. and Renn, D., 'The military effectiveness of arrow loops. Some experiments at White Castle', *Chateau Gaillard Etudes de Castellogie Medievale*, IX-X, 1978-80, Caen, 1982, 445-55.

20. An interesting account of a gatehouse is in Renn, D.F., 'An Angevin gatehouse at Skipton Castle', *Chateau Gaillard Studies*, VII, Caen, 1975, 173-82.

21. Mayes, P. and Butler, L., *Sandal Castle Excavations, 1964-73*, Wakefield, 1983.

22. Taylor, A.J., 'Castle building in Wales in the later thirteenth century: the prelude to construction' in Jope, E.M. (ed.), *Studies in Building History*, London, 1961, 104-33 on which the next seven paragraphs are based.

23. Rigold, S.E., 'Structural aspects of medieval timber bridges', *Med. Arch.*, XIX, 1975, 48-91.

24. Morley, B.M., *Henry VIII and the Development of Coastal Defence*, HMSO, London, 1976. Also a stimulating lecture given to the Society of Antiquaries by M. Biddle.

25. Shelby, L.R., 'Guines Castle and the development of English bastioned fortifications' in Taylor, A.J. (ed.), *Chateau Gaillard Studies*, III, Chichester, 1969, 139-43.

26. Biddle, M., 'Camber Castle' in Colvin, H.M. (ed.), *The History of the Kings Works, IV, 1485-1660* (Part II), London, HMSO, 1982, 415-47.

27. Turner, H.L., *Town Defences in England and Wales*, London, 1970.

28. Hassall, T.G., 'City walls, gates and posterns', *Victoria County History, Oxon*, IV, 1979, 300-4.

29. For the next section see Royal Commission on Historical Monuments (England), *City of York, II The Defences*, HMSO, 1972.

30. Aberg, F.A., (ed.), *Medieval Moated Sites*, Council for British Archaeology Research Report 17, 1978.

31. Spurgeon, C.J., 'Moated sites in Wales' in Aberg, F.A. and Brown, A.E. (eds.), *Medieval Moated Sites in North-West Europe*, Oxford, 1981, 19-70.

32. Smith P., *Houses of the Welsh Countryside*, HMSO, London, 1975, Map 1.

3 RELIGION

1. The Power of the Medieval Church

It is difficult to comprehend the extent of the influence of organised religion on the lives of people in medieval England. Nowadays the average man (apart from the 5 per cent who are regular church-goers) comes into contact with the church at perhaps three times in his life. He may be taken as a baby to the local church or chapel to be baptised or christened; he (or his wife) might choose to be married in a church; and, when he dies, it is likely that a clergyman will be involved in the funeral service. For the rest he will listen (or perhaps switch off) when community hymn singing is broadcast on a Sunday on the radio or TV; he will read from time to time the pronouncements of bishops and archbishops on political affairs; and he will be dimly aware from the empty and sometimes redundant churches which lie scattered over the landscape that there is, or has been, a world of religion which now has little impact on him.

Things were very different in the Middle Ages. The church was certainly the most important ideological influence on the lives of people, with an organisation potent enough to mould aspects of the lives of the whole population. Economic historians widely differ in their estimates of total numbers of people; in 1347 the year before the Black Death it has been computed that the population was either as small as 3.7 million or as large as twice that number. To minister to this flock were 23,000 priests in a country divided into 8,000 parishes, registered in a survey of 1291, assisted by perhaps 10,000 clerics in minor orders.[1] The clergy were able to control people's thoughts and influenced their actions from cradle to the grave. From the books of instruction compiled for them by pastorally-minded bishops we know that priests were encouraged to insist in annual confession before Easter, in which they examined their parishioners about the orthodoxy of their beliefs as well as their keeping of the moral commandments. In the thirteenth century the Holy Communion or mass was being celebrated much more frequently as can be seen from the multiplicity of altars which developed, particularly in the greater churches. Chantry chapels similarly proliferated in the town churches during the Later Middle Ages. There was, moreover, a greater emphasis on preaching, provided by the Franciscan and Dominican friars; large preaching churches in the towns were built for them. The naves of parish churches were made more spacious to accommodate large congregations.

The church in England was not merely a religious power. Its vast endowments meant that it exercised economic leverage and inevitably was a political force. As part of international Christendom its head was the Pope who increasingly intervened in its affairs from the eleventh to the thirteenth centuries, leading to an anti-papal nationalistic reaction in the fourteenth century. Like the rest of feudal society it was hierarchically organised in England, being divided into the two arch-dioceses of Canterbury and York. The successive occupants of these sees were traditionally among the king's closest advisers. There were 19 dioceses, each with a cathedral, a great church which housed the *cathedra* or bishop's throne. Of these Canterbury, Rochester, Winchester, Worcester, Norwich, Ely and Durham were also Benedictine monasteries.

Bath and Coventry were also cathedral monasteries but they shared their status in their dioceses with the 'secular' Wells and Lichfield. The great complexes of buildings which grew up in cathedral cities were maintained by the contributions of the faithful who flocked to the shrines and left their offerings by the holy relics collected in them.

Kings and barons had made their peace with God by massively endowing monasteries in the century after the Norman Conquest. By 1217, the beginning of Henry III's reign, there were about 180 larger monasteries with about 500 smaller communities. Within these there was a monastic population of about 12,500 in 1217 increasing to 17,500 by 1340. Between them these communities owned perhaps a fifth of the country's total wealth. Much of this wealth was used for the construction of ever more magnificent monastic churches and conventual buildings. The destruction of these at the Dissolution of the Monasteries was the greatest act of vandalism in our history.

This chapter begins with an account of the siting of greater churches and monasteries and in particular the water management associated with them. There follows an analysis of the component parts of monastic layouts. Conventual buildings rarely survive in their entirety and their ruins are difficult to comprehend without some explanation. An attempt is then made to describe how such enormous congeries of buildings were financed, and the important role of pilgrimage is touched upon. Parish churches provide the second main theme. Nothing is said of their architectural styles because this aspect has been overwritten in the past. Less familiar topics such as siting, dedications and functions are surveyed. A brief list of clues to look for when puzzling out the evolution of churches (or for that matter any buildings) is appended.

Examples of recent archaeological investigation of churches and cemeteries are given. Finally, disease and its treatment, especially in hospitals, is described. Taken together archaeological vestiges are a prolific source for reconstructing the powerful phenomenon of medieval religion.

2. Siting and Water Supply of Greater Churches and Monasteries

The essential prerequisite of the site of a great medieval church or monastery was a large piece of land, if possible fairly flat, on which the church, living-quarters and buildings to provide for various agricultural activities could be laid out. One difficulty arose from the extreme reluctance of medieval man to change the site of an ancient church and its sacred associations. From recent excavations at Wells it appears that under the later medieval cloisters there lie the remains of the Anglo-Saxon cathedral.[2] To the east it seems that the 'Lady Chapel by the Cloister' was retained through most of the Middle Ages despite the fact that this Saxon building was aligned 18° off a true east-west axis and 12° off the axis of the present buildings. This alignment was focused on St Andrew's well; the copious springs to the east from which the settlement took its name. It also decided the layout of the market place and the main street and property boundaries of the city. So what we are saying has happened here is that the whole of the subsequent development of the town of Wells was determined by the alignment of the original string of buildings which made up the Anglo-Saxon cathedral.

Another problem which had to be overcome was the uneasy juxtaposition of lay and ecclesiastical land-uses. There was no love lost between the military garrison of Old Sarum and the cathedral clergy. Such friction was one reason for Bishop Richard Poore's decision in c. 1220 AD to abandon the hilltop-site and begin a new cathedral at Salisbury down in the water meadows of the Avon (see Figure 4.7). Urban sites were noisy and led to conflict between monks and townsmen as happened at Abingdon and Reading. Serious riots led to a demand that the ecclesiastical premises be protected by fortifications: hence the embattled walls surrounding the cathedral closes at Salisbury and Lincoln and Wells.

The Cistercians solved this particular difficulty by seeking out sites in 'places remote from human habitation' (see Plates 3.1, 3.2). The white monks spread to scarcely settled mountain and marshland areas of Wales and the north.[3] Cwmhir was described as being 'in a mountainous district, remote from parish churches'. Sometimes the Cistercians created solitude by simply removing the former inhabitants. Margam took over a settlement in this way and erased the church of Llangewydd overnight. The monks of Valle Crucis also displaced the men of Llanegwestl. Such contentious beginnings at times reacted against the Cistercians. The Welsh claimed Valle Crucis 'had been built on land wrested from them' and forced a move. Aberconwy was founded in 1186 at Rhedynog Felyn and then transferred the site to the gently sloping land at the mouth of the Conwy River. Edward I, appreciating the strategic value of the site, removed the community in 1283-4 to another position, 12.9 km upstream. Occasionally wild sites proved too difficult. Barnoldswick, 152 m up in the Aire gap of the Pennines, was exchanged for the kinder Kirkstall, only 61 m above sea level. The monks of Stanlaw stuck it out in their frequently inundated site on the Mersey estuary between 1172 and 1296 but eventually moved to a more sheltered position on the River Calder near the old established vill★ at Whalley.

An ample *water supply* was necessary to serve the needs of a monastic community. The ideal situation, which was found at Fountains, included both springs and a stream.[4] The springs could provide pure drinking water and the stream was led under various buildings through stone-lined conduits, eventually passing under the rere-dorter flushing out the sanitation. There was also the difficulty of removing excess water from the monastic site. Great complexes of buildings meant problems of run-off. In recent excavations at Norton Priory (Cheshire) it was found that the twelfth-century buildings were provided with a simple ditch system, possibly backed up with timber linings. The T-shaped rere-dorter was first provided with drains of hollowed tree-trunks.[5] When the church was enlarged *c.* 1200 and a new rere-dorter built, masonry drains were supplied which received a regular water flow. Subsidiary drains took away the roof water. To begin with, these were stone-built

with squared ashlar bases. In the fourteenth century they were replaced by circular drains with corbelled tops. An increased fall meant more efficient waste disposal. In the kitchens at Norton were great circular cisterns supplied by lead pipes. The whole monastic *enceinte* (enclosure) was surrounded by a moated water system controlled by sluice gates.

Perhaps the most impressive example of monastic water management was at Rievaulx Abbey in North Yorkshire (Plate 3.1).[6] This Cistercian abbey was founded in 1131 in a remote, wild and uncultivated area of the Rye Valley. The buildings are perched on the side of the valley at the bottom of a steep bluff: the narrowness of the site forced the builders to orientate the church north-south. They brought their building stone from Billsdale, Hollingswood and Penny Piece by constructing two canals which straightened out the winding course of the river; the northern cut was 530 m long, 2 m deep and 15 m wide. The southern arm was 1,500 m long and 30 m wide and probably 130,000 cubic metres of earth and rock were moved in three river diversions each involving additional grants of land, first in 1145 from the neighbouring abbey of Byland, then in *c.* 1160 from Hugo Malabestia and thirdly between 1193 and 1203 from Richard Malebisse. In the meantime the drinking water for the abbey came from springs in the hillside to the east which were fed through a conduit house.

Cistercians never ate fresh meat in the Early Middle Ages and fish was therefore an important source of animal protein. River fisheries were a prized endowment. Tintern was fortunate in its situation by the salmon waters of the River Wye; it had three weirs, Plumweir, Staweir and Alflard's weir. Unfortunately, such interests led to irreconcilable clashes with others. In 1330 'the raising of the weirs obstructed certain openings that always used to stand open in all the weirs aforesaid . . . to the disturbance of men with boats and ships wishing to pass by the said water'. The monks of Tintern also had permission to fish up to the middle of the Severn opposite their lands at Moor Grange and Woolaston. Often there are signs of earth-worked fishpond complexes near monastic houses. Bordesley Abbey (Hereford/Worcs.) is

★ A territorial unit consisting of a number of houses with their adjacent lands corresponding to a modern township or civil parish.

Plate 3.1: Rievaulx, North York-shire. This aerial photo brings out the remoteness of the site chosen for this Cistercian abbey, perched below a bluff in a steep sided and nearly wooded valley. The curving River Rye has been canalised both north and south of the abbey to facilitate the transporting of stone. These canals and dams are now drained dry but their earth-works can be traced on the ground. Not far from the western end a wharf was constructed to land stone from the quarry of Penny Piece some distance up-stream (Photo: Cambridge University Committee for Aerial Photography, taken 10.9.71)

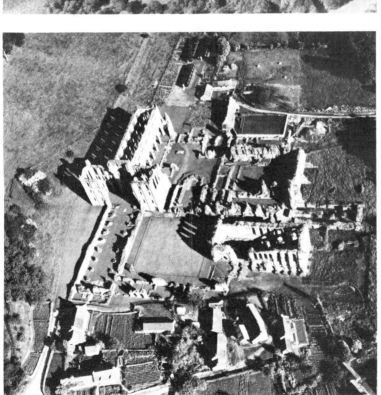

Plate 3.2: Rievaulx, North York-shire. The exigencies of the site forced its planners to orientate the church south-north with a result-ing swing of 90° round the com-pass for the whole complex. The church was unusually long, 112.8 m, and the Cistercian nave dated from 1135-40. The transepts are also Norman. Beyond is the mag-nificent Early English Gothic quire and presbytery with eastern ambulatory and chapels. To the right (in the photo) of the nave is the cloister; next to the church is the vestry and book room. Then an apsidal-ended chapter house with graves of the early abbots in the middle. Next was the parlour and the long undercroft to the dormitory, the foundations of which, insecure over falling ground, were buttressed on both sides. 'North' of the dormitory is the infirmary cloister with the infirmary complex, converted 40 years before the Dissolution into the abbot's lodging. South is the roofless ruin of the magnificent frater and the range in the fore-ground are the lay brothers' rather inadequate quarters (Photo: Cambridge University Committee for Aerial Photography, taken 5.7.48)

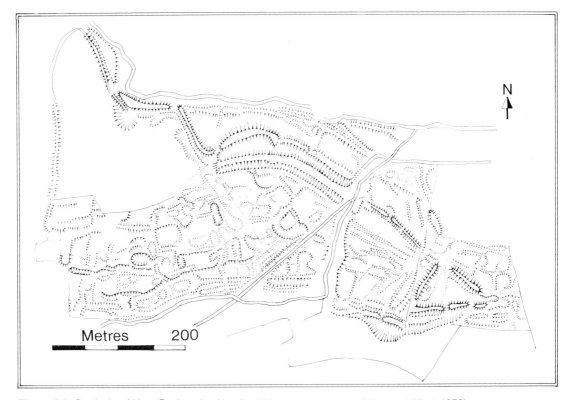

Figure 3.1: Bordesley Abbey Earthworks, Hereford/Worcestershire (after Rahtz and Hirst, 1976)

situated on a stretch of the Arrow Valley which has been extensively adapted for water power and fishponds since the thirteenth century (Figure 3.1).[7] There are two sites to the north of the abbey, one at Grange Farm where there are earthworks of the mill site, leats, dam and overflow channels. Further down the river is Weights Farm, where there is a series of parallel earthworks surrounded by deep channels, connected with some drainage or irrigation scheme. A survey of the banks, ditches and channels around the abbey site itself shows that there is a two-stage complex. It is thought that to begin with a smaller area with water courses was embanked around the abbey site. The second stage involved the diversion of the river around a larger low-lying area with a whole series of structures including fishponds, an elaborate drainage and irrigation scheme. Finally, a triangular mill pond was added beyond the precinct boundary bank.

3. The Outer Court

The chief buildings of the monastery or great church were generally concentrated in several courts and the whole complex was surrounded by a massive and lofty wall of stone entered through a main gatehouse. Often the wall has gone but the great gatehouse has remained with its vaulted passage. A room over this served sometimes as a court room, being connected to the ground floor by a staircase.

A number of cathedral precincts or closes are surrounded by walls, punctuated with gateways. At Peterborough the Minster Gate in front of the abbey (now the cathedral) surveys the market place. At Wells the close is entered by a series of embattled gates (Plate 4.8). At the north-west corner stands Brown's Gate, a fifteenth-century gatehouse with a separate pedestrian way. One can also penetrate from the market place into the close through the Pennyless porch built by Bishop Bekyngton in the fifteenth century; beggars used to gather here when soliciting alms. At the north-east corner of the close is an astonishing bridge with the Chaingate underneath. There is no entrance to the south-east where the close is guarded by the bishop's moated palace. Inside many monasteries was an outer court around which were ranged buildings concerned with the administrative side of the monastic estate. Here was stabling and accommodation for travellers and guests. St Benedict in his Rule, which provided the basis for regulating all early monasteries, positively encouraged a welcome to guests. These might include kings and barons who would arrive with great retinues, domestic staff, visiting ecclesiastics, farmers and travellers. There was also accommodation for poor people maintained at the monastery in return for bequests. Later in the Middle Ages there was a primitive form of insurance known as *corrodies*, whereby people made over sums of money or small pieces of property to the monastery in return for being allowed to 'live in'.

4. *The Conventual Church*

The most important building in the monastery was the church in which was performed the highly organised daily round of communal services including the series of daily offices. This started with Nocturns (now called Matins), the opening act of worship of the day. It was followed by Matins (the modern Lauds), Prime (which was sung at dawn), Terce, Sext, None, Vespers and the office of Compline which brought the monastic day to an end. In addition the major act of Christian worship was the Eucharist or Mass in which three officiating clergy might take part, and there were various other elaborations such as singing in Gregorian Plainsong and swinging the censer from which delicate blue smoke wafted heavenwards.

The complexities of medieval liturgy were constantly changing and careful inspection of the fabric of greater churches and parish churches shows clues as to these ritual developments. The ceremonies known as the Use of Sarum came into being first at Old Sarum under St Osmund and spread from the present Cathedral of Salisbury through the

other dioceses in the land.[8] At Salisbury, for instance, fixed to the pillar at the north end of the chancel is a wooden windlass with an iron handle; this was used during the Middle Ages to raise or lower the Lenten veil in front of the high altar. A hint of the impressive processions which were a normal and frequent event in a cathedral church is seen in the Lombardic lettering inscription on three Purbeck marble flags set in the choir pavement at Lincoln; 'CANTATE HIC' (Intone here). It marks a processional stopping place and it is claimed that this was one of the 12 spots acoustically chosen to be heard most effectively throughout the cathedral. Another example of ancient processional ritual embedded in the present building is seen at Salisbury. High up in the west front, now hidden by statuary, are nine quatrefoil openings. As the Palm Sunday procession approached the cathedral, the west front of which simulated the walls of Jerusalem, choirboys sang the hymn, 'All glory, laud, and honour' through these apertures. The development of beliefs connected with saints also took a tangible form. An obvious example is the multiplicity of representations in glass, paintings and images of the Virgin Mary from the twelfth century onwards as the cult grew, centred round the feasts of her conception and a little later her assumption.[9]

Each monastic or cathedral church has to be interpreted in the light of these ritual functions. The orientation was nearly always east-west with the monks' choir at the east end. This was for practical as well as liturgical reasons. As the major part of the monastic services came before midday, and all masses were said before this time (it was necessary to fast before a mass) it was desirable to make the best possible use of the rather thin and occasional English sunlight by having the monks' choir and as many as possible of the side chapels at the east end (there are nine at Fountains Abbey) where the morning sun could be expected. For the same reason the church was nearly always on the north side of the cloister because being the tallest building it would have blotted out the sun in any other position. Also it acted as a draught excluder on the north side.[10]

In plan the most popular shape was the

cruciform or cross-shaped church. The western arm or the nave was the longest. This was approached from the gatehouse by an imposing main door often set in a complex façade of windows and blind arcading. The main entrance to the parish church, it will be recalled, was by way of the south door. Inside the visitor would find the *nave* stretching out before him with arcades (pillars and arches) separating the main body from the aisles. Often a monastic church has been destroyed and all that we have left are pier bases: from these would have risen clustered columns and arches, above which was a *triforium* (a series of arches opening into the space below the lean-to aisle roof) and the *clerestory* (a range of windows at the top of the side walls). Some mighty naves such as Norwich and Peterborough are still twelve bays long. Fountains had eleven bays; other smaller houses had three or four. Again where the roof has gone its form can be recreated in the mind's eye by noticing the vaulting shafts from which a stone vault sprang or the slots from which tie beams spanned. Naves were allotted by the monks to local people for their services and this fact saved a number of them at the Dissolution when the rest of the church and the monastery was dismembered. Henry VIII allowed the parishioners to buy up the nave at such places as Bolton, Lanercost, Dunstable, St Germans and Worksop. But where they had no such rights often a parish church was constructed outside the gates of the monastery. Where this happened it had the unfortunate effect of causing a large number of the most magnificent English monastic churches to disappear virtually without trace except for their ground-plans. Glastonbury, St Augustine's Canterbury, Reading, Abingdon, Bury St Edmunds and Cirencester were almost obliterated. Their parish churches nearby were thought to be sufficient to satisfy the townsmen.

Medieval monastic churches were split into numerous divisions by building partitions against which altars were set. Sometimes the altar stones remain and they are marked with four crosses and one in the middle. Beneath them were enclosed relics. Behind them (this is seen well at St Albans where each nave pillar had an altar in front of it) were paintings of figures of saints or crucifixions or a carving in wood or alabaster. Close by the altar was a *piscina*, a shallow bowl in an arched recess through which drained away water used by the priest for washing his hands at mass and for cleansing the sacred vessels after the communion. A further recess, rebated for a door and known as the *aumbry*, was for holding the vessels used at the altar. A screen of stone or wood separated the nave from the retrochoir. This was to carry the rood, sculptured or carved representations of Christ on the Cross with our Lady and St John. A further stone screen known as the *pulpitum* was one bay to the east. A central door in this led to the choir stalls which were divided by it into two L-shaped blocks. These stalls were elaborately carved in wood and were protected from the damp by standing on stone bases. The seats had boldly projecting undersides each with a highly carved bracket known as a *misericord* (from the Latin word meaning 'mercy'). They were designed to give some sympathetic support to the monks who had to stand for long hours at church services. These seats are carved with floral patterns, grotesques, social scenes and well-known medieval stories such as Reynard the Fox. They are well worth study because they show many details of clothing and household equipment in their vivid carvings. Other pieces of furniture were housed in the *presbytery*, the area to the east of the choir; these included the bishop's chair (known by the Greek word *cathedra*, from which cathedral takes its name) when the monastery was also a cathedral — as at Norwich and Canterbury. Also the great book desk, or lectern, shaped like an eagle, with its wings spread to support the substantial service books. The lettering had to be large, partly because of bad lighting and also weak eyes, unaided by spectacles until the fifteenth century.[11] Altars had carved screens behind them of which fragments made of gilded and painted alabaster sometimes remain. Candlesticks and a crucifix of intricately worked metal were to be found on the altar. On the south side of the altar and at right angles to it ran the canopied stone seats or *sedilia* for the priest, deacon and subdeacon who would be needed to celebrate the mass. Finally, the floor of the presbytery would be richly tiled, but at

Westminster it was paved in Purbeck marble inlaid magnificently in Italian glass mosaic and coloured stone.

Lanfranc's *Constitutions* emphasises the tremendous importance that burial played in the ceremonial and sacramental life of Benedictine monastic communities. St Hugh of Lincoln was always ready to keep the king's council waiting while he scrupulously performed all the appropriate funeral rites of some perfect stranger! Archaeological excavations of monastic churches reveal that the interiors and the ground outside were honeycombed with graves. The main benefactors who added to the endowments would expect to be buried in the church with frequent masses said for their souls. At Norton Priory (Cheshire) 140 burials have been excavated. The less important members of the community were buried either outside the church or at the west end in wooden coffins. A number of wooden coffins, complete with nails, were found at Bordesley Abbey (Hereford/Worcs.). Those of higher rank were buried in stone coffins which were inserted mainly towards the east end of the church. This demand for burial led to extensions of some churches to accommodate them; at Norton the original North transept chapel was only 19 sq m in area. In the thirteenth century a larger chapel of 98 sq m replaced it; finally a large extension east brought up the size to 182 sq m. It seems that this chapel was the burial place of the Dutton family, by the sixteenth century the highest status landowners in Cheshire.

Most side chapels in cathedrals were utilised for the burial of important or wealthy persons. At Wells, where they wished to emphasise that the place had been a cathedral in Saxon times, a whole series of effigies of Saxon bishops was made in the thirteenth century. The richest graves, such as those of bishops, were marked by table tombs or great fretted and painted monumental structures with canopies. Bishop Beckyngton's tomb at Wells (1452) is brilliantly painted, the effigy of the bishop in full canonicals contrasting with the ghastly cadaver in a shroud below representing the transitoriness of his human glory. Railing it round is an imposing ironwork screen.

Effigies must always have commemorated a small minority. A cheaper but still impressive form of monument was made of engraved and inscribed sheets of latten, an alloy of copper and tin with some lead, imported from the continent. There were workshops specialising in the production of these *brasses* at York, Lincoln, Shrewsbury, London and possibly in Newcastle, Bristol and Corfe. Some of the earliest (late thirteenth-early fourteenth centuries) portrayed knights in chain armour and surcoats superbly engraved on thick sheets of metal. Most of the earlier brasses, however, were simple crosses or perhaps half figures with inscriptions made of individually cast Lombardic letters.[12] These were insecurely attached to Purbeck marble slabs by means of pitch. Only too frequently the brass has been removed, leaving the indent or recess shaped in the design of the monument. In the fourteenth and fifteenth centuries figures became almost universal and provide a typology of civil, ecclesiastical and military costume and armour. A warning is necessary because the brass-maker may well have used a design from an old pattern book rather than taking his inspiration from up-to-date fashion. Brasses are likely to be as inaccurate as manuscript illuminations in delineating the contemporary modes. These late medieval brasses were made of thinner sheets of metal but were more securely fixed by rivets, often socketed into lead filled holes.

The Reformation resulted in the destruction of many of these marvellous funerary monuments. Fragments of vandalised monuments are sometimes found by archaeologists in looted graves. At Wells Cathedral, Bishop Stillington's chantry chapel was destroyed in 1552 and his tomb was looted, but Rodwell's excavations in 1980 recovered fragments of the great painted and gilded stone tomb canopy from the site of Stillington's grave.

The *transepts* were the short arms of the cross plan and their chief practical function was to provide additional side chapels with altars. They were also useful in connecting the church to the other parts of the monastery. Access to the triforium and the roof was frequently by means of a circular staircase in the north-west angle of the north transept. The monks gained entrance into the church for the services in the early hours by descending the night stairs. The dormitory, which was at first-floor level above the cloister, was con-nected to the south transept by a door which led into the south transept, by means of a flight of stairs. At Bordesley a timber staircase was replaced by a stone one.

The stairs were often removed after the Dissolution but the blocked door can usually be traced. Finally, there was often a door in the north end of the west wall of the south transept leading from the church into the cloister. This was useful for the great proces-sion of the brethren who went from the church round the cloister and back again before the Sunday Mass.

5. The Cloister and Other Parts of the Monastic Complex

The *cloister* consisted of the cloister garth, an open plot of ground, usually square in plan and surrounded by four broad alleys. These had lean-to roofs which rested against the monastic buildings on one side and on their inner side had low walls with pillared arcades. The cloister was tucked in between the angle of the nave wall and the transept. Not many complete cloisters survive because after the Dissolution they served no useful purpose and were nearly always destroyed. The large square space is, however, unmistakable when it turns up on excavated monastic sites. The appearance of medieval cloisters with their vaulted roofs and glazed arcades can be reconstructed from the survivors, mostly in the cathedral monasteries at Norwich, Chester, Worcester, Gloucester, Canterbury, Durham and Oxford. Cloisters were at the heart of the monasteries. What were their functions? First, they had the extremely prac-tical one of connecting the major monastic buildings: the church was on one side and the chapter house, dormitory, refectory and kitchen lay on the eastern and southern sides of the garth. The cloister enabled the community to have a sheltered route from one building to another. The degree of elaboration of the door connecting the eastern end of the north walk with the church shows how important this entry was.

Secondly, the cloister was an area in which exercise could be taken at all times in the year.

Thirdly, the northern walk which adjoined the church was usually set aside for study. In this area, which enjoyed maximum sunlight, small desks for study known as carrels were set. The books were at hand because they were kept in niches or book presses at the northern end of the east walk. If a monastery had as many as a few hundred books, it was considered to have a large library. Not only were the materials for books extremely costly, every folio page of vellum represented one whole skin of a sheep which meant that each book was in effect a flock of sheep! Also each book was hand written and much painstaking work was devoted to the illumination of the initial letters.

Archbishop Lanfranc's *Constitutions*, drawn up about 1070, stated that all books were to be brought together into the chapter house on the Monday after the first Sunday in Lent.[13] Each brother would then hand in *the book* he had borrowed twelve months previously! If this seems a surprisingly slow reading-rate we must remember that manuscript books are not read so easily as printed works; also meditation on reading was encouraged and medieval volumes often contained several treatises.

The eastern range of buildings surrounding the cloister was of two storeys, the upper part forming the *dorter or the dormitory* of the monks. The dormitory, or communal sleeping place, was a long room running north-south which was connected to the south transept by a door leading to the night stairs. It was lit by lines of small windows in the north and south walls; this enabled partitions to be set up in the Later Middle Ages when more privacy was sought and each monk in effect had a 'bed-sitter'. Adjoining or near it were the monastic lavatories housed in the *rere-dorter*. The position of this was dictated by the course of the main drain. It usually projected eastwards from the dorter. The cabinets were generally arranged along both sides of a long narrow building at first-floor level; underneath was the great drain, often notable for its fine masonry which has led to its being connected in the popular imagination with secret passages! Lanfranc in his *Constitutions* thoughtfully ad-vised the monk acting as night watchman to go round last thing at night and inspect the rere-dorter in case any brother had fallen asleep!

At St Leonard's Priory, Stamford, the rere-dorter drain was an exceptionally well-built structure, rectangular at the top, with steeply battered west and east sides towards the base which was a long narrow channel flowing out under a semicircular arch. In the upper part of the deposits filling the drain were found the products of a late medieval laboratory.[14] These included fragments of glass distillation vessels, and crucibles connected with metallurgical working; also in the section were shining beads of mercury, in its elemental state, sulphur and copper. In an adjacent cellar was a buried group of clippings from the edge of silver coins dated to the reign of Edward IV. Finally, the deposit contained metal clasps from books and fragile laminated material which may have been the remains of books. Here in the pre-Dissolution levels of this Lincolnshire priory the strong suggestion is that alchemy was being practised; also coining; the preparation of mercuric compounds may also have a less sensational explanation such as medicine. It is noteworthy that similar finds of glass and pottery distilling vessels have been found at Selborne Priory (Hants.) and Pontefract Priory (West Yorks.) (see Figure 3.8).

The ground floor of the dorter range was divided into several rooms, each leading into the cloister. Next to the transept of the church was a *slype* or passage leading through the range to the cemetery to the east of the church or to the infirmary wing. It was customary to bury the founder of a monastery in the sanctuary and unusual at first for the church to be otherwise used as a burying place. The brethren themselves were buried east of the church in the cemetery garth. Gradually in the Later Middle Ages the practice grew up of cluttering up the church with elaborate monuments, as we have seen.

Next to the slype was the *chapter house*. The whole community assembled here each day in the morning to listen to a sacred reading followed by a chapter of the Rule (from which the room took its name). Monastic business was discussed, faults were confessed and punishment decreed. Chapter houses could be of many designs. At St Albans, Biddle has uncovered a whole series.[15] The earliest began in the eleventh century as apsidal-ended. This was lengthened and eventually became rec-tangular. Each increase in size reflected a growth in the monastic community. The extreme wealth here is indicated by the magnificent tiled floor, one of the earliest in existence. In sum, chapter houses were large, airy, often vaulted well-lit rooms and around the walls were the benches on which the monks sat. The chapter house at Wells whose roof is supported by a single central column from which rises, like spokes of an umbrella, a vault supported on 32 ribs, is one of the marvels of medieval architecture.

The planning of the rest of the ground floor of the dorter range was not standardised. There was often a *warming house* where there was a huge fireplace. Monasteries were extremely cold and draughty places and lacked methods of heating. The only way to over-come this was by donning large amounts of clothing, by using ample bedclothes, and by periodic visits in the winter to the warming house!

Other buildings which might well be found here were a *common room* and a *treasury* where were kept many of the valuables of the house and the deeds of its various properties. Adjoin-ing it, perhaps at the south-eastern corner, were the apartments of the head of the monastery. To begin with the superior lived a genuinely common life with the other monks, but towards the end of the Middle Ages it was customary for him to live apart from those he ruled, like a headmaster of a school. Suites of rooms of considerable magnificence were sometimes built and in these the abbot or prior entertained important guests. Such a complex, entirely separate from the monastery and equipped with its own chapel, has survived at the Cistercian house of Netley (Hants.).

Along the south range with its main axis running east to west was the usual position of the communal dining room or *refectory* — sometimes called the *frater*. It was rectangular in plan and might be on the ground floor or raised above an undercroft. When coming to the frater for meals the brethren washed their hands and combed their beards in the morning at the *lavatory*; this was usually a long trough in an arcaded recess in the frater wall or it might be in the cloister wall. Occasionally there was an independent circular or polygonal pavilion for this purpose. On entering the frater from the west end they would be in a building not differing substantially from the hall of a manor house. The tables were set parallel with the side walls, and the high table was at the east end where the officers of the monastery took their meals. A painting of the crucifix of our Lord in Majesty might be found on the wall behind. During meals a monk would read aloud from a pulpit reached by a stairway in the thickening of the south wall.

Not surprisingly the location of the monastic *kitchen* was adjoining the refectory on its western side. Here was the battery of ovens, hearths and troughs where food was prepared and cooked. It was generally rectangular but occasionally polygonal. The finest example remaining is the abbot's kitchen at Glastonbury. It has eight sides and is lit by a central lantern. Glastonbury was one of the richest abbeys so the numbers of its guests and visitors would justify having the provision of this second kitchen. Other buildings connected with the preparation of food included bakehouses and malthouses. At Fountains it has been established that the building formerly known as the bakehouse was in fact a wool shed and the various vats and tubs were connected with the preparation of wool including fulling.[16] The malthouse lies next to it and although much ruined it seems to have included a raised platform in the centre of the floor for drying the grain; the vat would be for steeping and draining the barley while the kiln at the north-west angle would have been for the final drying of the malt under heat. The building had an upper storey, probably used for brewing, as chases for waterpipes descend from it.

On the western side of the cloister was the *cellarer's range*. The cellar was the storehouse of the monastery. Here in a ground-floor room or basement vaulted from a central row of columns were kept the bulk provisions of the monastery: grain, bacon, salt and dried fish, clothes and wine. The practical reason for placing it here was that it was close by the outer court of the monastery through which the provisions were brought from the outside world. Another room on the ground floor of this range was the outer or *public parlour* where the monks met lay folk. The first floor in the

cellarer's range in Cistercian houses was occupied by lay brothers who did much of the manual work of the monastery but did not take a full part in the religious life of the house and therefore lived apart. In other monasteries here were guest rooms and at times the apartments of the head of the convent were situated here.

The last part of the monastery to be described was the *infirmary* or *farmery*. We must remember that once a monk had made his vows he lived the rest of his life in the community. The infirmary catered for him when he was sick and also when he grew elderly and could no longer maintain the arduous round of the monastic routine. Here he could enjoy better food, more sleep and obtain medical care. The essential parts of the farmery layout included a hall and a chapel and it usually had its own kitchen. The plan of these buildings was like a parish church with nave and aisles forming the hall, the beds of the inmates were ranged along the aisles. The chapel was in the place occupied by the chancel. The farmery was usually sited to the south-east of the monastery in a quiet place.

6. The Economics of Church Building

Great buildings cost money and it is a remarkable fact that such a poor society as medieval England generated a sufficient economic surplus to finance such great buildings as the cathedrals, monasteries and castles. The sources of income from which a great church was built or enlarged were numerous and varied. There might be a noble patron such as a king or a bishop who would take under his care the foundation of the new church and pay for the first stages of the building programme. Edward the Confessor, the last Anglo-Saxon king, refounded Westminster Abbey in this way. It is shown in the Bayeux tapestry having the finishing touches put to it before the king died: a man is climbing up to the topmost steeple to affix the weather cock. Edward is reputed to have devoted a tenth part of his revenues and also the money he would have spent on a pilgrimage to Rome on the building. When Henry III much enlarged and began to rebuild it in the

Plate 3.3: Netley Abbey, Hampshire. In 1251 Henry III declared himself patron of the abbey. A dedicatory inscription appears at the base of the crossing tower, seen here behind glass panels (Photo: J.M. Steane)

latest French style, he spent £40,000 between 1245 and 1272, the equivalent of the State's annual income for two full years of his reign. Colvin reckoned in 1963 that the modern equivalent could hardly have been less than £4,000,000.[17] Such royal patronage was commemorated in dedicatory inscriptions such as that incised on the pier bases at Netley (Hants.) (Plate 3.3).

King John, having quarrelled with the Cistercians, was induced by Hubert Walter to found an abbey by way of penance and the result was Beaulieu. In 1204 he ordered 100 marks to be paid to the abbot 'to build our abbey'. This was supplemented by a further £2,000 over the next ten years; his son, Henry III, continued to support the foundation allocating revenues up to £100 a year as well as donating valuable timber. It is likely that side by side or even in advance of the building of the church great barns were built for the receipt of tithe produce which went to swell the building fund. Such were the barns which have survived at Great Coxwell (Oxon.) (Figure 3.2), Beaulieu St Leonards (Hants.) and Glastonbury (Somerset).

A problem might arise if the founder died before any proper provision was made for the continuance of the work. Edward I, for instance, began the construction of a great monastery at Vale Royal in Cheshire in 1277. His intention was that it should be more magnificent than his grandfather John's foundation at Beaulieu and larger than his uncle's church at Hailes. Unfortunately, in that year he went to war in Wales, and embarked on an expensive castle building programme there. The church remained unfinished, its walls and vaults exposed to the wind and weather. In the great gale of 19 October 1360 the nave collapsed, its columns falling 'like trees uprooted by the wind'.[18] Another great royal builder, Henry VI, who was ambitious to found a school at Eton and King's College, Cambridge, was fortunate in having an able administrator, Bishop William of Waynflete, who carried through his educational projects after his master's death.

Royal patronage might be a source of strength in the first stages of a building enterprise. Financial prosperity could only be guaranteed if the foundation was backed by large landed estates. The oldest and wealthiest Benedictine abbeys like Peterborough, Ely and Glastonbury, were founded before the Norman Conquest. An abbey like Peterborough had tremendous endowments. It possessed practically the whole of the Soke of Peterborough, much of the middle and lower Nene valley and it had so expanded into the neighbouring counties of Leicestershire, Rutland and Lincolnshire that it was named 'the golden burgh'.[19] Not surprisingly it was able to finance a great rebuilding programme under its energetic Norman abbots. The huge church with a nave, eleven bays long, which

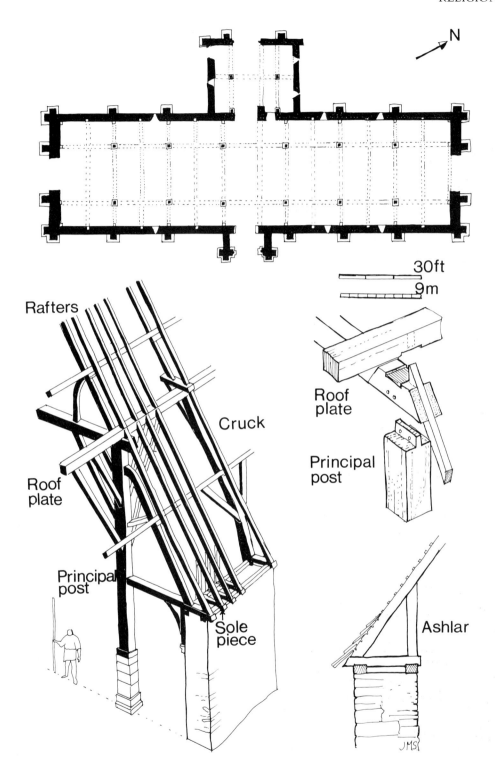

N

30ft

9m

Rafters

Cruck

Roof
plate

Roof
plate

Principal
post

Principal
post

Sole
piece

Ashlar

JMS

Figure 3.2: Abbey Grange Barn, Great Coxwell, Oxfordshire (after Horn and Born, 1965)

dominates the city, was the result. The abbey went on to make money out of clearing the forests and draining marshes during the twelfth century. Being situated on the western fenlands it was in a good position to reclaim land for pasture.

Another important source of money derived from the practice of 'appropriating' the revenues of parish churches. From the twelfth century onwards lords who possessed the right to appoint clergymen to livings and to enjoy the revenues accruing to parish churches (because their ancestors had founded the churches) frequently made these rights over to monasteries. The result is that the monks became responsible for maintaining the chancels of churches. Many parish churches show evidence of their chancels being rebuilt anew in a more stately style at this time. A less desirable effect was that they put in a miserably paid *vicar* (from the Latin meaning 'in place of') and pocketed the rest of the revenues. These were used to pay for building programmes. An example of a great church in financial difficulties, recouping its revenues by this system, was at Salisbury when in 1363 the revenues of the parish church of St Thomas were given over for six years to pay for repairs to the cathedral (Figure 4.7).

7. *Monastic Granges*

The monks of the new reformed orders of the twelfth century showed great economic enterprise. They were given large tracts of arable and pasture and in many cases their property lay in sparsely settled or developed areas and had therefore to be assarted (a term meaning 'clearing from the waste or forest'), or in the case of marshland, drained. Aberconwy's lands were situated in north-west Wales and Anglesey with a total of 15,379 ha. Strata Florida had some 13 granges, lying in five counties. Neath's land was particularly underdeveloped, being an area of 16 sq km of waste land between the Neath and the Tame Rivers. Tintern had about a dozen granges of which three were in Gloucestershire while eight lay in Gwent.[20]

This agricultural potential was realised through the institution of the monastic grange.

These were largely consolidated, independently controlled estates, between 40.5 and 405 ha in size, supposedly not more than a day's journey from the mother church (*Grangia juxta abbatiam*). In layout the farmstead was arranged round one or two courts (*curtes*). Accounts for Merthyrgeryn grange in the parish of Magor (Gwent) towards the end of the fourteenth century give some idea of the buildings to be expected. They mention a mill, the garden, the pigsty, the old byre and the new, the cow-house, the sheep-cote, the hen-house, the stable and the granary. Very occasionally complete buildings from such monastic granges have survived in the landscape. Such was the barn of the Cistercian abbey of Beaulieu at its grange of Great Coxwell in Oxfordshire (Figure 3.2).[21]

One method of turning their upland pastures into profit was to rear large flocks of sheep. We know from the *Taxatio Ecclesiastica* (1291) that the flocks of several Welsh houses ran into four figures. Margam had 5,285 sheep, Neath, 4,897, Tintern, 3,264 and Basingwerk, 2,000. These monasteries practised the prevailing medieval Welsh custom of transhumance. Their shepherds led the flocks to the upper pastures during the summer, occupying the '*hafotai*' (summer dwellings) and '*il vestai*' (shepherds' huts) and then bringing the sheep down to the valleys for the winter. They were found on the mountain pastures of the monasteries of Strata Florida and Aberconwy. Rights of way were important for the movement of stock. Gilbert de Clare gave Neath Abbey 'the easement of public ways' from the abbey to Briton, Ferry and Swansea and to Margam 'free and reasonable ingress and egress through his land for the use of Moor Grange, Cardiff'. Buildings connected with sheep farming included the *bercaria* or sheep fold and the *lanaria* or wool shed. At Wharram Grange, belonging to Meaux, there was a bercary 48.8 m in length. The *lanaria* at Fountains has recently been excavated.[22] It consisted of an aisled building entered by a wagon door in the gable end. There was a loft above and in the fourteenth century a fulling mill with two circular tubs was added, powered by an undershot water wheel.

The quantities of wool produced by Cistercian houses were a considerable item in the monastic economy. Tintern stands out because her best wool, though less in quantity than that of Fountains' 76 sacks and Rievaulx' 60 sacks, was much better in quality. It fetched the highest price of English monastic wool, 28 marks per sack, thus earning Tintern £150 per annum. Most of the wool trade was in the hands of Italians and by 1340 Tintern was in debt to the tune of £174 to Michael Simonetti de Lucca. The abbey had a house and two shops in Bristol and the abbot was a member of the Staple.

Tintern's monks went in for trading on their own account as well. The abbey could easily be reached by boats up to 70 tons, plying on the Wye. William of Worcester in 1453 notes a ship belonging to the abbey 'lying in Bristol harbour'. The remains of the water gate are still to be seen by the Anchor Hotel. From an examination of pottery and slates found on the abbey site it seems they were brought across the channel and up the River Wye from Bristol; tufa, for instance, a natural concretion, was brought in by river, and used for vaulting because of its lightness. The monks also mined iron ore and smelted it in their own furnaces.

Monasteries and cathedrals helped to finance their building programmes by the assiduous fostering of cults of saintly relics. It is perhaps cynical to assign an ulterior motive to Abbot John Thokey of Gloucester who decided to accept the body of the murdered Edward II for burial after it had been refused at the monasteries of Bristol, Kingswood and Malmesbury. He was in fact risking his freedom and even his life at the hands of Isabella and her paramour Mortimer. Nevertheless, the presence of the remains of Edward II, under one of the most spectacular pieces of Decorated style carving, was excellent business for the abbey. Pilgrims' donations financed the extensive rebuilding at Gloucester during the next one and a half centuries.[23] One would have expected the same to be true of Westminster Abbey and the cult of St Edward, but in fact this never really caught on and receipts from the offerings of the faithful tended to fluctuate according to the rising or waning popularity of the current king.[24] The boom occurred in 1372-3 when £120 was raised, reflecting the relative success of Edward

III in winning and keeping the affections of his subjects. At Canterbury on the other hand the relics of Thomas à Becket retained their drawing power and major building projects were accordingly undertaken there, and paid for, out of pilgrim offerings until the eve of the Dissolution.

8. The Archaeology of Pilgrimage

'Pilgrimage in the middle ages was more than a religious exercise, . . . (it was) a custom, a habit, an escape, an entertainment, or an act of profound faith.'[25] It required focal points, shrines of saints, the power of whose sanctity was proved by miracles. Among the most famous centres was the healing well and chapel dedicated to St Winifrede, a Celtic maiden saved from rape and restored to life, at Holywell in north Wales. Glastonbury was the greatest shrine of the south-west with a confusion, at times fraudulent, of legends and relics of Arthur, the Holy Grail, St Joseph of Arimathaea and St Dunstan, not to mention various worthy Anglo-Saxon kings. Durham on the other hand, had a splendid shrine dedicated simply to the one great northern saint, Cuthbert. Two shrines which were on the international pilgrimage routes were Walsingham and Canterbury. The Norfolk shrine arose as an imitation of the Holy House of Nazareth and it housed a famous statue of Our Lady. At Canterbury was commemorated the strong-minded, power loving and not very saintly Archbishop, Thomas à Becket, who had almost invited his own death by his rash actions. These were the most popular shrines, drawing pilgrims to them in thousands. Others, less magnetic, included the shrines of St Alban and that of Edward the Confessor at Westminster which was really a piece of royal idolatry, and finally the Holy rood of Bromholm, characteristic of the medieval cult of relics (Plate 3.4).

Undoubtedly one of the most potent reasons behind pilgrimage was the hope or expectation of a miraculous cure from illness. Modern medicine recognises that three types of illness are susceptible to 'cure' by any treatment: the self-limiting short illness whereby the sufferer is likely to get better on

Plate 3.4: Bromholm Priory, Norfolk. A Cluniac house, founded in 1113, the possessor from the thirteenth century of a relic of the Holy Cross, it became a famous pilgrimage centre. Henry III visited it frequently. 'By the Holy Cross of Bromholm' was the oath of Chaucer's Reeve. The site is on the windswept north-east Norfolk coast less than a mile from the sea. The aerial photo shows the course of a now filled-up river channel winding near the abbey site. This consists of the ruins of a gatehouse, precinct wall, north transept, chapter house and dormitory grouped round a farmyard (Photo: Cambridge University Committee for Aerial Photography, taken in drought summer of 1976)

his own; the chronic, but temporarily reversible complaint, such as rheumatoid arthritis which goes on from year to year, sometimes improving, sometimes subject to remission; the third, the psychogenic, induces 'real' symptoms such as paralysis, blindness or convulsions even when there is nothing obviously physically wrong. All three types figure in their hundreds in the registers of miraculous cures kept by medieval shrine keepers.

Such miraculous cures involved a number of tangible elements. The journey itself must have been increasingly euphoric, as groups joined with others on the way. They stayed at hospices provided by monasteries. Some of the routes are known — Erasmus went from Cambridge to Walsingham. The 70 odd miles of road is joined near Newmarket by others from the south and Midlands and winds its way to the shrine of Our Lady on the Norfolk coast. It is still called the Palmers' way (from the Latin *Palmerius* — pilgrim). There seems little historical evidence on the other hand to back up the claim that 'The Pilgrims' Way' in Surrey and Kent was an ancient pilgrimage route to Canterbury. Most references to it date from the nineteenth century.

Kirk has studied the church dedications of the Midlands and has noticed how certain dedications to saints, linked with pilgrimage shrines, are strung out along roads which may well have been used by pilgrims.[26] He suggested, for instance, that the cluster of churches dedicated to St Wolstan in Leicestershire was where pilgrims assembled before proceeding by the route of the Fosse Way and the Warwick — and Stratford — roads to the shrine of St Wolstan at Worcester. Perhaps more convincing is his mapping of dedications to the Assumption of the Blessed Virgin Mary which cluster near Wibtoft, Buckingham, Stony Stratford and Norwich, all close to one or other of the great historic roads of England. He considers that 'the evidence points to Walsingham as the goal to which all the routes are directed'.

Once arrived the pilgrim, in search of a

cure, tried to get as close to the relics as possible. Pilgrimage churches like Canterbury Cathedral were adapted architecturally to enable the thousands of the faithful to come literally in contact with the relics or at least the tomb of the saint. To this end processional ways, ambulatories, chapels and crypts for the display of holy bones were constructed. Events such as the translation of the martyrs' or saints' remains to ever more splendid shrines were stage-managed with awe-inspiring solemnity. The tombs of which substantial fragments survive, at Oxford (St Frideswide), Westminster (St Edward) and Salisbury (St Osmund), were so designed with arched apertures or large niches to enable those with afflicted limbs to introduce them into the tomb itself. One demented devotee of St Thomas à Becket squeezed through the holes in the outer casing of the saint's tomb and was only released after a miraculous intervention! Medieval pilgrims were as ruthless as modern souvenir hunters in purloining fragments of saintly shrines; the battered appearance of St Frideswide's or St Alban's shrine is not due solely to the iconoclastic attentions of Puritan reformers. Sometimes the dust on the floor was gathered up and taken home. Water used for washing a saint's corpse and the tincture of blood shed at a martyrdom were both widely used as healing substances. St Hugh of Lincoln, customarily given to excesses of this sort, went further. On a visit to the French monastery of Fécamp, he chewed off a piece of Mary Magdalene's arm: the guardian monks understandably hopped about wailing 'O, O proh nefas' 'for shame for shame'.

The beneficiaries of the cures carried or sent votives to the shrines. These were of four kinds. Animate votives could range from the offering of one lady who released all her rights over one of her serfs to St Edmund Rich, to the humble goose eaten with relish by the Canterbury monks. The tomb might be draped with inanimate offerings; cripples' crutches were common or bizarre objects like the halter used to hang a man miraculously revived. Exuvial objects were macabre bits and pieces of humanity dangled over the shrine; arm bones, human hair, stones ejected from the urinary system. Replicative votives were images, usually miniature, of the part cured or objects associated in some way with the miracle. On a ledge over the tomb of Bishop Edmund Lacy of Exeter (d. 1455) were found little hollow waxen images of arms, legs, hands, fingers, feet and fragments of animals. They had been made in moulds with strings for suspension over the episcopal anatomy.

Who actually went on pilgrimage? The answer is largely unknown. Only that tiny percentage, the accredited cures, were recorded by the shrine keepers. Distribution maps have been made of the places from which two or more cured people came who visited certain of the shrines. Becket's clientele were genuinely national if not international in origin. Nearly every British town from Dover, the Channel port, to Canterbury and to Aberdeen, is represented while Becket's own origins ensured plenty of foreign visitors, about a third of the known cures, from north France. Godric of Finchale, the twelfth-century merchant from Durham, who became a hermit in later life was, in contrast, visited almost entirely by locals; 89 per cent of his 200 pilgrims with known origins, came from villages within a 64.4 km-radius. Most of the early devotees of his cult were women, just as were the subjects of two-thirds of the 108 posthumous miracles of St Frideswide.

St Thomas Cantilupe's shrine at Hereford initially attracted royal patronage. Edward I, and both his queens, Eleanor of Castile and Margaret of France, came. Here there was a shift from female to male registered pilgrims after the first few frenetic years. Men were probably more mobile than housebound wives. It has been suggested that to begin with Cantilupe was appealed to as a remedy for common illness but after a passage of ten years or so he was approached more rarely and only for the emergency kind of happening, woundings, accidents and the like. Men and women now sought cures for their ordinary afflictions elsewhere.

Although the shrines themselves were swept away at the Reformation, occasionally buildings or fragments survive which are closely associated with pilgrimages. Such is the chapel of Bradwell Abbey (Bucks.) the subject of recent and continuing excavation.[27] It was built as an 'investment by the monks of this poverty stricken house' and is dedicated to St

Mary. Its focal point is a large niche which doubtless contained an image of the Virgin and was originally sited on the west front of the abbey. The little chapel was tacked on to shelter the cult which developed round the image. Its walls are powdered with red capital 'M's' (for Mary): scenes from the life of the Virgin are painted on both north and south walls. Most interesting, however, is the group of pilgrims painted, each kneeling with his staff by his side, each bearing a votive object, one a head, another a child, connected with the affliction he wishes the saint to cure.

Another building, whose peculiar architectural features have been connected with the large number of visitors likely to be on pilgrimage, is the ruined chapel of St Catherine on a hill overlooking the river by Guildford (Surrey). This has five doorways, two of them built into window spaces above the north and south entrances. The interpreta-

tion suggested is that these upper doors were reached by wooden stairs from outside which gave access to an interior gallery from which relics could be viewed. At Walsingham (Norfolk), the canons determined in the fifteenth century to cash in on the rising popularity of their miracle-working shrine; they completely enclosed the famous Holy House, a supposed replica of Christ's home at Nazareth, in a Perpendicular-style chapel called 'The New Work'.[28]

Medieval pilgrims left comparatively little written trace of themselves perhaps because pilgrimage was such an everyday event. Far more often do we find their souvenirs in the form of distinctive badges or pilgrim signs which they bought at shrines and displayed on their clothing as assiduously as any modern tourist who collects car stickers (Figure 3.3).[29]

William Langland describes the palmer in pilgrim's clothes

Figure 3.3: Pilgrim Badges from Museum of London. 1, 4 St Thomas of Canterbury; 2, 3 Henry VI

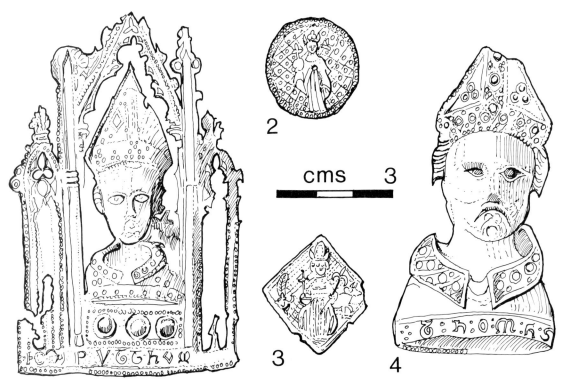

A bowl and a bag he carried by his side
And a hundred ampoulles on his hat set
Signs of Sinai, shells of Galicie and many
    a cross on his coat
And keys of Rome, and the vernicle before
For men should know and see by his signs
    whom he sought had.

Most pilgrim badges were made of lead or poor quality pewter. They were of two main kinds. *Ampullae* were miniature flasks designed to contain the holy oil or water that was dispensed at many shrines. They were made in moulds and small handles attached to them enabled them to be stitched to the clothing or they were suspended about the wearer's neck. More commonly found are *badges* which were decorated on one side only and designed to be worn as brooches. They were made in moulds in which several badges could be cast at once. The products of this medieval mass-production were sold in little shops which grew up outside the gate of the church. At Canterbury, for instance, the designs available included the mitred head of St Thomas, his effigy and shrine, the scene of his murder and his emblem, the Canterbury bell. One wonders sometimes if people collected the badges without going on the pilgrimages!

9. Parish Churches

Buildings have survived very unevenly from the Middle Ages. Manor houses and palaces have often been almost completely rebuilt and only small fragments of their medieval structures remain. Peasant houses have all been swept away and their plans can only be recovered by excavation. Of the greater churches some have been preserved as cathedrals; the monasteries are more often than not in ruins and in some cases hardly a stone is left upon another. One type of religious building, however, has come down to us relatively intact — this is the English parish church. In many villages it is the oldest building. There are 18,000 churches maintained by the Church of England and the greater proportion of these are medieval. They constitute field sites easy to hand and readily accessible (although nowadays frequently the key has to be fetched from the cottage down the road!). Their study can contribute a wealth of material about religious, cultural and social history.

10. The Siting of Parish Churches

Before inspecting the fabric of the church some consideration should be given to its siting. Why is it where it is? Many churches stand in or near prehistoric earthworks or stone circles, and it seems clear that such sites were deliberately chosen. Fimber Church (Yorks.) stands upon a Bronze Age barrow which was later used as an Anglian burial place. There is a barrow standing next to Berwick Church (Sussex). Edlesborough Church (Bucks.) stands on a mound in a circular churchyard. At Knowlton (Dorset) a roofless church stands in the centre of a prehistoric henge monument (Plate 3.5). There were originally a number of other earthen circles in the neighbourhood. The village, for which the church was provided has now gone, its site marked by a single farm. Such examples suggest that there was a continuity of use in sacred sites in many places. Pope Gregory referred to this when he instructed Augustine, his missionary to the Anglo-Saxons, 'Let the idols be destroyed, but let the temples be converted into churches, sprinkled with holy water and supplied with altars and relics'.

Other early churches were founded on hilltop sites. The Hampshire churches of Cheriton and Sopley were sited on artificial mounds; Barford St Michael (Oxon.) is on a steeply scarped hill; St Michael's Mount, an island peak off the coast of Cornwall, is topped with a church. The most frequent hilltop dedication is in fact that of St Michael; there is a possibility that churches built on these hilltops had earlier pagan shrines upon them. St Michael, it was hoped, would guard such positions of danger.

When reading Bede's *Ecclesiastical History*, it is seen time and time again that the support of the Anglo-Saxon leaders, whether king or thegn, was supremely necessary for the successful conversion of their followers. The

Plate 3.5: Knowlton, Dorset. On the chalk downland of Cranbourne Chase, scarred with numerous relics of prehistoric occupation, this ruined medieval church stands in the centre of a circular henge monument of *c.* 2000 BC. Such continuity of sacred function has protected the earthwork from obliteration by the plough. The farm to the top of the photo is enclosed by another large earthen circle partly lined by a belt of trees and partly flattened by cultivation in the adjoining field. At Knowlton and elsewhere such sites were the gathering points of popular assemblies of the Hundred, the Anglo-Saxon administrative division of the county (Photo: Cambridge University Committee for Aerial Photography, taken 19.10.72)

seat of the bishop was fixed at the place where the king customarily held his court, and similarly the church built with the help of the thegn was generally sited near his home. The Saxon law of Promotion stated that any ceorl who owned five hides of land, with a church and kitchen and a place in the king's hall, won the right to be considered a thegn. The church at Sulgrave (Northants.), which has Saxon work, stands beside the site of a pre-Conquest hall, doubtless the home of a fairly wealthy thegn. King Athelstan in 926 made it necessary to own a bell tower if one wanted to gain thegnly status. This may account for the fact that a large number of towers exist among the 400 or so surviving Saxon churches. Not surprisingly the thegnly builders of his family church claimed to have the right to appoint the priest, he retained the 'patronage' of the benefice and in effect was the proprietor of the church.

Consequently we often see village churches standing close to the gates of the great house or within its park, emphasising the fact that the building was the private oratory of the lord before it became the parish church of the village. At Hadstock, in Essex, a Saxon church which may well have been a minster church, stands only 100 m apart from the hall. Churches were not only closely associated with their lordly founders, they were also sources of profit. Naturally enough they needed protection and during the tumultuous years after the Norman Conquest we find many of them nearby or surrounded by defensive earthworks. At Cogges (Oxon.) the church stands side by side with the fortified enclosure surrounding the site of the Norman manor house. At Middleton Stoney, also in Oxfordshire, the mound of the motte and bailey castle overshadows the church. The physical link between the feudal lord and his proprietary church is close.

England during the period AD 950-1150 saw churches and chapels spread throughout the land. Side by side with the erection of worshipful buildings went the recognition of parochial status. Both were the fruits of hundreds of haphazard and impulsive legal and political decisions. Colswain of Lincoln, for instance, built 36 houses and two churches on former waste land outside the city. There are few traces of a systematic programme of religious organisation. The parish bounds in the country (as we shall see, p. 151) in many cases represent very ancient property boundaries going back to the Primary Anglo-Saxon settlements and beyond.

The church and its name can sometimes point to the way a settlement has developed in an area. Sometimes groups of parishes of the same name are differentiated by adding 'Great' or 'Little' or 'Upper' and 'Nether'. In these instances the parish has almost certainly been subdivided, probably when an old settlement grew overcrowded, and there was a new colonising offshoot in the Early Middle Ages. Hence in northern Norfolk we have Walpole St Peter and Walpole St Andrew, two subdivisions of the same settlement, both near the 'wall', a great seabank which helped to reclaim salt marshes from the sea.[30] In the same area are the four Wiggenhalls, on either side of the River Great Ouse, with churches of St Mary Magdalen, St Mary the Virgin, St Germains and the (now deserted) settlement of St Peter. What has happened here is a constant fight against the sea and the inundations of the river, resulting in the foundation of multiple offshoot settlements of the same name on the reclaimed pastures and cornlands. Each settlement ultimately obtained a separate church.

In the towns too churches multiplied and became dense on the ground. There were 46 in York, 22 in Canterbury, 17 in Oxford, 19 in Exeter, 60 in Winchester and in some of these places parishes were as small as 2 ha. Why were there so many and where were they sited? A number were, to begin with, private foundations, intended as chapels for the owners of substantial town houses. In the early stages of the church of St Mary, Tanner Street, Winchester, one doorway appears to have opened into a plot belonging to a substantial house 15 m to the south, while the other opened onto a lane or passage leading to the street.[31] Financial considerations are thought to have determined the siting of many late Saxon churches near or on gateways leading into towns. Such were the churches of St

Mary over the Northgate, St Swithuns over Kings Gate, St Mary, Westgate and another over East Gate at Winchester. The same phenomenon has been noticed at Oxford, St Michael Northgate and St Mary the Virgin (see Figure 4.6), and at Wareham, where the fabric of the church may well have been utilised in the defensive circuit. These town churches were very small. The nave of St Mary, Tanner Street, was only 4 m by 5 m and the early naves of St Pancras and St Peter *in Macellis*, Winchester, were about the same width. This again supports the theory that they were private in origin. As the town house and its associated land would soon be split up so the private chapel would come to be used by the surrounding townsfolk and emerged as the parish church.

Political circumstances following the Norman Conquest appear to account for the parochial peculiarities of Nottingham. Here there were only three medieval parishes. St Mary's is regarded as the original since it spreads well outside the borough to the north including the town fields. Nottingham is an example with two urban nuclei, one originating in an Anglo-Danish fort alongside which a Norman castle and borough evolved in two stages. These are represented by the churches (and parishes) of St Nicholas and St Peter. The first developed round the market at the gate of the Norman castle. The second marked an expansion of the successful Norman town. Parish churches and boundaries in medieval towns need close study. They were more subject to migration, absorption and subdivision than rural ones. They may provide a key to the fluctuations of urban size, prosperity and social complexities of town life.

11. *Parish Churches: Dedications*

The first feature that confronts the visitor to a parish church is a notice board containing the name and dedication of the church and then a list of the services together with the name of the current incumbent and churchwardens. The general practice of dedication of churches has been traced in this country to the era of Roman Christianity. The abbey of St Alban is perhaps 'the oldest continuously used site of

Christian worship in these islands'.[32] The custom was approved by Gregory and Augustine; when idols were destroyed, a new name had to be associated with a sacred building. The choice of a saint often gives a clue as to the relative age of the church. Those dedicated to St Laurence in Germany, for instance, can be shown to be of Roman origin. In Buckinghamshire churches dedicated to St Laurence appear to be grouped around known centres of Roman settlement. Those of Cholesbury and West Wycombe are actually sited in hillforts, giving another suggestion of a continuity of religious significance. Dedication to St Leonard may point to heavily wooded areas, because the saint is said to have possessed some of the attributes of the Celtic hunter-god, Cernunnos. A number, again in Buckinghamshire, are in well-treed areas near Roman sites. The age of missionary enterprise is also recalled in church dedications.[33] A group of churches with ancient dedications such as those to the Welsh saint, Samson, when plotted on a distribution map, gives us a good indication of the extent of the evangelising activities of this man. Dedications to St Samson at St Kew and Golant mark both ends of his journey across the Cornish peninsula. He also appears to have visited Guernsey and founded a monastery at Dol in Brittany. Anglo-Saxon kings, whatever their characters were like during their lifetimes, stood a good chance of being regarded as martyrs provided they suffered a sufficiently violent death. Such dubious saints as St Kenelm, who was adopted by Winchcombe Abbey, attracted pilgrims from all over the country: churches dedicated to him are generally in parishes where the influence of Winchcombe was strong.

The Norman Conquest introduced a new wave of dedications hitherto unknown or rare. Dedications in Winchester to St Valery, St Leonard, St Faith, St Margaret, St Anastasius, St Giles and three to St Nicholas are thought to belong to the period of the Norman Conquest or after. It is noteworthy that at Southampton, the Anglo-French community in the town was served by two churches with French dedications, to St Michael, patron saint of Normandy and to St John. The chains of churches, dedicated to the Assumption of the Blessed Virgin Mary, doubtless date from the twelfth century when the cult of the Virgin was increasing; they were strung out, as we have noticed, along some of the main roads of medieval England pointing towards the shrine of the Virgin at Walsingham.

12. Parish Churches: Functions

In order to understand the archaeological complexities of a religious building like a parish church, which has been altered and added to over a thousand years, it is important to realise that it has had a number of changing functions throughout its life. To begin with, as we have seen, there was perhaps no building on the site; the sacred meeting place was marked by a cross. Here people gathered to hear itinerant preachers and to take part in baptismal services. Once a church was built, it provided a building where these services could be held and the sacraments of baptism and marriage could be performed; the churchyard was a consecrated area where burial took place. At this stage all that was required was a nave where the congregation stood, and the chancel where the altar was and the priest performed the sacraments. As religious ideas changed in emphasis, new doctrines came to be believed in so the building was brought up to date. New beliefs meant new liturgical requirements and the parish church was adapted at every stage. At the same time changes meant that former features were obliterated or covered over. A simple example is the matter of the *piscina*. Pope Leo IV *c*. 850 directed that a place was to be provided near the altar for the disposal of water used for the ablutions of vessels and of the priests' hands after mass. Pope Innocent III nearly 400 years later deemed it unseemly that these two types of washings should be done in the same basin; consequently he ordered that there should be two *piscinas* in the same niche — the result is that a large number of churches gained double *piscinas* in the thirteenth century.[34]

The first major alteration that took place in many parish churches was the lengthening of the chancel in the thirteenth century. One reason for this was that monasteries frequently had *appropriated* parish churches (acquired the possession of their revenues and the responsibility for providing priests) and they rebuilt the chancel to bring it more in line with monastic practice to make more room for the choir and for ceremonial processions. The effect was to remove the high altar further from the congregation and to sever the priest from contact with them. He now entered the church through a door made in the south of the chancel. He, and perhaps a deacon, sat in specially made graded stone seats in the choir called *sedilia*.

The second major structural change in many alterations was the addition, first of a south aisle and subsequently of one to the north. The addition of the aisles was frequently done in the twelfth and thirteenth centuries to provide space for the swelling population. Squints or passages were cut through the masonry at the junction of the nave and chancel to allow people in the aisles a clear sight of the altar. Here Pope Innocent III had enjoined *c.* 1200 a more magnificent rendering of the office of the mass. Alternatively such enlargement may simply be the result of 'local boy makes good'. A successful chancery clerk or royal doctor might well come back to his village to spend the fruits of his career on rebuilding or refurbishing the church. Why else was a splendid north aisle added *c.* 1340 to the church at Cogges (Oxon.) by the de Grey family when the village was known to be in marked economic and demographic decline?[35] Subsequently the decline of the prosperity of a church frequently led to the loss of aisles or chapels. The fabric, in fact, may well be an index of the economic rise or decline of a community. Wharram Percy (Yorks.), as it declined in numbers, lost its aisles (Figure 3.6). The parish church at Hedon (Yorks.), formerly a flourishing port connected with the Humber, also lost its aisles and chapels as the port shrank into commercial insignificance (see p. 135).

As ritual developed in complexity in the thirteenth century so church furnishings and fittings became more elaborate. Thirteenth-century bishops' statutes laid down that churches should possess chalices, a cup of silver or pewter, a *ciborium* for holding the sacramental bread, a *pyx* (a little box of silver or of ivory) for the reserved sacrament, a *chrismatory* for the holy oils, a censer and an

incense boat, three cruets and a holy water vessel, a lockable font, an immovable altar with cloths, canopy and frontal, and so on.[36] Examples of all these items have survived from the Middle Ages and there is a trickle of new discoveries when they are dug up from the hiding places where they were cached at the Reformation (Figure 3.4).

More usually the fittings linked with these liturgical changes have remained because they were attached to the fabric of the church. On the north side of the chancel look for the remains of an Easter Sepulchre. This was used in connection with the rites of a Eastertide ceremony whereby the wafer, representing the body of Christ, was placed in a small receptacle on Good Friday and was transferred with the altar crucifix to a tomb-like structure, which was usually a recess in the wall covered by a cusped and crocketed arch; many of the finer examples were enriched with figure sculpture. All these features were simply the properties of an elaborate dramatisation of the Easter story. We see representations of such plays carved on alabaster panels, used as reredoses behind altars (Figure 3.5).

Another dramatic experience was the Palm Sunday procession in use in Jerusalem in the fourth century and repeated in English churches throughout the Middle Ages. This occasioned the erection of many churchyard crosses; sometimes a niche can be seen in the shaft of the cross or in its socket as at Great Malvern in which the pyx was deposited when the procession made its last station before entering the church. The reason why so many early grave slabs are incised with a foliated cross is probably connected with these processions. At the last station in the churchyard the plain cross swathed in plain draperies was exchanged for a jewelled cross, decked with flowers, symbolising the risen Christ. Processions in fact account for the multiple provision of doors. It might have been thought that only one door was necessary for entry and exit, and indeed the south door was the usual one; it is more highly decorated than the rest and nearly always is the one sheltered by a porch. The north door is often blocked and the west door (frequently in the tower) is locked. But processions, like the one described, required passage for the congregation out of the church

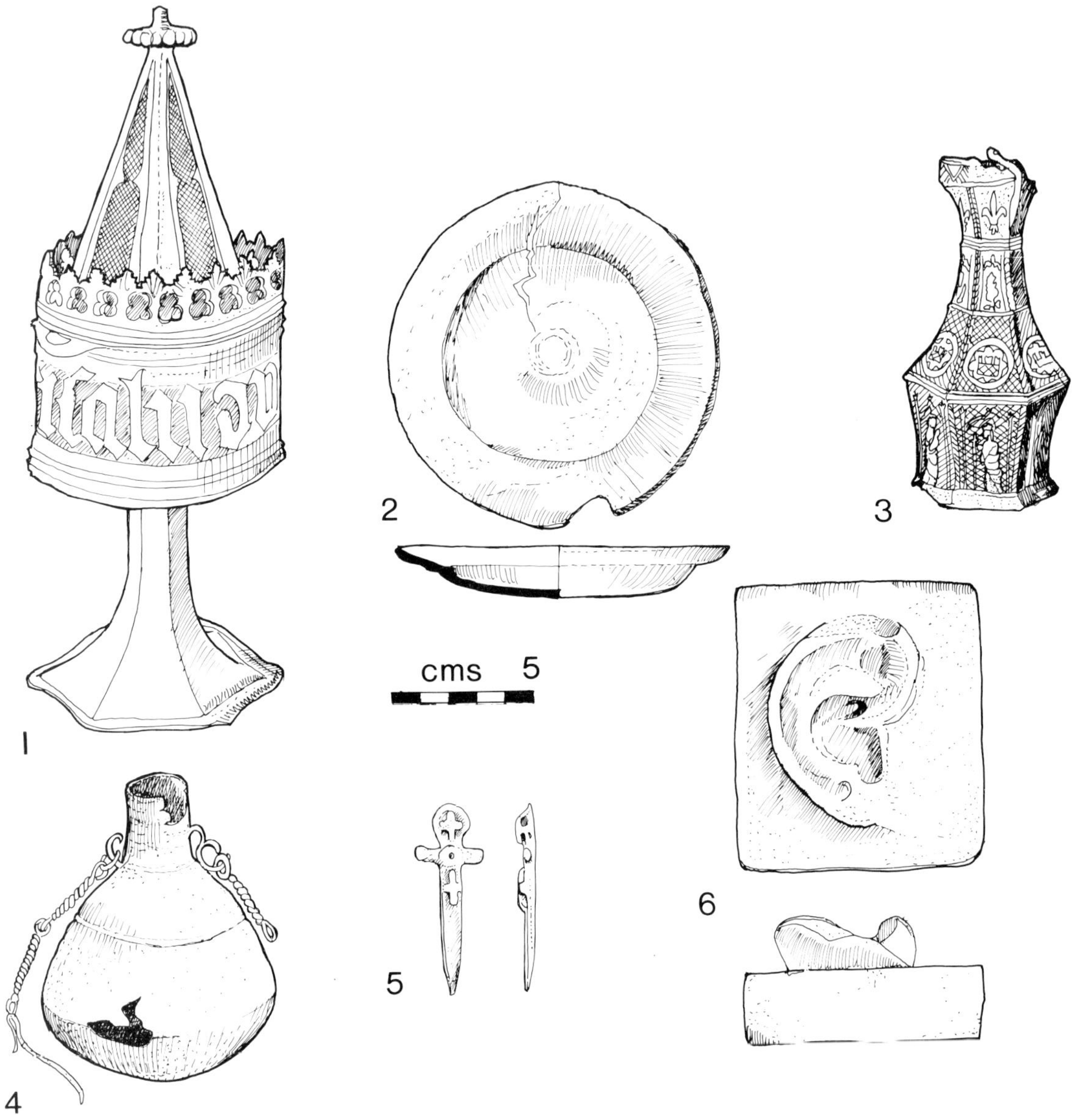

Figure 3.4: Religious Objects. 1. Ciborium, a container for the reserved sacraments, kept in a niche or tabernacle by the altar. Late fifteenth century. 2. Paten, pewter. 3. Cruet of lead. 4. Censer, a bronze container for incense. 5. Mortuary cross. 6. Votive object: ear carved in limestone. All from Ashmolean Museum, Oxford except 3 from Weoley Castle, Birmingham

on the north side; they then walked round the east and so to the churchyard cross. At Walpole St Peter's in Norfolk the churchyard is confined at the east end of the church so a tunnel-like processional way has been constructed under it.

One of the puzzling features frequently seen in medieval parish churches is a blocked door high up above the chancel arch. This originally led on to the top of the rood screens which were built in the late Middle Ages to fence the chancel and chapels off from the nave and aisles. This screen was topped by a beam bearing the wooden rood or crucifix with its

Figure 3.5: Two Alabaster Panels from Yarnton, Oxfordshire. Of Nottinghamshire alabaster, they depict scenes from the Nativity and the Betrayal

attendant figures of Mary and John on either side. At Cullompton (Devon) is a remarkable example of a carved wooden Golgotha, complete with skulls, bones, rocks and slots for the three crosses. The rood itself has, of course, vanished (Plate 3.6). The rood was generally provided with a loft from which these carvings could be cleaned, veiled in Lent and their candles attended to. The screens themselves were covered with carved panels and these were brightly painted with figures of saints. In East Anglia and Devon these screens often survive, but in other parts of the country only the slots for taking the beams and the doors leading to staircases in the chancel arch remain.

A further development took place in the Later Middle Ages. There was a multiplication of altars. The chancel walls were pierced and aisles or chapels were built north and south each with its side altar. Here masses could be said for the souls of the founders which might be rich men or guilds — that is to say clubs or associations of traders or craftsmen organised for the future welfare of their members in the next world as well as this. These side altars have often been swept away but the signs of them are the *piscinas* or arched stone drains which were used to wash the sacred vessels.

By the middle of the fifteenth century enormous numbers of relics had accumulated in English churches, particularly the great ones, many of which had virtually become 'museums of casual and uncomparative anatomy'.[37] This was part of the growing cult of the veneration of saints. Niches were filled with images; brackets were often added on the east walls of chancels to hold statues of saints. The Reformation cleared all these out, both relics and images, so we are left with empty niches or stains on the walls where they used to stand.

Plate 3.6: Cullompton, Devon. Carved timber Golgotha with slots for crosses. The base of the fifteenth-century rood screen (Photo: J.M. Steane)

One of the most profound developments in the life of the church was the increase in the practice of preaching. This originally owed its popularity to the work of the friars who succeeded in filling the vast preaching halls of their churches. Parish churches themselves were adapted in two ways to this change of fashion. The distinction between nave and chancel disappeared but for a wooden screen leaving one immense broad gallery of stone and glass. Moreover, the stone or carved wooden pulpit became a permanent part of the architectural screen of fifteenth-century churches such as Northleach and Cirencester (both in the Gloucestershire Cotswolds). Another effect of preaching was an increased need for the provision of seating. In the earlier Middle Ages the only seating was stone benches set against the wall on which the weak and elderly could sit — hence the phrase 'the weaker go to the wall'. The excavations of St Mary in Tanner Street, Winchester illustrate the process.[38] At first these benches were flimsy affairs held in position by stakes but they were replaced by stone benches. These were subsequently added to by a central bench and finally elaborate choir stalls were built at the eastern end of this small town church. From the fifteenth century benches were provided; even if the seating has been replaced, the elaborate carved ends often survive. They are good evidence for the important place which preaching had come to take in the religious life of the people.

13. Parish Churches: Study of the Standing Structure

There was no blueprint for a typical parish church at any period in the Middle Ages. Each church was built under a unique set of circumstances and consequently has a unique plan, often the result of a complicated series of alterations over the long period of its life. So the architectural development of a medieval church as, for that matter, any upstanding medieval building, can be a fascinating exercise in detection. Following Greening-Lamborn, the pioneer Oxford architectural historian, H.M. Taylor, the author of a classic work of architectural detection, *Anglo Saxon Architecture*, makes a plea for a closer scrutinising of structures. 'Detailed study and measurement are necessary, as well as carefully drawn plans, sections and elevations. Every feature needs study, for example to see whether it shows signs of later modifications, or whether it proves that another feature is earlier by resting on it or by partially cutting it away'.[39] Some classes of features are of especial importance in giving indications about the history of buildings.

(1) Straight Joints. where a straight vertical joint is seen in a wall without any bonding or with only occasional bonding it can be taken as an indication that the wall on one side of the joint is a later addition. The most frequent occurrences are seen at the west end where the junctions between aisles and an earlier nave can be seen; also where towers or porches have been tacked onto a church. Such an addition does not necessarily mean a lapse of a great many years. Financial constraints may have prevented the immediate carrying out of a plan conceived from the start.

(2) Changes of Quoining. Any single phase of a building will probably employ a uniform type of quoining — that is the treatment of the corners. Often an addition of a stage to the tower can be deduced from a change in the quoining. Again, changes in the type of string courses or plinths may betray additions or subtractions to the fabric.

(3) Changes of Roof Line. Early roofs in rainy Britain were of very steep pitch: the gable angle being sometimes one of 45° in a twelfth- or thirteenth-century building. These can be discerned high up on the east walls of western towers or on all walls of central towers. Water dripping down walls eventually destroys them so the drainage of such early roof coverings of tiles or thatch was accomplished by projecting the eaves well forward of the walls; the timbers were supported on corbels, rows of projecting and frequently carved stones. Later in the Middle Ages roofing became less steeply pitched for three reasons. Carpenters used shorter beams and rafters which were more common and cheaper.

The pitch of such roofs echoed the flattened four-centred arches which had become the distinguishing mark of the Perpendicular style. Most importantly, however, the development of lead mines enabled builders to cover their roofs with sheets of lead which would distort or fall from a steep pitched roof.[40] To hide these roofs stone parapets were built and the water drained away down lead-lined gutters through projecting spouts of stone known as gargoyles which shot the water by the force of its own volume clear of the building.

(4) Changes of Fabric in the Walls. Provided that they are not obscured by plaster, the walls themselves contain vital evidence about the evolution of the building. Before cement rendering was removed from the exterior of the chancel at Rivenhall (Essex) it was thought that the church had been virtually rebuilt in 1838-9. Rodwell showed that the western parts of the walls here were Anglo-Saxon with two original windows. A clear change of fabric had occurred in the fourteenth century when the chancel had been extended. The 'rebuild' of 1838-9 was seen to have been restricted to the parapets, buttresses and windows. Again a change in building material may well represent an addition even if the style remains the same.

(5) Inserted Features. Medieval builders were adept at inserting windows, doorways and arches leading to towers, side-chapels or aisles into previously existing walls. Clearly they were concerned to make it possible to go on using the building during these operations. Excavations have revealed holes for timber scaffolding in church floors; there are also putlog holes for taking the horizontal members in the walls themselves. When the holes had been cut through the walls wooden centring would have been introduced and the arch fitted. It is difficult to decide whether or not such features are contemporary with the wall in which it now stands except where arches cut windows or windows open into aisles which formerly were on the outside wall. Raking out the mortar is an essential preliminary. If the wall is carefully coursed the later insertion of a feature such as a door or window is likely to have left some clue such as 'broken faces of adjoining stones, small intrusive stones used to make good the gaps beside the feature, or even more subtle indications such as a lack of careful bonding between the courses of the original wall and . . . jambs or imposts of the inserted feature'.[41] There is much that can be learned from this 'vertical' archaeology and it can, of course, be applied to secular buildings.

14. Parish Churches: Evolution of the Plan

When the remaining masonry, its character-istics, mouldings and details, like doors and windows, have been surveyed, ideally the search should go below ground level because here, if anywhere, may be the foundations of the Anglo-Saxon churches; here are medieval floor levels; here is structural evidence for the phasing of the church which may have been hidden or removed in the remains above ground. A ground plan needs to be drawn in which the pieces of building from different periods are allotted a place. A hypothesis of how the church has evolved needs to be set up fitting all the observed features.

An attempt will be made to indicate how the plan of the parish church may have developed. We will then go on to discuss two churches whose full stories have been dis-entangled by excavation.

(1) Saxon Plans. The first stone churches built along the south-east coasts of England by St Augustine and his followers at the close of the sixth century AD were simple rectangular rooms with apses (semicircular rooms) at the east end. There may have been pillared verandahs or porticos round the remaining three sides. Bradwell (Essex), already men-tioned as standing in a Roman fort, was the most notable example. More typical were timber churches single or double celled, such as have been found by excavation at Wharram Percy (Yorks.) and Thetford St Michael (Norfolk) where they were encased by later stone buildings. At Rivenhall (Essex) the timber predecessor lay to the east of the stone church; at Asheldham (Essex) the timber church was to the north of the later one. Only one timber church actually survives in Britain, at Greensted-juxta-Ongar (Essex). The earliest stone buildings which have been recovered by excavation were also simple one or two-celled structures, such are the plans of St Mary, Tanner Street and St Pancras, Winchester (Hants.) and Raunds (Northants.).

Other slightly more ambitious plans were 'turriform', that is to say they incorporated a tower in the structure. This might be in the middle of the building with a nave and chancel on either side (as at Barton-on-Humber,

Lincs.) or the tower might act as the nave and a chancel would protrude from the east (as at Barnack and Earls Barton, Northants.). Cruci-form plans with arms developed from each side of the tower are also found (e.g. Netheravon, Wilts. and Breamore, Hants.). During the eleventh and twelfth centuries a plan which developed is the so-called pseudo-cruciform church where the turriform nucleus was dispensed with and its area was combined with the west nave. The lateral wings remained. An example is at Worth (Sussex).

(2) Norman Plans. The Norman Conquest ushered in a period when most great churches such as monasteries or cathedrals were either founded or were rebuilt on a larger scale. They were constructed with expanded monumental plans on a vast and extravagant scale, involv-ing such features as apsidal or semicircular ends, transepts with eastern chapels and great crossing towers. Smaller versions of these features became fashionable in the renewing or founding of smaller parish churches and field chapels throughout the land. Many Norman churches were built on a cruciform plan with a central tower over the crossing. Another frequent characteristic was an apsidal eastern end although this was seldom allowed to remain. It is often found underlying later chancels in church excavations. At Asheldham (Essex) for instance a fourteenth century two-celled church of nave and chancel with western tower was surprisingly found sitting on the foundations of a three-celled Norman building with an axial tower over the crossing and an apsidal-ended chancel.[42] Examples of such plans, nave, central tower and chancel, have quite often survived. Iffley (Oxon.), Steetley (Derbyshire) and Stewkley (Bucks.) are par-ticularly well preserved. The incentive behind the addition of aisles in the late twelfth and thirteenth centuries, as we have seen, was the necessity of accommodating the increasing population in a period of economic expansion. Such early aisles were usually narrow, perhaps less than 2.4 m wide, for the good reason that they had to be roofed by the simple expedient of extending the nave roof downwards.

(3) The Planning of Churches in the Later Middle Ages. The first big revolution in planning which was almost universal has already been referred to — the replacement of the apse or short rectangular chancel by adding a square-ended extension. These 'Early English' chancels of the thirteenth century were well lit, each with its own priest's door in the south wall. They were able to provide far more space for the entombment of important personages; often decorated tomb slabs, effigies and brasses were found lining the walls of these spacious chancels. During the fourteenth century aisles were widened and the 'lantern' system of lighting was introduced. Nave walls were heightened and pierced by rows of windows known as the clerestory. The aisles now had their own roofs. The plan which is found in perhaps half the late medieval churches of England is a clerestoried nave with wide aisles of at least four or five bays, while further east, transepts or wings are found. A wide chancel arch leads into a three-bay chancel lit by large windows. Further adjuncts which were extremely common were the south porch which might be two-storied, and the western bell tower entered from the church through a tall arch and leading to a processional doorway in its western wall. The church by the end of the Middle Ages in towns and prosperous country districts was now a great hall of glass and stone which we have noticed was suitable for the accommodation of large congregations gathered to listen to sermons. The only divisions within such a building were provided by screens of stone or wood between the various components. The chancels had intricately carved stalling for the clergy and the naves were now full of seating for the laiety.

15. The Excavation of Churches

The opportunity to investigate below-ground levels inside a parish church in normal use rarely occurs. When it does happen the excavator is sometimes disappointed by the discovery that the medieval floor levels have been badly cut about by the digging of multiple graves and by the later insertion of heating ducts. Datable finds are very rare; not surprisingly pottery is almost entirely absent. In many of the earlier phases only the foundations remain, with no distinguishing (and therefore datable) architectural detail. Something can be recognised from the tooling of the stone. Axe dressing, leaving a rough surface, is generally considered to be pre-Conquest in date. Using a chisel to dress stone which leaves diagonal tool marks over the surface was practised after the Norman Conquest. Unfortunately, there is constantly evidence that earlier material is reused in later periods. Other ways towards sorting out the tangle may be by analysis of mortar samples from different building phases; also radio carbon determination of charcoal samples from the foundations may help to provide dates for the origin of the church.

At Hadstock (Essex) the chance of detailed examination below ground came when it was proposed to replace a decayed Victorian wood block floor and to insert a damp-proof membrane under most of the interior of the building.[43] A trial excavation in the north transept indicated that as much as half a metre of chalk and earth floors survived in this part of the building. A massive internal levelling operation had removed all the ancient floor levels in most of the nave and south transept. It was possible to examine the lower courses of the walls by stripping back the plaster. It was known before that Hadstock was an Anglo-Saxon minster church but the evidence produced three periods of Anglo-Saxon work, the earliest of which probably belonged to the period before the Danish invasions and was a splendid five-celled cruciform structure which may be part of a seventh-century monastery founded by St Botolph. The second period saw the rebuilding of the choir — converting the area into a central timber-framed tower. A major rebuild took place in the late Anglo-Saxon period removing the timber tower, and replacing it with a new central stone-built tower. A symmetrical triple apse completed the east end. Rodwell, the excavator, associates this with Canute's Minster, dedicated in 1020 as a memorial church to the battle of Assandun. In the thirteenth century the central tower collapsed and was not replaced; the western wall was removed and the crossing and nave became one. The cause of the trouble was a shifting clay hillside which split the church through at the weakest point of its north-south axis. The dwindling community was unable to cope for the time being. A recovery occurred at the end of the Middle Ages when the north porch and west tower were added. The subsequent decline of the village saved the church from radical alteration apart from the redecoration of the chancel in the eighteenth century. So what was achieved at Hadstock? No less than a thorough understanding of the evolution of this interesting building. Excavation, moreover, has unearthed 135 post-holes representing many periods of scaffolding, some 20 floor and make-up layers of chalk, sand and earth in the north transept, six furnace pits including two lead-smelting hearths, a bell foundry and casting pits and, finally, 19 graves.

At Hadstock, a known Anglo-Saxon church was unravelled in its complexity. At Rivenhall (Essex) a structure previously thought to be a nineteenth-century rebuild was shown to have Anglo-Saxon beginnings.[44] To the north of the chancel were uncovered the foundations of a little timber church. When the cement was stripped from the chancel walls themselves they were revealed to be Anglo-Saxon in date. The inward curve of the foundation of an apsidal-ended chancel was seen to the east of the Saxon wall. Confirmation of this largely vanished feature was seen by the fact that the burials of this period are arranged in a concentric fashion which only makes sense when it is seen as reflecting the former curve of the apse. The other features reflect changing economic circumstances; the increasing prosperity of the village made it possible to demolish the apse and replace it by an extended chancel. The Black Death caused the postponement of the building of a west tower whose foundations were already dug. This was at length built at the end of the fifteenth century. A temporary timber bell cage had in the meantime done service. The tower appears to have collapsed in the eighteenth century and was rebuilt. There seem no reasons to contradict Rodwell when he claims that the Rivenhall experience, which has gleaned so much historical, archaeological and architectural information from an apparently unpromising structure, could be repeated at hundreds of other churches throughout England.

A church which mirrors most dramatically the changing economic fortunes of its community it served is St Martins, Wharram Percy (Yorks.) (Figure 3.6).[45] The roofless ruin still stands in a remote valley on the chalk wolds of North Yorkshire about halfway between York and Scarborough. Formerly it served four neighbouring townships as well as the village itself. It continued to be used until after World War II but during the 1950s and 1960s the state of the building rapidly deteriorated. From a visual examination of the walls it was realised that the church was a complex structure which had once been larger; blocked-up arcades revealed the former existence of aisles, the once larger chancel was shown by a scar of masonry. It was considered at this stage that there had been six basic phases of construction. Between 1962 and 1974 archaeological examination was undertaken both of the above- and below-ground structures. Plaster was picked from the walls exposing the masonry joints and blockings. The ground under and around the church was almost totally excavated. From such meticulous examination it now became apparent that there had been no less than twelve phases of building.

The emerging picture at Wharram is that first, perhaps in the eighth century, there was a small timber church, possibly preceded by a freestanding cross. The evidence for this first church were post-holes on a rectangular plan underlying the later east end of the nave. This was replaced in the late eighth century by a larger substantial church of sandstone ashlar set in a deep and wide foundation trench. A chancel was subsequently added to this. This church was completely rebuilt on a larger scale with a nave 15.2 × 7.6 m and a chancel 12 × 6 m built on a chalk rubble foundation over the sloping hillside. To this building was added an unusual Saxo-Norman overlap tower partly inside and partly outside the west wall. So far these first five periods reflect the gradual expansion of the small Anglo-Saxon village on the lower terrace of the valley: the population was also expanding in the other four town-

Figure 3.6: Evolution of Ground Plan of St Martin's Church, Wharram Percy, North Yorkshire (after Hurst, 1976)

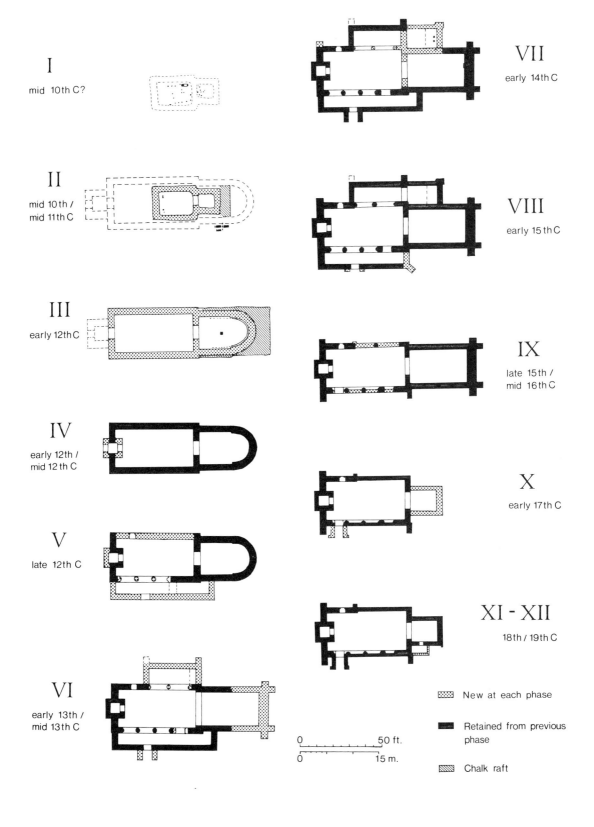

I
mid 10th C?

II
mid 10th /
mid 11th C

III
early 12th C

IV
early 12th /
mid 12th C

V
late 12th C

VI
early 13th /
mid 13th C

VII
early 14th C

VIII
early 15th C

IX
late 15th /
mid 16th C

X
early 17th C

XI - XII
18th / 19th C

0   50 ft.
0   15 m.

New at each phase

Retained from previous
phase

Chalk raft

ships in the parish necessitating a larger church.

With the arrival of the Percy family, as new lords of the manor in the twelfth century, a rebuilding programme was initiated. Not only was the manor house built but masons' marks found on stones here match those on the newly built apse and an aisle was added on the south side. Evidently prosperity came with the arrival of the new lords and the village spread on to the southern part of the western hillside. In the thirteenth century the continuing expansion of population to the north led to the addition of a further aisle on the north side and a chapel. Wharram Percy church had now reached its greatest extent. The village, in common with hundreds of other settlements in England, began to decline in the late Middle Ages. Four out of the five settlements in the parish were deserted. The church mirrored this economic and demographic decline. It sharply contracted in size; the aisles were pulled down, their arcades were blocked, the chancel was shortened in the seventeenth century. By the nineteenth century the only people using the church were the parishioners from Thixendale (the one surviving township) and they had to walk 4.8 km to services. When they built their own church in 1879 there was no longer any use for the mother church of Wharram Percy. The truncated remains finally fell into disuse and disrepair three-quarters of a century later.

16. Graveyards: Rural and Urban Examples

Clearly the excavated church has an important story to tell. Its complex structure epitomises the whole history of the village. But it does not give us information about individuals who lived out their lives in the village of Wharram Percy. Here study of the graveyard helped. The earliest evidence of the Saxon population came from the graveyard in the south-east angle between the naves and chancels of the first stone churches. These included three graves with limestone grave slabs and head and foot stones. In 1965 a further 200 burials were excavated from the graveyard to the north of the nave, while in 1971 168 more burials were examined to the west. These sample areas show that the graves were

regularly laid out in orderly rows at an average depth of 60 cm at four different levels. The ground has been deliberately made up over the centuries so that later disturbance of earlier burials was minimal. Among these burials were those of two vicars with pewter chalices and patens. These are normally the only grave goods found in medieval graveyards. The phenomenon of the raised ground surface of the graveyard has often been noted elsewhere. As one approaches churchyards the swelling mounds of turf studded with gravestones is seen to overtop the surrounding fields and the levels of the paths sunk deep through it give some impression of how much the yard has been raised over the centuries. Examination of the skeletons themselves should give us interesting information on the diet, habits and illnesses of medieval rural populations of north-east England. A full report of the Wharram graveyard has not yet appeared because a considerable length of time often elapses between excavations and the publication of their results. Something, however, can be said about the average life span for adult males and females at Wharram Percy during the Middle Ages. This has been worked out as 35.3 years for males and 31.3 years for females, a shocking fact.

It seems that only a very small proportion of people — perhaps a figure as low as 9.9 per cent — reached the age of 50 years and more. When one takes into consideration the appalling infantile mortality rates it seems that the life expectancy from birth was only 18.7 years. On the other hand, in terms of body size and shape, they appear to have been a fairly robust community; the males had a mean stature of 1.68 m which is larger than is commonly assumed. Signs of disease were noted on the bones. Rheumatic disease (osteoarthritis) was common; this is seen in the lipping and fusing of the vertebral column and in other joints. The Wharram peasants suffered seriously from dental troubles as well, dental caries was noticed in 8.1 per cent of all teeth examined. Another medical aspect which was noted as the result of very careful excavation was the recovery of gall bladder stones, tiny objects only too often missed by excavators!

17. A Town Cemetery

The largest single excavated medieval grave-yard group in England comes from the cemetery of St Helen's-on-the-Walls, Aldwark, York.[46] This small parish, which lies within the medieval walls, east of the legionary fortress, produced a total of 1,041 burials over a time span of 550 years. The church itself, whose site was unknown before the excavation, began as a single-cell structure in the tenth century. It was enlarged by the addition of a rectangular chancel. Later versions led to the extensions of the chancel and nave, each resulting in the enclosure of areas of the former graveyard. The methods followed in the excavation of the churchyard are of some interest. It was dug in its entirety by the open-area technique but several semi-permanent baulks were established within the church. As each skeleton was revealed it was defined and rapidly cleaned. A string rectangle with the sides marked in multiples of 5 cm was put round it, held by four metal pegs; each was photographed by a Polaroid camera. Then the skeleton was lifted, the skull placed in a box and the rest in polythene bags. The skeleton-recording card was filled in with data about associated finds, evidence of grave-cut, orientation, relationship to neighbouring skeleton and parts of the body present. The material was then submitted for analysis to a physical anthropologist.

It appears that two forms of laying out were practised at St Helen's-on-the-Walls. More than half the skeletons were interred with their hands resting on the pelvic region. A number were laid out with their arms at their sides. Nearly all were extended inhumations with their heads to the west and they lay roughly parallel to the long axis of the church. Evidence for only five coffins was found, in the form of nails. Bronze pins, doubtless for holding the shrouds together, were found in some graves. Some bodies were probably wrapped not in shrouds but in old clothes such as were used in the medieval cemetery at Herjolfsues in Greenland. Very seldom did personal jewellery accompany its owner to the grave. Three burials only contained finger rings. Apart from a silver penny of Burgred of Mercia (852–74), a pair of bronze tweezers

and a necklet of twisted wire, the skeletons were without grave goods. There were no traces for markers in the cemetery but the rows to the north-west of the church implies planning with wooden markers.

A great deal of interesting information emerged from the careful measurements of each bone. Anomalies of bone form, ante-mortem damage and disease signs were recorded together with the degrees of attrition of tooth surface. What did this population sample from medieval York look like? The average face was fairly broad and low, most had prominent and high cheek-bones. There was a noticeable tendency for the left cheek-bone to be higher and more prominent than the right. Both narrow and wide nasal roots were found. Most chins were pointed and foreheads were of a moderate height, either vertical or slightly receding. The average male height was 1.69 m, the female, 1.57 m. Most of the thigh bones were flattened from front to back in the upper part of the shaft. This may be attributable to cultural habits or to poor nutritional levels altering the conformation of the bone.

The low expectation of life was note-worthy. Although there were very few baby bones, possibly because they had been buried near the surface and had not survived, it seems that 27 per cent of the sample died as children and only 9 per cent lived beyond 60 years. As at Wharram Percy the men outnumbered the women at all ages over 35 which contrasts with the situation in modern Western societies where females can expect to live longer than males. It is likely that in medieval and Tudor towns females had lower rates of nourishment and suffered the special hazards of child-bearing.

Considering the violent tenor of life in this northern town, remarkably few bones showed signs of externally applied damage. Only 18 wounds were found, 13 on skulls, where four were probably caused by sword cuts and one of depressed contusions was dumb-bell shaped, perhaps the result of a blow from a mace or morning-star. The total number of fractures was low; only 26 men and 12 women had bones which had been broken. Osteo-arthritis was very common: 19 cases were found in neck bones and 119 in the lower thoracic and lumbar regions. Very few showed signs of infective diseases; one case of syphilis, one case of tuberculosis, one burial of a young woman with a new-born child and one of a grossly pathological individual suffering from von Recklinghausen's disease. There were 30-40 instances where the conformation of the femur or tibia indicated a period of soft bone which would have caused bowing: there was one classic case of rickets.

One last observation, and one of the greatest historical interest, is that there appears to have been a change in average physical type impressed in the mean cranial characteristics at about the time of the Norman Conquest, but there is no evidence for a mass immigration at the time of the Conquest sufficient to account for such a change. The total influx of Normans and other French was not more than 10,000 in a population of perhaps $1\frac{1}{2}$ to $2\frac{1}{2}$ million. That there was a change in skull type is undoubted, but the reasons for it remain mysterious.

18. Leprosy

The popular view of medieval England includes the sadly familiar figure of the solitary leper travelling the roads, his limbs maimed and stunted so that he hobbles or crawls, his staring eyes unseeing or unsightly, his hood drawn close round his disfigured face, his clapper or bell giving warning of his approach, his husky voice entreating 'Sum good, my gentyll mayster, for God's sake'.[47] It would seem from documentary sources that leprosy was very prevalent in England during the twelfth and thirteenth centuries and began to decline thereafter. The extent of the disease is difficult to calculate. For one thing diagnosis in the Middle Ages was uncertain and it was doubtless confused with other diseases such as impetigo, scrofula, lepra, lupus, tuberculosis, erysipelas or St Anthony's Fire, or even with venereal disease. One might think that archaeology would provide useful evidence since the disease is not only characterised by disfiguring skin lesions but by the inflammation, erosion and atrophy of bones. Bones displaying such damage, however, are almost unknown in the Anglo-Saxon period and continue to be scarce

during the Early Middle Ages when the disease was supposed to be at its height. Only three places in England have yielded skeletal remains with leprous lesions;[48] an immature specimen from Scarborough, seven cases from the period 1100-1350 at South Acre, Norfolk and a few, as yet unnumbered, further examples at Cathedral Green, Winchester. Maybe the reason is that no large leper cemetery has yet been excavated. Where this has happened in the medieval leper cemetery at Aarderup in Denmark, over 200 cases were found, testifying to the prevalence of the disease.[49]

The written record is much more abundant. Queen Maud, the wife of Henry I, was celebrated for her saintly care of lepers.[50] Ailred of Rievaulx describes how Prince David visited her and found the house full of lepers, she washed and even kissed their feet. Walter de Lucy, a twelfth-century abbot of Battle, similarly 'did not shrink from them, on the contrary frequently ministering to them himself',[51] while St Hugh of Lincoln actually dwelt among them, eating with them and declaring 'such to be blessed and called them the flowers of paradise and the lucent pearls in the crown of eternal king'.[52] As the disease became rampant these pious and sympathetic attitudes of the upper classes tended to be overtaken by a more vindictive reaction. The Canon De Leprosis of 1179, declared that lepers could not live with healthy men; they were expelled from London and other towns, while Philip V of France actually burned lepers on the pretext that they had maliciously poisoned wells.

Such a polarity of views fortunately yielded to a saner solution in many places, the foundation of hospitals for the treatment of the disease. The first Norman Archbishop of Canterbury, Lanfranc, pointed the way with his leper hospital at Harbledown, a mile and a half from the city.[53] This was their first obvious characteristic: the siting of most of such hospitals was nearby but well outside urban places. Henry I built his lazar-house, dedicated to St Bartholomew, the patron saint of plague-victims, about a mile from the centre of the town of Oxford.[54] Bartlemas Road, a turning off the Cowley Road, recalls it. The little fourteenth-century chapel with an almshouse block adjacent to it is still standing, almost engulfed in modern suburbs. This reminds us of the second recurring element, the belief, meted out in regular church services, in the spiritual treatment for illness. The reason was that this awful disease was popularly regarded as an expiation for sin. Gradually a more merciful view took over, it became to be considered as caused by the secret judgement of God, a visitation rather than a vengeance. In any case the chapel was an appropriate building and is frequently found where the layout of medieval hospitals has been recovered by excavation. A third feature of leper hospitals is that the living accommodation was usually detached from the chapel. It began as a common dormitory but subsequently each inmate was granted a room to himself. At Harbledown over a hundred inmates were scattered throughout a number of wooden houses. A more regular plan was adopted at St Mary Magdalene's, Winchester which was arranged around a quadrangle.[55] Here a row of habitations extended east and west and parallel to the chapel. The Master's house connected the two and the fourth side was occupied by a common hall. In the thirteenth century about 200 leper hospitals existed in England and it has been claimed by Wells that at the height of its spread 'about one person in every two hundred may have been a leper'.[56]

Leprosy is now known to be caused by an organism called *Mycobacterium leprae* which flourishes in the nasal secretions and saliva and is transmitted by close contact with a leprous patient.[57] The long-term eating of rotten and putrid meat and fish was a likely predisposing factor. Some understanding of this led to great care being taken in the leper hospital at Sherburn near Durham to provide patients with fresh and wholesome food. Sometimes medicinal waters were resorted to as when the Reading monk went in the twelfth century to take the waters of Bath. It is characteristic, however, that his cure was claimed to be effected by holy water from an ampoule of St Thomas when he decided to terminate treatment at Bath and make his way to Canterbury. Segregation, although official policy, was probably ineffective and only marginally reduced the incidence of leprosy. A

plausible suggestion is that leprosy declined when prolonged skin to skin contact became less common, perhaps because more clothes were worn as the climate deteriorated, perhaps because the reduced populations after the worst mortalities caused by the plague found fuel supplies more easily so people had less need to huddle together for warmth. In fact as living conditions improved throughout society in the late Middle Ages leprosy ceased to be such a widespread skin scourge.

Miracles, it might be suggested, offered a surer way of cure for most diseases and afflictions than the drastically unsuitable remedies offered by the 'medici', 'physici', 'sirurgici' and wandering barber surgeons. Patients in general were better off without flebotomy or bleeding, cauterisation or branding with a hot iron.[58] Roots and herbs, pills and potions, may illuminate the pages of manuscripts but they only succeed in obfuscating the mind in most cases.[59] Diagnosis was even more haphazard: feeling the pulse was simply done to impress the patient while application was made to astrological tables when it was desired to distinguish between different kinds of epilepsy, dropsy or leprosy. Medieval doctors were frequently depicted in manuscript illustrations holding flasks up to the light, they are carrying out urine inspections and colour charts were provided (Figure 3.7),[60] which showed 20 hues of urine arranged from dark yellows and browns, each accompanied by the appropriate diagnostic commentary. Pieces of the glass flasks are found in excavations while a fourteenth-century jug from Hertford,[61] with crystalline deposits of uric acid, is a reminder that urine was collected for use as a nasty medicine (as well as an ingredient in dyeing cloth).

The search for the philosopher's stone which would turn all to gold was one of the will-o'-the-wisps which medieval scientists followed but which also led to the beginnings of experimental chemical enquiry. Chaucer poked fun at the alchemist in the Canon's Yeoman's Tale and described his laboratory in terms verging on the fantastic

Earthen and glass-ware vessels piece by
   piece,
Our urinals, our pots for oil-extraction

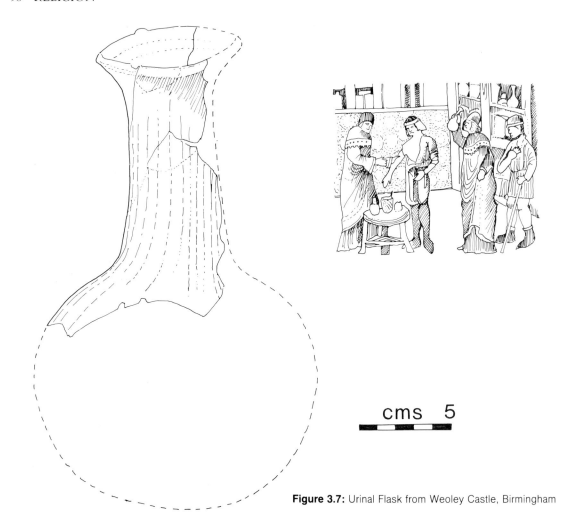

Figure 3.7: Urinal Flask from Weoley Castle, Birmingham

Crucibles, pots for sublimative action,
Phial, alembic, beaker, gourd-retort,
And other useless nonsense of the sort.[62]

but in fact some of these vessels in glass and ceramic have recently been recognised in deposits at Selbourne, Pontefract and St Leonard's, Stamford Priories (Figure 3.8).[63] The complete distillation apparatus consists of four parts: the still-head or alembic, the flask or cucurbit, the receiver and the lute. All have distinctive forms which are easily recognisable but when found in monastic contexts their use is considerably more dubious. Manufacturer's waste is one possibility, but it is perhaps more likely that they would have been used in the

Figure 3.8: Medieval Distillation Vessels (after Moorhouse, 1972)

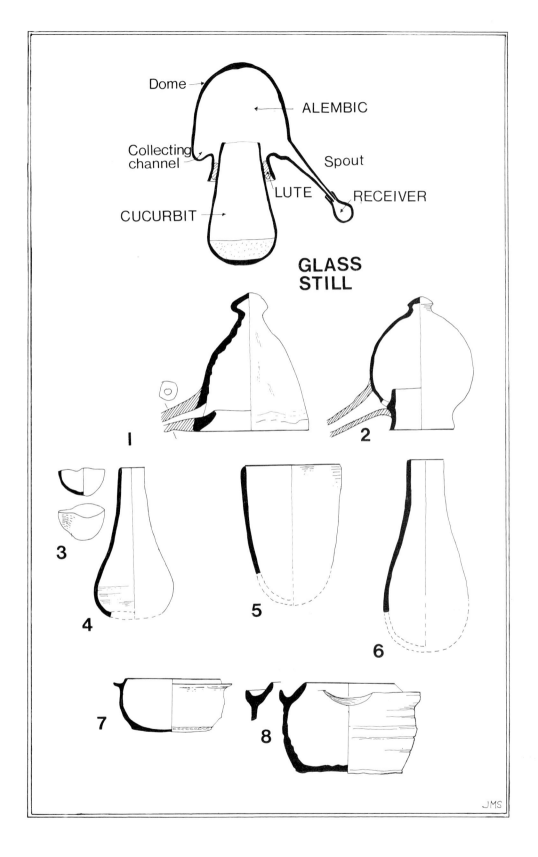

Dome

ALEMBIC

Collecting channel

Spout

LUTE

RECEIVER

CUCURBIT

GLASS STILL

1

2

3

4

5

6

7

8

JMS

monastic kitchen for making potable liquor, or
for distilling wine to make an *acqua vitae* or
infused with herbs to produce a liqueur. Such
traditions have continued in continental
monasteries — Chartreuse and Benedictine
spring to mind — but the consumption of such
strong drinks performed an important
medicinal function for fourteenth-century
people, debilitated and chilled with enteric
disorders; they generated a feeling of warmth
and well being. At St Leonard's Priory,
Stamford, it is likely that the fragments of
apparatus associated with deposits of chemicals
and metallurgical waste were the remains of
alchemical experiments or assaying processes.
The range of pottery forms and the chemical
analysis of residues found in them at Sandal
Castle (West Yorks.) also suggest that the two
workshops there were involved in alchemy.
The 150 near complete industrial wares
included two cucurbits and several conical
vessels called *aludels* used to raise the alembic
heads above the liquid being distilled. At
Sandal it is likely that the alembics themselves
were made of glass; these would have been
seated in bowls filled with sand. There is more
than a hint that at both Stamford and Sandal
the alchemical processes were being indulged
in illicitly.

19. Hospitals in the Later Middle Ages

Leper hospitals catered for a special type of
client whose affliction demanded isolation.
The word 'hospital' was used in the Middle
Ages to describe a much wider and less
specialised spectrum of institutions than those
devoted exclusively to the care of the sick.[64] It
derives from the Latin *hospes*, denoting a
stranger, foreigner or guest. The hospitals of
medieval England were designed to provide
shelter for travellers of all kinds, also to
minister to the needs of the poor, and succour
the elderly and the sick. They were nearly
always ecclesiastical institutions whose prime
motive was the salvation of the souls of the
inmates; the health of their bodies was very
much a secondary consideration, perhaps
because it was rightly recognised to be a
difficult task, if not impossible in many cases.
One or more priests usually were in charge,

but not doctors: general nursing, not medical
attention, was on offer, while strict rules of life
akin to the monastic were imposed on the
patients. It is hardly surprising that the buildings had a strongly monastic flavour.

The models for early medieval hospital
buildings were probably the infirmaries of the
greater monastic houses such as survive in plan
or in part at Ely, Christchurch, Canterbury
and Fountains. These were sited to the east of
and well separated from the busy hub of
the monastery round the cloister. They included
a large airy hall, with arcades, providing a
central space free for staff furniture and
utensils. The beds for guests, sick or elderly,
were placed in the aisles divided by wooden
screens or curtains rather as in wards in
modern hospitals. There were usually separate
kitchens (across a courtyard to reduce fire
risk), apothecaries, chambers for isolating
victims of contagious diseases, flats for retired
abbots and, most importantly, a separate
chapel. This might be physically joined to the
hall as at Canterbury, or separated as at
Fountains. The infirmary in fact was a self-
sufficient unit within the monastery.

Hospitals were founded in all the principal
towns of England (Plates 3.7, 3.8).[65] By the
twelfth century there were no less than 167; this
had increased to 800 by the Reformation
though many were short-lived. A favourite
siting was by the gates of towns or along main
roads. The five hospitals of Bury St Edmunds,
for instance, included St Saviours which was
outside the north gate, St John the Evangelist
outside the south gate, two, St Nicholas and St
Stephen, without the east gate, and St Peter's
hospital outside the Risbygate. Bristol had 13
hospitals built between the twelfth and the
fifteenth centuries. The little hospital of St
Bartholomew, Bristol[66] was built on the north
bank of the River Frome and was outside the
medieval town proper but very near to the
important road connecting Bristol to the
North. Excavations have shown that the first
building of the thirteenth century consisted of
the normal twofold elements, hall and chapel,
separated in this case by a courtyard. An
inventory taken in 1303 shows a well-equipped
kitchen, bakehouse and cellar with somewhat
more spartan arrangements in the hall and
guesthouse. By the fourteenth century men

Plate 3.7: Hospital of St Mary Magdalene, Glastonbury. The thirteenth-century hospital comprised hall and chapel (Photo: J.M. Steane)

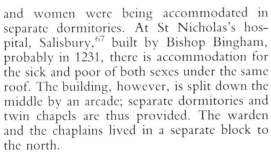

Plate 3.8: Hospital of St Mary Magdalene, Glastonbury. In the fifteenth century individual accommodation was provided in two terraces of two-roomed houses built within the shell of the former hall, whose gable ends can be seen in both plates. Half the houses were taken down in this century but the footings remain (Photo: J.M. Steane)

and women were being accommodated in separate dormitories. At St Nicholas's hospital, Salisbury,[67] built by Bishop Bingham, probably in 1231, there is accommodation for the sick and poor of both sexes under the same roof. The building, however, is split down the middle by an arcade; separate dormitories and twin chapels are thus provided. The warden and the chaplains lived in a separate block to the north.

The main changes in plan-forms which occurred during the Later Middle Ages accorded with greater standards of privacy and comfort demanded in upper class domestic accommodation (Plate 3.8). Here again

monastic planning probably led the way. The houses of the austere Carthusian order provided separate cells for each monk arranged round a courtyard as at Mount Grace Priory (Yorks.), and the Charterhouse, London. The same layout was used by William of Wykeham a few years earlier in his collegiate quadrangles at Winchester and New College, Oxford. It was followed in 1436-50 by William de la Pole's hospital at Ewelme, built in brick, a new-fangled material for Oxfordshire, made and laid by Flemings.[68] Each bedesman had a separate dwelling arranged round a cloistered courtyard, one up and one down, well heated by wall fireplaces, with a kitchen and garderobe. The bedesmen used the parish church as their chapel and a school below, 'God's House', completed the hospital complex. Cardinal Beaufort again used the quadrangular plan in his refoundation of St Cross Hospital, Winchester, in the 1440s but here he incorporated the common hall and a master's lodging on one side of the enclosure.

References

1. Edwards, D.L., *Christian England. Its Story to the Reformation*, London, 1981, 157-8.
2. Rodwell, W., *Wells Cathedral. Excavations and Discoveries*, Wells, 1980. Also *Current Archaeology*, 73, VII, no. 2, Aug. 1980, 38-44.
3. Williams, D.H., *The Welsh Cistercians*, Pontypool, 1969.
4. Gilyard-Beer, R., *Fountains Abbey, Yorkshire*, HMSO, London, 1975, 38-9.
5. Greene, P., 'Norton Priory', *Current Archaeology*, 31, March 1972, 216-21; 43, March 1974, 246-50.
6. Weatherhill, J., 'Rievaulx Abbey — The stone used in its buildings with notes on the means of transport', *Yorkshire Arch, J.*, XXXVIII, 1955, 333-54.
7. Rahtz, P. and Hirst, S., *Bordesley Abbey, Redditch, First Report on Excavations 1969-73*, British Archaeological Report 23, 1976.
8. Shortt, H. de S., *Salisbury Cathedral and Indications of the Sarum Use*, Salisbury, 1973.
9. Boase, T.S.R., *English Art 1100–1216*, Oxford, 1953, 110.
10. Dickinson, J.C., *Monastic life in Medieval England*, London, 1961, 15.
11. Rhodes, M., 'A pair of fifteenth century spectacle frames from the City of London', *Antiq. J.*, LXII, part 1, 1982, 57-73.
12. Blair, J., 'English monumental brasses before the Black Death' in Detsicas, A. (ed.), *Collectanea Historica, Essays in memory of Stuart Rigold*, Kent. Arch. Soc. 1981, 256-72. Also Bertram, J., *Lost Brasses*, Newton Abbot, 1976.
13. Quoted in Moorman, R.H., *Church Life in the 13th century*, Cambridge, 1945, 320.
14. Mahany, C.M., 'St. Leonard's Priory', *South Lincolnshire Archaeology*, 1, 1977, 17-22.
15. Biddle, M., *St. Albans Abbey. Chapter House Excavations 1978*, The Fraternity of the Friends of Saint Albans Abbey, occasional paper 1, 1979.
16. *Med. Arch.*, XXV, 1981, 193-4.
17. Allen, Brown R., Colvin, H.M. and Taylor, A.J., *The History of the King's Works*, London, HMSO, 1963, I, 157.
18. Ibid., 256.
19. King, E., *Peterborough Abbey, 1086-1310*, Cambridge, 1973, map on p. 1.
20. Williams, D.H., *The Welsh Cistercians*, Pontypool, 1969.
21. Horn, W. and Born, E., *The Barns of the Abbey of Beaulieu at its Granges of Great Coxwell and Beaulieu St. Leonards*, University of California, Berkeley/Los Angeles, 1965.
22. *Med. Arch.*, XXV, 1981, 193-4.
23. Harvey, J., *The Perpendicular Style, 1330-1485*, London, 1978, 78.
24. Harvey, B., *Westminster Abbey and its Estates in the Middle Ages*, Oxford, 1977, 43-4.
25. Hall, D.J., *English Medieval Pilgrimage*, London, 1965, 2. Finucane, R.C., *Miracles and Pilgrims*, London. 1977, an interesting book to which I am much indebted.
26. Kirk, K.P., *Church Dedications of the Oxford Diocese*, Oxford, 1946, 74.
27. Mynard, D.C., 'Excavations at Bradwell Priory 1968-73', *Milton Keynes Journal*, 3, 1974, 31-67; Rouse, E. Clive, 'Bradwell Abbey and the Chapel of St. Mary', *Milton Keynes Journal*, 2, 1973, 34-8.
28. Green, C. and Whittingham, A.B., 'Excavations at Walsingham Priory, Norfolk, 1961', *Arch. J.*, CXXV, 1969, 255-90.
29. Spencer, B.W., 'Medieval pilgrim badges', *Rotterdam Papers*, Rotterdam, 1968, 137-53.
30. Roberts, B.K., 'The anatomy of settlement' in Sawyer, P.H. (ed.), *Medieval Settlement*, London, 1976, 300.
31. Biddle, M. (ed.), *Winchester in the Early Middle Ages*, Winchester Studies 1, Oxford 1976, 332-5.
32. Biddle, *St. Albans Abbey*.
33. Anderson, M.D., *Looking for History in British Churches*, London, 1951, 11-12.
34. Cox, J.C., *English Church Fittings, Furniture and Accessories*, London, 1923, 265.
35. Steane, J.M. (ed.), *Cogges, Museum of Farming in the Oxfordshire Countryside*, Woodstock, 1980, 37.
36. Platt, C., *The Parish Churches of Medieval England*, London, 1981, 27.
37. Batsford, H. and Fry, C., *The Greater English Church of the Middle Ages*, London, 1944, 33.
38. *Current Archaeology*, 20, May 1970, 254.
39. Taylor, H.M., 'Structural criticism: a plea for more systematic study of Anglo-Saxon buildings' in Clemoes, P. (ed.), *Anglo-Saxon England*, I, Cambridge, 1972, 259-72.
40. Greening-Lamborn, E.A., *The Story of Architecture in Oxford Stone*, Oxford, 1912, 164-5.
41. Taylor, 'Structural criticism', 268-9.
42. Drury, P.J. and Rodwell, W.J., 'Investigations at Asheldham, Essex. An interim report on the church and the historic landscape', *Antiq. J.*,

LVIII, part 1, 1978, 133-51.

43. Rodwell, W.J., 'The archaeological investigation of Hadstock Church, Essex, an interim report', *Antiq. J.*, LVI, part 1, 1976, 55-71.

44. Rodwell, W.J. and Rodwell, K.A., 'Excavations at Rivenhall Church, Essex, an interim report', *Antiq. J.*, LIII, 219-31.

45. Hurst, J.G., 'Wharram Percy, St. Martins Church' in Addyman, P.V. and Morris, R.K. (eds.), *The Archaeological Study of Churches*, CBA Research Reports 13, 1976, 36-9.

46. Dawes, J.D. and Magilton, J.R., *The Cemetery of St. Helen-on-the-Walls, Aldwark, York*, York Archaeological Trust, 1980.

47. The closely observed symptoms are in fact described in great detail by Gilbertus Anglicus (*c.* 1230-40), Rubin, S., *Medieval English Medicine*, Newton Abbot, 1974, 155-6.

48. Manchester, K., 'A leprous skeleton of the seventh century from Eccles, Kent, and the present evidence of leprosy in early Britain', *Journal of Arch. Science*, 1981, 8, 205-9.

49. Wells, C., *Bones, Bodies and Disease*, London, 1964, 93.

50. Clay, R.M., *The Medieval Hospitals of England*, London, 1909, 50.

51. Searle, E., *The Chronicle of Battle Abbey*, Oxford, 1980, 261.

52. Douie, D.L. and Farme, H. (eds.), *Life of St. Hugh of Lincoln*, Edinburgh, 1962, vol. 2, 11.

53. *Victoria County History Kent*, London, 1926, II, 211.

54. Markham, M., *Medieval Hospitals in Oxfordshire*, Woodstock, 1979, 1.

55. Godfrey, W., *The English Almshouse*, London, 1955, 18.

56. Wells, *Bones, Bodies and Diseases*, 94.

57. Rubin, *Medieval English Medicine*, 153.

58. Bodleian Library M.S. Laud, Misc. 724, fols. 94, 96, 3v, 4-9.

59. A typical herbal is Bodleian Library M.S. Ashmole, 1462, thirteenth century.

60. Bodleian Library M.S. Digby 29, *c.* 1430.

61. Dunning, G.C., 'A medieval jug and its contents', *The Lancet*, 11 July 1942, 56.

62. Chaucer, G., *The Canterbury Tales* (trans. by Coghill, N.), Harmondsworth, 1982, 474.

63. Moorhouse, S., 'Medieval distilling apparatus of glass and pottery', *Med. Arch.*, XVI, 1972, 79-123.

64. Clay, R.M., *Medieval Hospitals of England*, London, 1909.

65. Godfrey, *The English Almshouse*, 16.

66. Price, R., *Excavations at St. Bartholomew's Hospital, Bristol*, Bristol, 1979.

67. Royal Commission on Historical Monuments (England), *The City of Salisbury*, vol. 1, 1980, 55.

68. Bond, C.J. and Steane, J.M., 'Stonor, Ewelme and the beginnings of brickwork in Oxfordshire', *J.B.A.A.*, forthcoming.

COMMUNICATIONS, TOWNS, PORTS AND TRADE

1. Stability or Mobility?

Comparatively little study has been given to the communications of medieval England and Wales. This has arisen partly from a misconception about the lack of mobility in medieval life styles. Society was regarded as largely static and peasants, in particular, were thought to have been 'tied to the land' and thus limited in their experience of travelling to within a mile or two beyond their village. In fact there was a constant interchange between town and countryside. The higher echelons of society, kings and barons and ecclesiastics with their sprawling retinues, travelled frequently and widely about the kingdom. Countrymen migrated to the towns, townsmen moved away from urban poverty and guild restriction. Moreover, the existence of hundreds of rural markets, urban centres and regional fairs presupposes much moving about, not merely by the mercantile groups. Again rectors and vicars, however fleeting their visits, acted as links between the rural backwaters and the wider world. All this implies an effective communications network.

Medieval roads are difficult to map and to date because they were not formally engineered except in towns and in one or two areas. Many of them are overlain by modern roads; others have declined into green lanes or have been ploughed up during the enclosure movement. What is beyond doubt is that many Roman roads continued in use.

2. Roads

The Romans had established a network of arterial roads which radiated from London and provided a communications system for the passage of armies and traders over the whole of their province of Britain. This system is now realised to have aided the Anglo-Saxons in their penetration of the country, but it required a strong central government if it was to be maintained. This was patently lacking in the fifth and sixth centuries AD. The decay of town life and the frequent collapse of bridges resulted in the loss of the conception of through-routes for long-distance traffic for a time.

It is evident, however, that stretches at least of Roman roads remained in use. In areas of the country not previously divided into estates Roman roads provided boundaries for Saxon parishes and they are often referred to in charters. The course of Watling Street forms a boundary for 17 parishes in Northamptonshire. The charter, for instance, granting land at Denshanger in Passenham, in 937 refers to the *Stanweg* of Watling Street which still forms the eastern boundary of the parish. The name *Stratford* found in several parts of the country may only be a reminder that stone-paved roads were sufficiently unusual to be recorded in the place name.[1]

New English settlements tended to draw traffic away from former routes. The declining importance of Watling Street as a through-route is suggested by the break in the alignment for 3.2 km which occurs between Kilsby and Crick. The Scandinavian settlement of Kilsby deflected the course of the road to itself. Northampton, a late ninth-century foundation, exerted a similar pull on traffic eastwards away from Watling Street and the most famous Roman road in Britain at this point degenerates into a derelict green lane.

Another example of the partial failure of a Roman road in the Middle Ages comes from the same area. The Gartree Lane, the Roman road which runs from Godmanchester to Leicester, disappeared in two places within the first 16 km of its leaving Alconbury hill. The Saxon settlement of Clopton enticed its traffic northward and there is a gap of about 3.2 km. It has also vanished from the map south of Titchmarsh, where again the Saxon village has apparently diverted the route northwards into its main street. The reason for these breaks may well be connected with the collapse of the Roman bridge with its causeway across the River Nene near this point. Remains of the Roman timber bridge have been recovered by excavation.[2] Its breakdown signed the death-warrant of the Gartree Lane as a through-route. The medieval roads in the area funnelled to the bridge across the Nene at Thrapston, 1.6 km to the south-west, first mentioned in 1224.

Recent study of roads further east in Cambridgeshire has revealed a similar pattern of Roman roads breaking down and being replaced by other routes in the Middle Ages.[3] Ermine Street, the Roman road which ran north-west from the town of Godmanchester skirting the Fens, fell into disuse for a stretch between Alconbury Hill and the River Nene, to the north. Again the collapse of a bridge, this time near the abandoned town of *Durobrivae*, may have been responsible. Two roughly parallel roads further inland developed during the Early Middle Ages. They run through the villages and former settlements of Upton and Coppingford, Sawtry and Glatton. One of these settlements is marked by a farm with the curious name of Ongutein Manor. This is near the site of the Knights Templars' property of Ogerston which is marked on the great Gough map of *c.* 1360.[4] The fact that this obscure place is mentioned is evidence that during this period the lane passing it was the main road to the north. Only in the turnpike era was the Roman road restored to its primacy among the communications of the area.

Turning to the West Midlands the survival or retention of the Roman bridge across the River Severn at Worcester seems to have been the all-important factor in explaining the radial pattern of routes continuing through the Anglo-Saxon into the medieval period. It is thought that the Roman bridge here went on being used until the eighteenth century.[5] The Anglo-Saxon communications system in this area has been reconstructed using charter evidence.[6] Two types of routes are in evidence, the '*weg*' roads which follow the watershed ridges are linked with prehistoric features like forts and barrows and lead out towards the south-east. Some of the made-up roads or '*straet*' routes refer to former Roman highways; those to the east of the '*port*' or '*burh*' of Worcester fan out towards the '*salt herpad*', the major saltway between Droitwich and the Avon Valley.

These instances show that while some major Roman roads decayed only to be revived again, other roads developed in the Middle Ages which have since declined into insignificance. Networks of salt ways, radiating out from the Cheshire Salt Fields, in the Middle Ages brought this vital commodity into eastern and southern England. Local roads were used by fish merchants bringing their wares from the ports on the Wash into Midland England.[7]

The idea of a national road system centring on London was as slow to grow as the concept of a unified free trade area. There are several approaches to the problem of building up a picture of the network of roads in medieval England.[8] The laws of Edward the Confessor (written down in the twelfth century) mirror the concept of the king's peace prevailing over the four great through roads of the kingdom. Only two, Ermine Street and Watling Street, were actually connected with London. The Fosse Way ran from Lincoln to Exeter and the Icknield Way was a prehistoric trackway, partly Romanised, running beneath the Chiltern escarpment. Neither of the two latter routes was greatly used by the medieval kings in their ubiquitous travellings.[9] The royal itineraries present the best data from which a road network can be inferred.[10] King John, for instance, is recorded as having made 360 moves in 1204-5, visiting 145 royal manors or demesnes, 129 castles, 46 religious houses, as well as 40 other places. Altogether John made 1,378 recorded moves, compared with 1,458

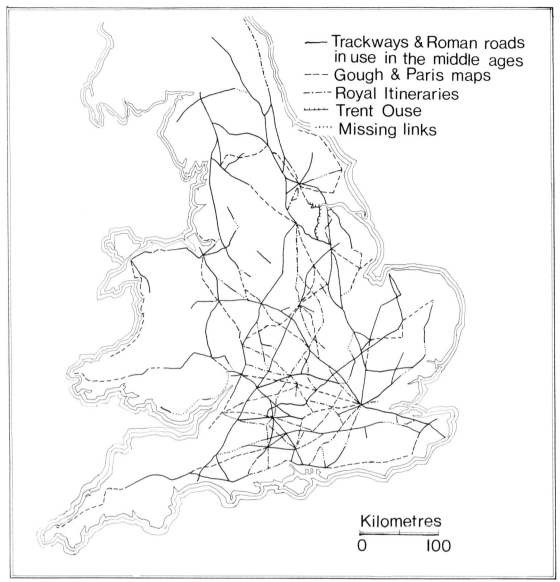

Figure 4.1: Map of Medieval Roads of England (after Hindle, 1982)

by Edward II. Edward I made twice as many, 2,891. Clearly these itineraries give vital information about the general directions of travel and if a route was traversed at all frequently, it is reasonable to suppose that the line of travel must have been represented on the ground by a track or road. These have been mapped and superimposed on another map containing information from Matthew Paris' map of *c.* 1250 and the Gough map of *c.* 1340 (Figure 4.1).

The Gough map appears ostensibly to show roads and distances but it is not certain that the lines connecting the towns on the map denote the actual roads or whether they are merely drawn as a cartographic convention on which a figure was placed representing the distance.[11] The map certainly suggests that by the mid-fourteenth century London had once again become a route centre with five through roads running to distant parts of the kingdom. One runs from London via Winchester, Salisbury and Exeter to Cornwall. Another ran via Maidenhead, Reading, Marlborough to Bristol: a third ran via Witney to Gloucester and eventually to Brecon and St Davids. The fourth road follows much of the line of Watling Street to Lichfield and thence via Newcastle-under-Lyme to Carlisle. The last of these five main routes was the Old North Road which we have already seen was diverted somewhat to the west of its present course. From Wansford bridge, where it crossed the Nene, it ran north through Stamford, Newark, Doncaster, Boroughbridge and then, instead of aiming for Newcastle, crossed the Pennines and arrived in Carlisle. This is a salutary reminder that the mapmaker was not as objective as the Ordnance Surveyors. He may have been a churchman intent on showing a highly selective number of routes between ecclesiastical institutions; an alternative explanation is that it was 'an official compilation for government use'. The Gough map certainly leaves out several well-known roads such as London to Dover and York to Newcastle which was the main route to Scotland.

Other important route centres were York with ten converging routes, followed by Marlborough and Leicester with nine, Salisbury with eight, Winchester and Woodstock with seven and Lincoln, Chester, Shrewsbury, Lichfield, Gloucester, Oxford and Windsor all with six converging routes. The information about the south-west is very incomplete owing to the fact that the kings never penetrated that far into Devon and Cornwall. The northern routes similarly, apart from the Scottish campaigns of Edward I, are not so completely known but the majority were along Roman roads.

So far the emphasis has been on the slow and haphazard growth of a national communications network and it might be concluded that properly laid out and surfaced roads were rare if not unknown during the Middle Ages. There are two obvious exceptions to this rule: military roads and Fenland causeways. During Edward I's 1277 campaign of conquest in north Wales, we are told 'a large part of this forest being cut down, the king opened for himself a very broad road for an advance into the prince's land'.[12] Cumbersome siege

engines and their ammunition were moved along these military roads for use against the Welsh supporters of Prince Rhys. One particularly heroic haul involved the transport of an engine within five days from Dryslwyn 17.7 km east of Carmarthen to the siege of Emlyn, 25.7 km north of Carmarthen by way of St Clears and Cilgerran.[13] Forty oxen and four four-wheeled wains were used.

Tradition insists on a military origin also for one of the Fenland causewayed roads. William the Conqueror may have built the Aldreth causeway in his determination to crush the revolt of Hereward the Wake, holed-up in the Isle of Ely. More likely it was constructed by the bishopric in the twelfth century. Darby[14] shows that these three causeways, Aldreth, Earith and Soham-Stuntney-Ely, strung together the Fenland islands and the mainland to the south-east and south-west. They were economic in function, connecting the monks with their outlying granges, and enabling them to reach the outside world. The Deeping causeway was also attributed to a monk: Egelric of Peterborough 'caused a solid highway for travellers to be made through the middle of most dense forests and the extremely deep marshes of Depyng as far as Spalding, constructed of timber and sand, a most costly work and one of the greatest utility'.

Travelling monks compiled guides or itineraries to help their brethren plan their journeys. One such early precursor of an AA-type route guide was written at Titchfield Abbey (Hants.), for the use of Premonstratensian houses.[15] Naturally enough since Titchfield is on the south coast it gives a greater emphasis to north-south routes.

One of the Titchfield Abbey roads runs north to Winchester and thence to Oxford and to Brackley. This is the southern portion of a road which already existed in the late Anglo-Saxon period, connecting Northampton to Southampton. It is now followed by the trunk roads A43 and A34. Down the northern part of this route was carried the corpse of Edward I's beloved queen, Eleanor of Castile, after her death in Lincolnshire in 1290. On its way to Westminster Abbey, Edward erected an elaborate monument at each of the twelve places where the bier rested.[16] Only three of these

'Eleanor crosses' remain, those at Geddington and Hardingstone in Northamptonshire, and Waltham Cross in Essex. An attempt has been made to reconstruct the line followed by the sad procession in detail as it passed through various Northamptonshire villages, using field archaeological techniques.[17] For the first part of the route from Stamford to Easton-on-the-Hill the route of the medieval and modern roads coincide. At Duddington, however, a fine modern road bypasses the intricate corners of the medieval village round which must have wound the cortège of Queen Eleanor. South-west of Bulwick a large and deeply worn hollow-way runs across Bulwick Park some 7.6 m below the present course of the road which was an eighteenth-century improvement. This was the medieval predecessor of the A43. Its muddy rutted surface must have been extremely difficult to traverse in wet weather. The hollow-way joins the present course of the A43 1.6 km to the south. Similar stretches of hollow-ways are seen south of Deenethorpe and running through Boughton Park before Weekley village is reached. In Boughton Park the hollow-way is up to 35 m across and $1\frac{1}{2}$ m deep. In each of these cases the modern road now bypasses the medieval village and also usually takes a higher route than the miry medieval trackway.

In some places, in fact, it seems that when rural roads became worn out, their courses were moved to another site in preference to maintaining them. The hollow-way which served as one of the streets of the clayland village of Lyveden, some kilometres to the east of the road mentioned above, became boggy in the thirteenth to fourteenth centuries.[18] The site of it was shifted a few metres up the slope to the south. A more dramatic example is found 1.6 km east of Marlborough.[19] Here the medieval Bath Road on Forest Hill is deeply rutted. As one route became churned up another parallel to it was used. Eventually the road at this point spread over the surface of the unfenced down for about 0.8 km. When the modern Bath Road came to be built this particular corner was straightened out and the medieval ruts became covered with grass.

The medieval road system of England, if that is not too grand a word for it, suffered from crimes of commission as well as omis-sion. At times damage was deliberate. The Abbot of St Mary's, York was said to have dug up the King's Street which ran from York to Huntingdon and taken earth to repair his wall outside the city. This, it was claimed, had narrowed the street until it was a mere ditch, whereby none could pass.[20] The men of Titchmarsh in Northamptonshire were accused of digging wells in the king's highway between Thorpe and Thrapston.[21] The Abbot of Chertsey allegedly allowed two wells, 3.7 m and 2.4 m deep, to exist on the highway between Egham and Staines thus causing the bizarre death by drowning of an unknown man whose goods the abbot claimed as a deodand! The majority of cases of disrepair, however, arose out of neglect.[22] Two Oxford-shire cases may be cited. The jurors claimed that Sokebryges Lane at Crowmarsh Gifford was full of water in summer and winter and blamed the Abbot of Battle for the lack of maintenance. Another slack cleric, the Abbot of Dorchester, was at fault over the state of Cobble Lane in Nettlebed where the road was so dangerous through the caving in of the banks that two men could not meet and pass. Very seldom do roads appear to have been metalled; it is altogether exceptional to hear of a road such as that between Glapthorpe and Southwick in Northamptonshire which 'was wont to be made of great stones'.

So far we have been discussing the cart ways which were known as *viae*. The *via regia* was common to all while the *communis strata* belonged to some city, or town, or private person. Medieval lawyers recognised two other types of routeway. Lesser tracks for packhorses were known by the name of *vicus*; footways were known by the term *iter*. Villages surrounded by open fields had numerous lanes and trackways leading out into the fields. Some led from one village to another. Where they go reasonably directly they may be quite ancient. Where the course has frequent dog-legs it clearly post-dates the furlong blocks and had to pursue an indirect course to avoid pre-existing arable. The other type gave access to the fields themselves. They are shown on pre-inclosure maps such as the splendid series by Brazier made for the Dukes of Montague at Boughton (Northants.) in the eighteenth century. In the Midland coun-

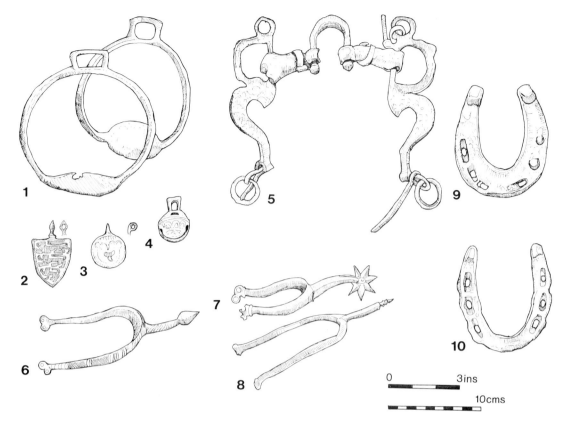

Figure 4.2: Horse Harness, Oxfordshire County Museum. 1. Stirrups, late medieval. 2, 3. Harness pendants. 4. Packhorse bell, fourteenth/fifteenth century. 5. Snaffle bit, late medieval. 6. Bronze prick spur, thirteenth century. 7. Rowel spur, fourteenth century. 8. Prick spur. 9. Horse shoe, later medieval. 10. Wavy-edged early medieval horseshoe

ties of Buckinghamshire, Northamptonshire, Warwickshire and Leicestershire they can be seen in the landscape itself. At times they run along the headlands, those linear mounds weaving between the furlong blocks, and in other places they are unploughed access-ways between two blocks of ridge and furrow.

Medieval travellers left scarcely any other discernible traces behind them, apart from the roads themselves. The wagons have vanished but we know about their appearance from MSS such as the Luttrell Psalter. Here carts with wheels, studded with iron nails, are shown. Doubtless the toll granted to William Caldecote of Aylesbury of a penny on 'every loaded cart with irons and of a halfpenny from every loaded cart without irons' is a reference to them. Occasionally pieces of iron tyre with strakenails are recovered from excavations —

an example occurred at Lyveden. William Caldecote also received 'a farthing from every horse carrying goods'. Packhorses must have been a very common sight along medieval roads. Many hundreds of horseshoes have been recovered from medieval sites (Figure 4.2); doubtless one day someone will be able to submit them to analysis and produce a picture of the size of the medieval pony. Oxen of course were also shod with curved pieces of iron roughly the shape of half a horseshoe for each hoof.

3. Fords and Bridges

One of the determining factors for the sites of towns were fords and bridging places. Here land and water routes converged and merchants were attracted by the prospect of an increase of traffic, bringing an opportunity for commerce. Lords might well fortify settlements at these points. Tolls would be easy to collect at such crossing places.

Two Midland towns, Oxford and Stamford, illustrate these points well. Oxford retains in its place name a reminder that here were crossings of the braided course of the River Thames by one of the most important north-south roads in Saxon southern England. This road ran north from the channel port of Southampton past the capital, Winchester, and so over the Thames at Oxford to Northampton. It determined the shape of the original town which grew up in the eighth/ninth centuries along a north-south axis. Recent excavations have shown that below the present street known as St Aldates there is a massive clay bank perhaps datable to the reign of King Offa.[23] The latest discovery (in 1982) of a paved surface of limestone rubble lying deep under layers of river silt and modern build-up seems to be the ford itself.[24] Both bank and ford were supplemented by a series of timber bridges and causeways. Robert D'Oilli, the Norman Constable, replaced the timber by stone arches. These may still be seen, semicircular and barrel-vaulted, encased in later widenings under the present busy Abingdon road, as it approaches Folly Bridge from the south. Robert's engineering works were known as the 'Grand Pont' and the long embanked mound carrying it can be traced for 1.2 km southwards over the flood plain of the River Thames.

At Stamford (Lincs.) there has been an equally interesting sequence of roads, fords and bridges.[25] There had been no important Roman settlement in the area and Ermine Street, the main north-south Roman road, crossed the River Welland upstream on its way to Lincoln. Owing no doubt to the collapse of its bridge, Ermine Street became unusable at the end of the Roman period. A Saxon village developed a little to the east where the river flows through shallows. Here was the 'Stony Ford' from which the later town took its name. The Danes established a fort in this part of Lincolnshire in c. 877.

The river crossing was moved further to the east for the second time when Edward the

Elder seized Stamford and ordered 'the burh on the south side of the river to be built'. The road was now diverted through this English burh and crossed the River Welland at a point narrow enough for it to be bridged. In this way the 'Stony Ford' was replaced by a stone bridge. The road then pushed up the hill, turned a right angle round the Danish burh, pursued its way round to the west, and ultimately joined its original alignment to the north of the town.

This complicated story is largely the product of surmise, an uneasy mixture of scrappy documentary evidence, allied with arguments derived from urban topography. Who actually ordered the first bridges to be built at Oxford or Stamford is unknown. It may well be connected with the so-called *Trinoda Necessitas*, the three common dues exacted in England in the eighth century involving service in the field army, the building of fortifications and the construction of bridges. Strategy certainly decided the location of a number of bridges and one element was to prevent the Vikings sailing upstream of them. The 'Curatbrygan' was built on the Severn at Quatford in 895; at Nottingham a bridge joining two burhs was built on either side of the Trent in 923; Redbridge straddled the tidal Test in Hampshire before 956. At London the bridge has been there as long as the city has. The Thames estuary forms the main inlet into the country from the continent of Europe.[26] The river was about 4.6 m lower on average in Roman times and the site of the city was near the tidal limit. London grew up at the lowest point at which the river could be conveniently bridged. Geography offered a double advantage; on the north side two low gravel-capped hills (later crowned by St Pauls and the Bank) and on the south a further bench of gravel. Here then was the ideal place for a pair of bridgeheads. The bulky timbering of the north end of the Roman bridge has recently been uncovered. It was followed by a succession of Saxon and medieval structures, timber piled, multi-arched, and finally topped with houses, shops, gates and drawbridges. Defence again was paramount. The defended bridgehead to the south was known as the 'Southwork' or Southwark. Even so redoubtable a warrior as William the Conqueror did not attempt to

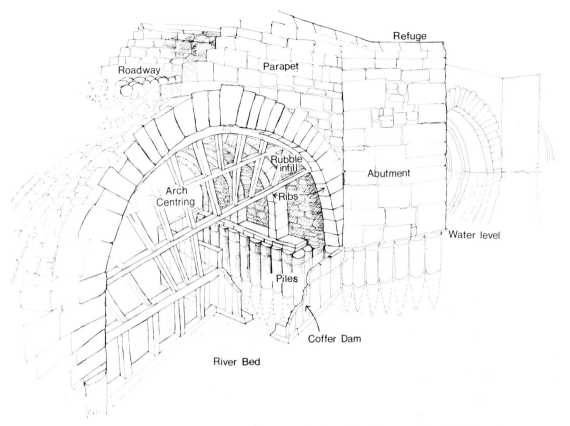

Figure 4.3: Bridge under Construction. A conjectural reconstruction based on the excavation of a bridge at Waltham Abbey, Essex

carry London by storm across its bridge.

During the next four centuries the Thames was crossed by a great series of bridges dictated by the needs of state rather than by commercial convenience. The proximity of royal residences and the availability of great timbers from royal forests were deciding factors. This succession of bridges included Kingston by 1219, Staines by 1222, Henley by 1225, Marlow by 1227, Caversham by 1231, Windsor by 1242, Maidenhead by 1297 and Chertsey by c. 1360. They appear in seventeenth- and early eighteenth-century prints and watercolours of the River Thames, their picturesque and ramshackle appearance contrasting with the genuine strength of their pile-driven structures.

Among the techniques already available in the twelfth and thirteenth centuries for building bridges were pile-driving and coffer dams (Figure 4.3). The pile-driver (called a *ram* or *mouton*) consisted of sheer legs carrying a pulley by means of which a heavy block of wood or iron could be hoisted and let fall on the head of the pile.[27] Old Rochester Bridge, rebuilt in 1383-93 had 10,000 of these piles of elm each 6.1 m in length. Pile-driving on the river bed was facilitated if the water was temporarily excluded by means of a coffer dam. Remains of such dams, which involved piles connected by timber sheeting, were found during excavations of a medieval bridge at Waltham Abbey.[28] Dense concentrations of piles could then be driven in and the abutments built over the top.

The superstructure of the great timber bridges varied according to the length of the space to be spanned and the depth of the river.[29] In a number their trestles were closely but irregularly spaced, having between two to five unsquared but accurately-driven projecting piles rising straight from the bed to a lintel. There was no longitudinal bracing but sometimes a rough traverse bracing of scissors or single oblique members trenched or bolted across the piles. A medieval bridge, which survived at Chepstow until the early nineteenth century, was erected on a series of transverse sole-plates set in platforms on the river bed. From these arose accurately worked trestles of well-squared posts which carried the lintels. Over these ran the bearers, arch-braced to the posts between the piers.

These timber bridges have now all disappeared (at any rate above water level) but there are dozens of smaller stone-built medieval bridges surviving, some of them uncomplainingly carrying immense loads of modern traffic. Their characteristics are instantly recognisable. They include massive projecting piers or cutwaters, triangular (or more rarely semicircular) in shape, and found pointing upstream to protect the abutments from the force of the current, and the impact of trees and other objects borne along by the water. The upper parts of these piers have refuges for pedestrians at roadway level. Medieval bridges are usually multi-arched, their spans varying from 1.52 m to 6.1 m or more. The arches were raised on wooden centring. Early arches were barrel-vaulted, but from the late twelfth century, ribs of cut ashlar were used and rubble infill as in ecclesiastical vaulting. Many early medieval bridges were humped where the roadway rose over pointed Gothic arches (a good example is the thirteenth-century Newbridge, Oxfordshire). Towards the end of the Middle Ages arches tended to flatten and become four centred; bridges reflected this stylistic change and in turn lost their humps (the early sixteenth-century bridge at Burford, Oxfordshire, is an example). The approach to such bridges was usually along a causeway which raised the road above the flood plain. A sixteenth-century writer described such a 'causey' as being 'a bridge over dirt'. These causeways were occasionally revetted in stone and frequently were pierced by subsidiary arches which were used at times of flood to allow the swollen waters to escape instead of ponding up behind the obstacle. Folly Bridge, Oxford, had a

causeway with no less than 42 arches in the sixteenth century. Bridges in towns, such as Bedford and Lincoln, attracted buildings. The most famous example was London Bridge where a stone structure of 19 pointed arches was surmounted by a street lined with buildings, houses and shops whose rents helped to defray the city's considerable investment. London Bridge was defended from the south by a stone gateway; the seventh arch was crossed by a drawbridge. A superb fortified gateway still protects the bridge into the border town of Monmouth. There is a less impressive one at Warkworth. A fortified sluice-cum-bridge protects the monastery of Bury St Edmunds on the north-east of the precinct (Plate 4.1). The thirteenth-century south gateway at Oxford obtained the undeserved reputation of being Friar Bacon's observatory. Capped with a seventeenth-century storey (which earned the nickname of Folly) it straddled the bridge crossing the Thames here until 1776. One last recurring feature of medieval bridges were the chapels built on or at the approaches, and lived in by chantry priests, or bridge hermits.[30] These were the equivalent of toll-houses because the hermits were licensed to collect from passengers crossing the bridge. Only four such chapels survive, at Wakefield, Rotherham, Exeter (Figure 4.4; Plate 4.2) and St Ives, but there were originally many more.

This last point raises the whole question as to who financed the construction and maintained the fabric of medieval bridges. They owed their existence to five main sources: acts of religious charity, orders from the government, the calls of commerce, the opportunities of levying tolls by lords and the thoughtfulness or necessities of great persons. In many parts of the country monasteries or great churches are said to have been responsible for building bridges. A whole string of bridges across the River Wey in Surrey has been attributed to Waverley Abbey. The Abbot of Ramsey undoubtedly built St Ives' bridge and equipped it with a chapel. During the Later Middle Ages it was laymen who increasingly left legacies to the bridge funds. Maidenhead bridge was maintained by multiple donations in this way. Often different authorities or individuals were supposed to co-operate or

Plate 4.1: Abbot's Bridge, Bury St Edmunds, Suffolk. The bridge proper dates from the twelfth century. It is a *pont a trous* with portcullis or penstocks formerly attached to each arch. (The slots are visible behind the cutwaters.) Behind it is a wall, built in the fourteenth century, carried across it (Photo: J.M. Steane)

Plate 4.2: Exeter, Devon. The multi-arched bridge across the River Exe, which has now been embanked and narrowed leaving this section high and dry. Originally built in the late twelfth/early thirteenth centuries with semi-circular arches (seen at right) and cutwaters, subsequently repaired with ribbed gothic arches (centre). Three building materials are visible: a vesicular volcanic rock known as 'trap' found at Ide and Thorverton; cretaceous limestone from East Devon; and coarse red breccia known as Heavitree stone. The Victorian replacement of the medieval bridge church of St Edmunds is seen top right (Photo: J.M. Steane)

contribute and the result is the very patchwork appearance of many medieval bridges. At Rochester there were no less than 53 places mostly on the Medway and its tributaries responsible for different portions.[31] The Archbishop of Canterbury was supposed to maintain the fifth and ninth pier, the Bishop of Rochester the first, the king the fourth, and so on. Only very gradually did the idea of communal responsibility creep in.

One other archaeological aspect of bridges remains to be noticed. The sands, mud and silt below the roadway are likely to retain objects thrown or dropped by those traversing the bridge and provide a good date-range of use of the crossing. The river bed below London Bridge has yielded an immense number of objects. Similarly below Wallingford bridge a rich hoard of coins, lead tokens and other metal objects have been painstakingly recovered in difficult conditions by divers. They can only operate in the murky and icy waters of winter owing to the number of boats using the river during the summer. An indication of the ancient nature of the crossing of the River Cherwell at the eastern end of Oxford (later Pettypont and subsequently Magdalen bridge) is given by the recovery of

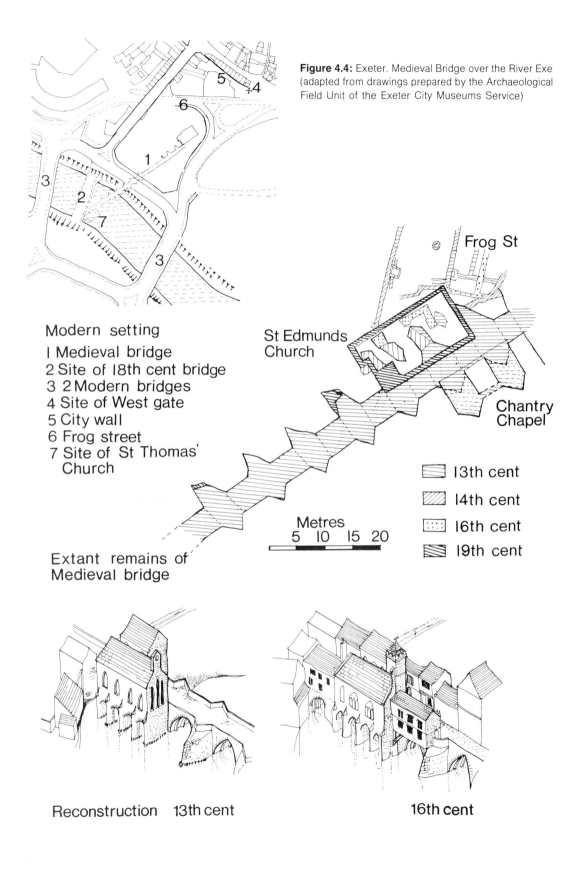

Figure 4.4: Exeter. Medieval Bridge over the River Exe (adapted from drawings prepared by the Archaeological Field Unit of the Exeter City Museums Service)

Modern setting

1 Medieval bridge
2 Site of 18th cent bridge
3 2 Modern bridges
4 Site of West gate
5 City wall
6 Frog street
7 Site of St Thomas' Church

Extant remains of Medieval bridge

Frog St

St Edmunds Church

Chantry Chapel

13th cent
14th cent
16th cent
19th cent

Metres
5 10 15 20

Reconstruction   13th cent

16th cent

two inlaid Viking stirrups,[32] a prick spur and a horse-shoe — all connected with transport.

The building of a bridge could have far-reaching effects on the pattern of trade. Not everyone was prepared to pay the toll for the privilege of crossing the bridge. In this case it acted as a barrier rather than a junction. The distribution of pottery types found in excavations at Bedford suggests that this happened here.[33] Glazed jugs were brought into the town from the Northamptonshire potteries at Lyveden and others were imported from the Oxfordshire potteries. Most of the Lyveden vessels were found in the town to the *north* of the River Ouse. Most of the Oxfordshire material was picked up *south* of the river. It seems that 'despite the existence of a stone bridge from the late twelfth century, or perhaps because of tolls levied upon it, there were two commercial foci in the town'.

Bridge-building again was sometimes a critical factor in the growth or decline of towns and could have a curious knock-on effect. At Salisbury the building of a new bridge across the Avon in 1244 led to a diversion of the main road leading to the south-west that bypassed Wilton, the old county town and contributed to its demise.[34] Wallingford was similarly eclipsed by Abingdon.[35] It was already losing prosperity in the thirteenth and fourteenth centuries and the building of the Burford bridge at Abingdon which diverted the main road from London to Gloucester and South Wales through the town in 1416, allegedly put paid to the economic hopes of Wallingford. The numerous obstructions to the free navigation of the Thames, in the form of weirs, mills and bridges, are thought to have contributed to the commercial weakening of Oxford in the thirteenth and fourteenth centuries. This, however, was to be a positive stimulus to the university: new foundations like Merton and New College took advantage of falling land values and bought up blocks of central town property.

4. Inns

At the end of a hard day's journeying the weary traveller would seek shelter in a ditch, a barn, hospital or an inn. Hospitals (see p. 97) were designed as guesthouses as well as for the elderly and the sick. The term 'inn' was used in a number of ways. It could refer to a lodging or dwelling house, maybe the town house of an ecclesiastical or lay magnate. Lawyers in London lived in Inns of Court and students in Oxford lived in inns or halls (before colleges were founded), while from *c.* 1400 the word could mean a public house for the accommodation of travellers.

Not very many medieval inns survive in recognisable form because the English 'pub' has suffered from radical reconstruction at irregular intervals. A very few remain from the fourteenth century, rather more from the fifteenth. In plan-form most medieval inns fall into two categories, courtyard or gatehouse.[36] In the courtyard-type the main buildings lie back from the street, grouped round a courtyard with ranges of chambers at first-floor level, reached by means of galleries with stabling under. Such are the George Hotel, Dorchester-on-Thames (Oxon.) (Figure 4.5; Plates 4.3, 4.4)[37] and the New Inn, Gloucester.[38]

In the block or gatehouse type the main part of the inn facing onto the street is a solid block of rooms incorporating a gateway or passageway. This leads travellers through to a courtyard where the offices and stables are found. The inspiration for such a plan came from monastic gateways and it is perhaps not surprising that a particularly well-preserved example from the fifteenth century, the George or Pilgrim Inn, Glastonbury, was a monastic investment (Plate 4.5). With its elaborately reticulated facades, stone-vaulted cellars, panelled ground floor hall, half-timbered corridors and well-heated guest rooms, it was the gift of Abbot Selwood (1457-93) to endow the office of monastic chamberlain. The siting of the George Hotel, Dorchester, is immediately opposite the abbey gate, ideal for pilgrims to the shrine of St Birinus whose relics were translated in 1225. The New Inn at Gloucester similarly was built in 1457 by the abbey to accommodate pilgrims. These three inns remind us of the way that life was shot through at all levels with religion. Pilgrims in fact were as numerous as traders on the routeways of medieval England and Wales.

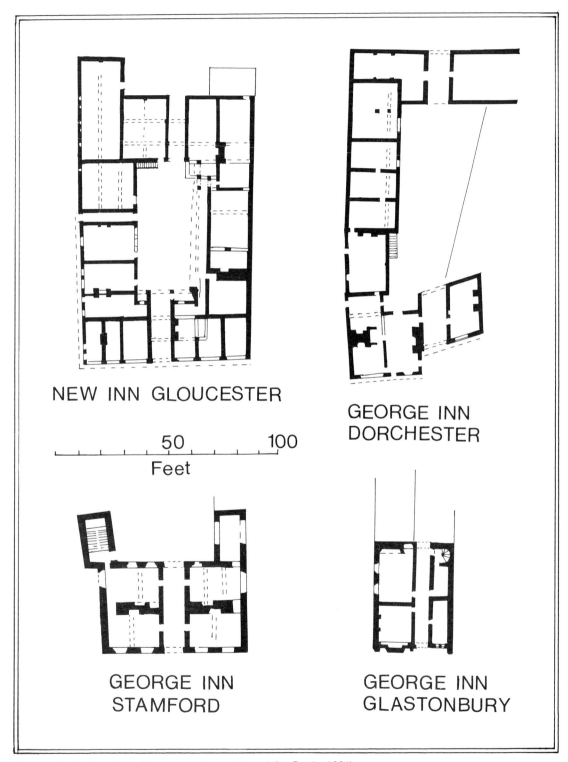

NEW INN GLOUCESTER

GEORGE INN
DORCHESTER

50   100
Feet

GEORGE INN
STAMFORD

GEORGE INN
GLASTONBURY

Figure 4.5: Medieval Inns: Comparative Ground Plans (after Pantin, 1961)

Plate 4.3: The George Hotel, Dorchester-on-Thames, Oxfordshire. A timber-framed courtyard-type late medieval inn. The courtyard is entered through the archway in the centre (Photo: Oxfordshire County Council Department of Museum Services)

Plate 4.4: The George Hotel, Dorchester-on-Thames, Oxfordshire. The gallery runs along the side of the rear range. Stables were below and a series of chambers above (Photo: Oxfordshire County Council Department of Museum Services)

5. *The Topographical Study of Towns*

Comprehensive redevelopment, financed during the economic boom years in the late 1960s and early 1970s, posed an ugly threat to the archaeology of historic town centres. Some, like Worcester and Gloucester, were virtually gutted without much effective response to begin with. Rescue archaeology was born and a crop of urban surveys quickly resulted. Oxford was the subject of the first in 1967; the most dynamic was a plan for rescuing London's past in 1973. By the 1980s most historic towns had their archaeological strategies aimed at focusing limited, and dwindling, financial resources for excavation on the most productive areas.

Such strategies were based on the compilation of a series of maps showing the evolution of the urban plan-form at different periods. The techniques used were an amalgam of field archaeology, the present topography, maps and documents. Hoskins, as so often, pointed the way, by suggesting that a start was to be made by walking the ground and thus 'to study what the documents are talking about'. The different levels do much to explain the siting of the town, the position of its defences and water sources. The present plan, despite frequent widenings and straightenings of main streets, may well perpetuate the medieval layout. Market places rarely change location though they can be infilled. Every medieval town has some narrow and tortuous lanes

Plate 4.5: The George Hotel, Glastonbury. Originally the Pilgrims' Inn of the Abbey. A gatehouse-type inn, stone faced, panelled, three-storied and embattled with a grand set of chambers on the first floor, taller than the others. The original panelling inside and stone newel staircases makes it 'one of the most sumptuous of the small number of surviving English inns of before the Reformation' (Pevsner) (Photo: J.M. Steane)

often perpetuating the names of ancient thoroughfares which recall long vanished families or, maybe, the site of a church or friary which has disappeared. The Lincolnshire port of Boston has a Spain lane from the de Spayne family of the fourteenth century, and Emery Lane from another late medieval family. Street names locate sectors in the town occupied by specialist craftsmen or traders.

Boston again had its *Fleshe ware Rowe*, *Les Barber Rowe* and *Fysshe Row*. A study of the surviving historic buildings pinpoints both change and continuity. The two medieval halls in Boston, for instance, show that the line of the High Street frontage has scarcely changed since the Middle Ages between Bridge Street and the Co-op Car Park. The siting of the mother church in towns, like Brackley and

Thame, indicate the Saxon core to which have been tacked planned elements including broad linear market places. Parish boundaries within towns are informative about the direction of growth. Churches outside the fortifications at Lincoln (Wigford) and Oxford (St Giles and St Clements) demonstrate that extramural suburbs had developed respectively in the late Saxon and early medieval periods. If datable artifacts dug up in service trenches or controlled excavations are plotted on urban maps, the extent of the town at various periods can be demonstrated. Jope pioneered this approach in Oxford, and Waterman in York in the 1950s. Their maps, peppered with symbols, are effective at showing the extent of the late Saxon and Danish towns.

6. Saxon Urban Planning

It is when attempts are made to push back the layout of towns into the Saxon and Roman periods that the documents dry up and archaeology provides virtually the only evidence. It has long been realised that a number of towns which flourished in the Middle Ages had Roman predecessors on the same site. London is the most famous example: within the Roman walls arose the medieval capital of England. Lincoln, York, Gloucester, Chester, Canterbury and Winchester were other examples. What was not so obvious was whether urban life in those places had been continuous. Practically no archaeological evidence has been found for the early Saxon occupation of London. Almost the entire Roman street pattern vanished while at the same time the Roman defences lasted intact into the Middle Ages and provided a foundation for the later London wall except along the water front.[39] Only in two places did lengths of the Roman streets survive to provide the courses for later medieval streets. The great street markets of Cheapside and East Cheap, however, are both roughly aligned along Roman streets. The same is true of Canterbury.[40] Here there are few points of contact between the layout of the medieval city and the Roman grid which has emerged from systematic and recent excavation. The siting of the Roman gates has forced the later streets for

short distances onto an ancient axis but this is all.

In Winchester, where a comparatively large area has been carefully excavated, apparent correlations between the Roman and Saxon street plans are shown to be parts of a more complicated story.[41] Here the principal thoroughfare of the High Street runs downhill from the site of the Roman Westgate. It lies over the site of the Roman road for about a third of its course but even here constant traffic had eroded a hollow-way where the ground slopes downhill. As the road progressed towards the east gate it diverged from the Roman street until it ended up 16 m to the north of the site of the Roman east gate. In fact the remains of Roman buildings have been found under the High Street. All this implies is that far from being evidence of a continuity of street pattern, the Anglo-Saxon road seems to have disregarded the Roman property boundaries and buildings facing one of the most important streets in the Roman town. In fact a case has been made out for interpreting the layout of the streets of Winchester, complete with an intramural way running right round the town, as having been organised in one operation. The date is thought to have been within 60 years either side of 902 AD. This fits in very well with the reign of Alfred, famed as a military leader and a builder of burhs.

Such planning, however, was not unique to this late stage of the Anglo-Saxon period. Precursors of the Alfredian burhs are found both in Wessex itself and in Mercia. Already in the seventh century AD, in the reign of Ine, a Saxon settlement called Hamwih was laid out along the peninsula between Test and Itchen about 0.8 km east from the present site of Southampton.[42] Its grid of eight or nine gravelled streets was located when brick earth was being dug out in the nineteenth century. The streets seem to run back from the shore with cross streets at intervals at right angles; within this undefended area a commercial entrepôt with continental connections grew up and flourished for about 100 years. At Hereford, in Mercia, defence from the Welsh was necessary from the first but here also in the eighth century there was a number of streets with alignments strongly suggesting townplanning.[43] The main streets ran east-west and intersect with a north-south street which joined the north gate to a ford across the River Wye. A series of metalled surfaces was also found suggesting a road running along the back of the defences on the western side.

A combination of these features, namely a gridded layout of streets and an intramural street system, is found in the layout of a number of Alfred's burhs which he built for the defence of Wessex following his victory over the Danes at Edington in 878.[44] These places, 30 in number, are listed in a document called the Burghal Hidage which has now been plausibly dated to 886/90.[45] They are very varied in character, some, like Sashes (Berks.), an island in the Thames, were little more than forts, blocking routeways. Others like

Lydford (Devon) and Shaftesbury (Dorset) were fortifications perched on promontories. Others like Winchester, used Roman defence systems. In a further group, the large rectangular defended sites previously not fortified, we gain the clearest impression of planning, if by planning we mean the laying-out of a town in a regular pattern at one moment in time, with the intention of dividing and distributing the ground for a permanent settlement.

These Alfredian planned towns included Wareham, Wallingford, Cricklade and Oxford. The earthen ramparts of the first three of these towns have survived and are still formidable, if grass-grown elements, in the urban scene. Around them on the inside were

Figure 4.6: Plan of Saxon and Medieval Oxford (after Rodwell, 1975)

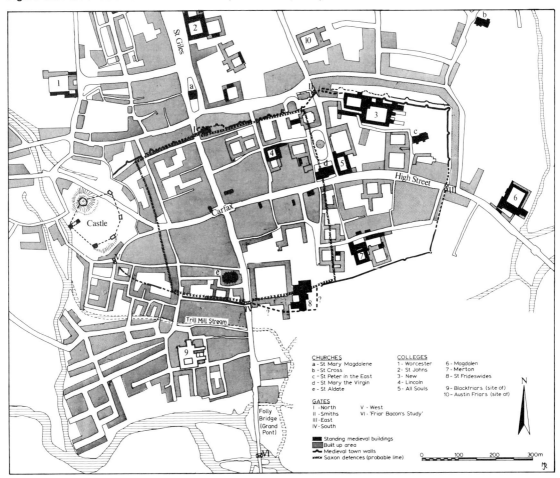

intramural streets serving two purposes, to ensure the rapid movement of troops from one part of the fortification to another, and to provide rear access to the more important properties, facing onto the main street. These burhs also had a planned layout with a High Street serving as the principal axis and lesser streets and paths laid at right angles to it.

Two interesting refinements of our model for these early fortified towns of Wessex have come from Oxford (Figure 4.6). Excavations in 1982 on the southern edge of the Saxon town revealed that it was bounded by a 30 m wide branch of the River Thames.[46] This was known later as the Trill Mill stream, when the main navigation stream had shifted southwards to its present position where it is crossed by Folly Bridge. Evidently the Saxon

town was defended on this side by the river but there is no trace of an intramural road in this area. Instead a gravel path and a series of boundaries, revetted with wattle fences, ran along the water front. The defences were set back from this tow path. Properties inside the town backed up against the defences. A similar feature was noticed on the west side of medieval Southampton where the harbour road runs outside the town wall. The other observation from Oxford is that when Queen Street, the main east-west street of the Saxon town, was cut through in 1970 it was found to have been repaired and resurfaced on 19 occasions in Saxon and medieval times.[47] No less than seven surfaces dated from the tenth and eleventh centuries. In Winchester where the street system, as we have seen, was laid out c.

Plate 4.6: Lincoln. General view of excavations at Flaxengate, 1975, tenth-century levels, timber buildings and associated pits. Cobbled surface at extreme right (Photo: N.H. Hawley)

880-6, it was noticed that the first surfaces of the Anglo-Saxon streets excavated were formed of small broken flints.[48] These were knapped and stockpiled for the initial surfacing. This task, it has been calculated, involved 6–8 km of streets and required something like 8,000 tonnes of flint cobbles. It implies a co-ordinated system of public works which is not so surprising for the capital town of Wessex.

When we turn north to the Danelaw, to Lincoln, we find that excavation has again complicated what was previously thought to be a simple story (Plate 4.6).[49] A large site on the centre of the slope between the ridge occupied by the Roman legionary fortress (and later by the Norman castle and cathedral) and the river front has been examined. Flaxengate and Grantham street were laid out early on in the period of Danish occupation, but neither proved to be superimposed on Roman streets. They did, however, respect a pre-existing framework and it seems that some surviving Roman buildings were still sufficiently upstanding in the ninth century to affect the urban topography. The street plan of Lincoln was not so precise as those of Winchester and comparable Alfredian burhs, although the systematic resurfacing of Flaxengate implies central direction of some sort. Another town in the Danelaw, Northampton, has also produced evidence for an informal layout paying little attention to exploiting street frontages in its early phases.[50]

7. Early Medieval Town Development

Recently it has become fashionable to belittle the effects of the Norman Conquest on English social and economic life. The contribution of some 10,000 Normans to the lives of a population of $1\frac{1}{2}$-2 million is seen in some ways to have been exaggerated. The main stream of Anglo-Saxon traditions in government, administration, law, even architecture, continued largely unchanged through the tumultuous years of invasion. Although undeniably accomplishing a revolution in landownership the Norman invaders do not seem to have stimulated trade or urban life to a marked degree between 1066 and 1140. That is not to say that the towns remained unmarked with the imprint of their conquerors. Castles

made their unwelcome presence felt (Plate 4.7). Religious houses often linked with alien monasteries sprang up in towns. Colonies of Frenchmen were established in a number of boroughs. New and enlarged market places were laid out.

Two towns, Winchester and Windsor, received an obvious impetus from the activities of the Conqueror himself. Winchester, the capital of Alfred's Wessex, continued to act as the seat of the treasury for the Norman kings. William I built a castle at the top of the hill overlooking the city whose great hall was used as one of the ceremonial centres of the Anglo-Norman kingdom. In the south-east quadrant was a great group of churches, the cathedral and the New Minster, the royal and episcopal palaces. The royal palace was to the west of and close to the cathedral; its site is as yet unexcavated. The frequent visits of the court stimulated the growth of urban crafts and industries. Moneyers and goldsmiths were among Winchester's leading citizens. There had also been a tradition of royal residence at Windsor since the ninth century. The late Saxon kings, no doubt attracted by the hunting potential of nearby forests and heaths, had built a timber palace by the River Thames furnished with an impressively large water-mill. William I fortified the great crag which towers over the Thames Valley and New Windsor grew up under its walls in the twelfth century. Norden's plan of 1607 shows two routes, now St Albans Street and High Street, converging on the gate of the castle. The church stands in the triangle so enclosed, and this was also the probable site of the market which was encroached upon in the Later Middle Ages.

Fortification boosted trade in the uncertain century after the Norman Conquest. In Nottingham there had been an Anglo-Danish fort; the new conquerors established a borough and castle alongside.[51] They laid out a special market lying in close proximity to the castle, from which all the roads of the Norman borough radiated. This pattern of castle in close conjunction with market is found at Stamford (south of All Saints Church), Canterbury (Wincheap), Lincoln (High Market at Castle Gates) and Colchester. The bishops of Lincoln similarly encouraged the growth of

Plate 4.7: Corfe, Dorset. The ruins and earthworks of the royal castle begun by William the Conqueror stand on a great natural mound north of the village. The view is from the keep looking down towards the outer bailey ringed round with bastions, some of which have fallen down the slope. The gatehouse is in the centre with a bridge connecting it to the village. Economic life of the medieval villagers was dominated by the Purbeck stone industry. Many of the 'marblers' or quarry owners had their yards at Corfe (Photo: J.M. Steane)

markets under the walls of their castles at Banbury and Sleaford.

Ecclesiastics were foremost among lords in founding or enlarging towns deliberately aimed to generate or capture trade. The abbots of Ramsey in Huntingdonshire, for instance, built a bridge over the River Ouse at St Ives (Cambs.), and laid out a broad market-cum-quay 0.8 km long with a row of houses alongside it.[52] They clearly hoped to draw traders there along the network of Fenland waterways. The great market street or *strata* was fully $36\frac{1}{2}$ m wide. Funnelling into it were side streets whose names — French Row, Lincoln Row, Beverley Row and Leicester Row — show that the market at St Ives was of European as well as of regional significance in the Middle Ages. The medieval bridge remains with its remarkable chapel, but the market place has shrunk in size. It had already been partly built over by 1808 and since then there has been further encroachment. St Ives is now a sleepy little market town, considerably less important than it was 600 years ago.

It is paradoxical that some monasteries, orginally intent on creating an environment apart from the hurly-burly of ordinary living, actually ended up by attracting markets and even towns to their gates. Their congeries of estates produced surpluses of commodities which could be sold there. Great complexes of monastic buildings generated the need for servicing; plumbers, carpenters and masons were required to build and repair their ever growing fabrics. Merchants meeting for a trade were a taxable asset. Consequently the gates of a number of monasteries led out directly into market places and round these grew up towns. Both Battle (Sussex) and Wymondham (Norfolk) have triangular market places at their gates. The great Anglo-Saxon foundation of Abingdon adjoined a large market place and ultimately had to be defended against the irascible townsfolk who clustered round it. At St Albans the abbey chronicle has preserved the tradition that Abbot Wulsin created the town in c. 950.[53] The Roman town, bisected by Watling Street, lay on the west bank of the River Ver. The Benedictine monastery grew up round the burial place of the Roman soldier-martyr, St Alban, on the hill to the east. The abbot diverted Watling Street, led it to the monastic gate, and then back to its old course 1.6 km further on. There are churches at three key points, one dedicated to St Michael where the Watling Street left its course in the Roman town, one, St Stephen's where Watling Street rejoined its old course to the south and St Peter's at the end of the market place. The market place is the one obviously planned element and has been claimed to be late-Saxon in date. Archaeology has not so far supported this interpretation. No pottery earlier than the twelfth century has come from excavations along the market frontage. It now seems likely that the Saxon urban nucleus lay along Fish-pool Street immediately to the south of the small bank, called Kingsbury. The market place whose wedge-shape can be seen so well from the top of the abbey tower, with its medieval clock tower, seems to be an early medieval afterthought to this piece of Saxon monastic enterprise.

Monastic landowners were at times powerful and imaginative enough to shift the whole centre of gravity of the settlements growing up at the gates of their houses. At both Peterborough and Bury St Edmunds there are clear indications that their market places, and the grids of streets aligned on them, have been moved bodily westwards from the original nuclei. The Anglo-Saxon centre of Peterborough, marked by a straggle of lanes to the north-west of St Peter's monastery, was replanned by Abbot Martin in the twelfth century who laid out a rectangular market place in front of the minster gates. Abbot Baldwin of Bury[54] (1065-98), who came from S Denis and doubtless knew of the Roman grid pattern that survived in Paris, created a new planned town on a grid running west

from the west front of the abbey church. The Great Market was located in the north-west corner of the town; Moyses hall, a twelfth-century house (Plate 6.6), still faces onto it. A second market place at Bury, Angel Hill, just outside the Great Court of the Abbey, was the scene of one of the great medieval European fairs.

The layout of these medieval markets tells us a great deal about the conditions of medieval trade. Their entrances and exits had to be in public positions so that they could be well regulated. The stream of rural traffic had to pass along narrowly controlled channels so that tolls could be easily extracted. Often roads were diverted to direct travellers and merchants into the desired space. Thame in Oxfordshire[55] was not a new town but its cigar-shaped market was an ecclesiastical promotion of the Bishop of Lincoln, who in 1219 had royal licence to divert the Oxford-Aylesbury road through the new town. By 1230 there were 63 burgages in the New Thame laid out over the ridge-and-furrow. A similar investment was the Bishop of Winchester's town at Witney where a wedge-shaped market, focused on the church, is first mentioned in 1209. The great size of these markets such as Marlborough (Wilts.), Banbury (Oxon.) and Brackley (Northants.), was dictated by the large areas required for the tethering and penning of herds of animals.

Often the urban archaeologist will have to look hard for the telltale signs of the former existence of a medieval market place. For as the patterns of trade fluctuated, some market places became gradually built over. Wallingford (Oxon.) seems originally to have had a long central strip devoted to marketing. This was encroached upon by blocks of building as the town lost its commercial prosperity towards the end of the Middle Ages. The south-west quadrant of the borough became vacant and only four of the eleven churches were left by the fifteenth century. A similar story of encroachments on a market place laid out in a more optimistic age is seen at Thame where the Bishop of Lincoln himself tried to capitalise on a wasting asset.

In some towns like Winchester and Oxford there was no special provision for market places; their streets became the markets. One

Plate 4.8: The Market Place, Wells, Somerset. On left behind the bank is Bishop Bekynton's *Nova Opera* – a remarkable row of town houses dating from *c.* 1450. They were originally embattled and the shops, of course, are later. The fountain replaced a medieval conduit in 1793. Behind it to the right is Bekynton's 'Bishop's Eye', one of three medieval gatehouses and leading from the market place into the Bishop's Palace, which is also *c.* 1450 (Photo: J.M. Steane)

was held at Winchester outside the west-gate, another inside the walls in North Street. By the twelfth century parts of the High Street indicate specialisation in marketing certain goods. There was a great annual international fair on top of the eastern hill outside the city known as St Giles' Fair which was laid out in a rectilinear fashion. Biddle considers that the fair may go back to the tenth century.

Just as there was a close link between parish church and manor house in hundreds of rural sites so there was frequently a significant juxtaposition between church and market place in medieval towns. The church is often sited (Plate 4.8) close by the market place, together with the market cross in the centre. Both served as constant reminders to men of the need to keep the peace and to hold to the sanctity of contracts. The churchyards may even have been used as the market place. Sundays were sometimes the days for the ordinary weekly markets and the patronal festival of the parish church was often the occasion for local fairs. At King's Lynn, the so-called Saturday market abutted onto the church of St Margaret. At Northampton, after the Norman Conquest, a wide market place grew up to the north of All Saints Church. At Stamford the market place of the Norman borough lies under the shadow of All Saints Church. The church of St Dionysius at Market Harborough rises up from the market place with no intervening green space of a church-yard around it.[56] The reason is that the town grew up on the edge of the open fields of the neighbouring village of Great Bowden 3.2 km away. Traders gathered round this crossing place of the River Welland and a growing town soon required its own church. St Dionysius was a dependent chapel of the parish church with no right to bury its dead. Similarly Hull, a new town founded by the king,[57] had the chapel of Holy Trinity, but the rights of the mother church of Hessle were strictly safeguarded. Burials had still to take place there. It was not until the Archbishop of York met a mournful procession wending its way over the mudflats of the Humber shore in a storm that he felt impelled to consecrate a churchyard. The king granted a vacant plot of land in 1302.

8. Rural Markets

So far in our discussion of medieval markets we have linked 'markets' with 'towns'. This tendency to think of markets as urban phenomena is a notion which probably stems from the fact that by 1700 most markets in England were urban, specialising in particular commodities. Recent studies have pointed to the periodic rural marketing of contemporary Asia and Africa as possibly more relevant models for medieval society. In a survey of medieval markets in Nottinghamshire, for instance, it is observed that markets which were distant in space and also removed temporally could have circuits which would have encouraged traders to 'travel to a different market each day of the week'.[58] Also these rural markets were spread pretty evenly through the county; the average distance between all neighbouring markets was 5.2 km but the mean distance between markets on the same day was $1\frac{1}{2}$ times as much. It was recognised by medieval lawyers, such as Bracton, that markets should be at least 10.8 km apart if their competition was not to be hurtful. But provided that neighbouring markets were held on different days in the week this need not have mattered. There were only two boroughs in Nottinghamshire, Nottingham and East Retford, plus one ecclesiastical centre, Southwell; perhaps significantly their markets were held on Fridays and Saturdays. By 1600 only nine markets out of 30 in 1300 were left in the county and these were all in places which developed into towns linked by an efficient communications network. It seems likely that the growth of markets was connected with the increased taxation of the peasantry, associated with grain shortages and commutation of labour services in the late thirteenth century.

This induced the peasants to market their produce and thus enter the money economy. Doubtless lords encouraged this by taking tolls. By the fifteenth century, however, since food shortages were also frequent and population levels reduced, there was no longer such a necessity to sell grain: rural markets decayed and a centralisation of the market economy resulted in the increasing dominance of small market towns.

A similar story has emerged from Suffolk.[59] Here 70 grants of markets were made between 1227 and 1310. By 1547 no less than 98 towns and villages in the county had a market or a grant of one but it seems that many of these had already dwindled and died in the century or so following the Black Death. The Bigod family's market at Kelsale disappeared, owing to being superseded by a market and fair granted at Saxmundham just a mile down the road. Oxfordshire shows a parallel network of rural markets. Everyone was within 8-10 km of a market. In the Vale of the White Horse around Faringdon it is noticeable again that each market was held on a different day in the week so travelling merchants and pedlars could move in a circuit.

9. New Towns and Planned Urban Elements

Most medieval urban growth resulted from promotion by individual or corporate owners. Claims have been made that no less than 171 English and 88 Welsh towns, founded during the Middle Ages, show signs of having been deliberately 'planted' with a more or less conscious attempt to plan them. During the last 15 years since Beresford's seminal book *New Towns of the Middle Ages*[60] the emphasis has shifted away from this thesis in two directions. Archaeological excavation has shown that the tradition of planned burhs can be tracked back to Mercia and Wessex in the eighth and ninth centuries AD. Moreover, first recorded references do not provide us with the origins of towns; frequently lords, whether royal, baronial or ecclesiastical, simply added planned components to pre-existing urban nuclei. Also intensive analysis of topographical maps allied to excavation of central-town sites has shown that towns (and villages) can contain a number of planned elements added at different times.

Two examples, both from Oxfordshire, illustrate these last points.[61] Old Woodstock was a linear settlement promoted by Henry I along both sides of the Oxford-Stratford road. Henry II added a new town to accommodate his swollen court on a wedge-shape of wasteland between the royal park and the main road. New Woodstock was laid out on a grid plan with a large market place, subsequently encroached upon by building and cut by the diagonal line of the present High Street. Aerial photographs of Eynsham, 8 km to the south, show clearly three phases of planned development. The first was represented by a small market place focusing on the gate of the Saxon abbey and encircled by Acre End Street and a back lane. This was followed by phase 2, Mill Street, at right angles to the north. Finally 'Newland' with long tenements stretching back from the street, was tacked on by 1215. Archaeology, here and in many other places, has provided a technique for recognising the extent of medieval town-planning; it is silent on the motives which activated the planning.

The regular organisation of internal space is a marked characteristic of planned medieval towns. There are three approaches when attempting to reconstruct the medieval urban plot patterns.[62] One technique used with success in Oxford, Winchester and Canterbury is to make use of deeds of transfer to trace groups of properties back from the known modern boundaries to a hypothetical medieval pattern. Surveys of properties and rights, exchange of lands, rents, tolls, customs and court pleas are invaluable in reconstructing early town topography. The Hundred Rolls of 1279 provide for Oxford and Cambridge the most detailed, large-scale and systematic surveys made in boroughs before the end of the Middle Ages. This detail probably arose because a uniquely large number of clerks was available in these places to assemble the evidence! There are 50,000 medieval deeds in the case of Oxford alone. At Canterbury the monks of Christ Church Priory, lords of between a third and a half of the domestic property of the city, left more than 500 charters, rent rolls and surveys mostly dating before 1300 relating to their holdings.[63] Urry's

studies have shown that the medieval plot boundaries have survived in the modern plan in many instances in depth, in length, or occasionally in both. A few alleys have disappeared and the odd new street (e.g. Guildhall Street) has been cut through. Inside the walls he reckons, the layout of Canterbury is much the same as in the reign of King John. Outside the walls the extramural suburbs show 'there was little change between the age of the crusades and of the Napoleonic Wars'.

The second method, favoured by geographers, is to analyse burgage dimensions by using large-scale town plans. Conzen pioneered the method using a large-scale late eighteenth-century plan of Alnwick; he found that five-sixths of the plots in the oldest part of the borough fitted a standard burgage width of 8.5 m–9.8 m or some fractional division of it. Such findings suggest landscapes of deliberate creation.

An extension of this method has been tried in several medieval towns recently by measuring modern plot frontages. At Stratford-on-Avon the initial burgage width of $3^1\!2$ perches and length of 12 perches recorded in the foundation charter of 1196 is still detectable in the modern layout. Such quarter acre (0.1 ha) plots were frequently divided lengthways into halves and thirds within 50 years of the borough's foundation. At New Sarum the burgage plots were initially 3 × 7 perches (15 × 35 m). In Oxfordshire the planned extension to Eynsham was laid out in quarter-acre plots, while the Bishop of Lincoln's new town at Thame was provided with one-acre burgages (0.4 ha). The fact that all these places had plot patterns of different sizes reminds us that medieval urban development was the result of a great number of small scale and diverse decisions of local moment. Only in one area and at one time, the Edwardian Conquest and concurrent urban plantation of Wales, is there a development which can vie in scale with the Roman urbanisation of Britain.

We shall now briefly look at two case-book examples of new town foundations, one episcopal and one royal, which, although familiar, will vividly show the extent to which medieval lordship was able to create and control the urban environment *de novo*. New Sarum or Salisbury began in a remarkable way.[64] Old Sarum was founded on a high chalk hill, overlooking the valley of the River Avon, which had been fortified in Early Iron Age times. By the tenth century it was a minting place and a trading centre. The Normans built a massive ring-motte in the middle of the defended area. They then transferred the see from Sherborne and Ramsbury to Salisbury and a stone cathedral was built next door to the castle. At the foot arose a small and cramped medieval town. It was an unhappy combination. Apparently friction grew between soldiers and ecclesiastics on this hilltop site. The chronicler, Henry of Avranches, graphically wrote that the site was sodden with rain and dew and that nothing would grow but wormwood. The chalk dazzled the eye and provoked thirst which the town wells were unable to satisfy.

At last, in 1223, Bishop Richard Poore decided to make a clean break. He founded a new Sarum in the water meadows by the River Avon which seemed a garden of Eden by comparison with the old centre. The layout of the town was on a generous scale, the urban area was unusually extensive; about 105 ha of the bishop's land was set aside for the new city, of which the cathedral close occupied approximately 33.6 ha. The form of the new town was determined by the decision to provide it with a supply of water running in shallow channels down the centres of most streets. Another constraint was the pre-existing route pattern. The streets were laid down in a grid of twenty chequers, the standard plot being 7 × 3 perches or about 35 m × 15 m, an ample size, the standard rent being 12d a year. The plan moreover comprised a spacious market, two churches within the town, and a third outside. The cathedral close stood physically separate from the town and largely independent of it. In the second quarter of the fourteenth century it was defended by the building of a close wall with gates. In this way the two problems which had bedevilled Old Sarum were solved. The new town had an ample water supply; the cathedral clergy had achieved their privacy, independence and safety. The result was a great success. By 1377 New Salisbury ranked sixth among the provincial towns in England; in the fifteenth century it reached third place. Its prosperity, based on the wool trade, is reflected in the remarkable number of substantial medieval houses which still survive in the town.

Salisbury was restarted by a bishop; a far more prolific town-founder was the king. Perhaps the most famous of the royal towns of the Middle Ages was New Winchelsea in Sussex (Plate 4.9).[65] The old town, one of the Cinque Ports, had been threatened by massive marine erosion; the threat reached crisis proportions in 1250 and 1252, when there were heavy losses of houses. Ten years later the sea reached the market place. When the waves began to batter at the parish church itself, Edward I decided to act. He removed the whole town to a new site, on the top of nearby cliffs. Thirty-nine *insulae* were laid out by the royal surveyors, in as near rectangles as the strongly defended site would allow. The streets were named in military (and later American) style, *Prima Strata* (first street), *Secunda strata* (second street), *Tertia strata* (third street), and so on. The building plots within each *insulae* were also rectangular. Despite the fact that the town has now decayed and there are many vacant spaces in the original layout, there are plenty of pointers to the former mercantile prosperity of New Winchelsea. Below many of the houses are capacious stone-vaulted cellars for storing the merchandise brought from the town quay at the foot of the cliff. Within the impressive fragment of the unfinished fourteenth-century church which occupies one of the *insulae* are the tombs of the Alard family, who produced two admirals of the Cinque Ports (Plate 4.9).

10. *Pottery as a Trade Indicator*

Archaeological research in the last 30 years or so has amplified our knowledge about trade in three ways. It has illumined the late Saxon and early medieval periods, virtually devoid of records regarding internal and external trade. Tangible evidence has been collected of commodities carried and in particular their containers. Assiduous mapping of the distribution of finds has suggested the geography of routes, the extent of trading areas and the fluctuations in patterns of trade, reflecting

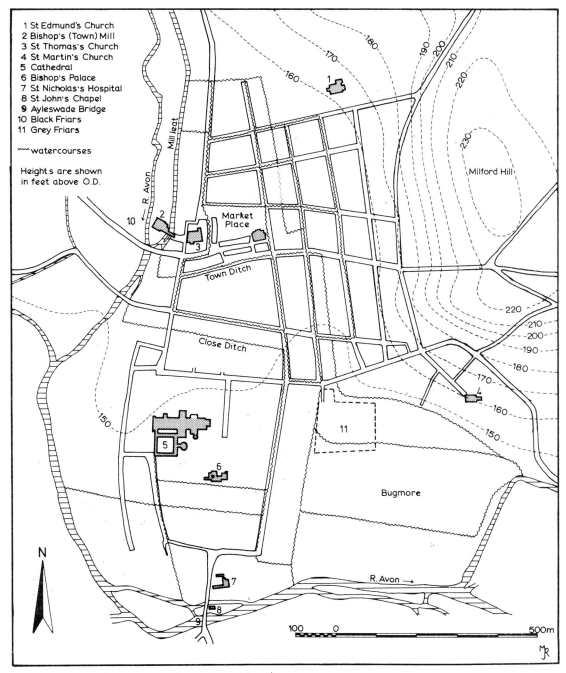

1 St Edmund's Church
2 Bishop's (Town) Mill
3 St Thomas's Church
4 St Martin's Church
5 Cathedral
6 Bishop's Palace
7 St Nicholas's Hospital
8 St John's Chapel
9 Ayleswade Bridge
10 Black Friars
11 Grey Friars

~~~watercourses

Heights are shown
in feet above O.D.

Figure 4.7: Plan of Salisbury (New Sarum) (after RCHM, 1982)

political events and social trends.

The main source of this new sort of information is pottery. This was made in bulk in highly distinctive and localised styles of manufacture in England, France, the Low Countries and Scandinavia. It was easily transported with other commodities and was equally frequently broken. Consequently it has

Plate 4.9: Winchelsea, Sussex. The classic planned town of medieval England, laid out with a grid of streets (*strata*) at right angles to one another forming 39 quarters (*quarteria*) mentioned in the survey of 1292. This aerial photo shows the strongly defensive site, a tree-covered plateau high above the marshes connected to the sea by the estuary of the Brede. Plagues, French attacks and the relentless silting up of the estuary caused its decline, so that now only about a third of the medieval town is still built upon, while the harbour is green fields 3.2 km from the sea (Photo: Cambridge University Committee for Aerial Photography, taken 26.6.58)

been found in quantity at excavations in towns and ports on both sides of the Channel. Medieval potsherds, discarded from cargoes, are picked up from the foreshores of the southern coast of the Humber and from the north bank of the Thames, on both sides of London Bridge. Gerald Dunning pioneered the study of pottery found round the North Sea littoral.[66] He first mapped the distribution of pottery of different fabrics, forms and functions in England, France, Holland, the Rhineland and Scandinavia and sketched patterns of early medieval trade. This work has been continued, with ever increasing scientific exactitude, by Hodges who has mounted a search in French and other continental museums for parallel material.[67] It is not suggested that pottery was traded as such. What is far more likely is that it was carried with the trade in a major commodity of a region. French jugs would accompany the import of French wines into England. Dutch pottery would reach England in cargoes of

other goods in return for English wool which went to supply the Flemish weavers in the Low Countries.

Most traders between England and Europe in the late Saxon and early medieval periods seem to have concentrated their activities across the North Sea to the Rhineland. Distinctive red-painted pottery made at Badorf and Pingsdorf in the Rhineland has been found as far west as Southampton and as far up the east coast as York. Similar Rhenish wares have been traced on the west coast of Jutland and they travelled north to Bergen. The Norman Conquest is thought to have reinforced the consumption of wine in England. For a time there was evidently competition between the French and Rhenish wine industries. Pingsdorf wares appear in quantity at London perhaps providing ceramic confirmation for the notorious drunkenness of the German merchants! The Norman wine importers saturated the southern markets judging from the large quantities of Beauvaisais red-painted and

Normandy gritty wares in such places as Southampton. As one would expect the Norman Conquest tended to shift English trade in the direction of the short Channel crossing.

In the twelfth-thirteenth centuries the centre of gravity of England's trade with Europe moved down Channel in response to the political fact that she was now only part of the Angevin Empire based on both sides of the Channel. The ports of Southampton and Plymouth grew in relative importance compared with the Cinque Ports. The collapse of King John's interests north of the Loire, and the conquest of English Normandy by the French King Philip IV helped this. An instance is the flourishing wine trade which developed between Gascony and the British Isles. This accounts for the very distinctive French type of pottery known as Saintonge ware which is found mainly in English abbeys, castles and wealthy towns. The wine has disappeared beyond recall but the fragments of the imported jugs in local Gascon pottery with their characteristic creamy fabric, parrot beak spouts and painted floral and heraldic decoration (which earns them the name 'polychrome' — many-coloured-ware) remain. This evidence can be compared with what is known from documentary sources. The written records, which give us the average annual tunnage of wine imported during the years 1407-19, show that the bulk of it was moved up the English Channel to London, and that lesser amounts entered the country by way of Southampton and Bristol. Some ships bearing cargoes of wine passed up the east coast to the ports of King's Lynn, Boston, Hull and Newcastle. When this picture is compared with maps showing the distribution of Saintonge polychrome ware the overall pattern is seen to be virtually the same — a pronounced emphasis on the large ports of southern England.[68] What is particularly interesting is that the pattern of the wine trade between England and France seems to have been almost the same a hundred years before the tunnage records begin their testimony. Archaeology has in fact extended our knowledge of the trade backwards by a century.

The study of ceramics has also shed light on the nature of internal trade. By identifying the kiln sources of pottery found in a medieval town like Southampton or Oxford — maps of the trading hinterland at different periods can be built up. Trade routes, moreover, can be postulated. Three instances from Oxford of the useful indicators given by study such as this may be cited. The fact that distinctive Stamford ware pottery has been found in early ninth-century levels at All Saints, Oxford, witnesses to the use of the Northampton-Southampton route via Oxford in late Anglo-Saxon times.[69] There are few continental or regional imported wares into Oxford known from late eleventh-century assemblages, and this apparent insularity of the town may have been affected by the impeded navigation of the Thames by the construction of multiple weirs. The presence of St Neots' ware pottery brought in from the north-east Midlands may be associated with the settlement of a Danish element in the town. A cellar pit under All Saints Church reflects a wealthy merchant household with contacts in Wessex and on the continent. In fact the pottery found in early medieval Oxford suggests that different parts of the town were connected with diverse cultural groups. Not surprisingly the main street frontages such as those along Queen Street and the Carfax end of High Street are found to have earlier occupation than the other late Saxon areas of the town.

11. Ports and Havens

Recent excavations along the waterfronts of medieval ports have produced tangible evidence for the existence of substantial docks and quays.[70] At King's Lynn, a port and a new town grew up on the east side of the Wash where the River Great Ouse enters.[71] This town was started by Herbert Losinga, Bishop of Norwich (1091-1119), who founded the parish church of St Margaret next to a wide space known as the Saturday Market Place. The waterfront of the port of King's Lynn was some 60 m from the present east bank of the River Great Ouse. A portion of the massive retaining wall of the quayside was uncovered some 3 m below modern ground level in 1964.[72] It consisted of upright oak posts supporting horizontal planks both acting as a retaining wall for the river bank. The practice grew up of dumping refuse into the river, thus blocking the harbour, and making it necessary to extend the quayside further west. This had the double advantage of enlarging the town and increasing the scour of the tidal river as it was narrowed.

When one walks through the streets of King's Lynn, the visible signs of the town's former mercantile greatness are obvious.[73] The two market places, one in the old borough to the south, the Saturday market; one in the new borough laid out by Bishop de Turbe (1146-74) to the north, the Tuesday market. The two mighty churches of St Margaret and St Nicholas, with their spacious naves, are perfectly designed to serve as preaching houses to the large populations of the late medieval town. In St Margaret's Church are impressive memorial brasses to Adam de Walksoken (d. 1349) and Robert Braunche (d. 1364) probably made in Germany and very like brasses of the same period at Lübeck, Stralsund and Thern. Leading down lanes to the River Ouse are long tenements with merchants' houses at the street end and yards and warehouses at the back. Here was the Steelyard, the premises of the Hanseatic traders in Lynn. The Hanseatic league was a confederation of German merchants created to exploit the trade of the Baltic and North Seas. It handled the import trade of corn, timber, fish, naval stores and furs from northern Europe. In addition it arranged the exports of the most valuable commodity of the English medieval export trade, wool, and later woollen cloth. The Lynn steelyard occupied an extended site about 21.3 m wide and 61 m long stretching from St Margaret's to the quay and built around four sides of a quadrangle. Another complex of merchants' dwelling house, shops and warehouse built around a courtyard is Hampton Court. Such a flourishing community of merchants organised themselves into guilds which were part religious, part friendly, societies. Two of their possessions survive. Behind the chequered flint and stone façade in Queen Street, pierced by huge Perpendicular-style windows, met the members of the Guild of Holy Trinity, founded in 1421. Their wealth and importance is expressed in the magnificent gilded, embossed and enamelled loving cup, now part of the civic regalia and kept in this building.

King's Lynn was not just a port handling overseas cargoes. It was also a centre for internal trade. All round the Wash in the late eleventh and early twelfth centuries huge efforts were being made to drain the marshes and make new farms and villages. Large quantities of farm produce came into little market towns and were carried down the Fenland rivers to Lynn for shipment overseas. Many of the Fenland pastures were stocked with sheep, scientifically bred, and managed by the great Benedictine abbeys such as Peterborough and Crowland, which had over 16,000 sheep between them. Without English wool the looms of Ypres and Ghent would have stopped working. Large amounts of the profits from this East Anglian wool trade were invested in church building. The twelfth- to fifteenth-century spires and towers which point to heaven are marks of the prosperity of the medieval Fenland.

A second medieval port where archaeology has contributed some new information is Southampton.[74] Here on the western edge of the peninsula formed by the junction of two rivers, the Test and the Itchen which flow south into the great inlet of Southampton water, a town grew up in the tenth century. There had been an Anglo-Saxon settlement further to the east of the peninsula at Hamwih, but alluvium silted up the earlier haven. The new settlement was first sited in the northern sector of the parish of All Saints but when a rampart and ditch and a gate (known as the North Bar) were built in the thirteenth century the focus of the town shifted south. The Anglo-French community settled in the south-west quarter of the town, 'in the French Street known as Bugle Street' and the two churches bear French dedications, to St Michael, patron saint of Normandy and St John. Judging from what archaeologists have found in the rest of the walled area, medieval Southampton was largely patronised by middling-to-prosperous burgesses. There were no rows of artisans' cottages such as those found in Winchester. Maybe they were out of town in the extra-mural suburbs. The prosperity of these burgesses was largely based on overseas trade. The main outlets of Southampton's trade remained fairly constant from the thirteenth to

COMMUNICATIONS, TOWNS, PORTS AND TRADE 133

the sixteenth centuries. Much is known about it from surviving customs' accounts and other records. Wool from the sheep which grazed the chalk downlands of southern England was in great demand first in Flanders and then, later in the Middle Ages, increasingly in Italy. The pattern in fact is the same as that of King's Lynn in the matter of wool exports. In exchange Southampton imported dyestuffs for the textile trade and luxury goods such as spices and silks from Italy. Ships also docked from northern France and Flanders carrying cargoes of linen and canvas, haberdashery and household stores. Timber and naval stores were brought in from the Baltic, and salt, so vital to an economy which had no refrigeration, from the Bay of Bourgeneuf. In addition, as we have seen when discussing pottery, the best wines came from France via the ports of La Rochelle and Bordeaux. Cheaper wines, together with fruits, oil and iron, were imported from Portugal and Spain.

Not all these commodities were retailed all over southern England. Some were consumed in the port of Southampton itself. One vivid illustration of the variety of objects employed daily by a thirteenth-century burgess, Richard of Southwick (d. 1290), can be taken from those found in a stone-lined cesspit at the rear of his house in Cuckoo Lane, Southampton.[75] Some of the silk found was probably Iranian; in the same pit were rope and string made of palm fibres, perhaps the wrappings of bales of spices. Amongst the earthenware pottery there were jugs from northern France and from Saintonge. This French pottery comprised 70 per cent of the total. Lustre ware from Spain made up a further 11 per cent and there was a jar of Near Eastern origin. From northern Europe came a bucket bowl and a number of pieces of glassware were Venetian in origin. Among the food remains found in the pit there were fig seeds, grapes, plums, innumerable cherries, raspberries, hazelnuts and walnuts. The quantity of non-food animals thrown into the pit again has a touch of the exotic. There were five dogs, a ferret, two sparrow hawks and a pet monkey — a Barbary ape — probably brought in with a recent shipment of goods from southern Spain!

Such remains suggest that a high standard of living was attained by one of the leading members of Southampton's merchant body. During the Later Middle Ages, this prosperity, derived largely from the Italian trade, helped to pay for a programme of public works in the town. The Guildhall was rebuilt in the fifteenth century, the walls were strengthened and brought up to date by being adapted for guns. A new quay, sited outside the water gate and equipped with a crane, improved the port's facilities. What is more, the paving and drainage of the streets were undertaken, while common latrines, down by the quays, were a further improvement to the urban environment. Similar civil engineering works were carried through in other ports. Wharves of stone and timber have been excavated at Pevensey, Harwich and Lincoln. At Portsmouth a timber-built cistern, probably a ship's watering tank, was added to the waterfront in the fifteenth century.

A parallel process went on in the port of London, England's capital city. The Normans had quickly realised that London with its strong Scandinavian commercial links was an admirable international port. Its trade was stimulated by the fact that foreign kings demanded foreign luxuries. Also traffic was encouraged by the fact that kings and barons, with interests both in England and Normandy, frequently crossed the Channel. Hundreds of French settlers were soon joined by Germans, the so-called 'men of Cologne'. All this growth is reflected in the archaeology of the waterfront.[76] Between 1000 and 1550 London expanded in area of reclaimed land and docks by 10 per cent (Plate 4.10).

By the late Anglo-Saxon period there were a number of anchorages and wharves, but the safest havens for the shipping of all sizes, which crammed the Thames, were inlets in the river bank. Billingsgate was to the east of London Bridge, Dowgate was at the mouth of the Walbrook. Queenhithe was below St Paul's and the mouth of the Fleet River was another creek which offered shelter. On both the New Fresh Wharf and Dowgate sites the late Saxon and Norman waterfronts were merely beaches indicating that boats were expected to run aground to be off-loaded. Pieces of planking from a clinker-built ship were found lying on the sloping surface of the shore, possibly to facilitate boats being hauled

Plate 4.10: London. Trig Lane excavations looking south-west. The modern course of the river lies to the south behind the fencing at the rear of the fifteenth-century river wall. In the fore-ground is the back-braced timber revetment of the fourteenth-century river front. The space between represents the extent of less than a century's reclamation. Excavation took place in 1974 (Photo: Museum of London)

ashore. Fragments of their cargoes lay strewn along the foreshore; three-quarters of the pottery comprised spouted pitchers of Pings-dorf ware and related types. It is clear that the main direction of trade from London was towards the Rhineland and the Low Countries in the Early Middle Ages.

It has long been realised that extensive land reclamation was carried out in early medieval London. In three main waterfront excavations the Department of Urban Archaeology exca-vated sites at New Fresh Wharf, Seal House and Trig Lane, and found evidence for this reclamation. It was usually effected by erecting a series of timber revetments upon the fore-shore to the south of the contemporary frontage: the intervening area was then filled up with dumps of refuse and sealed with a gravel or stone surface. The sequence at Trig Lane shows how the front-braced revetments were superseded by the development of back-braced revetments (Plate 4.10). This method in turn was further refined by being constructed in two distinct levels, separated by a horizontal plate. It enabled the upper part, constantly exposed to a fluctuating water line, and thus shrinking and swelling all the time, to be renewed without moving the lower members which were permanently submerged. It is clear that the motives were not simply to gain land but also to provide a deep water berth, to overcome problems of silting and to maintain a sound frontage.

Two further characteristic structures were found on London's medieval waterfront — buildings and docks. Thames Street coincided with the general edge of the river bank in the earliest medieval period. From this line long narrow plots stretched south. These properties were between 3 m and 11 m wide; many had an alley down one side. The buildings, which were held by fishmongers, chandlers and vintners, consisted of halls and were equipped with stone vaults and cellars. Finally there were indentations forming docks. The dock west of Baynard's Castle was cleared out exposing a complete rectangular basin of the fourteenth/fifteenth centuries (Plate 4.11). Oak rubbing posts originally lined the dock to protect boats being damaged by the rough stonework. On the west side they had been renewed several times before the dock was filled in in the fifteenth century. Towards the back of the dock were signs of an unloading platform. Although an oak mooring post was found there was no trace of a crane. It is known from sixteenth-century drawings that cranes were employed but in this case it is likely that yard arms were used for unloading.

New uses are now being found for London's decaying and disused dock facilities. Many medieval ports have gone the same way for a variety of different reasons. The port of Hedon was founded c. 1115 by the Earls of Aumale on a convenient creek which led from

Plate 4.11: London. Fifteenth-century stone-lined dock, situated west of Baynard's Castle. Timber rubbing posts protected vessels moored in the dock from damage by the stone wall. Excavation in 1972 (Photo: Museum of London)

the Humber into the parish of Preston in Holderness (Plate 4.12).[77] They cut out a small part of the land of Preston (Hedon means 'the small hill overgrown with heather'), and laid out streets, a market place, burgages and three arms or havens, to enable ships to come up the River Hedon from the Humber and so into the town. Hedon was meant to tap the wealth of one of the greatest areas of marshland colonisation in medieval England, Holderness, between the Yorkshire wolds and the sea. At the height of its prosperity in the thirteenth century it had three churches. The king acquired the port and re-roofed the Hall of Pleas. Clearly as seigneur of Hedon he hoped to profit from justice here. The fortunes of the town soon wavered, however, and as early as 1280 we hear 'the men of Hedon are straitened and poor; many of them wish to move away on account of being tallaged: they have near them two other good towns, Ravensrodd and Hull, which have good harbours and grow day by day'. What finally halted Hedon's economic hopes was not commercial rivalry, it was the relentless and gradual silting of the River Hedon. When Leland visited Hedon in the reign of Henry VIII he noticed 'it is evident to see that some places where the ships lay be

overgrown with flags and reeds, and the Haven is sore decayed'. To the eye of the field archaeologist today, the decay is evident. The havens have been infilled, grass grows over the wharves. The churches have been reduced to one, and that has been stripped of much of its former splendour: the tower and transepts rise gauntly but their aisles and chapels are nothing more than scars on the walls. The grid of streets retains its ancient names, Fletchers Gate (Fleshwares gate), Souter Gate (the gate of the shoemakers), Magdalen Gate and Sheriff Highway. There are square fields with humps and bumps where the houses of merchants used to be.

What happened to the other rivals of Hedon? Hull survived to become one of the greatest ports of modern England but Ravensrodd disappeared under the sea, eroded away so completely that even its site is imperfectly known. The situation of Hull was favourable from the start. The Cistercian Abbey of Meaux founded a town called Wyke on the marshy edge of Hessle parish at the junction of the River Hull and the Humber. The Hull was a considerable enough river to scour the haven free of silt. The deep water channel of the Humber approached the

Plate 4.12: Hedon, East Yorkshire. A twelfth-century port and planned borough planted by the lords of Preston in Holderness on the stream known as the Hedon Haven, 3.2 km from the Humber and 9.7 km east from Hull. The installations included three 'arms' of the canalised stream enabling ships to unload their cargoes in the middle of the town. One is seen being filled in on the left of this photo. The other, fringed with bushes, is visible on the right. The port was eleventh in the list of English port dues, 1203-5, but thereafter declined so that today houses only cover about a third of the borough area. One church, St Augustines (centre), survives of the three. The railway's arrival in 1854 carefully avoided the place, and is seen crossing the middle of the photo. Its unloading shed was sited in Preston parish to escape the borough tolls (Photo: Cambridge University Committee for Aerial Photography, taken 17.6.51)

northern shore at this point. Edward I realised the admirable possibilities for water traffic from Hull, situated as it was halfway up the east coast *en route* for Scotland. He persuaded the monks to exchange the port for other lands in Holderness, and immediately began to redevelop it as Kingston-upon-Hull. The results can be traced in the urban topography of the modern town.[78] A gridded layout of streets was tacked on to the west of the earlier monastic nucleus. The chapel of Holy Trinity in the market place was provided with a *placea* for a cemetery. The mighty church was rebuilt during the 1330s using brick from the corporation brickworks. Defence was provided by a ditch and wall and 21 towers also of brick. These were systematically removed in 1767-84 to make way for a new dock but their foundations have been recovered by modern excavation. Edward I improved the communications network by linking Hull to its hinterland by means of three approach roads with Beverley (north), York (north-

west) and Hessle (west).

German bombing of Hull during World War II opened up areas of the old town; archaeology is now beginning to expose the plans of medieval merchant houses. A number of interesting observations have been made. It seems that the town suffered from tidal incursions during these formative years. Many of the earth or gravel floors of the earlier timber houses were raised by approximately 30 cm by the addition of loads of clay which formed new floors at a higher level. The production of the local brick industry was sufficient for public works and for a private market; bricks were used as a building medium for houses. Leland tells us that Michael de la Pole built himself a palace and three houses with towers of brick.

Pottery found in excavations at Blackfriargate and Myrtongate, Hull, illustrates the wide flung commercial connections of the town in the Middle Ages.[79] A massive orange-glazed drip pan came from Holland, olive oil jars and a costrel from south-west Spain, a chafing dish and a jug used for serving wine from the Saintonge district of south-west France, an ointment or cosmetic pot from the Beauvais region, and a salt-glazed stoneware jug from Germany. Population growth and the increased need for warehousing led to pressure on available land that resulted in many subdivisions of the thirteenth-century messuages and plots even before 1320. These demands on the commercial centre have fluctuated throughout Hull's history. Today the main shopping centre has shifted away to the west of the old town; the haven along the Hull has been superseded by enormous dock complexes along the Humber. But now (1983) the modern port in its turn seems to be in decay.

To contrast with this the history of Ravensrodd was comparatively short and it ended disastrously by natural causes.[80] 'In the reign of King Henry [probably *c.* 1240-50] at first, by the casting up of the sea, a certain island was born which is called Revenserodd. And afterwards fishermen came to dry their nets there and men began little by little to dwell and stay there, and afterwards ships laden with divers kinds of merchandise began to unload and sell at the town.' These were the words of a jury given in 1290 when the King was hearing complaints from the royal borough of Grimsby about the town 'newly constructed' only 8 km away across the Humber estuary.

The site was a little to the east of the present Spurn Point at the south-eastern tip of Holderness (Plate 5.9). Here the sea had built up and then eroded a succession of headlands connected to the main land by narrow bands of sand and shingle. North and north-westerly gales battered the town. A flood devastated the Abbey of Meaux' church there, washing the bodies and bones from their graves in the cemetery.[81] In 1346 two-thirds of the town were said to have been swept away within 20 years. Finally 'a towering wall of water' persuaded the inhabitants to flee and the site was engulfed under the sea.

12. Shipping

So far we have considered the archaeological evidence for medieval trade and ports. There remains a further element to complete the picture, the ships themselves.[82] Over a period of 500 years many changes took place in shipping which can be traced in literary sources, contemporary pictures, and in the remains of the ships' structures. Literary sources give us the names of major ship types of the period and an insight into their relative size and frequency. Contemporary pictorial records provide representations of ships on seals and coins, in stained-glass and benchends, as well as in illuminated manuscripts. Such designs, however, are frequently conventional, the artist clearly has no technical expertise to depict what the ship really looked like. He drew the ship's hull on a seal design with an exaggeratedly semicircular line to make it fit (Figure 4.8): on a bench end a vertical distortion occurred. Potentially the best source of information would be the remains of the ships themselves. Fragments of ship's timbers, sometimes clinker-built with rivets *in situ*, quite often turn up in excavations of medieval wharfs.[83] Much less frequently in England have wrecks been recovered. We often have to look abroad to supplement the meagre maritime material available at home.

While improving the drainage system on the Graveney marshes near Faversham in 1970 a mechanical excavator driver uncovered the oaken timbers of a clinker-built boat.[84] The vessel was more than 14 m long, less than 3 m broad with a keel 7.5 m in length. The sternpost was unique, 90 cm aft of its scarf with the keel plank. The tapering lower edge of the post turned through a sharp angle and formed a distinct keel. There were probably ten strakes a side. Carbon 14 analysis established that it was ninth century in date. 'The boat would have been fully capable of crossing the North Sea.'[85] Clearly such a vessel was related to the Viking long ships. These of course figure in the Bayeux tapestry: they also inspired the smith who made the ironwork for the twelfth-century door of Stillingfleet Church.[86] The stern, with its steering oar and dragons' head terminals, survives more or less intact, as does the hull, represented by two strakes. A mast, a figure and the prow are lost, but nail holes in the wood show the position. Representations of such ships are also found in models and sketches incised on a timber plank

Figure 4.8: Seals Showing Three Types of Medieval Ships. 1. A representation of a *hulk* on an angel of Henry VII dated to the late fifteenth century. 2. A ship reflecting the Viking tradition of shipbuilding on the thirteenth-century seal of Winchelsea, Sussex. 3. A *cog* represented on a seal of Elbing, Poland, dated *c.* 1350. From photographs in National Maritime Museum

found in early medieval levels at Dublin.[87]

We have to go to Denmark to see substantial remains of the sort of ships which used English waters within two centuries either side of the Norman Conquest. A series of wrecks of five ships were found in 1956, filled with stones and sunk so as to block one of the channels giving access to the Danish town of Roskilde from the sea.[88] A coffer dam was constructed and the water pumped out from the timbers embedded in the mud.

All five ships turned out to be of different types. There were two warships; one was 18.3 m long, 2.4 m wide with twelve pairs of oars, a typical Danish Viking ship as seen in the Bayeux tapestry. The long ship was 27.4 m long, had a continuous deck, and could carry 30 to 60 oars. Such ships were beautifully adapted to beaching on a sandy shore or lying at anchor offshore. Horses could jump the low gunwale and thus land with ease. The long ships' speed, and large complement of oar-rowing warriors, struck fear into their enemies all over Europe. There were also two merchant ships with accommodation for cargo amidships, a half deck fore and aft and rowing facilities confined to a few oars near the bow and stern. The square sail was the principal means of propulsion. The deep sea trader was heavily built, with keel and lower parts of ribs of oak, the rest of lime and pine planks. Such a craft could withstand the really heavy weather on the north Atlantic run between Norway to Scotland, Iceland, Greenland and Finland. The coaster was smaller in scale, 13.7 m long and 3.2 m across, with a half deck forward and aft, intended for service in the Baltic and on the North Sea, small enough to have been hauled overland for short distances, with shallow draught to enable it to sail far up rivers. All these five types are clinker-built, i.e. the planks overlap one another, the hulls have elegantly curved double pointed shapes with ends almost identical and, a great source of strength, they had keels. In fact the English referred to them as 'keels' perhaps to distinguish them from the flat-bottomed Frisian ships.

Changes in ship design had occurred by the thirteenth century. The town seal of New Shoreham (formerly called Hulkesmouth) has a distinctive picture of a ship with the legend, *hoc hulci signo vocor os sic nomine digno* — 'by this picture of a hulk I am called mouth which is a worthy name' (Figure 4.8).[89] The characteristic shape of the hulk is a strong curved one constructed from stout boards, all converging on the ends of the vessel without any sternpost — and in some cases were held together by a coil of rope. That such curious vessels were not figments of the seal engraver's imagination is covered by the discovery of a banana-shaped vessel dated as early as 800 AD in the bed of a former arm of the Rhine near Utrecht, Holland.

A second type of vessel which dominated the maritime trade of northern Europe from the beginning of the thirteenth century to *c.*

1400 was the 'cog'.[90] This type appears frequently in town seals of the period, especially those of the Hanseatic towns of north Germany. The planks were laid edge to edge, the sides being clinker laid at an acute angle. Such vessels probably developed from coastal shipping in the tidal areas of the Frisian Wadden Zee where loading and unloading could take place when the ship was high and dry at low tide. They developed into craft of a considerable size: large cogs needed 3 m of water whereas Viking ships could use any natural harbour so long as the depth of water was at least 1.52 m.

In the fifteenth century further developments took place. The single large square sail was supplemented by smaller square sails at the top of the mainmast, and small sail-bearing masts were fixed for and aft. In this way the three-master came into existence. A bench end carved c. 1420 for the rebuilt church of St Nicholas at Lynn shows vividly the new type of ship which was doubtless used in the North Sea and sailed across the Atlantic to Iceland.[91] Its mainmast is square rigged as of old, but its mizzen has the new fashioned lateen sail. Great changes also took place in the construction of the hull. The accepted practice in the Mediterranean since the time of the Roman Empire was now used by northern shipwrights. Here the planks were laid edge to edge leaving the ships' sides smooth and rendered it possible to work with far heavier planks than in clinker-building.

One English late Medieval ship, Henry V's 'Grace Dieu', built at Southampton in 1416-18 was wrecked in the River Hamble.[92] The visible timbers of the ship still lie out in the stream, the bows touching the east side of the deep channel. They are exposed for only brief periods during the equinoctial spring tides. The 'Grace Dieu' was clinker-built with planks overlapping but the construction was triple giving five thickness of planks at every overlap. The draught would appear to have been of about 4.6 m. These are the remains of the only carrack surviving from the European Middle Ages.

13. Lighthouses

Strong political ties and powerful economic motives bound England closely to the continent in the Early Middle Ages and were sufficient to overcome any reluctance on the part of sailors to navigate the stormy waters of the Bay of Biscay, the English Channel and the North Sea. Shipping was furnished with certain navigational aids which must have marginally reduced the risks of sailing round the coasts.[93] Medieval lights and, at times, lighthouses, are confirmed by documentary or structural evidence at Aberdeen, Tynemouth, Spurn Point, Great Yarmouth, Orfordness, Dover, Camber, Winchelsea, Fairlight, Rye, Chale, St Aldhelm's, Carn Brea, St Michael's Mount and Ilfracombe. In addition there were lights at St Anne's Head, Wales, and Hook Head and Youghal, Ireland.

Most medieval lights were the result, either directly or indirectly, of the influence of the church. The building of the lighthouse at St Catherine's, Chale, Isle of Wight illustrates the effectiveness of the church's authority in the fourteenth century, its concern for seamen, and its interest in safeguarding its own merchandise (Figure 4.9).[94] In 1314 a chartered ship laden with wine, the property of a monastery in Picardy, foundered off the southern tip of the Isle of Wight. The crew salvaged the cargo and sold it to the islanders. The owners successfully sought redress from the courts and the receivers, including Walter de Godeton, a local squire, were heavily fined. The case went further to Rome and Godeton was forced to expiate his crime of sacrilege by building a lighthouse with an oratory attached, endowed to maintain a priest to say masses for the souls of those lost at sea. The tower which still survives, stands on top of the down, 213 m above sea level; it is of four stages, square within and octagonal without, terminating in a pyramidal roof. The light must have come from a cresset set near the top where there is a series of slits radiating out. It is doubtful whether it was very effective on this fog-wrapped down and probably owed its preservation to its greater utility as a sea mark.

On the top of the fourteenth-century tower of the church on St Michael's Mount (Cornwall), is a well preserved medieval

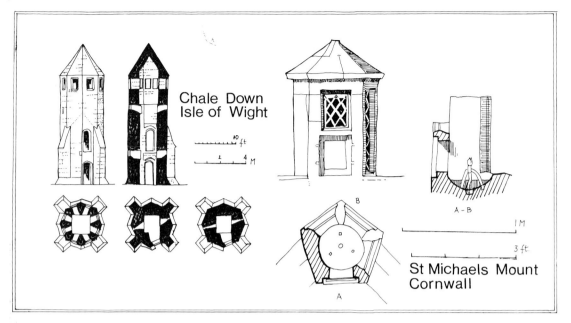

Figure 4.9: Medieval Lighthouses (VCH Hants. and Hague, 1975)

lighthouse cresset. It was built on the south-west corner of a crenellated parapet to guide ships into the small harbour — the most important tin-exporting port in west Cornwall. The light burned in a stone basin which is near 0.4 m across and 75 cm deep with a central hole for the wick end and three smaller ones for the legs of an iron tripod. Around was a pentagonal stone lantern pierced by mullioned windows, glazed with leaded lights. The light gave a coverage of about 200° towards the south-west approaches.

A third surviving medieval lighthouse, a chapel appropriately dedicated to St Nicholas, stands on a rock at the entrance to Ilfracombe harbour. The lantern was displayed from a projecting bay window on the northside.

Such charitable and useful works which aided navigators were often (like bridges) looked after by hermits. In 1427 the king made a grant to the Mayor of Hull to collect dues from every ship entering the Humber for the completion of a tower which Richard Reedbarrow, the hermit of the chapel of St Mary and Anne at Ravensersparne (The Spurn) had begun.

The oldest lighthouse in the British Isles still in use is at Hook Point, Waterford. This was built as a small isolated keep or watch tower by Raymond Fitzgerald c. 1170-82 and was meant to be defensive. It was designed to have an open fire in a brazier. Subsequently its crenellated parapet was removed and a succession of turrets with glazed lanterns were mounted from the seventeenth to the nineteenth centuries.

References

1. Steane, J.M., *The Northamptonshire Landscape*, London, 1974, 130-1.
2. *Current Archaeology*, 9, 1968, 229-30.
3. Taylor, C.C., *Roads and Tracks of Britain*, London, 1979, 120-1.
4. Parsons, E.J.S., *The Map of Great Britain, c. 1360, known as the Gough Map*, Bodleian Library, 1970, 18.
5. Carver, M.O.H. (ed.), 'Medieval Worcester. An archaeological framework', *Trans. of Worcs. Arch. Soc.*, 35, vol. 7, 1980, 2.
6. Hooke, D., 'The hinterland and routeways of late Saxon Worcester. The Charter evidence' in Carver, ibid., 39-53.
7. Hooper, M.D., 'Which Winwick?', *Northamptonshire Past and Present*, V, 4, 1976, 305–8.
8. Hindle, B.P., 'Roads and tracks' in Cantor, L.

(ed.), *The English Medieval Landscape*, London, 1982, 193–218.

9. Stenton, D.M., 'Communications' in Poole, A.L. (ed.), *Medieval England*, Oxford, 1958, 197.

10. Hindle, B.P., 'The road network of medieval England and Wales', *Journal of Hist. Geog.*, 2, 3, 1976, 207-21.

11. Parsons, *The Map of Great Britain*, 17.

12. Morris, J.E., *Welsh Wars of Edward I*, Oxford, 1901, 130.

13. Ibid., 213.

14. Darby, H.C., *The Medieval Fenland*, Newton Abbot, 1974, 106-18.

15. Dickins, B., 'Premonstratensian itineraries from a Titchfield Abbey MS at Welbeck', *Proceedings of Leeds Philos. & Literary Soc.*, 1938, IV, part I, 349-61

16. Allen Brown, R., Colvin, H.M. and Taylor, A.J., *History of the Kings's Works*, London 1963, I, 480-1.

17. Taylor, *Roads and Tracks of Britain*, 116-19.

18. Steane, J.M. and Bryant, G.F., 'Excavations at the deserted medieval settlement of Lyveden', *Journal 12*, Northampton Museum, 1975, 24.

19. Crawford, O.G.S., *Archaeology in the Field*, London, 1953, Frontispiece, 70-1.

20. Flower, C.T. (ed.), *Public Works in Medieval Law*, Selden Soc. 40, 1923, xvi-xvii.

21. Ibid., 104.

22. Ibid., 208.

23. *Council for British Archaeology Group 9, Newsletter 10*, 1980, 158-9.

24. Durham, B. (personal communication).

25. Royal Commission on Historical Monuments (England), *The Town of Stamford*, London, 1977, xxxvii-xxxix.

26. Wheeler, R.E.M., *London in Roman Times*, London Museum Catalogue 3, London, 1930, 12.

27. Salzman, L.F., *Building in England Down to 1540*, Oxford, 1952, 86.

28. Huggins, P.J., 'Excavation of a medieval bridge at Waltham Abbey, Essex in 1968', *Med. Arch.*, XIV, 1970, 126-47.

29. Rigold, S.E., 'Structural aspects of medieval timber bridges', *Med. Arch.*, XIX, 1975, 51.

30. Robins, F.W., *The Story of the Bridge*, Birmingham, n.d., 143-9.

31. Ibid., 131.

32. Seaby, W.A. and Woodfield, P., 'Viking stirrups from England and their background', *Med. Arch.*, XXIV, 1980, 114, 116.

33. Baker, D. *et al.*, 'Excavations in Bedford, 1967-1977', *Bedfordshire Arch. Journal*, 13, 1979, 294.

34. Reynolds, S., *An Introduction to the History of English Medieval Towns*, Oxford, 1982, 64.

35. Rodwell, K. (ed.), *Historic Towns in Oxfordshire*,

Oxfordshire Archaeological Unit, 1975, 155.

36. Pantin, W.A., 'Medieval inns' in Jope, E.M. (ed.), *Studies in Building History*, London, 1961, 166-91.

37. *Victoria County History, Oxon.*, VII, 1962, 41.

38. Verey, D., *Buildings of England, Gloucestershire. The Vale and the Forest of Dean*, London, 1970, 248.

39. Biddle, M. and Hudson, D., *The Future of London's Past*, Worcester, 1973, 21.

40. Urry, W., *Canterbury under the Angevin Kings*, London, 1967.

41. Biddle, M., 'Winchester: the development of an early capital', *Vor und Früh formen der europäischen stadt in Mittelalter*, Göttingen, 1972, 229-61.

42. Biddle, M., 'Evolution of towns before 1066' in Barley M.W. (ed.), *The Plans and Topography of Medieval Towns in England and Wales*, London, 1976, 22-3.

43. Ibid., 23-5.

44. Hinton, D.A., *Alfred's Kingdom, Wessex and the South, 800-1500*, London, 1977, 30-41.

45. Davies, R.H.C., 'Alfred and Guthrum's frontier', *English Historical Review*, CCCLXXXV, 1982, 803-10.

46. Ex. inf. Durham, B. (personal communication).

47. Hassall, T.G., 'The topography of pre-University Oxford in the light of recent archaeological excavations' in Smith C.G. and Scargill, D.I. (eds.), *Oxford and its Region*, Oxford, 1975, 33.

48. Biddle, M., 'Excavations at Winchester, 1971', *Antiqs J.*, LV, 1975, part I, 103.

49. Perring, D., *Early Medieval Occupation at Flaxengate, Lincoln*, Council for British Archaeology, London, 1981, 44-5.

50. Williams, J.H., *St. Peters Street, Northampton Excavations 1973-76*, Northampton Development Corporation, 1979, 141.

51. Rogers, A., 'Parish boundaries and urban history', *J.B.A.A.*, 3rd ser., XXV, 1972, 46-63.

52. Beresford, M.W. and St. Joseph, J.K., *Medieval England, An Aerial Survey*, Cambridge, 1979, 182-3.

53. Aston, M. and Bond, J., *The Landscape of Towns*, London, 1976. I acknowledge the help of M. Biddle in discussing recent archaeological work at St Albans.

54. Scarfe, N., *The Suffolk Landscape*, London, 1972, 156-9.

55. I owe these comments on Oxfordshire planned towns to discussions with my colleague James Bond.

56. Hoskins, W.G., *The Making of the English Landscape*, London, 1979, 293-4.

57. Armstrong, P., 'The old town of Kingston upon

Hull' in Symes, D. (ed.), *North Humberside, Introductory Themes*, Hull, 1978, 9.

58. Unwin, T., 'Rural marketing in medieval Nottinghamshire', *J. of Hist. Geog.*, 7, 3, 1981, 231-51.

59. Scarfe, *The Suffolk Landscape*, 165-7.

60. Beresford, M.W., *New Towns of the Middle Ages*, London, 1967, 637-41.

61. See ref. 55 above.

62. Slater, T.R., 'The analysis of burgage patterns in medieval towns', *Area*, Institute of Br. Geography, 13,3, 1981, 211-16.

63. Urry, *Canterbury under the Angevin Kings*.

64. Royal Commission for Historical Monuments (England), *Salisbury*, vol. I. HMSO, 1981, xxix-xlvi.

65. Homan W. Maclean, 'The founding of New Winchelsea', *Sussex Arch. Coll.*, 88, 1949, 22-41.

66. Dunning, G.C., 'The trade in medieval pottery around the North Sea', *Rotterdam Papers*, 1968, 35-58.

67. Hodges, R., 'Some early medieval French wares in the British Isles; an archaeological assessment of the early French wine trade in Britain' in Peacock, D.P.S. (ed.), *Pottery and Early Commerce*, London, 1977, 239-55.

68. Dunning, 'The trade in medieval pottery', 53.

69. Mellor, M., 'Late Saxon pottery from Oxfordshire. Evidence and speculation', *Medieval Ceramics*, 4, 1980, 17-27.

70. Milne, G. and Hobley, B. (eds.), *Waterfront Archaeology in Britain and Northern Europe*, CBA Research Report 41, 1981.

71. Carus-Wilson, E., 'The medieval trade of the ports of the Wash', *Med. Arch.*, VI–VII, 1962–3, 182-201.

72. Parker, H., 'A medieval wharf in Thoresby College Courtyard, King's Lynn', *Med. Arch.*, IX, 1965, 94-105.

73. Hoskins, W.G., *Local History in England*, London, 1972, 92-5.

74. Platt, C. and Coleman-Smith, R., *Excavations in Medieval Southampton 1953–1969*, 2 vols., Leicester, 1975.

75. Ibid., vol. I, 293-4.

76. *Archaeology of the City of London*, Dept. of Urban Archaeology, Museum of London, 1980, 50-1. Marsden, P., 'Early shipping and the waterfronts of London', Milne, G., 'Medieval riverfront reclamation in London' and Schofield, J.A., 'Medieval waterfront buildings in the city of London', all in Milne, G. and Hobley, B. (eds.), *Waterfront Archaeology in Britain and Northern Europe*, CBA Research Report 41, 1981, 10-16, 21-36, 24-31.

77. Boyle, J.R., *The Early History of the Town and Part of Hedon*, 1895. Also English, B., *The Lords of Holderness 1086-1260*, Oxford, 1979, 213-22.

78. Armstrong, P., 'The Old Town of Kingston upon Hull' in Symes, D. (ed.), *North Humberside. Introductory Themes*, Hull, 1978.

79. Seen in the archaeological museum, Hull, 1981.

80. Beresford, *New Towns of the Middle Ages*, 513-14.

81. Gransden, A., 'Antiquarian studies in fifteenth-century England', *Antiqs. J.*, 1980, LX, 83.

82. McGrail, S. (ed.), *The Archaeology of Medieval Ships and Harbours in Northern Europe*, British Archaeological Reports International Series 66, 1979. Unger, R.W., *The Ship in the Medieval Economy*, London, 1980.

83. *Med. Arch.*, XV, 1971, Fig. 24, XI, 1967, 228.

84. *Med. Arch.*, XV, 1971, 127.

85. Greenhill, B., 'The Graveney boat', *Antiquity*, XLV, no. 177, March 1971, 41-2.

86. Addyman, P.V. and Goodall, I.H., 'The Norman church and door at Stillingfleet, North Yorkshire', *Archaeologia*, CVI, 1979, 93-5.

87. *Med. Arch.*, XIV, 1970, 186; XV, 1971, 77, Fig. 27.

88. Crumlin-Pedersen, O., 'The Vikings and the Hanseatic merchants 900-1450' in Bass, G. (ed.), *A History of Seafaring Based on Underwater Archaeology*, London, 1972, 183.

89. Ibid., 187.

90. Ibid., 187-8.

91. *Med. Arch.*, VI-VII, 1962-3, 199, Plate XXII.

92. McKee, A., 'The influence of British naval strategy on ship design, 1400-1850' in Bass, G. (ed.), *A History of Seafaring Based on Underwater Archaeology*, London, 1972, 227-9.

93. Hague, D.B. and Christie, R., *Lighthouses. Their Architecture, History and Archaeology*, Llandysul, 1975. I owe this reference to S. McGrail.

94. *Victoria County History, Hampshire*, 5, 235.

THE MEDIEVAL COUNTRYSIDE

1. Archaeology and the Anatomy of Settlement

When trying to understand the medieval countryside there are several basic questions to tackle. The first is the location of settlements. Where did the Anglo-Saxon and medieval farmers live? Did they favour individual farms, hamlets or villages? Did the locations of these settlements remain stable or did they shift and change over the generations? Was an increase of population accommodated by enlarging original sites – or by founding new offshoot settlements? Another group of problems concerns their exploitation of the rural environment. Did they find an orderly landscape already cleared, already split into estates, or did they create a new one hewing it out from primeval forest and fen? How did they gain a living from the fields, woodlands, marshes and moors?[1]

Archaeology has made two major contributions to the problems of the location and plan-forms of early settlements. With the new dimension of aerial photography whole panoramas have been delineated for the first time (Plates 5.3, 5.5).[2] Villages and farms are now seen in the context of their fields, woods and waste. Features which had escaped earlier map makers are now recognised. The corrugations of ancient and obsolescent field systems, the earthworks of abandoned settlements, the network of hollow route-ways, display the fact that these Saxon and medieval landscapes were in a constant state of flux, as the economy expanded and then contracted. Archaeologists have also recorded and analysed the complex history of individual rural settlements in a series of major village excavations. The most valuable of these have been in places as widely separated as West Whelpington in Northumberland, (Plate 5.1), Faxton and Raunds in Northamptonshire, Thaxton in Norfolk, Upton in Gloucestershire, Gomeldon in Wiltshire, Hound Tor in Devon (Figure 5.1), Wharram Percy in Yorkshire, (Figure 5.2) and Tresmorn in Cornwall. For generalisations, however, we still have to rely on the geographers. They are fortunately no longer content with simplistic classification of plan-types of villages. Roberts has put the problem well. He sees all settlements developing within a 'matrix composed of two distinct but interlocking frameworks, on the one hand there is the physical environment, with the limitations and possibilities inherent in variations in location, altitude, soil quality, local climate and biological response, on the other, there are the man-imposed organisational frameworks of kingdom and honour, estate and manor, parish and township'.[3]

2. The Choice of Site

As practical farmers Anglo-Saxons were quite capable of recognising the type of site most useful to them. Water supply was of prime importance to animals and men. Banks of rivers were, however, not necessarily desirable locations because of the difficulty of control and drainage. Springs and places where shallow wells and ponds could be dug were sought after. In north-west Berkshire, for instance, many of the major Saxon place-names are connected with drainage, water supply, water-control and crossing places.[4] Very small streams are used as names of Baulking, Ginge, Lockinge, Wantage,

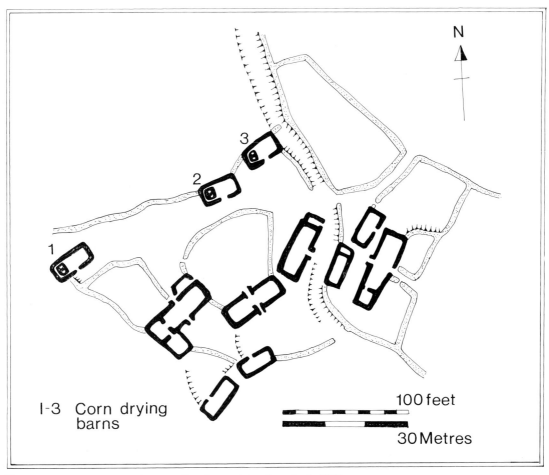

Figure 5.1: Plan of Village of Hound Tor, Devon (after Beresford, 1979)

Hendred and Hagbourne. Crossing places are referred to at Garford, Lyford, Shellingford, Wallingford, and so on. In many areas of the country we find lines of settlements strung out like beads along spring-lines, where water gushed out at the junction between permeable sands, chalk or limestones, and impermeable clays. This helped to create a linear distribution of settlements, each with long strip parishes such as are seen in the remarkable series on Lincoln Edge, the South Downs in Sussex, or along the Vale of the White Horse, Oxfordshire. The dense mesh of Iron Age and Romano-British field-systems to be seen over the Downs above these settlements implies that these linear strings of settlements in the vales below cannot possibly be primary. In the chalky regions of Wiltshire and Dorset, where

water was scarce, settlements are found along valley bottoms near the permanent streams. In lowland Staffordshire only a third of the nucleated settlements were on a stream or river and another quarter near them.[5] Too close a contact with water was avoided where water was a hazard, however, and well drained sites were at a premium. The Fenland villages are built on the silt lands along the rim of the Fen or are perched on drier 'island' sites. It has been noticed in Yorkshire that early settlements favoured the high terraces along major rivers, or were built on isolated hillocks and banks of better drained material in the Vale of York itself.[6] In the Vale of the White Horse dry sites gave rise to village names in 'ey' (from O.E. – ieg – island, dry ground in a marsh), e.g. Charney, Goosey and Hanney.[7]

The proximity of warm, well drained and easily worked soils was another marked feature of such early settlement sites. Studies of Gloucestershire and Warwickshire show that many villages adjoin patches of glacial sand and gravel.[8] A clue to the location of these early arable areas is that they are often referred to in field names as the 'Old Field'. It is likely that when the population began to grow markedly in the twelfth and thirteenth centuries it was from these light-textured, tractable and free draining soils that expansion took place on to more marginal land. In lowland Staffordshire, islands of glacial sand and gravel provided dry, lightish and easily cleared soil, suitable for initial occupation and later, in many places, the policy was undertaken of clearing the easiest soil first as at Shredicold and Bradley.

This description of a steady continuous expansion of settlement from a core of easily worked soils is one model which has tradition, if nothing else, to commend it. Another has received an impetus from archaeological field work and may be referred to as the process of 'balling'. Briefly, settlement is seen to have taken place as a series of isolated farmsteads over large areas of land in the Pagan and Middle Saxon periods. Many of these were abandoned for the sake of concentrating settlement on certain favoured nuclei; maybe these had the permeable, warm, easily worked soils. The nucleated villages and hamlets thus grew up in the Middle to Late Saxon periods. The sites of abandoned farms account for the scatters of Saxon pottery and building materials found over such areas as the Northamptonshire uplands and the chalk downs of Hampshire.

3. Settlement Shapes

Much thought has been devoted by geographers to the classification of medieval grouped settlements on the basis of size, compactness, shape and regularity. There are considerable difficulties, however, in discussing the plan-forms of medieval villages in terms of their present shape or the shape seen on the first maps. We have an early map of the Buckinghamshire village of Boarstall, dated 1444: when we compare it with the contemporary scene it is quite clear that the village-plan has changed radically over the intervening five centuries.[9] Similarly, if we have a sixteenth-century estate map which shows a village-plan this is no guarantee that the village was the same shape two or three centuries before. In fact archaeology has often proved that individual settlements have evolved through their lives into shapes wholly dissimilar from those occupied during their earlier stages. More disturbing, field work in places as far apart as Norfolk, Yorkshire and Hampshire, has shown that the locations of settlements bearing the same name have moved round the countryside. Settlement shift, in fact, rather than stability, seems the rule rather than the exception. One other problem is that documentary records are usually silent about the shape of the places they are recording. Only occasionally, as in parts of the East Midlands and Cambridgeshire, do they mention groups of houses set some distance away from the centre of the village as clearly identifiable units called 'Ends'. Hence North Leigh in Oxfordshire has an 'East End' and Witney has a 'West End'. Also, in County Durham, a fifteenth-century document describing the holdings of people living in the village of Kirk Merrington, mentions the 'Southraw' and the 'Northraw', unequivocally referring to the north and south rows of a two-row village with a linear layout.[10] At Cuxham in Oxfordshire, where splendid documentation describes each holding in detail, they can be identified with confidence on the ground although all medieval buildings except the church have now been replaced.[11] The layout in fact here is undoubtedly much the same as it was six or seven hundred years ago.

With these reservations in mind, we can still claim that there appear to have been two basic village shapes; either the assemblage of structures and enclosures can be linear, forming a row, or non-linear, forming an agglomeration (Plates 5.2, 5.1). The simplest shape of a settlement, though not the most defensible was a single row of houses with holdings at the back of them, facing onto one side of a street. This plan has survived where the road faced a river as at Deeping (Lincs.) A more usual shape was the village with houses facing

Plate 5.1: West Whelpington, Northumberland. Excavations on this deserted village site on the edge of a crag 213 m above the Wansbeck have revealed a rationally laid out village of stone-built houses, each within its croft grouped round a village green. Occupation was during the twelfth to fourteenth centuries (Photo: Cambridge University Committee for Aerial Photography)

Plate 5.2: Middleton, near Aislaby, North Yorkshire. A regularly planned linear village along the road skirting the southern edge of the north Yorkshire moors. The lines of the tofts surrounding the homesteads are continued into the crofts and so across the whole landscape and up the slopes of the hills to the north. The lines of ridge-and-furrow are contemporary with the long narrow field boundaries. Numerous hedgerow trees are another indicator of their considerable age. Clearly the landscape retains the marks of a former economy largely devoted to cereal production (Photo: Cambridge University Committee for Aerial Photography, taken 15.7.52)

one another across a street, or facing one another across a junction of two streets. The church and the manor house are often at one end of a street village, inhibiting growth in that direction. As the village expanded it grew along the street, the holdings extending outwards in long strips using the street frontage as a base. In many street villages there are traces of a strict regularity of layout. Such villages as Appleton-le-Moors or Middleton in Yorkshire are extreme examples of this regulated planning (Plate 5.2). The planning went further than deciding the topography. A regularly planned village went hand in hand with a symmetrical ordering of agriculture and tenure. Such holdings were regulated by similar customs and obligations – all produced by a single act of rearrangement.

These are isolated examples of the regulated layout of settlements. An instance of large-scale redevelopment of an area involving village planning is seen in the so-called 'green villages' which are particularly characteristic of the plains and low plateaux of north-east England between the Tweed and the Humber.[12] The greens which appear to be integral parts of the plan, not tacked on to it subsequently, are areas of open land now used by the community for playing games and for grazing animals. The regularity of their design makes it appear inevitable that they were planned. Not only are the roads and lines of homesteads bordering the greens rigidly straight; there are also belts of small walled enclosures leading onto back lanes which may be continuous around the settlement. Thorpe, who made the first systematic study of the 101 'green villages' of County Durham, considered that their function was defensive. He saw the green serving as a compound in which cattle, the chief source of wealth in early medieval society, could be driven at night out of the way of wild animals or human marauders. He also suggested that each end was kept open and more homesteads could be added as the population grew. More recently Roberts and Sheppard have argued that the most regular village plans of Durham and Yorkshire are the result of settlement refoundations following the devastations of the north by William the Conqueror's punitive campaigns of 1068-70.[13] This is linked with the presence of landlords,

the Bishop and Cathedral Priory of Durham, mighty enough to impose such a wholesale reordering of the landscape.

The presence of regularly planned nucleated settlements, some with greens, some without, in other parts of the country, unconnected with any cataclysmic event of the magnitude of 'the Harrying of the North' emphasises the importance of this last point. Such topographical rearrangements were doubtless the results of decisions of individual lords, royal, baronial or ecclesiastical.

Two further settlement shapes which both appear to be fortuitous and unplanned may be briefly mentioned. The double-loop plan was first noticed as appearing along the Ouse Valley in north Bedfordshire. It has also been found in twelve places in Northamptonshire, especially in the wooded country on the western boundaries.[14] Here certain villages are built round two complete loops or a figure of eight. Such a random and sprawling plan may be associated with clearance in former woodland. At Badby (Northants.), for instance, on the Warwickshire border 'the medieval village had carried through into its period of expansion something of its earliest form of a group of houses in a clearing'.

Where some settlements have more than one green, major road junction or group of buildings they have been termed 'polyfocal'.[15] A number of suggestions attempt to explain this lack of nucleation. The simplest is that different focuses of settlement grew up as the result of differences in ownership, land tenure or social grouping. Two contiguous manors, with separate parish churches perhaps only a stone's throw away, might grow up side by side. Another possibility is that they reflect a situation which may have been much more widespread in the Anglo-Saxon period, namely a completely dispersed settlement of small hamlets or farmsteads scattered widely. In many areas this pattern has been broken up by the process of 'balling' into nucleated villages. A further possibility is that a village might acquire new focuses as a result of planned additions.

So far we have been considering mainly the evidence on the ground surface. It is when we turn to villages which have been the subjects of intensive archaeological work that insta-

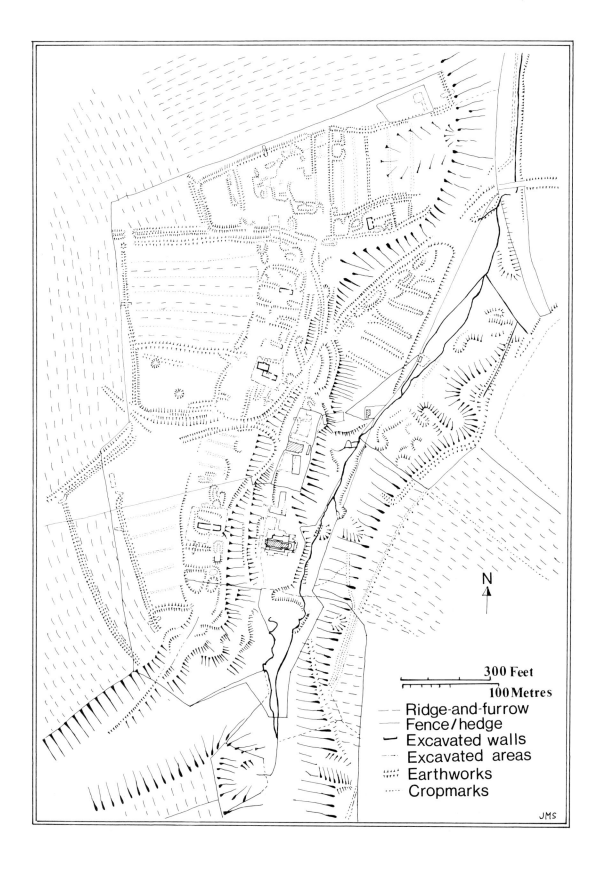

300 Feet
100 Metres
Ridge-and-furrow
Fence/hedge
Excavated walls
Excavated areas
Earthworks
Cropmarks

N

JMS

bility, settlement shift and a general air of fortuitousness seem to become dominant.

At Wharram Percy, Yorkshire, 25 years of excavations of the deserted village on the chalk wolds have shown that there were three major growth phases before the site was deserted (Figure 5.2).[16] First, the Saxon village seems to have lain around the church on the slight terrace above the stream. A second phase of expansion took place in the twelfth century when tofts 5-8 were laid out on the ridge top above the church. A fine stone-built manor house, associated with this period, was found on toft 10. During the thirteenth century the population appears to have grown, and a second manor house was built to the north of the village. Further tofts, numbers 9-18, are associated with this phase of development. It is possible that tofts 1-3 and 19-22 were also part of this activity. Here then is an example of a village whose plan was continually changing until it was largely deserted in the fifteenth century.

Even more dramatic changes took place at Maxey (now in Cambridgeshire).[17] Here on a gravel ridge above the River Welland aerial photography showed a complex of cropmarks dating from Neolithic ritual sites to mediev-al ridge-and-furrow. The Saxon and early medieval settlement was continuous but shift-ing. The present village lies some 0.8 km to the south-east of the twelfth-century church which incidentally sits on a large circular mound possibly dating from the Bronze Age. Speed's map of Northamptonshire, 1611, refers to the village as Maxey East. Both documentary and archaeological evidence (in the form of eleventh- and twelfth-century pottery scatters) indicate that there was an early medieval settlement around the church. This has now vanished but it evidently re-placed a Middle Saxon settlement lying be-tween the two, consisting of hall houses and sunken-floored buildings which were exca-vated in the 1960s.

A similar pattern, emphasising the insta-bility of Saxon and early medieval settlements, has emerged from field work in Norfolk.[18] At Longham, for instance, a Middle and Late

Saxon village was traced near the church which now stands isolated in fields. Then in the twelfth century settlement started about 0.4 km south around Southall green. This is shown on a sixteenth-century estate map. By this time settlement had begun to shift again, this time to the north-east to Kirtling common. So in this parish there are two deserted areas of settlement, one largely pre-Conquest and the other medieval.

In sum, archaeological excavation and field work have demonstrated that the stability of the immemorial English village is an illusion. The present settlement shape has frequently been shown to be only the last phase of a shifting process of kalaedoscopic complexity.

4. Field-systems and Estate Boundaries: the Prehistoric and Roman Legacy

Twenty-six years ago, W.G. Hoskins wrote his seminal work on *The Making of the English Landscape*. His view then was that 'the great majority of the English settlers faced a virgin country of damp oak-ash forest or beech forest on and near the chalk'. He envisaged the Anglo-Saxon farmers hewing their way through this woodland so that by the time Domesday Book was surveyed the job of clearance had largely been done. Studies undertaken since then have emphasised the widespread clearance undertaken at an earlier period by prehistoric and Romano-British farmers. The fact that the traces of ancient field-systems are mostly found only on the chalk hills of the south no longer blinds us to the evident fact of considerable prehistoric and even more Romano-British settlement in the river valleys and the midland plain.[20] The earthworks of ancient fields have been obliter-ated here by the intensive and continuous cultivation but scatters of pottery are equally effective indicators. Where intensive field work has been carried out, as in the Nene Valley, Roman settlements appear to have been in the region of one per 2.5 km.[21] In the fertile valleys of the Chelmer and Brain in Essex fragments of extensive field-systems and associated trackways of prehistoric date sur-vive in the modern landscape.[22] They were cut across diagonally by the construction of a

Figure 5.2: Ground Plan of Wharram Percy, North Yorkshire (after Hurst, 1982)

Plate 5.3 (above) Over Chalford, Oxfordshire and **Plate 5.4** (below) Nether Chalford, Oxfordshire. Two late medieval deserted village sites. Depopulation was perhaps caused by enclosure by the lessees of Oriel College in the late fifteenth or early sixteenth century. Much evidence remains of ruined farms, mills and cottages along hollow-ways. The ends of the crofts are clearly delineated. In Plate 5.3, well preserved lynchets are seen behind the village (Photo: Cambridge University Committee for Aerial Photography)

Roman road from Little Waltham to Braintree. In both places the Anglo-Saxons took over a landscape which had already been mostly cleared and was densely settled in many places. Far from being primary colonists, they are now seen as peacefully settling down and adapting slowly an already existing agrarian landscape to their own purposes.

It used to be thought that parish boundaries were created comparatively late in the Anglo-Saxon or even early medieval periods. Certainly many of these have survived intact since the late Anglo-Saxon period when they were recorded in detail in charters. The charters not only demarcate the boundaries but also locate features of the pre-Conquest landscape.[23] Lynchets, furlongs, chalk pits, even individual trees, are singled out as landmarks. There is now growing evidence from field work done in different parts of the country that parish boundaries may perpetuate estate divisions which go back into the Roman period or even into the pre-Roman Iron Age. The division of the countryside into parishes was a process begun in the late Saxon period and not completed until the twelfth century.[24] These boundaries are characterised in many places by deep ditches and massive linear banks topped by hedgerows with multi-species. They owe their antiquity to the fact that they defined estates for perhaps a thousand years before they became parish markers.

One interesting line of reasoning has been pursued in Wiltshire.[25] Here the courses of Roman roads in the eastern part of the county are seen to cross a series of parish boundaries. In these areas there were many Iron Age settlements. The roads were comparatively late features crossing a landscape, already sub-divided into estate units. In the western part of the county, on the other hand, the Roman roads coincide with long stretches of parish boundaries. There seem to be good grounds here for believing that the roads were among the *first* permanent features in the landscape. When settlement began, perhaps in the late Roman or Saxon periods, and estate units began to be demarcated, the Roman roads were chosen naturally as one fixed line. This apparently happened in central Northamptonshire where the 17 parishes take the line of the Roman Watling Street as one of their boundaries. It is also seen in Oxfordshire where the Roman Akeman Street crosses the county from east to west and forms part of the boundary of a number of parishes which lie in the formerly thickly wooded area of Wychwood.

Bonney has also made the interesting observation that in Wiltshire many very early pagan Saxon cemeteries are situated on or near parish boundaries, which seems to support his contention that they perpetuated ancient land-holding divisions. In other areas, however, such as Oxfordshire, this juxtaposition of burials and boundaries is not noticeably close.

A process involving the early breakup of large estates probably took place in Dorset where villages which today retain the element *minster* in their name are seen to have served large territories which were later subdivided.[26] Charminster parish, for instance, contained no less than ten medieval settlements and their land units. Sturminster Marshall again was once much larger and contained Lytchett Matravers, Corfe Mullen, Mamworthy and Lytchett Minster.

If it is accepted that estate boundaries lasted on from the Roman into the Saxon periods it is not very surprising to find that in a number of places earlier underlying field-systems appear to determine to some degree the layout of medieval open fields.[27] In Cambridgeshire, for instance, a gas-pipeline cutting across two medieval headlands exposed ditches under them and on the same alignment. What is more important is that these contained datable material in the form of Romano-British pottery. Moreover, ten years of work on the fields and boundaries of the Yorkshire village of Wharram Percy has shown similar evidence.[28] Sections cut through parts of the village and its furlongs have shown that they lie on Roman ditched boundaries. Again in Essex considerable tracts of land remained laid out in a rectilinear framework which apparently dates from the Romano-British period.

All this does not add up to there being any proof for a continuity of cultivation from the Romano-British into the Anglo-Saxon period. It can be interpreted in a number of conflicting ways. Saxon farmers may have taken over some Roman fields as a going concern.

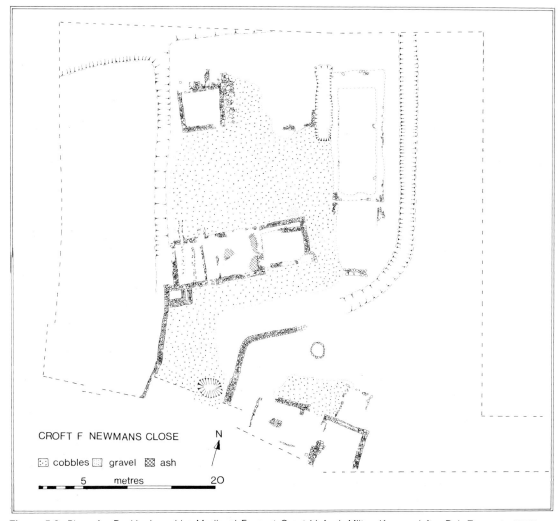

CROFT F NEWMANS CLOSE

N

cobbles   gravel   ash

5   metres   20

Figure 5.3: Plan of a Buckinghamshire Medieval Farm at Great Linford, Milton Keynes (after R.J. Zeepvat, 1979)

Alternatively, if we accept the current theory that there was no widespread devastation or 'conquest' in the fifth century, many Britons may well have gone on cultivating their 'ancient fields' well into the so-called Anglo-Saxon period, or it may simply be the case that many Roman field boundaries were still visible features in the landscape and were reused by later Saxon farmers as a matter of convenience.

5. The Origins of the Open-field System

Vigorous controversy surrounds 'the origins of the open-field system'.[29] There are not many people who still believe with Seebohn and the Orwins that the Anglo-Saxons brought their field systems ready made from their continental homelands and imposed them on their conquered English acres. It is increasingly coming to be held that an early form of settlement all over Britain was the hamlet and its associated infield-outfield system.[30] A small cluster of farmsteads occupied by kinship groups would have constituted the normal settlement. Nearby, perhaps ringed around by a low turf wall, was a plot of intensively cultivated arable; all the manure produced by the animals of the settlement was used on this 'infield' which may have been laid out in undivided block fields or perhaps as sub-divided strip fields. Surrounding the area were a number of plots which were brought under cultivation for short periods of from two to eight years and followed by periods of fallow from six to 25 years. This was the 'outfield'. Other pasture land, grasslands, woodlands and heaths were used extensively.

How then did open fields with their characteristic strips develop and ultimately cover much of midland, eastern and southern England? Dr Thirsk has argued that early Saxon communities held their land in severalty but later population pressures and the operation of the principle of partible inheritance resulted in the division of many holdings into strips.[31] Doubtless some strips resulted from groups of colonisers clearing land and allocating it communally. In the Chilterns, for instance, in the thirteenth century, lords are found dividing freshly cleared lands among their tenants. Again in the Lincolnshire Fens, land, newly reclaimed between 1230 and 1250, was partitioned first among the seven hundreds involved, then among the villages and finally among individual farmers. Other strips were formed when manorial lords gave up farming themselves and parcelled their demesnes among lessees.

Archaeology, being concerned only with the tangible traces of cultivation, the marks made by farmers on fields such as pits, ditches and banks, is unlikely to be able to contribute very much to this discussion of origins. It cannot hope to know what the overall tenurial arrangements were or how the fields were organised by the society which developed them. Great strides, however, have been made recently by using field-archaeological techniques in recognising features of field-systems and in particular in mapping systematically areas of ridge-and-furrow, the principal physical remains of open-field cultivation.

6. Ridge-and-furrow

Viewed from the air large parts of central and southern England were, until recently largely eliminated by modern farming techniques, covered with ridge-and-furrow which made the land look like a patchwork of pieces of corduroy material (Plates 5.5, 5.6). Ridge-and-furrow is the term given to corrugations in the field surface made by generations of peasant farmers ploughing lands in a clockwise manner with a heavy iron plough drawn by draught oxen.[32] The effect was gradually to build ridges on the field surface with parallel furrows between them. Generally furrows were aligned down the steepest natural gradient to assist drainage. In many cases a good crop was likely to grow in the furrow even in drought conditions and in a rainy summer a crop would have survived on the better drained ridges. Modern studies of grassland have shown that ridge-and-furrow provided two strongly contrasted habitats – wetter and drier. Two other features of ridge-and-furrow are of interest. Along the edge of a block of strips (the furlong) was the headland. This was the point at which the plough team turned and over the years the extra soil deposited from the plough scrapings led gradually to a rise in the surface along the line. These banks are important archaeologically because they are often the only substantial feature to survive from the open-field system when it has been repeatedly ploughed flat using modern techniques.

Secondly, the shape of furlong blocks of ridge-and-furrow often has a slight reversed S-bend, supposed to have been deliberately fashioned to help the oxen in their long swing round at the end of the furlong. The lengths of furlongs vary greatly in different parts of the country. In Holderness there are particularly long strips, a distance of 1.6 km in some townships. In the Midland clay region shorter lands may have been necessary so that each one could be ploughed in a day and there were more resting places for draught animals. In some places furlongs have been shortened and this may be connected with a change over to horse traction. The horse, while more energetic, tired more easily.

How old is ridge-and-furrow? In three places so far it has been proved to be Pre-Conquest in date. At Gwithian in West Cornwall, narrow parallel undulations were found in part of a contemporary field bounded by a headland, a ditch and a marsh.[33] The ridges varied in width from 2.13-6.09 m and 24-38 m in length. Sherds, the debris from manuring, dated the field to c. 950-1050/1100

Plate 5.5: Isle of Portland, Dorset. Despite diminution by quarrying, houses and later cultivation these 'lawnsheds' (their local name) survive along the east coast of Portland. Most of the furlongs in this aerial photo (taken 20.6.48) extend end to end but there is a group at right angles stretching to the coastline. Where least disturbed they are divided by grass baulks; in places the furlong blocks are walled while other hedged fields in the distance show signs of their former division into strips. Those in the centre show the reversed curve. At the tip of the island was an area of common grazing (Photo: Cambridge University Committee for Aerial Photography)

Plate 5.6: Isle of Portland, Dorset. Looking east from the hill above the road to the Coastguard Station at Portland Bill. The strips are still being cultivated, are separated by baulks of grass and are up to 300 m long, varying in width from 10 to 70 m. They have begun to take the stepped configuration of lynchets. Of the 825 acres of open-fields shown on the Tithe map of 1842 about 150 acres survive. Today they are scheduled as an Ancient Monument (Photo: J.M. Steane)

AD. At Hen Domen, Montgomeryshire, a similar feature of ridge-and-furrow was recorded beneath and outside the bailey bank of the castle built by Roger de Montgomery in the period 1070–4. Here the ridges averaged 4 m in width; pollen analysis proved the former presence of cereals and the weed of cultivation, *Plantago major*. The same telltale traces of ridge-and-furrow ploughing were noticed at Sandal Castle (West Yorkshire) underlying the timber-phase bailey bank.[34] This was recognised to be part of an infield and again the presence of cereal pollen and bindweed (*Convolvolus cf. arvensis*) confirmed pre-Conquest arable cultivation.

It is one thing to demonstrate the antiquity of some ridge-and-furrow but another to prove a similar age for a system of divided holdings. Here again archaeology has produced some useful evidence for considerable modifications if not total replanning of landscapes being undertaken in the Middle Saxon period. Field walking in Northamptonshire has indicated that many scattered farms were abandoned at this time as the pattern of settlement began to move towards nucleation in villages.[35] It may well have been at this stage that open-fields were laid out. In the chalk downland around Chalton in Hampshire a similar sort of settlement shift has been noticed.[36] Here early Saxon sites on the tops of hills were in occupation during the sixth and seventh centuries. The Church Down settlement was abandoned at about the same time as

occupation began in the valleys below on the sites of the villages of Chalton, Idsworth and Blendworth.

Cunliffe considers that the creation of the arable here must date back to the foundation of the villages in about the ninth century. Sometimes, as we have seen when discussing settlement, the complete replanning of a landscape can be tied to a political event. In Yorkshire, for instance, William I carried out extensive devastations during the years 1069-70. It has been suggested that lords who owned widely dispersed estates repopulated their devastated manors in the Vale of York by moving tenants from other places in the uplands which had escaped William's ravages. Such a situation led to a widespread reapportionment of land on new and planned lines in the late eleventh century.

7. Agricultural Implements (Figure 5.4)

In the previous sections we have been trying to

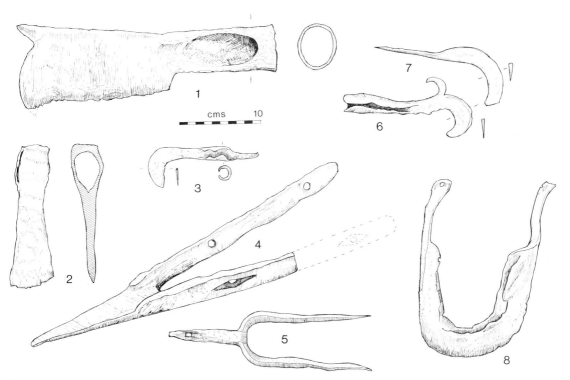

Figure 5.4: Agricultural Implements, Oxfordshire County Museum. 1. Billhook. 2. Felling axe. 3. Pruning hook. 4. Plough share. 5. Hayfork. 6. Pruning hook. 7. Small sickle. 8. Spade shoe

explain the imprint of the tools and muscle power of medieval farmers on the landscape. Another approach is the examination of the tools themselves. Recently a comprehensive study has been carried out of those made of iron.[37] Much agricultural ironwork survives but is nearly always found in a fragmentary and corroded state. It is difficult to interpret because the wooden handles and other fittings have almost entirely vanished. By a close comparison with medieval manuscript illustrations, which at times (as in the Luttrell Psalter) show a considerable degree of technological expertise, it is usually possible to make sense of them.

When one considers how widespread was the use of the plough it is disappointing to record how seldom pieces survive. Basically medieval ploughs were of wood with ironwork restricted to three parts.[38] The coulter was a heavy knife-like blade fixed vertically in the beam which cut a furrow slice in front of the plough share. The iron share itself protected the tip of the share beam, undercut a slice made in the ground by the coulter, and created a furrow. Finally there were the chains and associated fittings used to attach it to the plough team. The yokes of course have vanished, but the oxen are represented by iron ox shoes.

Spades were used for cultivation, for clearing overburden and waste from quarries, for digging building foundations, farm ditches and for moving fuel and ashes.[39] They were also used for digging wells (one was found at Lyveden in the well pit) and for cleaning out garderobes. It has even been claimed that they might have been responsible for the original construction of ridge-and-furrow. Archaeological excavations have produced a number of wooden spades, some with the blade and shaft in one piece, some with the two separate. They were commonly of wood with an iron edging to prevent wear to the blade. Such spade irons are of three types, those with triangular mouths, round mouths or straight mouths. The two former may well have been shrunk onto wooden blades since they do not have any signs of nail holes. From illuminated manuscripts it seems that many spades were asymmetrical and presumably were meant to be pressed into the ground by the foot on one

side only.[40] Forks were much less frequently found than spades but one was retrieved at Old Manor, Askett (Bucks.) where it had been used for cleaning out a garderobe.

Further tools used in cultivation include turf cutters, used during excavation and earthmoving, as well as gardening. At Weoley Castle, near Birmingham, one was found in the bottom of the moat (see Figure 7.2). It is thought to have been used for cutting blocks of turf before they were lifted out by using a spade or a shovel. Medieval hoes, which were socketed and chisel shaped, were probably used in gardening, for weeding and breaking-up soil surfaces. Hand rakes were used during threshing and gathering individual corn stalks together on the field surface. These were probably entirely made of wood but a number of iron rake-teeth with a characteristic long taper to the base and a short taper to the clenched tang tip have been found. Billhooks were used for coppicing, lopping stems and branches of young trees, trimming posts and rails of wattle and for laying hedges. Hedge bills or slashers were fashioned out of one piece of iron and their bevelled backs effectively gave them two cutting edges – one stouter, and one narrower and sharper. The hooked blade backs found on others were probably used to spike pieces of wood required for chopping.

Medieval open-fields were rife with the menace of weeds. The strips in the hands of a careless or sick farmer could easily spread weeds to those of others. The major weeds to be removed were 'thystles', 'dockes', 'cockle-drake' or corn cockle (*Lychnis* (or *Agrostemma*) *githago*), which were poisonous to stock and 'gouldes', presumably buttercups or marigolds. The weeding was done using weed-hooks and crutches. The latter was a long wooden forked stick, used to hold the weed in place while its stalk was cut. It seems that cereal crops were hand-weeded in late May-early June. Action was delayed against thistles until July; if cut earlier each root was likely to throw up three to four plants, if dealt with later, the plants had time to disperse their seeds.

The haycrop was harvested using scythes which frequently figure in medieval illustrations of the labours of the months. They were almost identical with those used today, having long handles with pairs of hand grips and long gently curving iron blades. They were attached to the handle with a short clenched tang at right angles to the blade. This was triangular in section with a strengthened and thickened back rib. Cereal crops were normally cut by sickles or reaping hooks. These rarely survive in complete form but consisted of a blade which curves fairly sharply away from the end of the tang before straightening out. Sometimes the edge was filed on the underside to produce a sharp and toothed edge which would have sawn the stalks being harvested. The arduous task of cutting the crop involved the reaper sawing the stalks quite low down where they were stiffer. Bound sheaves of corn, and bundles of hay and thatching straw, were moved about by pitchforks. These are usually tanged and have pairs of tines which can either be straight or curved in side view. Other iron tools used on the farm included spuds – with flat rectangular blades and round shoulders used to clean earth from ploughs and digging tools, and ox goads mounted as prods on the ends of long sticks.

8. Common Land

In the previous sections we have considered the areas of open-field farming which were devoted to a predominantly arable use. There was, however, a second element in Anglo-Saxon and medieval agriculture which is already found established in Wessex, eastern Yorkshire, and throughout the eastern Midlands before the Danish raids of the eighth century. This was the use in common by these farmers of primeval woodlands, heaths and pastures. What are common rights?[41] They are exercised by a considerable number of ordinary people who have legal rights over the surface of such lands. The most generally recognised common right is the right of common pasture – the right to allow one's animals to graze the herbage and, connected with stock rearing, the right to cut bracken for fuel or cattle bedding. Common lands were also the source of wood for fuel (the right of 'estovers'), turf for fuel or roofing (the right of 'turbary') and at times there was the right to fish in common waters ('piscary').

The origin of these common rights is obscure but it does seem that they may antedate the idea of private property in land and therefore are of vast antiquity. On Dartmoor, for instance, where 11,736 ha are still subject to common rights men have been using the upland grazing during the summer months since the Early Bronze Age (c. 1800 BC).[42] All who could reach the moor used its herbage and hunted its wild animals. By the thirteenth century, when written records begin, it seems that the moor was the common grazing of all the inhabitants of the Devon countryside, from the springtide of the year and throughout the summer. In Oxfordshire a number of places in the Cherwell Valley in the north of the county had common rights in the great area of woodland and heath called Wychwood in the south of the county.[43] Bloxham, for instance, was linked with the 'wood of Blocksham' at Stonesfield. Drayton was linked with 'Draytonsmore' in Kidlington. The same sort of thing is found in Warwickshire. Here farmers in the valley of the River Avon from Evesham to Warwick intercommoned in a stretch of woodland situated several kilometres to the north. In the 'Andredsweald' of Kent, Sussex and Surrey particular clearings, known as 'denns', were attached to individual villages near the borders of the great wood.

A similar system is found on the fens and marshes bordering the Wash, in Lincolnshire, Norfolk and Cambridgeshire.[44] Here groups of villagers grazed their animals on the level wastes of the fens as they gradually dried out. Also, because any attempt to drain the area by digging dykes and banks required an immense corporate effort on the part of the men of several villages, it was natural that the resultant pasture would be used in common.

Towns, too, had their common land; we must remember that medieval townsmen were farmers as well as traders and craftsmen. They still relied on their food from open fields and grazed their animals on common pasture. The inhabitants of the port and borough of Liverpool, for instance, grazed their animals on the wastes to the south of the town near Toxteth. Newcastle-upon-Tyne still possesses a 'town moor' of well over 405 ha, which is now a source of surprise in the middle of the great

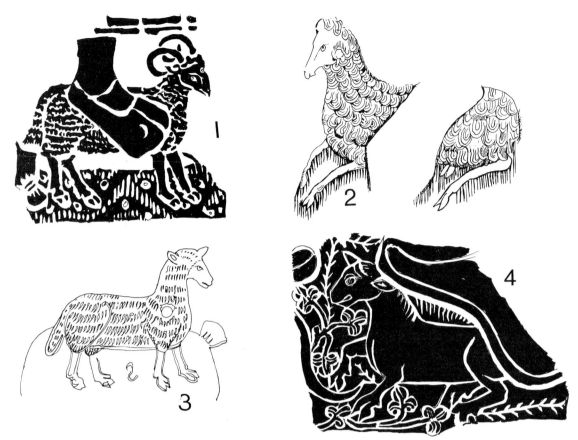

Figure 5.5: Sheep Represented in Monumental Brasses. 1. Northleach (Gloucs.) brass to a woolman (*c.* 1485). 2. Northleach (Gloucs.), John Fortey (1458). 3. Northleach (Gloucs.), John Taylour (*c.* 1490). 4. Northleach (Gloucs.), Thomas Bushe (1526) (after Armitage and Goodall, 1977).

city. When an American visitor asked Freeman, the Victorian Professor of History at Oxford, to show him the most ancient monument in Oxford, Freeman walked him out to Port Meadow. This takes its name from the Anglo-Saxon word meaning a market town. It is a great stretch of common grazing lying by the River Thames north of the City of Oxford, which has belonged to the freemen since time immemorial. The freemen still control the use of Port Meadow; an instance is the notices hung on the gates forbidding the dumping of refuse and the feeding of horses. Such common grazing over a thousand years has had an interesting effect on the herbage and the flora it contains.[45] Since the grazing has been continuous all the year round the vegetation has been impoverished and contains fewer flowering plants. This contrasts markedly with other areas of common meadow lying a few hundred metres to the north, the so-called Yarnton and Pixey meads. Here grazing by the commoners of Yarnton, Begbroke and Wolvercote has been restricted until after the hay harvest with the result that flowering plants have not been prevented from flowering and re-seeding each year. The resultant flora is extremely rich and these meadows in June and the first weeks in July are covered with a sheet of yellow, white and mauve flowers. They still give an impression of what a portion of the Anglo-Saxon landscape must have looked like.

9. Woodland

When we look at an Ordnance Survey map of

almost any part of England we realise that only a small proportion of the country is now covered with woodland. Domesday Book reveals that this situation had already been reached by the mid-eleventh century. Only about 15 per cent of England was still woodland in 1086.[46] Many villages were 6.4 km from any wood and many others were a day's journey from a substantial piece of woodland. This had been accomplished not by burning down the forests. Rackham comments 'native woodland burns like wet asbestos; even if there is enough bracken to support a fire as in the South Essex woods in spring, the fire is not hot enough to kill trees'. In fact the woodland had been removed by the exertions of generations of farmers who, with axes and twybills in hand, carved out clearings and called them 'leys' and 'hursts'. The result is clear in zoological as well as botanical terms. The mammals which one would expect to haunt remote and extensive forest tracts showed signs of dying out in the Early Middle Ages. The beaver, bear and lynx were all extinct before the Conquest; wild swine were hunted to extinction by *c*. 1260.

Woodland, although reduced in this way, nevertheless had a vital part to play in the economy of the medieval countryside. Medieval woods produced three types of product which are distinguished by the terms 'timber', 'wood' and 'firewood'.[47] 'Timber' (referred to in the medieval Latin records as *maeremium*), was the big stuff used for making structures, posts, beams and planks. It was cut from trees called standards, or maybe from maidens grown from seed or suckers. 'Wood' on the other hand (the latin word is *subboscus*, literally underwood), was taken in the form of poles, produced by cutting coppices, pollards or young suckers or maybe by chopping off branches of trees felled for timber. Maple, wych elm and hazel all can be cut down at intervals, and the stumps become stools which send up further shoots. If these are protected from the browsing habits of deer and other animals they grow rapidly within a few years to become crops of poles. The third commodity, fuel, was produced from dead or dying trees, the so-called *robora*.

It seems that a tradition of intensively managing woodland and using it as a self-renewing resource, developed in the Early Middle Ages. We know from the detailed surveys made and accounts kept by the great religious houses that coppice cycles were well understood. They varied from four to 28 years with a tendency to lengthen the time from six years in the thirteenth century to 14 or 15 years in the nineteenth century. This, it has been suggested, can be explained by a change from faggots to burn on an open hearth to billets and logs for chimneys, but it also might be linked to falling growth rates owing to the removal of phosphates in successive crops of underwood. Hand in hand with intensive management went a belief in the importance of conservation. Bishop Herbert de Losinga left detailed orders concerning the conservation of woodland at Thorpe Wood near Norwich *c*. 1100. The Crown similarly from the thirteenth century recorded its anxiety that trees should not be felled if this did harm to the forest. Felling for timber donations was stopped in 1257 for this reason.

There are many archaeological traces of medieval woodland management. Ancient woods are found in places which were not so much good for growing trees as areas that were bad for anything else. They are not located on river terraces, fens or meadowland, because these lands were too valuable for other purposes. Rather they are likely to be on steep and damp slopes, greater than 1 in 10, and also on flat clay hilltops which were difficult to drain. A characteristic site is that of Graven Hill near Bicester (Oxon.). This site means (in Anglo-Saxon) 'the wooded hill'. The Priors of Bicester took timber there for building works at the priory in the fifteenth century.[48] It has the typical curving shape of ancient woodland and has one massive woodbank to the south. It is also on ill-drained clay land.

Ancient woods are usually in remote places, on parish boundaries and away from villages. Main roads are avoided. In 1284 a statute ordered that underwood and woodbanks were to be removed a distance of 200 ft (61 m) from the main roads. Interesting examples of this can be seen in Cambridgeshire where the Ermine Street (now the A1) runs north of Alconbury. Parallel to the course of the road and set back about 61 m are the hedgerows and patches of woodland which were the result

Figure 5.6: Hayley Wood, Cambridgeshire at Three Dates (after Rackham, 1975)

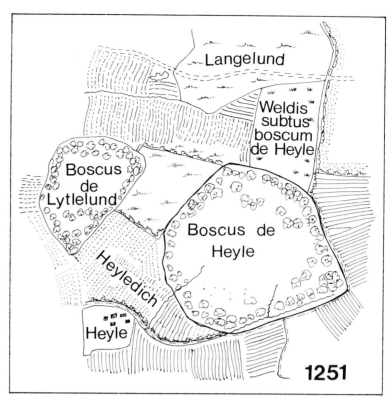

Langelund

Weldis subtus boscum de Heyle

Boscus de Lytlelund

Boscus de Heyle

Heyledich

Heyle

1251

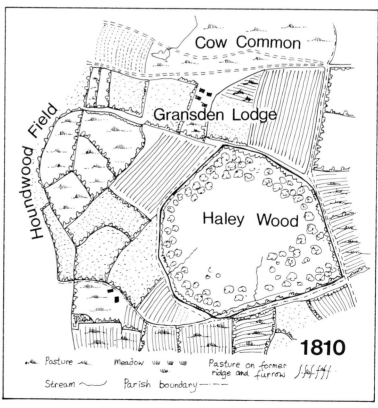

Cow Common

Houndwood Field

Gransden Lodge

Haley Wood

1810

.·ıll.. Pasture ..ıu.   ɯ Meadow ɯ ɯ ɯ   Pasture on former ridge and furrow

Stream ⁓   Parish boundary — — —

300 Metres

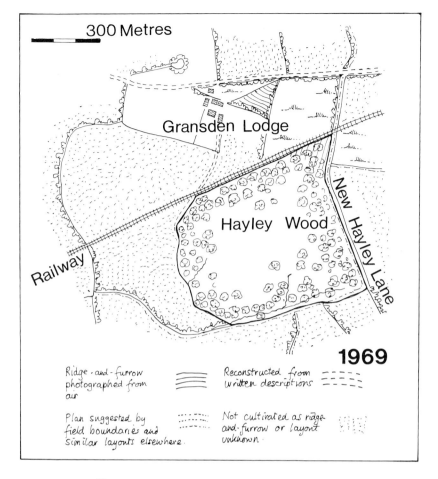

of this order.[49] Similarly it can be observed on
the roads out of Canterbury.

Many medieval woods have survived
virtually intact into the modern landscape. We
know their names, their areas and values from
surveys made by medieval monasteries and
other landlords from the thirteenth century
onwards. Such is Hayley wood in Cambridgeshire, the subject of recent intensive studies.[50]
This was on one of the estates belonging to the
Bishops of Ely. Its shape, like that of many
medieval woods, is irregular in outline.
Medieval woods either have sinuous boundaries which wander across country in a series
of curves – or are zigzag in shape with abrupt
changes of direction at larger intervals. These
may result from medieval peasant farmers
hacking successive small intakes from the
woodland.

Hayley Wood has a massive bank and ditch.
These woodland banks are characteristic of
medieval boundaries. They usually measure a
total width of 10 m across and follow the
sinuous or zigzag outlines of the woods. Often
where the wood has been reduced in size later,
the medieval boundary survives as a hedge in
the fields outside the wood. Sometimes when
this has been ploughed flat the former course
of the woodland boundary can only be traced
as a soil mark across a field. It is possible to
construct the history and alterations to a wood
by studying the earthworks. Later additions
are marked by straight stretches of less massive
banks and steeper ditches.

Within the wood are other earthworks. To
keep out browsing deer and other animals
from freshly sprouting stools of hazel, maple
or elm, it was necessary to fence off individual
sections of coppice. Such compartments have
been found in the Bradfield Woods in Suffolk.
These used to belong to Bury St Edmunds
Abbey and were being coppiced before 1252.[51]
Further ditches, more irregular in outline,
were drainage grips, which were skilfully laid

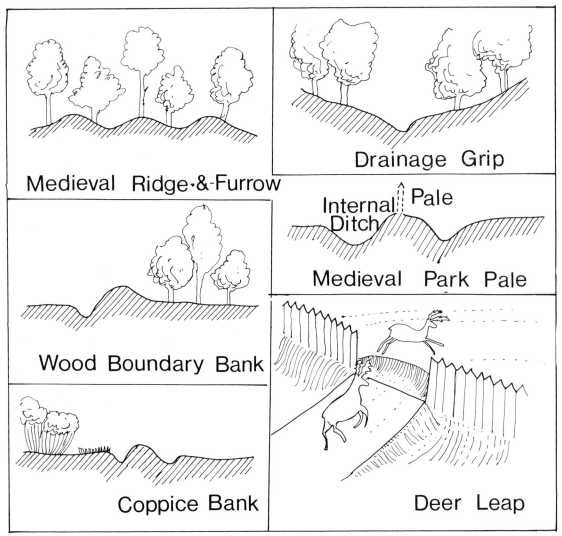

Figure 5.7: Woodland Earthworks

out following the lie of the land using existing streams and often leading into ponds. Depressions may be filled-in rectangular saw pits. The grass is sometimes greener where charcoal was made. Other features to look for in medieval woods are the random sprawling outlines of gravel pits, brick pits and marlpits. An area riddled with these is in the Chilterns south of Nettlebed. To find these often rather faint and eroded earthworks it is best to investigate woodland during the winter. February is a good month because vegetation has died down by then and the outlines of

banks and ditches can be discerned between the trees.

It is now being increasingly realised that the botanical composition of woodland can contribute useful information to the history of the landscape. Botanists call woodland, which has never been completely felled, grubbed out and ploughed up, *primary* woodland. Woods which have been planted or allowed to develop naturally are called *secondary* woodland. As one would expect, surviving areas of 'wildwood' are likely to have a richer flora than recently established woodland. Moreover, they are likely to retain some particular plants which are slow to colonise more recently planted woods. A good approach to recognising primary woodland is to look for these indicators.[52] A well-known example which is confined to Cambridgeshire. Suffolk and Essex, is the oxlip, a yellow flower which has something of the characteristics of a primrose and a cowslip. This plant is found only in ancient woodland. Many secondary woodlands, even up to 350 years old, fail to contain it. Other plants which, in East Anglia at any rate, are good indicators of ancient woodland are the woodland hawthorn, wild service, herb paris and wood anemone. Bluebells and dogs mercury too are very slow colonisers and are nearly always confined to ancient woodland. It is not good enough evidence to have only one of these species, but a group of them in a wood is a reasonable indication that the wood is ancient.

The plants growing between the trees in secondary woodland are widespread in hedges and other habitats and have no particular connection with woodland. Ivy, for instance, is very common in secondary woods but is only found on the edge of primary woods; it may well mark out areas which have been added to a primary wood. Another typical plant of these later woods is cow parsley.

10. Forests

Nowadays the term 'forests' conjures up areas of dense woodland, populated by roaring boars or merry outlaws and huge trees luring the traveller into their limitless depths. Medieval forests in reality were simply tracts of land governed by special laws aimed at protecting the royal deer. Each forest contained areas of royal wood pasture where the deer actually lived but they also contained ordinary farmland, private woodland and parks, villages and even towns. The Norman and Angevin kings were continually adding to their extent and they covered huge areas at their height.[53] The New Forest, for instance, extended over 32,376 ha of heath and woodland and Sherwood had about 20,235 ha. There were some 80 wooded forests with an average of 2,023 ha of wood pasture each. The

legal area of forest jurisdiction covered about a third of the country but the actual physical areas of forests covered approximately 404,700 ha, only 3 per cent of England. The increase of the forests was one of the causes of friction between King John and his barons, and Magna Carta curtailed these abuses. Henceforward the boundaries of forests began to shrink.

The extent of a medieval royal forest can be mapped using a number of techniques. Celtic place-name elements may provide hints that a heavily wooded area continued under British control well into the Saxon period. The old English 'hursts', 'leys', 'dens' and 'groves' can all be plotted on maps and will give some indication of the distribution of former woodland and clearings within it. Domesday evidence can be mapped although the figures are difficult to deal with. In places linear measurements are given; the wood is so many leagues in length or breadth. In some areas the commissioners recorded swine rents; in others the number of swine which areas of woodland would support. The aggressive afforestation of the Angevins led to disputes which are recorded and eventually to perambulations in the thirteenth century which fix the now shrunken bounds closely for the first time. An example of mapping using these sources of information is the Forest of Bernwood in Oxfordshire and Buckinghamshire now threatened by the extension of the M40 motorway (Figure 5.8).

The most publicised use of medieval forests was the protection of *vert* and *venison*, the green food and the deer which fed on it. There were three species of deer (Plate 5.7). The most prized were the red deer (Latin *cervus*, feminine *bissa*) which came mostly from the northern forests. These were supplemented by the fallow deer (male buck – *damus*, female doe – *dama*) which were introduced from the Levant at the time of the Crusades. Roe deer (Latin *capreolus*), were a third type but these were thought to drive out others and were no longer protected after the middle of the fourteenth century. Archaeological evidence for poaching by the peasants of the village of Lyveden in Rockingham Forest was found in the deer bones here which made up 2 per cent of the total of animal bones found on the site.[54] The whole skeleton of a red deer had

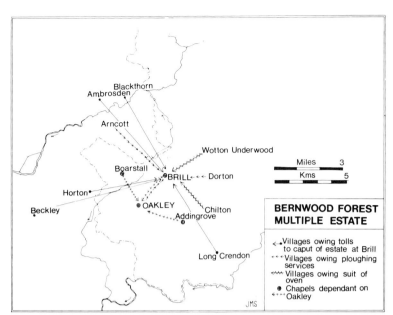

Figure 5.8: Bernwood Forest
(a) Multiple estate (after Reed).

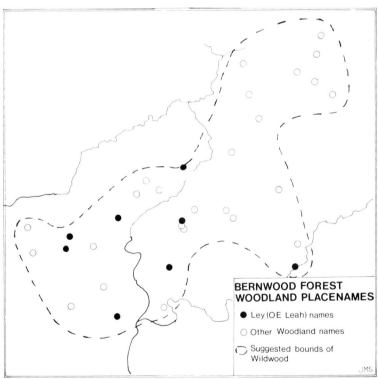

(b) Woodland placenames.

(c) Domesday woodland
(after Darby and Campbell).

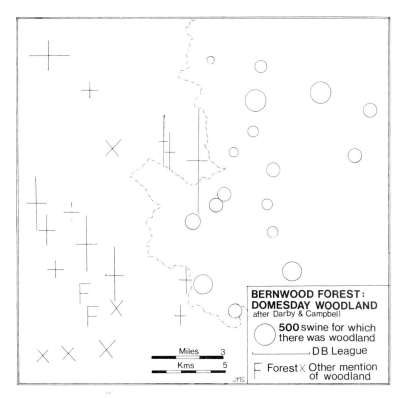

BERNWOOD FOREST:
DOMESDAY WOODLAND
after Darby & Campbell

500 swine for which
there was woodland

⌐ DB League

F Forest X Other mention
of woodland

Miles 3
Kms 5

(d) 1298 perambulation
(after Reed).

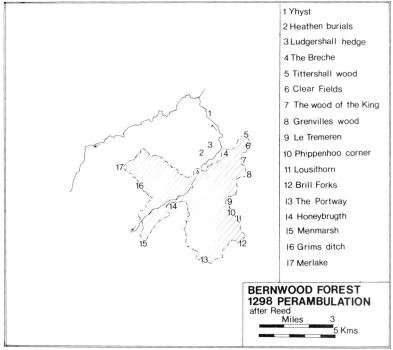

1 Yhyst
2 Heathen burials
3 Ludgershall hedge
4 The Breche
5 Tittershall wood
6 Clear Fields
7 The wood of the King
8 Grenvilles wood
9 Le Tremeren
10 Phippenhoo corner
11 Lousithorn
12 Brill Forks
13 The Portway
14 Honeybrugth
15 Menmarsh
16 Grims ditch
17 Merlake

BERNWOOD FOREST
1298 PERAMBULATION
after Reed

Miles 3
5 Kms

(e) Modern woodland

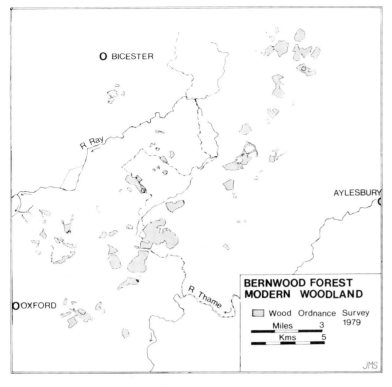

Plate 5.7: Savernake, Wiltshire. Detail of fourteenth-century horn with enamelled mount with hunting scenes. The horn may have been in the possession of the Sturmy family, hereditary wardens of Savernake Forest (Photo: British Museum)

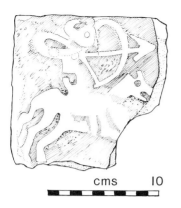

cms 10

Figure 5.9: Three Tiles Showing Hunting Scenes, Dorchester Museum, Dorset

been partially stripped of meat before being jammed down a well. Whether this was a novel way of getting rid of the evidence is not known, but villagers from Lyveden certainly figure frequently as poachers of the king's deer in the forest records. They used the deer bone, which is peculiarly dense, for making tools.

Other predators of the king's deer were wolves, regarded for generations as every man's enemy. The rich reward paid by King John, 15 shillings to two huntsmen who killed two wolves in Dorset, probably emphasises that they were an unusual phenomenon. One must have been caught lurking in the Forest of Rockingham in the thirteenth century because a wolf bone was identified at Lyveden. By 1200, however, they were virtually confined to the mountainous areas of Wales, Westmorland and the Peak and by 1500 they survived only on the north Yorkshire moors and other high parts: henceforward shepherds no longer needed to lead their flocks from the front. The sheep dog now replaced his mastiff or wolfhound.[55]

Deer fitted in well to medieval wood pasture because they were mainly grass feeders but took some sustenance from dead leaves, brambles, fruit and nuts. They attacked saplings and coppice regrowth and were very difficult to capture in continuous woodland especially in underwood. It was therefore necessary to ensure that forests were divided into compartments – i.e. where the coppices were fenced in during the time new shoots were forming. In the meantime deer had to make do with feeding on the grass which grew

on the plains, lawns or '*launds*'. These place-names are often found in ancient woodland and indicate mainly open grassy areas of wood pasture. Another aspect of medieval wood pasture is mentioned in Domesday Book which measures large parts of the country's woodland by calculating how many swine foraged on it. This seasonal practice of taking domesticated pigs into the woods to fatten them on acorns or beechnuts before slaughtering them and salting them down, was known as pannage. Pannage was pretty unreliable because the acorn crop varied from year to year and beech mast often failed for years on end.

The royal forests were a source of valuable timber and the chief reservoirs of great trees were the forests of Dean, Windsor and Sherwood. It must have been one of the prized privileges of being a medieval king to be able to bestow great oaks on one's subjects. Henry III particularly enjoyed giving trees away. Within 25 years, 1228-53, 568 trees were given away or used by the king from the Forest of Windsor.[56] Most travelled east or west along the communications artery of the River Thames from Abingdon some 56 km to the west to Grays Thurrock, 72 km to the east. This timber was used to repair bridges which in the thirteenth century were mostly of timber, to construct boats and for fuel (frequent donations to cold and clammy monasteries were noted). Much was used for royal building works because Henry III began to gratify his architectural tastes on a larger scale during the 1230s and 1240s. Timber was also used to reward civil servants; gifts varied in generosity from 30 'robora' to the king's treasurer, Henry of Patishall, to a couple of 'robora' slipped, for old times sake, to Alice, the nurse of the daughter of Henry de Burgh.

It is possible by studying the timbers in a building to calculate how many trees were cut down to provide the raw material. The Black Friars of Gloucester were among the lucky recipients of oaks from the Forest of Dean (see Plate 7.9).[57] They received 71 between 1241 and 1265. Each tree was about 15.2 m in usable length and about 67.6 cm in diameter at the middle. They were sawn lengthwise into four or six rafters. Grundle House, Stanton, in West Suffolk, a slightly larger than usual farmhouse of c. 1500, contained 332$\frac{1}{2}$ trees built into it of which 80 per cent were oak and 20 per cent elm.[58] This represents one year's growth of oak on roughly 121 ha of woodland and Rackham has calculated that West Suffolk, with some 8,499 ha of woodland, was capable of producing 70 Grundle Houses a year. Of course once a great tree was chopped down it would take several hundred years to replace it. If we lay too much stress on the poor economic return from 404,700 ha of the forests – less than a thousand deer and a few hundred great oaks annually, – we shall misunderstand the nature of medieval society. More emphasis was placed on the social assets of forests. They certainly contributed to the prestige of monarchy which had at its disposal gifts which money could not buy, while the hierarchy of forest officials provided 'jobs for the boys' on a large scale. Also the 'real income' from forests may well have come from the fines levied by the forest courts. You could make *assarts* (clearings) and *purprestures* (enclosures, sometimes buildings) in royal forests, provided you paid for the privilege.

11. Parks

The other members of the ruling class, barons, bishops and abbots, were anxious to share in the social status which the possession of deer-bearing land and hunting rights gave them. They sought permission from the Crown to create parks. These differed from forests in that they had perimeter fences to retain the deer and were wholly private property, not having any special laws or administration. In their heyday, at the beginning of the four-teenth century, it is reckoned that there were about 3,200 parks, amounting perhaps to 259,000 ha, or 2 per cent of England. The greater nobles had ten or more parks each; the Crown had about 20.

The archaeologist has begun to give parks some attention and already detailed studies have appeared of parks in Dorset, Leicester-shire, Staffordshire, Buckinghamshire and Northamptonshire.[59] The first obvious feature which is discernible in the landscape is the remnants of the park pales. The shape of these was ideally a rectangle with rounded corners – which meant that the maximum area was enclosed with a minimum of cost. The bank often tended to have the ditch on the inside, the reverse arrangement to wood banks, since the pale was intended to keep animals in. The pale itself was sometimes set back from the boundary of the property and the interval, usually one perch wide, was called the free-board. It was apparently used to provide access to the pale for maintenance purposes. The maintenance of park pales posed a problem. The royal park of Moulton near Northampton was maintained by the surrounding town-ships.[60] Their obligations were recorded on stones carved with their names which were inserted at intervals in the park pale, in this case, a wall. The remains of park pales can be recognised because they are marked by curv-ing hedgerows which more recent field boundaries respect.

Parks, like forests, could be uncompart-mented with pollards and large timber trees, or they could be compartmented and divided by internal fences into coppices. Another separation between livestock and trees occur-red by the access of the animals to the grassy plains or *laundes* frequently found in parks. Other features of parks include lodges, some-times moated enclosures, where the park keeper lived, fishponds and rabbit warrens.

Early medieval parks are often found in remote parts of the country, on the edges of parishes, far from village centres. It is clear that they occupied less valuable land. Towards the end of the Middle Ages, however, it is apparent that they were being created on land which had previously been under cultivation. A sure mark of this is the presence of ridge-and-furrow. A typical example is the corrugated marks of earlier cultivation by the villagers of Geddington and Weekley in the late medieval park of Boughton in Northamptonshire. Gradually the concept of the park changed from being a reservoir of meat and fuel, to being a foil to set off a grand house. The Tudor courtiers required their elaborate display houses to be set in a park.

12. Mills and Milling

We have seen that one of the most important determinants of the sites of settlements was water supply, essential if men, animals and crops were to survive. Villagers might find their water in springs, streams or wells. Running water, where it was suitable to harness, could also be used to drive mills. Domesday Book records 5,624 mills in England, each catering for about 250 people.[61] They are widely distributed; in Lincolnshire, for instance, they are mentioned in connection with 256 out of 755 manors; in Suffolk, in 178 out of 639 manors. The sites of a great number are known. Their positions were determined by the gradient of the stream, not by the spacing of settlements. At times the parish boundary has obviously been altered by the presence of a mill – a long strip for an access path and a mill race has been carved out of the land of a neighbour.[62] Mills are often found on the upstream sides of fords. Clearly access was a consideration of some importance. The water usually needed diverting some way upstream where the main channel was directed over a weir, the mill race was led along embanked leats to a pond. This was dammed by an earthen or stone-revetted bank in order to build up a sufficient head of water to drive the mill. Watermills were used in the Anglo-Saxon period and throughout the Middle Ages to grind corn. Later in the medieval period water was harnessed to drive fulling mills, and hammers in iron forges. Only a very few sites have been excavated but it is clear that there were three types of mills: horizontal, undershot and overshot.

A horizontal mill, found at Tamworth,

demonstrated the sophistication achieved by Saxon carpenters as early as the eighth century.[63] The structure consisted of two rectangular 'boxes' at different levels; the upper of these apparently acted as a mill pool from which water was led by an outfall trough to the lower structure with a plank floor, the undercroft of a mill. The wheel, of which one spoon-shaped paddle was found, provided the power; it was a horizontal overshot wheel of the type known from the Atlantic Isles.[64] The Click mills in Orkney are examples of the same principle; they derive their name from the noise they make as water flows under them from the blade, and are simply a development from the old hand quern operated by what is in effect a water turbine.[65] They may well be a Norse introduction and traces of them have been found in Ireland, Isle of Man and Faroes, as well as the Orkneys and Shetland. It is debatable to what extent the Domesday mills were horizontal or vertical. One type of vertical mill could be undershot and here the water comes in at low level and a masonry breastwork keeps the water in touch with the wheel. In overshot mills, such as that illustrated in the fourteenth-century Luttrell Psalter, the water came in over the top. An example of the wheel pit framework, and part of the wooden wheel, was found in situ at the fourteenth-century mill at Batsford in Sussex.[66] Numerous wooden pegs would have fitted into a gear wheel which, driven by the water wheel, would have transferred its drive at right angles to another similar gear wheel, turning in a horizontal plane. This second wheel would then have powered the mill stones. Mill stones were often brought from afar. The Tamworth mill had fragments mostly of the local millstone grit but some of Mayen-Niedermendig lava. This coarse gritty black stone was imported into the country from the central Rhineland from Roman times until the late Middle Ages.

There is plenty of evidence for multiple wheels, either stepped or in tandem, under the same roof. Little survives of medieval mill buildings. One has been embedded in a later rebuilding at Rievaulx in Yorkshire and a fifteenth-century tent-shaped mill (with nineteenth-century machinery) has recently been restored at Nether Alderley in Cheshire.

The tide was also harnessed in the Middle Ages. At Tamar in Devon the water comes in under the thirteenth-century base of the mill at high tide and is trapped by sluices; as it drains away, it drives several water wheels. There were three tidal mills in Devon and Cornwall in the thirteenth century, five in the fourteenth, and nine in the sixteenth century.[67]

13. Windmills

Many people in the east and south-east of England where rivers ran too slowly to turn a wheel forcefully, or where the building of a dam might have threatened flooding, had an alternative form of powered milling, from the last quarter of the twelfth century. This was the wind-driven mill. The idea may have come via Crusaders from the Orient.[68] Arabian writers claim that they were used in Seistan in eastern Persia to raise water for irrigation purposes. A survey of the Knights Templars' estates made in 1185 locates two windmills, one at Weedley in Yorkshire. The idea soon caught on. By 1189 one of Henry II's constables handed over one in Buckinghamshire to Oseney Abbey. Within a hundred years windmills became one of the most familiar features of the landscape all over northern Europe. To adapt the windmill to Europe one important alteration was necessary. In the Near East and on the Mediterranean seaboard the wind nearly always blows from the same direction. In Western Europe the more variable winds made it necessary to devise a mill which could turn its sails to the wind.

The result was the post mill, consisting of a box-like wooden body, carrying the sails, and containing the gearing and the stones (Figure 5.10).[69] This was mounted on a suitably braced post on which it was turned so that the sails could face the wind. The post was fixed to cross timbers which could either be sunk into the ground or rested on brick or stone piers. No post mills survive above-ground from a period earlier than the seventeenth century. Their sites, however, can easily be recognised in the field. Ideally they were built on high ground to catch the wind but not too far from the village or its cornfields. Often lanes or hollow-ways can be seen converging

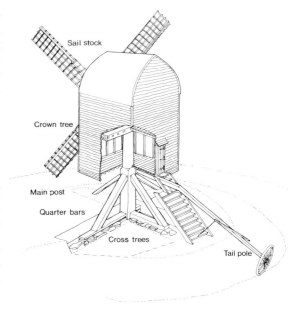

Figure 5.10: Post Mill, Great Linford, Buckinghamshire (after R.J. Zeepvat, 1979)

across the ridge-and-furrow of the open-fields on the circular mound with a crisscross shape cut into it. This is like a hot cross bun and the cuts are the remains of the slots for the timbers. These mounds, sometimes mistaken for prehistoric tumuli, were necessary to support the legs of the mill. The ditch outside was simply a spoil pit from which the soil of the mound was dug. Fragments of millstones often litter windmill sites. Excavation of two windmill sites in Northamptonshire revealed the constructional details.[70]

A technological advance was marked by the invention of the tower mill in the fourteenth century. In this type a tower of brick or stone contained the machinery, and the only part turning to face the wind was the top or cap carrying the sails. A fifteenth-century stained-glass window at Stoke-by-Clare (Suffolk) shows a tower mill, and they are common in Flemish and English manuscripts of this date. A further development was pioneered by the Dutch who in 1408 invented the *wip molen*, or hollow post-mill, and applied it first to draining marshland by pumping water out of the polders.

The windmill owed its success to the fact that it offered obvious advantages over the water mill. In winter it could not be stopped by freezing; also winds were far more constant than water which tended to dry up in summer.

This extraordinary progress towards substituting water and wind-power for human labour eventually overtook all the basic industries. In England during the thirteenth century, in place of the traditional methods of fulling cloth by hand or foot, mechanical fulling using water power tended to shift the centre of textile production from the south-east to the north-west. Mills for tanning, laundering, sawing, for crushing anything from olives to metal ores are found in the Later Middle Ages. There was even an idea in a book by Walter de Millimete in 1326 for using a post mill for flinging beehives into a besieged town! Tower mills were particularly useful for erecting on the walls of castles and town walls. Watermills were finally harnessed to operate the bellows of blast furnaces and the hammers of forges. They still had nearly four centuries of useful life ahead of them at the end of the Middle Ages.

14. Fishponds

Recent field work has suggested that fishponds were normal appurtenances to manors over much of lowland England during the Middle Ages.[71] Far from being the sole preserve of monasteries they provided a vital addition, scarce animal protein, in the diet of the

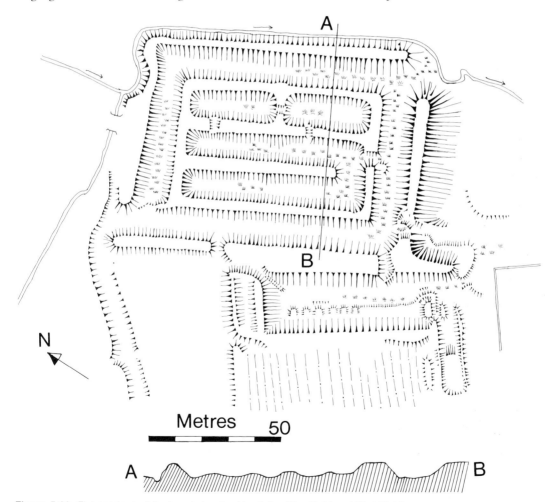

Figure 5.11: Fishponds, Lyddington, Leicestershire (after Woodfield and Woodfield)

aristocracy, both lay and ecclesiastical. The Close Rolls show that during the thirteenth century the royal ponds were producing large quantities of fish for the king's table and for stocking the ponds of favoured subjects. Moreover, research in the area of Warwickshire shows that they were not a seignorial monopoly; villagers as well as manorial households drew fish from them. In some instances, such as during Prior More's time at Worcester, enterprising investment resulted in substantial commercial returns.[72]

In most cases medieval fishponds have now been breached; they have lost their water and it takes some stretch of the imagination to recreate them. But their earthworks are quite distinctive.[73] In some cases they were small rectangular excavations fed by a small stream or spring, in others streams running down valleys were blocked by dams which might be revetted with stone. A third type was perched on the sides of hills. The water level was controlled by means of sluices. Overflow channels looked after excess water and side leats sometimes acted as tributaries. The ideal was a pool of moderate depth with a gentle flow of oxygen and mineral rich water moving through it. Islands were common and are thought to have been used for growing reeds, rushes and acting as refuges for waterfowl. More complex series had auxiliary breeding chambers and separate ponds for different types of fish (Figure 5.11). The most fully developed series like that seen at Harrington in Northamptonshire, near a preceptory of Knights Templars, consisted of a battery of different shaped embanked ponds, in a shallow valley, with deep supply channels and linked by a complex system of overflow channels, leats and sluices. A mighty dam at the royal fishpond site at Silverstone, created what was the largest lake in Northamptonshire until the late eighteenth century. Even the parish boundary here at Silverstone appears to have been altered to follow the stream which no longer runs down the valley but is carried round the pond by a high-level leat. Evidently the idea was to have the royal fishpond in one parish, in somewhat the same way as the county boundary with Bedfordshire was moved to enclose the whole of the ducal park of Higham Ferrers in Northamptonshire.

Little excavation has yet been done on fishpond sites but it seems that large quantities of timber were used in the construction of sluices and in lacing the earthen banks. We know from writers such as Norden in the sixteenth and seventeenth centuries that great attention was given to the building of dams. Clay was used, ramming was advised, great stakes 15 cm square of oak, elm or ash were scorched, and then driven in as piles and consolidated with staves. Faggots and earth were piled over the top. It seems that ponds were drained every so often and that cattle and sheep were encouraged to graze on them; their dung was thought to encourage flies on which the fish fed when the pond was refilled!

Occasionally, as at Bredwardine (Herefordshire), remains of the fish themselves are found. Perch scales were dredged up here from the pond silts. We know from the documents, however, that pike was perhaps the most popular fish; eels, tench, bream, perch and roach were all common. Prior Morton of Worcester, an early sixteenth-century fish producer on a commercial scale, experimented with carp. Chub do not feature unless present accidentally. Trout were still a fish of the future. A variety of freshwater fish was served at the lordly table of Castle Barnard, Durham (see p. 26).

15. The Making of the Broads

One of the common rights we have mentioned was the right of cutting turf or peat, which is the accumulated vegetable debris of the fresh water fens, in *turbaria* or turbaries. Peat is of course found extensively on the tops of moors in the highland parts of the country but medieval fuel was more intensively sought in the low-altitude peat deposits. These are found in the Lincolnshire and Cambridgeshire Fens, in the Norfolk Broad area, in the Somerset Levels and in the 'raised bogs' of the Welsh marshes. It has recently been realised that the series of lakes called the Norfolk Broads, connected by rivers and used nowadays by countless boating and yachting enthusiasts and holiday makers, came into existence in the late Middle Ages. They are in fact the flooded hollows of former extensive peat workings in

Plate 5.8: Barton Broad, Norfolk. Such sheets of water are the sites of great medieval peat diggings cut down into the brushwood deposits at a time when the land stood somewhat higher in relation to the sea than it does at present. The basins have roughly rectangular profiles which have been cut by medieval fuel gatherers. The process also left linear processions of islets and narrow peninsulas of uncut peat as seen in this photo. Flooding in the fifteenth century put an end to such turbaries. Barton Turf is now a hamlet more than 1½ km to the west (Photo: Cambridge University Committee for Aerial Photography, taken 11.6.52)

shallow river valleys.

This conclusion came about through the combined researches of archaeologists, historians, botanists and geomorphologists.[74] The main strands of evidence can be summarised. It was noticed that the Broads had steep margins, whereas one would have expected them to have gently sloping sides if they were the remains of an open estuary which had been partially filled in by sedimentation (the alternative theory of their origin). Moreover, there were upstanding islands or ridges of peat with vertical sides found in the basins of the Broads themselves (Plate 5.8). These lines were found to correspond with the limits of different properties shown in old tithe award maps. Clearly they were baulks of uncut peat left standing between adjacent diggings.

The fact that the Broads are not mentioned as place-names at all in the Early Middle Ages indicates that they were not in existence at this time. On the other hand there are plenty of references to turf digging in parishes which are now devoid of peat or have little left. What happened initially was that turves were cut and gradually the cuttings became wetter. Turf cutting gave way to the extraction of '*mora*' which meant wet peat and mud. This was shaped into 'bricks' and left to dry out before it could be used as fuel. A parish like South Walsham was producing over 200,000 turves a year in the 1260s. One of the biggest consumers was Norwich Cathedral where kitchens were burning roughly double this amount each year in the early fourteenth century. Soon, in the fifteenth century, references begin to come in from fisheries instead of turbaries. Clearly the turf diggings had begun to be flooded and the making of the Broads had started.

It is not quite so clear as to why this flooding happened. There may have been a fall in the general level of the land relative to the sea. Certainly, as we shall see when considering coastal changes, there is plenty of evidence for erosion taking place along the East Anglian coast in the Later Middle Ages. The flooding may be connected with the climatic deterioration which is known to have taken place in the fourteenth and fifteenth centuries. Whatever the reason it seems that when the waters returned to these Norfolk valleys they had a greater space to fill. It has been estimated that nearly 23 million cubic metres of peat were taken from the Norfolk Broads. The fact that there was now less fuel available to offset the worse weather must have been a contributing factor to later medieval misery.

16. Climate in the Middle Ages

The extent to which the weather continues to fascinate Englishmen is reflected by the fact that it remains one of the dominant themes in everyday conversation, fuelled by the detailed information provided by the daily recording of radio, TV and press. To medieval society whose economy was based so largely on agriculture the overall effects of weather could be a matter of life and death. Monkish chroniclers recorded remarkable events such as great storms which blew down trees and buildings. They also remarked on severe winters which resulted in frozen waterways, or droughts in July and raininess in August producing flooding on ruined crops. Such conditions might spell the death of livestock, create famine conditions, and put whole human populations in jeopardy.

Many lines of evidence make it now seem certain that the period _c._ 1150–1300 experienced a climatic optimum.[75] Summers appear to have been warmer and drier than in subsequent centuries. Ocean temperatures were at least as high as today and probably rather higher. Winters during the warmest decades of the twelfth to fourteenth centuries were at least as warm as the warmest decades of the twentieth century.

One effect of the climatic optimum was to make it possible to cultivate at remarkable heights above sea level, far higher than anything attempted in the present century, even in wartime. The characteristic traces of ridge-and-furrow, the marks of medieval tillage,

have been found up to 350 m above sea level on Dartmoor and up to 320 m on the fells of Durham and Northumberland. There was probably a similar extension in the Scottish highlands and it has been suggested that the general tendency towards cooler and wetter weather after 1300 may have contributed towards the unsettled state of that country. Raininess induced a raiding mentality!

A similar pointer is provided by the documentary evidence for a flourishing wine industry in the south of England during the eleventh to thirteenth centuries, particularly vineyards at Tewkesbury and in the Isle of Ely and the Essex valleys. This indicates that either May frosts did not occur or were much rarer than in the present century. It also implies higher average sea temperatures around Britain. The climate in fact was probably more like northern France with summer temperatures generally about 1°C higher than now.

Information about the environment is also being collected from excavations. The remains of insects are probably the greatest potential source for data about climatic fluctuations. A large number of species have their northern or southern limits in the British Isles, in many cases around Lincolnshire and Yorkshire. Only small changes in climate can cause quite large extensions or contractions of range. The remains of about a dozen species of beetle, whose northern limits are now in the twentieth century well south of Yorkshire, have been found in early medieval deposits from the City of York.[76] It is possible that this may be accounted for by the warm micro-climate of the very organic environment of the City, which may have produced an artificial habitat favouring species such as the beetle _Aglenus brunneus_ (Gyll.). The bug _Heterogaster urticae_ (F) shows a strong preference for nettlebeds in open sunny places. It is a phytopage with the stinging nettle, _Urtica dioica L._ as its principal host. It is now extremely rare north of Huntingdonshire. Early medieval deposits in York have, however, produced numerous specimens. This marked change in distribution and abundance can only be attributed to a climatic deterioration which has taken place since the early medieval period.

Historical meteorologists seem undecided as to whether there were wetter or drier conditions during the period of climatic optimum. On the one hand they point to the distribution of water mills in south-east England and conclude that for the streams to be sufficient to drive them, the rainfall must have been heavier in the eleventh and twelfth centuries. On the other hand, this rainfall may have been offset by evaporation in many warm and dry summers, 1100-1310, to cause excessive drying out and compaction of the soil resulting in subsidence of a number of Norman churches and cathedrals (including Carlisle and Ely).

There was a fluctuating but on the whole progressive trend towards wetter summers and more frequent severe winters in Europe during the thirteenth to fourteenth centuries. Great storms and sea floods are reported in 1251 which took a large area of Holland-Friesland and formed the northern half of the Zuider Zee; further losses of land round the North Sea and Baltic occurred at intervals in the thirteenth and fourteenth centuries. Wet, cold summers in the decade starting 1310 were particularly disastrous and in 1315 there were harvest failures with famine conditions all over Europe. The increased wetness of the ground led to recurrence surfaces on the peat bogs of the uplands. A retreat from marginal highland cultivated areas began and many villages which subsequently became deserted seem to have suffered a serious decline in the years of disastrous summers and famine 1311-19.

Archaeologists have noticed a number of other indications of deteriorating climatic conditions.[77] It is striking that during the warm epoch in the Early Middle Ages peasant houses were built on the old ground surface, only surrounded by shallow gullies on land which is quite low-lying and now liable to waterlogging (see p. 190). During the Later Middle Ages signs of worsening weather are seen in the frequent re-cutting and deepening of ditches. Houses were surrounded by eaves' trenches and also had drains running along the insides of walls. At Goltho (Lincs.), Tresmorn (Cornwall), and Dinas Noddfa (Glamorgan), these same features have been noticed. Moreover, houses were now built on mounded platforms in an attempt to keep them out of the wet and yards were frequently paved and thresholds cobbled to cope with mud.

It has been suggested that some moated

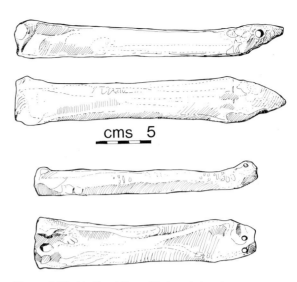

Figure 5.12: Medieval Bone Skates, Ashmolean Museum, Oxford

sites were dug at this time to improve drainage (see p. 58). The material from the ditches was often heaped inside to form a drier base. Finally the increasing wetness may well account for the fact that timber buildings all over the land in the Later Middle Ages were now provided with dwarf stone walls instead of the posts and beams being set directly on the ground as had happened in the earlier period.

Certain archaeological artefacts have also been used as indications of past climatic conditions. The discovery of large numbers of worn and polished bone skates in deposits of Anglo-Scandinavian date at York and Oxford have been considered to imply fairly frequent long hard winters (Figure 5.12).[78] This might be thought to conflict with the evidence of the climatic optimum but it has recently been realised that the comparatively inefficient land drainage systems of the period would have led to large areas of low-lying countryside spending at least part of the winter under shallow water. Similar skates have been found in medieval London and remind us of William Fitz Stephen's description of 1170-83 which begins 'When the great marsh that washes the north wall of the City is frozen over, swarms of young men issue forth to play games on the ice . . . put on their feet the shin-bones of animals, binding them firmly round their ankles . . . ' These low-lying areas would have been more prone to freezing than the main rivers themselves particularly if the climate was experiencing an episode of increased continentality.

17. Coastal Change in the Middle Ages

The coast of Britain offers dramatic demonstrations of the ever-changing nature of the landscape. An archaeological study of the sea coast reveals that man has played an increasing part in these changes.[79] Along many stretches of coast the sea has cut back rock strata with its top-soil capping, exposing man's disturbance of the surface in the form of pits, ditches, wells and buildings. In other places the unstratified remains of human occupation such as pottery, bones and coins lie at the foot of cliffs, or along the shores of creeks. Elsewhere it seems that the ancient coast is to be found inland, either because of slow-moving geological processes, building up deposits of shingle, mud or silt or because generations of farmers have painfully reclaimed coastal marshes by means of dykes, levees and drainage works.

The post-glacial shore of the western Grampians, relieved from the great weight of ice, has been uplifted to a maximum of 15 m since its formation and the process is still going on at a rate of 2-3 mm a year. The result has been the retreat of the coast leaving medieval havens on the west coast high and dry. At Harlech, for instance, the castle, built in the 1270s as part of Edward's campaign to conquer Wales, was originally connected to the sea by a port which lay at the foot of the rock. The sea gate now leads only to grass, sand dunes and a golf course; the waves can be dimly seen 3.2 km to the west.

On the other side of the country, on the eastern coast, this tilting process has been going on the other way and here the sea is still actively eroding the coastline (Plate 5.9). In its heyday in the reign of King John c. 1200 Dunwich (Suffolk) was a gated town on a hill about 12 m above the sea.[80] It had eight or possibly nine parish churches, and a number of monastic houses grouped round markets which were held every day of the week. It

does seem, however, that by the time of Domesday Book (1086) the sea had already begun to threaten to submerge the town. The haven was constantly blocked by storms and liable to shift. There was also great erosion of the cliffs. St Felix' Church, the mother church of East Anglia, was the first church to go, followed by St Leonards' c. 1300. On 14 January 1328 the sea, sweeping in, completely choked the ancient harbour with shingle and in 1350 'upwards of 400 houses' with shops and windmills were reported overrun. From a study of maps made in the sixteenth century it seems that the sea has gained about 457 m in the four centuries since 1587. All that is left in the present village is the western suburbs of the medieval town of Dunwich.

Less dramatic but of greater economic importance was the constant struggle of medieval peasants and landowners to extend the land at the expense of the sea. This can be illustrated by three examples, in south Wales, on the south-east coast of Kent and Sussex, and around the Wash in Norfolk and Lincolnshire.

During the Early Middle Ages religious houses had been founded close to the sea in south Wales: the alien priory of Goldcliff, a few miles east of Cardiff in 1113, and the Cistercian abbeys of Neath and Margam, in 1130 and 1147.[81] The monks soon began to build embankments to enclose portions of the sea marsh and to dig drains to turn these areas into profitable pasture and, at length (when the salt had been leached out), arable. We know from charters (documents concerned with land tenure), that the *walla* or *walda Anglorum* (The Englishmens' embankment) was on Afan's marsh near the present town of Port Talbot. Margam Abbey had a farm which can be located at Grangetown, an inner suburb of Cardiff. A new embankment was built here in the early thirteenth century and the monks were granted 'all our moor which lies outside the new *walda* of Cardiff, between the *walda* and the sea . . . besides ten acres of land within our new *walda* to build themselves a sheepfold'. When we look at the landscape itself, we see flat fields intersected by winding roads on causewayed banks and a mesh of drainage ditches. The sea, unfortunately, gained the upper hand along parts of this

Plate 5.9: Spurn Head, Holderness, Humberside. This dramatic photo illustrates the cyclical changes which have overtaken this part of the north-east coast. These include rapid coastal erosion at a rate of 12.3 m a year which has led to a loss of 21,578 ha or about 215 sq km since Roman times (Steers, J.A., *The Coastline of England and Wales*, Cambridge, 1946, 412). The point at the mouth of the Humber builds up with sand and shingle, the detritus of this erosion lengthens, is breached, becomes an island, moves eastwards. Then the whole process begins again. The medieval port of Ravenserodd (1235-1360) was about 2.4 km to the east. The earliest lighthouse, Reedbarrow's of 1427, and Edward IV's landing place, was about 1.2 km to the east of this view. (Photo: Cambridge University Committee for Aerial Photography, taken 5.11.68)

stretch of the coast in the fourteenth and fifteenth centuries. The church at Goldcliff was half undermined by the sea and much of the land of the priory drowned. To counteract these inundations the late medieval churches of St Brides, Peterston and Marchfield were all built a safe distance inland.

An even more radical series of transformations of the sea coast has occurred at Romney Marsh on the borders of Kent and Sussex.[82] Here four processes were at work which changed this stretch of coast in two thousand years out of all recognition: the growth of the beach, the work of the rivers, the changes in sea level and, a decisive factor, the operations of man. Briefly, in the Roman period it seems that the Wealden rivers all flowed north-east into a series of tidal creeks and inlets. The position of the Roman coastline can be inferred from the location of Roman settlements found some kilometres inland from the present one. Gradually through this period the west-east currents of the English Channel began to build up a headland of shingle composed of pebbles torn from the eroded chalk cliffs of Sussex. At the same time the sea wore away the shingle at the

western end of the headland and eventually burst through, the overflowing waters capturing the rivers which now flowed south instead of north-east. What had been a series of creeks in the north-east part became clogged with silt and reverted to marsh. The Saxons during the next five centuries made a major effort in reclaiming and planting settlements in this swampy region. The drainage changed and for a time the River Rother reached the sea through an estuary known as Romney Creek. Here there were two ports, Old and New Romney, which engaged in profitable cross-channel trade and were numbered among the Cinque Ports. In an effort to keep the channel scoured, a major canal known as the Rhee wall was cut through from Appledore to Old Romney in the twelfth or early thirteenth centuries. A series of great storms, however, frustrated these designs. Exceptionally high tides destroyed ships and flooded houses at Old Winchelsea in 1250, 37 years later they totally destroyed this town. All the marshland south of the Rhee wall was flooded and the River Rother was now diverted into the southern estuary. This spelt doom for the ports of Romney.

Old Romney was probably in decline as early as the eleventh century. Its parish church, large enough to accommodate the modern population of Romney Marsh, lies with a few houses in fields which mark the site of the former town. New Romney was founded 3.2 km nearer the sea. The quayside was positioned south-east of the churchyard on the curving estuary of the River Rother. It is now completely silted up and covered by a modern housing estate. The great Norman parish church still towers over the village, a symbol of the early medieval wealth and importance of the former Cinque Port dependent upon and ultimately defeated by the sea.

Success by medieval farmers in reclaiming land from the sea and controlling its waters was therefore short-lived along both the south Welsh and south-eastern coasts. When we turn to a third area, the Fen region around the Wash in Norfolk and Lincolnshire, we find that the struggle here, though arduous, was ultimately profitable and long-lasting. Here reclamation proceeded from two directions, the sea and inland.[83] Between 1150 and 1300, peasants living in villages on the silt-lands situated on the rim of the Wash, began to construct banks and dig dykes to drain the fen and the marsh. Many of these banks have major east-west roads. At the same time they started to win land from the sea by building groynes and walls which trapped the silt laden waters. The tides as they swept in across the Wash, tended to build up salt marsh. This could be embanked, turned into rough pasture for a number of years until it dried and the salt leached out, and then converted into fertile arable. Features in the present landscape recall the process of winning this so-called 'Newland'. The sea-banks themselves run circuitously along and are used as causeways by roads; they are now sometimes miles from the coast as the process of reclamation has long passed them by. Their tremendous bulk together with the massive fen-banks emphasise their origin in thousands of hours of hard labour and co-operative action. The land so won was held in severalty, each owner using it as he wished. Cattle were driven to common pastures along the fen banks. Even the settlement pattern had to be modified by the increasing distances between parent villages

and new land. Some parishes stretched as much as 27.4 km into the Fen. The effect of this effort still enriches the landscape today. The breezy Norfolk coast is studded with tremendous churches, totally out of scale with the small villages which they straddle. They speak of rich harvests of corn and wool gathered in from the fenland fields and pastures. They were the result of no sudden spurt of energy which was quickly spent but were constructed over centuries. The Norman churches of Tilney and Walsoken, the Early English bell tower of West Walton, the magnificent Perpendicular buildings of Walpole St Peter and Terrington St Clement, record the same tale of wealth and prosperity throughout the Middle Ages.

18. The 'Black Death' and the Dissolution of the Medieval Landscape

An event which has produced lively controversy among social and economic historians during the last 20 years is the so-called 'Black Death'.[84] This silly nick-name, now applied to the plague in all its three forms (bubonic, pneumonic and septicaemic), was invented by a Mrs Penrose in 1823. During the fourteenth century and earlier, it was known as 'The Great Mortality' or 'The Great Pestilence'. The debate has concentrated on whether the disease was a new and unheard-of phenomenon; the means by which it spread; its relative toll on population in towns and the countryside; and its long-term effects on the social fabric and its underlying economic base. In each respect archaeology might be expected to have something to contribute.

Doubt has been cast on the tradition that the plague first made its appearance in England during the late 1340s.[85] Black rats, house rats or ship rats (*Rattus rattus*) are accepted as the principal carrier and transmitter of the primary vector, the flea *Xenopsylla cheopsis* of the bubonic plague, caused by the bacterium *Yersinia pestis*. During excavations of a Roman well at Skeldersgate, York, a rodent skull was recovered and identified as the black rat. Other black rat skeletons have been found in Viking Dublin, in a fourteenth-century context at Doncaster, in early medieval pits at Southampton and in a fifteenth-century drain at Barnard Castle. It has been suggested that the plague appeared from time to time in Anglo-Saxon England and particularly affected monastic houses which had regular contacts with Italy, France and Belgium. If we accept this it can no longer be maintained that the black rat was introduced into the country during the Norman period or was an unwelcome import associated with returning crusaders. The plague in fact haunted the Dark Ages.

The notorious means by which a virulent outbreak of disease entered England in the summer of 1349 was in bales of woollen cloth brought into the south coast port of Weymouth. Wool and its products provided excellent cover for the passive transport of the house or ship rat and its fleas. There were many wool stores in the Cotswold and East Anglian towns; also the rats could hide securely in wagonloads of grain, straw, hay and hides. The speed at which the plague spread was dictated by the fastest speed of human transport, the horse-drawn wagon. What was so alarming to contemporaries was that the disease appeared in many places when there was no visible human contact; the plague of rats (as we now realise), simply walked from one isolated farm to another spreading the disease to other rats on the way. Fairs were important focuses for plague carriers, Northampton, Boston, Stamford, Winchester, St Ives (Cambridgeshire) and Bury St Edmunds. Pilgrimage centres such as St Davids, Hailes (Glos.), Peterborough, Walsingham and Canterbury acted also as catalysts for spreading the disease. Fugitives flocked from plague centres to miracle-working shrines in hope of escaping what was wrongheadedly attributed to divine wrath. The most powerful encouragement to the spread of the disease was the nature of urban and rural housing. Two- or three-roomed dwellings, one used for living, one for a communal bedroom and one for domestic animals (see p. 190) produced ideal conditions for the propagation of the human flea (*Pulex irritans*) and the rat flea (*X. cheopsis*). The building materials themselves – wattle, daub, cob (made of dung and mud) – combined with dark, unventilated, earth-floored, humid interiors provided a happy home for the multiple infestation of both rats and fleas. Where these dwellings crowded together in fourteenth-century urban places, clustering around warehouses, corn stores, mills and harbour frontages, large populations of rats would be generated sufficient to sustain severe epidemics of bubonic plague.

Dramatic and tangible expressions of the horror of the plague in medieval London are the vast pits hurriedly dug to receive the bodies dumped in them *en masse* as the hot and foetid summer of 1349 progressed. Two hundred plague dead were buried almost every day in a cemetery at Smithfield. Walter de Manny, one of Edward III's captains in the French war, donated another burial ground and, according to Stow, 50,000 corpses were interred there.[86] Two others were outside the city wall at the east end. The Museum of London preserves a pathetic group of crosses roughly cut out of lead strip which accompanied some of the bodies to their hurried burial.[87]

Two broad generalisations can be made about the relative mortality and geography of the plague. It was most devastating in its effects on the population of England south and east of a line drawn from York to Exeter. The fairs and the pilgrimage centres just mentioned are all (with the exception of St Davids to which the plague was probably carried by sea), within this part of the country. Secondly, its ravages were much more serious in the towns than in the country. Shrewsbury reckons that as much as a third of the population died in the more densely populated urban areas and perhaps only a twentieth in more rural regions. He thinks that it is improbable that an epidemic would have spread through areas with a human population of less than 60 persons per 2.59 sq km.

He also points out that it is a disease with a fixed seasonal periodicity, normally occurring in the late summer season.[88] Some other disease like smallpox or typhus is likely to have been at work if the death rate in any epidemic is recorded as continuing high during the winter. The low mortality rates of Shrewsbury's calculations which amount to only 5 per cent of the population over the country as a whole, run counter to the figures suggested by every other historian:[89] it is difficult to reconcile them with the heavy mortality among beneficed clergy which ranged from just under 40 per cent in the dioceses of Lichfield and York to 48 per cent in Norwich and Winchester.

Whatever one's view of the magnitude of the death rate brought by the 'Black Death' it does seem that its effects on the economy have been exaggerated in the past. Recent historians in fact take a more optimistic view. It is undeniable that in the short term profits from demesne farming dropped in many places including the estates of the Bishops of Winchester.[90] At Witney (Oxon.), for instance, the profits in 1349 were reduced to half what they were a year previously. Thirty years later the situation had largely returned to normal. Rents had been slightly raised, an average from 5s–6s 8d per annum and most labour services appear to have been dispensed with. The bishops by now had gone in for stock farming on a larger scale, breeding and selling cows and sheep, especially the latter. Sheep numbers, in fact, had doubled on the Witney estates from 700 head to 1,485. They had also decided to cease direct farming and had leased out the demesne. Profits from the manor 30 years after the Black Death brought in £115, about the same as before the alleged cataclysm.

Such attempts by both lords and peasants to come to terms with the Great Pestilence are echoed in other areas where mortality struck hard. The end of demesne farming on monastic and seignorial estates was far advanced by the end of the fourteenth century; increased wage levels combined with a shortage of men contributed to this decision, as well as to the increasing tendency to change over to stock farming on a larger scale. The field evidence for these changes has been long recognised;[91] the fossilisation of field-systems under permanent pasture, the decay of holdings, the consolidation of farms within village centres, the abandonment of outlying hamlets, particularly those on the poorer marginal land, and in general the contraction and shifting of settlement.

The Black Death was only one among a number of predisposing factors causing rural depopulation and the dissolution of the later medieval landscape. It was undoubtedly a disaster for some but turned out to be a blessing and an opportunity for others. It resulted in an easing of the pressure of population on land. Some men were able to start building up their fortunes by renting or buying land cheaply. Others were no doubt turned out of their holdings when their manorial lords attempted to recoup their failing fortunes in an increasingly inflationary age by changing over from cereal cultivation to sheep farming. Most peasants who were hard workers and go-ahead tenants found that it was to their advantage to pay rent. Those living on poor land or suffering from grasping landlords might do better by moving to another village on richer land but where holdings were vacant because of the plague.

These opportunities were offset by an obvious decline in the community of the village. As hard-nosed peasant dynasties came to the fore, individualism tended to triumph over the communal system which had guaranteed a more egalitarian share-out of land and rights in the thirteenth century. There was probably less equality but possibly more opportunity in the English countryside in the later fourteenth century and one reason for this was the Great Pestilence.

If the Death had been so momentous as contemporaries depicted it, one would have expected to see signs of it in the social fabric and architectural expressions of the age. The church certainly suffered huge losses of clergy and the institutions of replacements recorded in episcopal registers provide our only systematic statistical estimates of the mortality rates caused by the plague. The survivors were often of inferior calibre; many inadequate parsons fled, the more devoted died side by side with their stricken parishioners. The fabric of churches serving outlying districts often deteriorated.[92] In 1437 in Lincolnshire, for example, Dunsthorpe was united to Hameringham, the reasons given being 'the lack of parishioners, the fewness of peasants, their low wages, the bareness of the lands, the lack of cultivation, pestilences and epidemics, with which the Lord afflicts his people for their sins'. But the process of contraction is seen sometimes before the Pestilence. In 1338-9 the rector of the Lincolnshire village of Brant Broughton was granted episcopal permission to take the wood and stones from the superfluous chapel at Stapleford for his own church's bell tower, 1½ km away.

There was destruction on the one hand, as settlement contracted; and yet the spate of towers, porches, clerestories, chapels and chantries, all in the Perpendicular style, seemed to continue unabated in the century after the Black Death. Fear of the disease may well have accelerated the endowment of chantries. The new architectural fashion, despite Ruskin's denigratory dismissal ('as much imagination as a builder's sieve'), was not a cheap and easy substitute for an age of poverty. Certainly some building programmes were postponed and a few grand projects were cut down in scale as a result of the Pestilence.

Harvey has noticed by looking closely at Hollar's and Wyck's drawings of Old St Paul's Cathedral, London, that the upper stages of the chapter house appear to have been left unfinished. The Pestilence stopped the work and, later, it can hardly have appeared worthwhile to re-erect the scaffolding. He reckons that this truncated appearance of one of the key buildings in the capital had 'an unintentional psychological effect'.[93] It was the predecessor of the cut-off towers of Perpendicular England – Lavenham (Suffolk) and Wells Cathedral are among the most famous, – so the Black Death is inadvertently commemorated by a lack of spires in the fifteenth century.

Winchester also provides two interesting instances of its influence. The Death hit the city just as Bishop Edington was planning to rebuild the west end of the cathedral. The Norman west front had already been knocked down and Edington ran up a temporary replacement which still stands 600 years later. The economy of the diocese was so undermined for the time being that it was unable to afford any more. But within 35 years Bishop William of Wykeham had collected sufficient resources to encase the Norman nave of the cathedral and recast it in the new style. Moreover, he plugged the clerical manpower gap within the see by founding two educational institutions, a boys' school at Winchester and a *Novum Collegium* at Oxford.

The terror inspired by the disease lasted longer than its economic effects.[94] It imprinted itself on the psychological make-up of the men and women of later medieval England. People

had become inured to the effects of bad harvests, droughts, floods, famines and frequent wars. But the plague was something new to their experience; it was disgusting, mysterious and all powerful. It produced a spirit of gloom, dread and depression. People lapsed into pessimism, cynicism and selfishness. The upper echelons of society alternated between riotous 'living it up' and wallowing in self-pity. Artists and writers combined in producing works steeped with the all-pervading presence of death, hell and damnation; depictions of torture, agony and corruption became an artistic obsession. A special type of two-tiered tomb was developed. The commemorated one was in full robes or armour, an epitome of worldly success, in effigy on the upper level; below, behind a grill was a ghastly cadaver crawling with worms, toads and corruption. Didactic versions of the contrast between life and death were seen in paintings of two grand themes – 'The three dead and the three living' and 'The Dance of Death'. These were painted on church walls, where the astounded traveller was confronted with grinning skeletons beckoning or trampling down, emphasising the transitoriness of human life or the futility of hope in this world. Gone are the calm and lofty versions of Christ in Judgement, the expression of the twelfth-century feudal order. The artists now draw attention in their representations of Christ's passion to his humanity, his sorrows and sufferings. The alabaster images or panel paintings pinpoint every laceration, drop of blood or bead of sweat.

References

1. These questions are dealt with in Sawyer, P.H. (ed.), *Medieval Settlement*, London, 1976.
2. Beresford, M.W. and St. Joseph, J.K., *Medieval England. An Aerial Survey*, Cambridge, 1979.
3. Roberts, B.K., 'The anatomy of settlement' in Sawyer, P.H. (ed.), *Medieval Settlement*, London, 1976, 300.
4. Gelling, M., 'The effect of man on the landscape: the place name evidence in Berkshire' in Limbrey, S. and Evans, J.G., (eds.), *The Effect of Man in the Landscape of the Lowland Zone*, CBA Research Report 21, 1978, 123-5.
5. Peters, J.E.C., *The Development of Farm Build-*

ings in Western Lowland Staffordshire up to 1880, Manchester, 1969, 38-9.

6. Roberts, B.K., *Rural Settlements in Britain*, Folkestone, 1977, 88.

7. Gelling, 'The effect of man on the landscape', 125.

8. Ford, W.J., 'Some settlement patterns in the Central Region of the Warwickshire Avon', in Sawyer, P.H. (ed.), *Medieval Settlement*, London, 1976, 290-3.

9. Beresford and St. Joseph, *Medieval England. An Aerial Survey*, 110–11.

10. Roberts, B.K., 'Village plans in County Durham: a preliminary statement', *Med. Arch.*, XVI, 1972, 44-5.

11. Harvey, P.D.A., *A Medieval Oxfordshire Village: Cuxham 1240-1400*, Oxford, 1965, 25-9.

12. Thorpe, H., 'The green villages of County Durham', *Trans. Institute of British Geographers*, 15, 1951, 155-80.

13. Roberts, 'Village plans in County Durham'; and Sheppard, J.A., 'Metrological analysis of regular village plans in Yorkshire', *Agricultural Hist. Rev.*, 22, 1974, 118-35.

14. Steane, J.M., *The Northamptonshire Landscape*, London, 1974, 66-7.

15. Taylor, C.C., 'Polyfocal settlement and the English village', *Med. Arch.*, XXI, 1977, 189-93.

16. Beresford, M.W. and Hurst, J.G., 'Wharram Percy: a case study in microtopography' in Sawyer, P.H. (ed.), *Medieval Settlement*, London, 1976, 114-44.

17. Addyman, P.V., 'A dark-age settlement at Maxey, Northants', *Med. Arch.*, VIII, 1964, 20-73.

18. Wade-Martins, P., 'The origins of rural settlement in East Anglia' in Fowler, P.J. (ed.), *Recent Work in Rural Archaeology*, Bradford-on-Avon, 1975, 141-6.

19. Hoskins, W.G., *The Making of the English Landscape*, Harmondsworth, 1979, 44.

20. Taylor, C.C., *Fields in the English Landscape*, London, 1975, 27.

21. Taylor, C.C., 'Roman settlements in the Nene valley; the impact of recent archaeology' in Fowler, P.J. (ed.), *Recent Work in Rural Archaeology*, Bradford-on-Avon, 1975, 116.

22. Rodwell, W., 'Relict landscapes in Essex' in Bowen, H.C. and Fowler, P.J. (eds.), *Early Land Allotment*, British Archaeological Reports 48, 1978, 95.

23. Gelling, M., *The Placenames of Berkshire*. Cambridge 1976, III, 615-34.

24. Addleshaw, G.W.O., *The Development of the Parochial System from Charlemagne to Urban II*, University of York, 1970, 13.

25. Bonney, D., 'Early boundaries in Wessex' in

Fowler, P.J. (ed.), *Archaeology and the Landscape*, London, 1972, 184-5.

26. Taylor, C.C., *Dorset*, London, 1970, 79-81.

27. Taylor, C.C. and Fowler, P.J., 'Roman fields into medieval furlongs?' in Bowen and Fowler (eds.), *Early Land Allotment*, Bristol Archaeological Reports 48, 1978, 159.

28. Beresford and Hurst, 'Wharram Percy: a case study in microtopography', 141.

29. Rowley, T. (ed.), *The Origins of Open Field Agriculture*, London, 1981, for the most recent discussion of this.

30. Baker, A.R.H. and Butlin, R.A., *Studies of Field Systems in the British Isles*, Cambridge, 1973, 655-6.

31. Thirsk, J., 'The common fields' in Hilton, R.H. (ed.), *Peasants, Knights and Heretics*, Cambridge, 1976, 19.

32. Hall, D.N., 'Modern surveys in medieval field systems', *Bedfordshire Archaeological Journal*, 7, 53-66.

33. Fowler, P.J., 'Agriculture and rural settlement' in Wilson, D.M. (ed.), *The Archaeology of Anglo-Saxon England*, London, 1976, 28-9.

34. Jones, G.R.J., 'The pre Norman field system and its implications for early territorial organisation' in Mayes, P. and Butler, L., *Sandal Castle Excavations 1964-73*, Wakefield, 1983, 70-3.

35. Hall, D.N., 'The origins of open-field agriculture – the archaeological fieldwork evidence' in Rowley, T. (ed.), *The Origins of Open Field Agriculture*, London, 1981, 35.

36. Cunliffe, B., 'Chalton, Hants; the evolution of a landscape', *Antiqs. J.*, LIII, part II, 1973, 173-90.

37. Goodall, I.H., 'Ironwork in medieval Britain. An archaeological study', PhD thesis for University of Cardiff, 1980. I have drawn heavily on this for the next five paragraphs.

38. A good contemporary illustration of a medieval plough was published by Colvin, H.M., 'A medieval drawing of a plough', *Antiquity*, 107, 1953, 165-7.

39. Gailey, A. and Fenton, A., *The Spade in Northern and Atlantic Europe*, Belfast, 1970.

40. Hassall, W.O., 'Notes on medieval spades' in Gailey and Fenton, ibid., 30-5.

41. Hoskins, W.G. and Stamp, L.D., *The Common Lands of England and Wales*, London, 1963, 4.

42. Ibid., 6.

43. Ford, W.J., 'Some settlement patterns in the central region of the Warwickshire Avon' in Sawyer, P.H., *Medieval Settlement*, London, 1976, 280.

44. Darby, H.C., *The Medieval Fenland*, Newton Abbot, 1974, 71.

45. I owe this example to my student A. McDonald

of Wolfson College, Oxford.

46. Rackham, O., *Ancient Woodland*, London, 1980, 126.

47. Rackham, O., *Trees and Woodland in the British Landscape*, London, 1976, 23.

48. *Victoria County History, Oxfordshire*, V, 221.

49. Hooper, M.D., 'A History', in Steele, R.C. and Welch, R.C., *Monks Wood, a Nature Reserve Record*, Nature Conservancy, Huntingdon, 1973, 22-35.

50. Rackham, O. (ed.), *Hayley Wood. Its History and Ecology*, Cambridgeshire and Isle of Ely Naturalists Trust, 1975.

51. Rackham, *Ancient Woodland*, Figs. 3.1, 3.2, 3.3.

52. Ibid., 50-6.

53. Bazeley, M., 'The extent of the English forest in the thirteenth century', *Trans. Roy. Hist. Soc.*, 4th ser., 4, 140-72.

54. Steane, J.M. and Bryant, G., 'Excavations at the deserted medieval settlement of Lyveden', *Journal 12* of Northampton Museum and Art Gallery, 1975, 156.

55. Thomas, K., *Man and the Natural World*, London, 1983, 273.

56. Steane, J.M., 'The medieval forests, woods and parks of Berkshire', *Arboricultural Journal*, August 1981.

57. Rackham, O., Blair, W.J. and Munby, J.T., 'The thirteenth century roofs and floor of the Blackfriars Monastery at Gloucester', *Med. Arch.*, XXII, 105-22.

58. Rackham, O., 'Grundle House: on the quantities of timber in certain East Anglian buildings in relation to local supplies', *Vernac. Archit.*, 3, 1978, 3-8.

59. Cantor, L.M. and Hatherly, J., 'The medieval parks of England', *Geography*, vol. 64, part 2, April 1979, 71-85.

60. Steane, J.M., 'The medieval parks of Northamptonshire', *Northants Past and Present*, V, 1975, 211-33.

61. Hodgen, M.T., 'Domesday watermills', *Antiquity*, XIII, 1939, 261-79.

62. A vivid example of this was pointed out to me at Grove, Bedfordshire by Evelyn Baker.

63. *Current Archaeology*, 29, 1971, 166-7.

64. Williamson, K., 'Horizontal water mills of the Faeroe Islands', *Antiquity*, 78, 1946, 83-91.

65. Laing, L., *Orkney and Shetland – an Archaeological Guide*, Newton Abbot, 1974, 212-13. Recent work on Irish mills in tree-ring studies by Baillie does not support a Norse derivation for them (inf. from L. Alcock).

66. Bedwin, O., 'The excavation of Batsford Mill, Warbleton, East Sussex, 1978', *Med. Arch.*, XXIV, 1980, 187-201.

67. Gimpel, J., *The Medieval Machine*, London, 1977, 23.

68. Slicker van Bath, B.H., *Agrarian History of Western Europe AD 500-1850*, London, 1963, 185.

69. Wailes, R., 'A note on windmills' in Singer, C. and Holmyard, E.J. *et al.*, *History of Technology*, II, Oxford, 1957, 623-8.

70. Steane, J.M., *The Northamptonshire Landscape*, London, 1974, 114-15.

71. Roberts, B.K. 'Medieval fishponds', *The Amateur Historian*, 7, 4, 1966, 119-26.

72. Hickling, C.F., 'Prior More's fishponds', *Med. Arch.*, XV, 1971, 118-23.

73. Steane, J.M., 'Medieval fishponds of Northamptonshire', *Northants Past and Present*, IV, 1970-1, 299-309.

74. Lambert, J.M. et al., *The Making of the Broads*, Royal Geographical Society Research Series No. 3, 1960, esp. 63-106.

75. Lamb, H.H., 'The early medieval warm epoch and its sequel', *Palaeogeography, Palaeoclimatology, Palaeoecology* 1, 1965, 13-37.

76. Addyman, P.V., Hood, J.S.R., Kenward, H.K., MacGregor, A. and Williams, D., 'Palaeoclimate in urban environmental archaeology at York, England: problems and potential', *World Archaeology*, 8, 2, 220-33.

77. Beresford, G., *The Medieval Clayland Village. Excavations at Goltho and Barton Blount*, Soc. for Med. Arch. Monograph series 6, London, 1975, believes in the archaeological evidence for deterioration of climate.

78. Radley, J., 'Economic aspects of Anglo-Danish York', *Med. Arch.*, XV, 1971, 55-7. Also MacGregor, A., 'Bone skates: A review of the evidence', *Arch. J.*, 133, 1976, 57-74.

79. Thompson, F.H. (ed.), *Archaeology and Coastal Change*, Society of Antiquaries, London, 1980.

80. Scarfe, N., *The Suffolk Landscape*, London, 1972, 207-8.

81. Boon, G.C., 'Caerleon and the Gwent levels in early historic times' in Thompson, F.H., (ed.), *Archaeology and Coastal Change*, Society of Antiquaries, London, 24-36.

82. Cunliffe, B.W., 'The evolution of Romney Marsh. A preliminary statement' in Thompson (ed.), ibid., 37-55.

83. Darby, H.C., *The Medieval Fenland*, Newton Abbot, 1974, 43-60.

84. Shrewsbury, J.F.D., *A History of Bubonic Plague in the British Isles*, Cambridge, 1970; and Turner, D., *The Black Death*, Harlow, 1982.

85. Rackham, J., 'Rattus rattus: the introduction of the black rat into Britain', *Antiquity*, LIII, no. 208, July 1979, 112-120. Donaldson, A.M. *et al.*, 'A dinner in the Great Hall, Barnard Castle. Report on the contents of a fifteenth century drain', *J.B.A.A.*, CXXXIII, 1980, 92.

86. Stow, J., *Survey of London*, Everyman edn, London, 1945, 384-5.

87. Spencer, B.W., *Chaucer's London*, Museum of London, 1972, Plate 15.
88. Shrewsbury, *A History of Bubonic Plague*, 124-5.
89. Slack, P.A.'s review of Shrewsbury's book in *English Hist. Review*, LXXXVII, 1972, 112-15. I owe this reference to John Blair.
90. Hyde, B., 'The Winchester Manors of Witney and Adderbury, Oxfordshire, in the later Middle Ages', Oxford B. Litt. thesis 1954.
91. Beresford and St. Joseph, *Medieval England. An Aerial Survey*, 117-36.
92. Beresford, M.W., *The Lost Villages of England*, London, 1965, 171.
93. Harvey, J., *The Perpendicular Style*, London, 1978, 75.
94. Huizinga, J., *The Waning of the Middle Ages*, London, 1950, Chapter 1, 'The Vision of Death', 124-35.

6

HOUSING

1. The Techniques of Rural Archaeology

Our understanding of the physical remains of medieval villages has increased enormously over the last 20 years owing to improved techniques of excavation. It is now realised that medieval village sites are very complex. In the first place the houses are likely to have been rebuilt or substantially repaired at least once every generation over the hundreds of years of the life of the village. It may be that this was intentional, that in each generation the son taking over from his father would build anew. An added complication is that during this time the alignment of the houses was often changed – even to the extent of moving them round 90° on the same site. Moreover, the centre of gravity of the settlement might well have altered. The likely causes for settlement 'shift' have already been mentioned (p. 149) and it adds one more complication to the problem of understanding medieval villages. Finally, medieval peasant houses have been found to be so insubstantial, their foundations were so flimsy and the floors were kept so remarkably clean by their occupants, that frequently there is little left to excavate. Only a very thin level of occupation is all that has survived. A sequence of up to ten periods might be represented by only 30 cm of deposit.

Obviously special methods have had to be developed to deal with these problems. In particular what is called 'open area' excavation is now recognised as being the only way of gaining a complete picture. This means the large-scale stripping of the remains of each period in its entirety before going down to the next level. The technique was first developed in Denmark but the English site which has led

the way in developing 'open area' excavation is the deserted village on the chalk uplands of the North Riding in Yorkshire, Wharram Percy.[1] Here since 1952 the Deserted Medieval Village Research Group has been engaged in excavations.[2] Aerial photographs and ground observations very clearly pinpointed house-sites, roads and field systems. First the area to be excavated was divided into 1.52 m squares, and a contour survey was made. The turf was then stripped and the soil removed to expose a rubbly level. This is material from the collapsed walls of the buildings. In the second stage, all the small stones which were obviously not part of walls were removed, leaving in place all stones larger than 15 cm across. These might be parts of walls in situ or they might be simply tumble or odd boulders lying about. They had to be recorded in detail so that if it was found at a later stage that they had been removed in error, the missing parts could be reconstructed. Gradually the tumble was then removed to expose the wall lines underneath. It became apparent at this stage at Wharram Percy that there was a complex series of buildings, and that the earlier ones were often on different alignments. As the buildings of each period were recorded they were removed exposing the earlier remains beneath. These were built of timber, and the post-holes and slots, even more difficult to trace than the flimsy stone walls, could only be seen when the whole site was cleared to this level. Baulks were left which recorded sections across the site at each level. When these were recorded they were removed to expose the whole level. The next level was then peeled off leaving again a baulk exposing the section. In this way it was possible to make a vertical record of the stratigraphy which did not get in the way of the main purpose which was to expose a large area, a level at a time. The final technique used was to record the finds. To begin with this was done by plotting all the finds three dimensionally but it was subsequently realised that it was only necessary for small finds and significant potsherds to be bagged according to the level and 1.52 m grid square. Only the datable finds are fully recorded three dimensionally.

2. Highland Housing

The techniques tried out at Wharram Percy have now been applied in a series of excavations of peasant housing in different parts of England and Wales. On the granite uplands towards the eastern side of Dartmoor (Devon), Mrs Minter recovered the plans of three medieval settlements at Hound Tor, Hutholes and Dinna Clerks (Devon).[3] Hound Tor village and its fields lie on a gentle north-eastern facing slope about 350 m above sea level. The settlement is protected by Hound Tor Down, rising 45.7 m above the house sites. There are few trees at this altitude, only thorns, holly and a group of stunted oaks; the surrounding moorland is mainly covered with grass, as well as some heather, brambles, gorse and blewberry. The medieval fields of irregular size and shape extend along the 1,200 ft (366 m) contour; beyond them is open moorland.

The haphazard layout of clustered houses, barns and little gardens, all lying within a single enclosure, differs from the type of settlement found elsewhere in the highland zone of south-west England and is more closely related to prehistoric settlements such as Chysauster, (Cornwall). The buildings date from two periods. In the first, the early medieval, the houses were built of turf, and probably needed to be replaced or extensively repaired by each succeeding generation. The turf with a strong matt of grass and roots was carefully selected and after being trimmed, the sods were cut and lifted. The blocks were usually 90 cm long and 60 cm wide. Such a material is reasonably durable if protected from undue saturation, but the interior surfaces need to be stabilised by wattles to prevent the turf crumbling away when dry. The position of 1.2 m-thick walls of these earlier houses of Hound Tor was easily visible because the rows of stake-holes for the wattles showed up as dark brown or black pockets in the light buff-coloured gravel or 'growan'. The stake-holes were connected with the hard edges of floors; these, together with hearths and the signs of heavy wear of the floors, showed that turf houses lay under stone-walled ones.

In the second period, c. 1250–1350, stone buildings replaced the turf structures. There were three types of building – houses, barns and corn-drying kilns. The homesteads were long-houses, long rectangular buildings, planned so that men and beasts could live at opposing ends of the same building under a single roof, sharing a common doorway in a lateral wall. The houses were usually built on a slope and the byre with its central stone-paved drain was on the lower side. The walls of these long-houses were built of roughly coursed, undressed and weathered granite blocks, gathered from the skitter slopes and some were cleared from arable field surfaces. The positions of doorways were clearly marked in the higher standing walls; post-holes show that they were hung from wooden frames. Some of the houses had porches, usually added as an afterthought. The living rooms were heated from central hearths, defined by granite hearth-stones, and cooking-pits were found in four of the houses; some of the houses had wattle and daub chimney hoods. The cows were tethered to timber posts and the byres were equipped with wooden mangers. It is likely that a thin layer of hardened manure and straw was allowed to accumulate over the drain cover to act as a filter, down to which level the byre was periodically cleared out.

The surviving houses, both those excavated and those still standing, of this long-house type are largely confined to the Highland zones of the country, to Devon, Wales and the north-western counties, but it is suggested that the type was formerly more widespread at least in the north. In west Yorkshire the Court Rolls of the manors of Bradford and Wakefield have been trawled for references to rural peasant dwellings. When in 1316 it was alleged

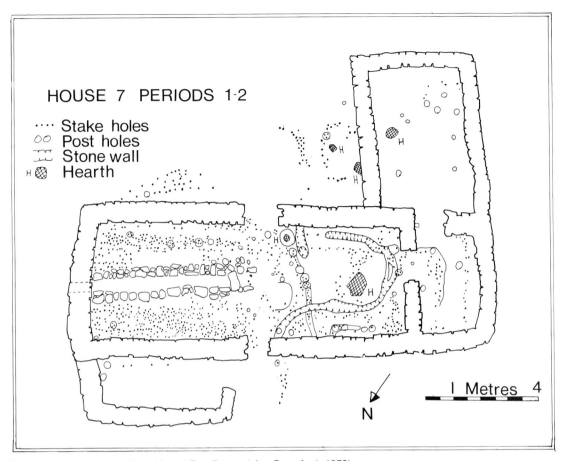

Figure 6.1: House Plans from Hound Tor, Devon (after Beresford, 1979)

that William de Thurgerland 'opened the door of Peter de Grene and stole a horse and a cow' it certainly seems likely that a long-house is being referred to. Another possibility is that it was an example of the so-called laithe house where there was separate access from house to byre, although the earliest examples of this plan-form date from *c.* 1650.

The barns at Hound Tor were rectangular structures usually smaller than the homesteads but with the same rounded corners which indicate that the roofing was hipped in shape. The roof cladding of both the smaller houses and barns is likely to have consisted of turves, straw, heather or rushes which were heaped on top of rafters laid like joists horizontally from wall to wall. The thatch was held in position by a network of ropes of heather or straw weighted down by stones. Such primitive roof

structures were still in use in Oxfordshire in the nineteenth century and examples of 'bundle thatch' roofs can be seen at Cogges Manor Farm, Watlington and Stanton St John.

Several barns in these settlements on Dartmoor are located within the central farm complex; in parts of Northern England such as the West Riding of Yorkshire dispersed barns are found isolated in the field-system. Their function was to shelter cattle and sheep during the winter months. They served as collecting places for valuable animal manure, the barns often being sited so it could be cast downhill on to the fields. About 1212 Alan, son of Nicholas de Shippen, granted Pontefract Priory the right to pasture 200 sheep in Shippen, together with a barn for keeping the sheep, but specifying that 'the dung shall remain to me and my heirs'. These barns

188   HOUSING

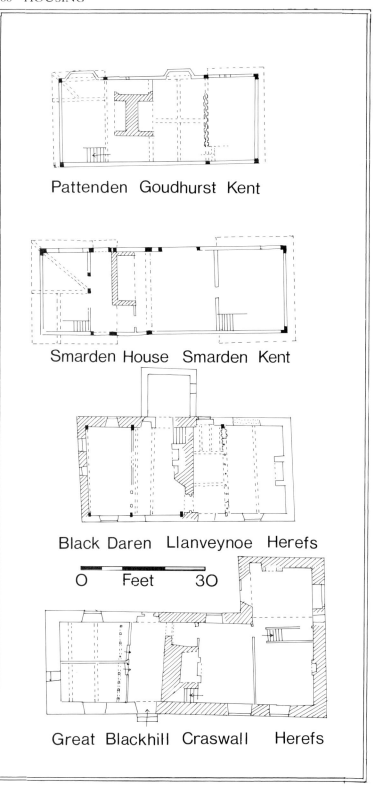

Figure 6.2: Medieval House Plans (after Smith, 1970)

Pattenden Goudhurst Kent

Smarden House Smarden Kent

Black Daren Llanveynoe Herefs

O   Feet   3O

Great Blackhill Craswall   Herefs

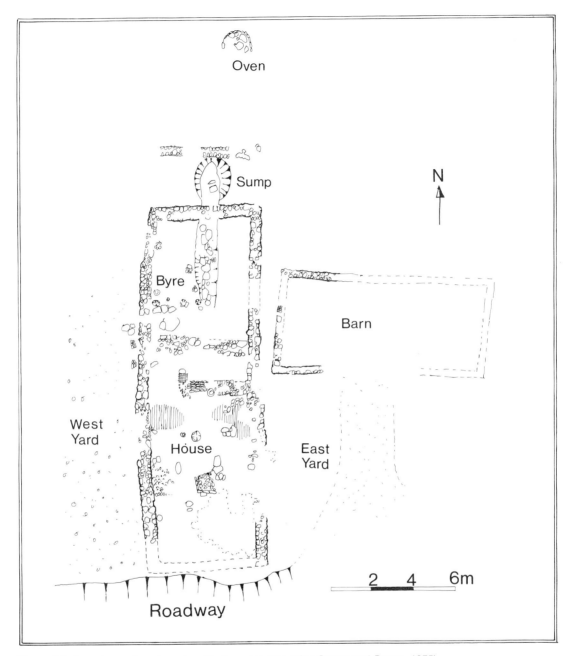

Figure 6.3: Long-house from Lyveden, Northamptonshire (after Steane and Bryant, 1975)

rarely, if ever, survive but can be located on hill slopes by their foundations, footings and fragments of stone slates or pottery tiles with which they were roofed.

3. Lowland Village Houses: Plans

If we now turn to the Lowland zone of medieval England interesting variations of peasant housing are met with. These are partly to be explained in terms of availability of building materials and are partly the result of different economic circumstances.

The plans of medieval peasant houses have been divided in a recent attempt at synthesis into three types.[4] There was first the peasant cot, a small one-roomed house measuring about 5 m x 3.5 m; here lived the cottar or bordar who had no land of his own and who was at the lower end of the social scale in the countryside. The medieval villein or more prosperous peasant would have lived in a long-house which had accommodation for men and animals under the same roof. In the upper or living end was the hearth and here in one or two rooms the peasant and his family would live. Access was by means of two opposed doors connected by a cross passage which would give an entrance into the byre or lower end. Here there was stalling for animals as well as an open paved drain leading off liquid manure outside. These long-houses varied in size up to 15 m in length. They could be as long as 25 or 30 m. The farm was the third type of peasant house (Figure 5.3).[5] Here the byre or the barn was in a separate building and was placed at right angles to the farmhouse forming two sides of a rectangular, sometimes stone-paved courtyard. The development had social as well as economic reasons. These farms are clearly the homes of yeoman farmers who were prospering and acquiring their freeholds in the Later Middle Ages.

4. Lowland Houses: Walling

The early medieval houses excavated in the Lowland zone are nearly always built of timber. Those examined by Beresford at Goltho (Lincs.) and Barton Blount (Derbyshire) showed up as lines of post-holes and timber slots.[6] Little survived of the walls: they were of clay tempered with chopped straw, between 38 to 46 cm thick, their strength dependent on studs of unsawn timber, set in the ground. Predominantly dry climatic conditions account for the lack of drainage channels and the absence of cobbled thresholds and paths. During the next period the houses, which were rebuilt every 20 years or so, were located by spreads of occupation material and by wear of floors. A change of construction

methods had occurred. Now timber studs were placed on the ground surface and were not buried on the ground surface or fitted into slots. This probably prolonged the life of the posts. Wetter conditions are implied by the eaves trenches, which surrounded the houses, and cobbling surfacing the thresholds. In the third and final phase, which began in the mid-thirteenth century, the posts were set on a padstone foundation. Stone was apparently so scarce that padstones were used in preference to dwarf stone walls used in other parts of the country.

A changeover from turf, clay or timber to stone-walled buildings occurred all over the country during the late twelfth and early thirteenth centuries. It seems to have begun in the south and south-west and then later in the thirteenth century it spread to the north. The reasons may be connected with a shortage of timber arising out of the fact that with the increase of population and the consequent large-scale clearances, timber became scarcer. In East Anglia, for instance, stone was scarcer than timber so half-timbered buildings continued to be built. In the undulating fields of the Midlands as at Faxton[7] and Lyveden (Northants.), where limestones and sandstones are masked with boulder clay, the glacial erratics were gathered and built into the foundations and dwarf walls. These were capped with the upper structures of cob, a mixture of clay, straw and dung, which would be perfectly durable provided it was 'well capped and shod'. At times worked stone was robbed from ecclesiastical or manorial buildings. This has happened at Wharram Percy (North Yorks.), where peasants have also used rough natural chalk quarried from their tofts or backyards.

5. Peasant Housing: Heating and Flooring

Among the structural characteristics of medieval peasant houses was the use of wattle and daub for infilling between the timber uprights. Sometimes fragments of fire-hardened daub are found where the house has burned down. The entrances are sometimes marked by thresholds or the presence of paving outside the doorway. Large stones with socket holes to

Plate 6.1: Meare, Somerset. This fourteenth-century fisherman's house was built on the rim of a lake whose circumference in the Middle Ages was 8 km; it was drained in the late eighteenth century. The house was used for salting and storing fish caught in the mere. There were work rooms on the ground floor; access to the living rooms on the first floor was by means of an outer staircase (Photo: J.M. Steane)

take the door pivot are found *in situ*. Often hinges, latches, keys and padlocks are picked up on the sites of peasant houses indicating that they had solid doors. Window glass never occurs and such openings as there were for light and air were probably shutters hinged on iron pivots. Sometimes the presence of large numbers of nails near an entrance suggests a collapsed porch or perhaps simply a rotted door. The central hearth was found in houses – both great and small – throughout the medieval period. At Lyveden (Northants.), in one late medieval long-house, three hearths were found in different parts of the living end (Figure 6.3).[8] The first had simply been lit directly on the floor producing a burned area; it had been replaced by a pitched stone oval-shaped one; during the final stages of occupation in the late fifteenth century this had in turn been superseded by a rectangular one made of clay covered with tiles in a setting of brick. Information about fuel used is available if the charcoal fragments are studied. The cell structure of carbonised wood is preserved in amazing detail and under low-power magnification the species can usually be identified. At Lyveden, again, oak, hazel, field maple and hawthorn were found to have been used as fuels. Floors of peasant houses were either of clay, stone, cobbles or covered with stone flags. In many, constant sweeping by medieval

housewives has brushed away the floor surfaces – so that this has produced a U-shaped depression. It does away with the old view that the peasants lived in dirt and squalor and incidentally accounts for the problem which afflicts archaeologists, the scantiness of depth of deposit on medieval house sites. Byres, where animals were stalled, frequently have stone paved drains.

6. Peasant Housing: Roofing

If it is difficult to reconstruct the doors and windows of medieval peasant houses in the imagination, it is well nigh impossible to restructure the roofs. From the archaeological remains sometimes the presence of padstones, or maybe sloping post-holes in the wall footings, suggest that here there were crucks.[9] Crucks were long curved timbers cut from the halves of a tree of suitable shape. They were framed together in pairs and were joined together by collars or tie beams using wooden pegs or tree-nails. They rose from ground level to support the horizontal beams or purlins on which the rafters rested. Medieval building agreements recorded in Worcestershire confirm that most peasant houses in the West Midlands involved crucks in their construction.[10] The tenants of one-bay houses were at the foot of the social ladder but such

Plate 6.2: Meare, Somerset. The summer house of the abbots of Glastonbury. An L-shaped house, entered through a projecting porch with a first-floor hall with three large pointed (blocked) windows. At the rear (to the left) another large upper room with its original fireplace and substantial chimney stack. Sited on the edge of the mere, the drained fields of which can be seen in the background (Photo: J.M. Steane)

cruck dwellings were more often two or three bays in length and three- to five-bay houses were occupied by richer peasants.

Such substantial houses have survived in considerable numbers. The latest count of cruck buildings is over 2,000, most of which are in the north and west – there are none in the south-east – and many now serve as farm buildings. It is very unlikely that most peasant houses had as good carpentered roofs even as these rather primitive buildings. If they had, they would surely have lasted more than a generation. Flimsy timbers resting on ridge poles and covered with thatch or turves are likely to have been almost universal. Rarely are stone slates found, and only a few tiles. Perhaps these were used around smoke louvres to diminish fire risks. Ridgetiles may have been used to make the apex of the roof watertight.

It is unreal to consider the peasant house separately from farming, its economic base. The Court Roll and other documentary evidence suggests that in the West Midlands during the fifteenth century there was specialisation in pasture farming by some peasants, and that flocks and herds carried by many tenements were larger in 1500 than they had been in 1400. The main reason was the increased local demand for wool and meat. Wool production had already fuelled the cloth industry of the towns in the area and the demand was now spreading out into the countryside. An increased market for meat tempted peasants to overstock their animals on common land. The main stimulus for these two developments was the changed condition of the land market after the Black Death.

An abundance of land was thrown onto the market. Lords, faced with an economic crisis as a result of demographic decline, were forced to make concessions to find tenants for vacant holdings. As the climate deteriorated so peasants brought their cattle indoors into the longhouses. The cruck-framed multi-bayed longhouses are the archaeological expression of these three economic tendencies – a rise in pastoral farming, a more prosperous peasantry, the contracting size of rural settlements.

Similar tangible evidence for a more effective exploitation by the peasantry of pastoral farming is found in eastern England. A notable feature of the clayland villages of both Goltho and Barton Blount was the provision, during the fourteenth and fifteenth centuries, of *crewyards*, near the sites of peasant houses.[11] The position of these are shown in aerial photographs as hollows in the ground; they are caused by the treading of cattle penned up within them and the subsequent removal of manure. They seem to be a peculiarity of the eastern part of the country, and are another indicator of the change to pastoral farming as the climate deteriorated. Many of the settlements on the more difficult soils of eastern and central England were deserted; many more contracted in size; by the end of the Middle Ages, for instance, villages on the claylands within a 14.5 km radius of Goltho had been abandoned. What was disaster for some was an opportunity for others. Some farmers survived by turning over to livestock. The somewhat drier eastern arable counties produced more straw enabling cattle to lie out in open yards during the winter. In the western and northern areas where the rainfall is higher and straw less plentiful they were brought indoors as we have noticed. It is just possible that the strange distribution of cruck-framed houses which seems to defy explanation may be connected with this divide in farming techniques between western and eastern England. Cruck-framing perhaps provided the solution to housing men and animals under the same roof.

So far in our consideration of 'peasant' houses we have been relying entirely on the evidence of 'below-ground' archaeology. Towards the end of the Middle Ages between *c.* 1430 and 1530, and particularly in well wooded south-east England, vernacular houses of sufficient substance to have survived, appear in the countryside in large numbers (Figure 6.2).[12] They were timber framed, with jettied wings (projecting upper storeys) and close studding (walling with closely set timber uprights) and are found in Essex, Kent, Suffolk, Sussex and Surrey. The sheer numbers of such houses make it certain that they were the homes of peasants. They vary greatly in size from two to six rooms and this implies a considerable differentiation of wealth among the peasantry of south-east England. Most of them had a central lofty open hall with two, two-storeyed ends. The chief peculiarity about them was that by the fifteenth century they had become completely detached from their farm buildings, in itself a sign of increasing prosperity.

The multiplicity of rooms in such houses is paralleled from documentary sources referring to houses in the West Midlands. Here in the fifteenth century a house might well be divided on the death of a peasant between his daughter, who took the hall and the lower rooms, and his widow who was allotted the upper rooms. A specific mention of an upper storey is made in the case of the old man who handed over his tenement to his heir but retained 'a room over the hall' and free access to it. These upper rooms may have been more often used for storing bulky goods than housing elderly relatives.

In the south-west, Wales and the north, the earliest houses which have survived and which date from the Late Middle Ages are derivatives from the long-house where animals and men were housed under the same roof. Several, reconstructed, can be seen at St Fagan's Museum, Cardiff. The cross passage here, instead of leading into the pantry and buttery as was usual in the economically more advanced south-east, was used for access by the cattle to the byre, and for feeding the cattle once they were tethered. Its presence has often been detected even after the byre has been transformed into a parlour or kitchen as the house was upgraded during the first 'Great Rebuilding' (*c.* 1540-1640). In particular the beam containing a number of slots designed to take the tethering posts has remained in a number of such long-houses. Otherwise these long-houses usually conceal their diagnostic features. Open hearths have been replaced by chimney stacks, either inserted centrally or at the gable-end; and the halls have been split at first-floor level, making them warmer and more comfortable with greater privacy. Differences in their size and plan-form again probably reflected social or economic gradations among men. In the East Riding manor of Settrington, for instance, a survey made in 1600 describes the housing of husbandmen, grassmen and cottagers, in descending order of prosperity; four-bay houses for husbandmen, three-bay houses for grassmen, and so on. One can sympathise with the puzzlement of Celia Fiennes on her travels in Kent in the late seventeenth century when she remarked on the 'old timber houses' of Goudhurst as 'occupied by a sort of yeomanly gentry'.

7. *Rural Manor Houses*

So far we have only studied the remains of houses providing shelter for people in the lower levels of medieval society and have had to rely almost entirely on the evidence of below-ground archaeology. Most studies of medieval domestic architecture inevitably concentrate on the stone-built remains of the houses of the upper social strata.[13] Although these rarely survive intact, and are frequently encumbered with later additions, their features can still be recognised in above-ground archaeological investigations. In plan they were collections of buildings, groups of halls, chambers, wardrobes, kitchens, brewhouses, all separately roofed, loosely linked together, of different dates, and added to when required. The fact that most of these houses are stone-built should not blind us to the fact that very many of the more important houses were constructed in timber, and these have survived less well.

At Goltho (Lincs.), Beresford found a series of Saxon and Norman halls on the manor site.[14] During the late Saxon period the hall was defined by post-pits about 1.52 m wide and 90 cm deep. It had a single aisle on the south and there were partitions between the aisles forming small chambers at the side of the hall. At the west end was the bower or sleeping quarters, and hall with bower occupied one side of a courtyard which was surrounded by other ancillary buildings. There was apparently a steward's house to the east, marked by two parallel lines of post-pits, indicating a quasi-aisled structure. This complex was surrounded by a defensive work, enclosing a larger area than the later earthwork castle. It was replaced *c.* 1100 by a small but strongly entrenched earthwork castle built by the Kyme family. The banks, 15-18 m wide, were so thick that they left a space 16.8 m wide, only just wide enough for a single hall with a small yard in front of it. It was twice built on the same foundations and, during its later phase, was divided into three rooms, a parlour, a hall and a kitchen with a pantry and garderobe against the south wall. Around the mid-twelfth century, when presumably the needs of security were less pressing, the top of the earthen banks was levelled and thrown into the centre of the earthwork. A new hall, a timber-aisled structure, partitioned at both upper and lower ends to form two small chambers, was built. It was linked by a covered passage to a detached bower close to the south-east of the hall. Little pottery or domestic debris was found associated with this phase of the building, and it seems that the

Kyme family removed themselves to a new site – 1.2 km to the south. Possibly they wished to distance themselves from the peasant houses of the settlement, possibly they just required more room than could be found on the top of a truncated Norman ringwork.

It seems clear from surviving examples that by the twelfth century there were three main types of hall in larger medieval houses.[15] The aisle-less *ground-floor hall* was heated by a central hearth and this mode of heating demanded a lofty roof for the escape of smoke; a low ceiling would have been a fire risk. The central hearth very rarely survives to the present day since it has nearly always been replaced by a chimneyed fireplace. Archaeology has established that it was usually made of pitched stone (stones set on edge) or was tiled. Smoke rising from it would have encrusted the timbers above it with soot. Frequently such smoke-blackened timbers in a roof space, subsequently floored, betray the fact that the house at an earlier stage in its history had such an open hall. Beyond the hearth was the 'upper' end of the hall where there was a high table for the lord or the owner, perhaps placed on a dais as still happens in college halls. Substantial masonry to support such a dais still survives in Henry III's great hall at Winchester Castle. The lower end of the hall was for the servants, and doors led into the service apartments, a buttery for storing drinks, and a pantry for storing bread and table utensils. Between them was a passage leading to the kitchen which tended to be an isolated building, at any rate until the fifteenth century, standing by itself as a precaution against fire (see p. 265).

The second type of hall followed the Saxon timber tradition, the *barn-like hall* with two rows of posts or arcades forming nave and aisles. The twelfth-century hall in the Bishop's Palace at Hereford has the remains of such a structure embedded in it. A number of medieval barns, such as Great Coxwell (Oxon.), give one a very good impression of this type of building. The subdivision into nave and aisles was an attractive structural proposition when long roof timbers were not available. Gradually carpenters experimented to get rid of the obstructive posts and the result, as we shall see, was a series of ingenious roofs such

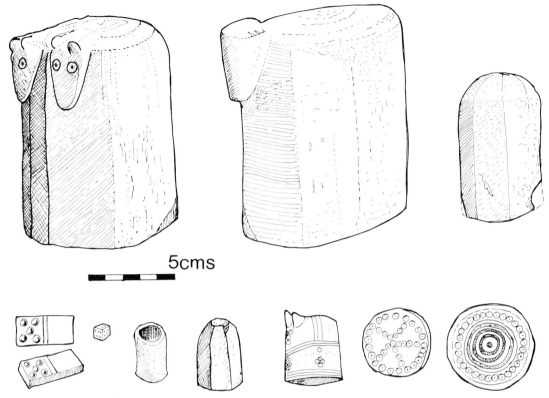

Figure 6.4: Games – Chessmen and Dice from Museum of Oxford and Dorchester Museum

as the arch-braced collar beam and the hammer beam. At times the service end retained its posts even when the rest of the hall was roofed in the span; such a roof is at the early fourteenth-century hall at the Abbey, Sutton Courtenay, (Oxon.), where the posts were kept because they were serving as the screen's divisions and were known as 'spere trusses'.

A third type of hall found in the twelfth century was the '*first-floor hall*'. (Plate 6.2) These were more defensible if they were built on a stone basement which was often vaulted and lit by narrow splayed loops. A classic instance is the manor house at Boothby Pagnell (Lincs.). These upper halls were heated normally by wall fireplaces, although the tradition of the central fireplace was maintained when the hall was lofty enough as at Ludlow (Shropshire), and was even used at the end of the Middle Ages at Hampton Court, (Middlesex).

The second structural element of these hall-houses was the series of chambers which could be attached to one or both ends of the hall, usually in the form of a two-storey chamber-block roofed at right angles to the hall.[16] The principal chamber was generally on the first floor and was often referred to as the *solar*. Access to it could be either by way of an internal stair rising from a position near the hall entrance or by an external staircase. It offered comparatively luxurious accommodation, being heated by a large fireplace with perhaps a projecting stone hood on carved corbels, and was lit by windows as large as possible with stone window seats. Finally, it was provided with a garderobe. The lower chambers in these blocks offered inferior accommodation, with no separate external access, no fireplace and no garderobe. They were probably used for storage if they were sited under first-floor halls, or for servants' quarters.

These arrangements in effect provided self-sufficient accommodation for the lord and his family in the chamber-block. The question arises, what was the function of the hall? To begin with, it is likely that the hall would have provided shelter and warmth for the head of the household and his family. The upper and lower end mirrored the hierarchical state of medieval society, just as the chancel and nave separated priest from people in parish churches. Its size and magnificence reflected the social status of its owner. There seems little doubt that in palaces and castles the function of the hall became more and more that of a ceremonial chamber, a place where courts were held and accounting took place, the necessary background to the pomp and state dear to the medieval nobility.

8. The Evolution of Timber Roof Structures (Figure 6.5)

Often the part of the house which has been least changed is the timber framework supporting the roof. One has to climb into the loft, armed with torch and tape-measure, to study the remains of medieval roof construction. The earliest and simplest type of roof which has survived from the thirteenth century was not divided into bays. It simply consisted of pairs of rafters each joined by means of a lap-joint to a cross piece or collar creating the coupled-rafter roof (Plate 7.9). Sometimes a scissors-type of cross bracing was used. The rafters were held in precarious place by the battens and roof covering. There were in fact no longitudinal timbers in these roofs at all and clearly this gave rise to severe structural weaknesses. Racking★ was only too often the result.

Carpenters began to design various forms of roof trusses to deal with these problems.[17] One of the earliest, being used about the turn of the fourteenth century, consisted of tie beams in the centre of which were placed crown posts. These were chamfered, provided with capitals and were joined to the collar to which they were diagonally braced. They were also braced to the crown plate which ran along between the collars (it was sometimes called a collar purlin). Such crown posts were obvi-

★The collapse of a wooden structure by horizontal movement.

ously meant to be seen. They are found in large numbers in eastern and south-eastern lowland England.

Their place was taken by a development whereby carpenters divided the building into bays by cross frames. Here the main posts (in a timber-framed building) or the walls supported long timbers laid along their tops known as wall-plates. The wall-plates were fastened together at eaves level by tie beams which crossed the building transversely and formed the base for a roof truss. Tenoned into the ends of the tie beams were pairs of heavy and slightly tapering principal rafters. These were linked together by collars. All the joints were cut when the timber was green; as it seasoned they tightened with shrinkage. They were fastened together with wooden pegs – very little, if any, iron was used in early roof construction. The principal rafters were joined by horizontal longitudinal beams called purlins. These could be trenched by being borne on the backs of principal rafters. Others were 'clasped' underneath the principal rafter and on top of the collar. Others were tenoned or butt jointed into the rafters. Further strength was provided by flat curving pieces of timber connecting the principal rafters to the purlins, known as wind-braces. The common, or lesser rafters, lay in rows on top of the purlins and the wall tops and carried the roof covering.

Other forms of roof development towards the end of the Middle Ages included king posts, queen posts and arch-braced collar beams. Many medieval halls in the Pennines of West Yorkshire are of king-post construction. Here a stout post rises from the tie-beam to give direct support to the ridge of the roof; the post is tenoned into the principal rafters which rise on either side. With queen-post trusses which are found in some East Anglian buildings there are two posts rising from each tie beam and on these rest the purlins. The tie-beams are dispensed with in the open arch-braced collar trusses where arch-shaped pieces support the collar and make up impressive arch-shaped features.

The culmination of the development of medieval timbered roof structure came with the hammer beam. This was evolved to strengthen the arch-braced roof over a wide hall and it solved the problem of spanning a

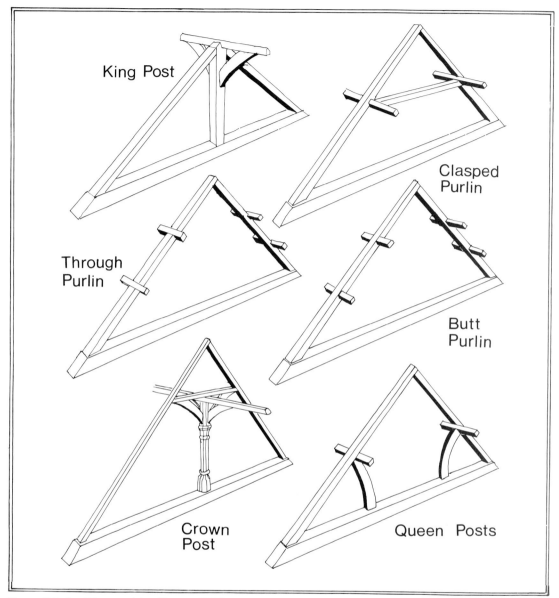

King Post

Clasped Purlin

Through Purlin

Butt Purlin

Crown Post

Queen Posts

Figure 6.5: Roof Trusses (after Mercer, 1975)

space of more than 9 m. In effect the carpenters extended the sole piece, the horizontal timber set at right angles to the wall-plate. The outer end was gripped by the rafter foot; into the inner end was socketed the arch-brace. Above the arch-brace was a pierced and traceried frame concealing the collar. Roofs thus constructed were capable of further extension and the double hammer beam was developed. Hugh Herland's superb roof at Westminster Hall of 1395-9, spanning $20\frac{1}{2}$ m combines hammer beam and arch-brace; it is the largest timber-roofed space in medieval Europe. Ultimately great pendants were added at the junction of the arch-braces and the hammer beams, while the arches themselves became wider and four-centred. Such roofs were still being constructed on the eve of the

Reformation; examples are Wolsey's at Christ-church, Oxford, and Henry VIII's at Hampton Court.

The massive timber framework of medieval roofs quite often survives. The evidence for roof coverings is more difficult to come by, because they were replaced as they wore out, burned up or fell down. Early buildings were covered with thatch; the old English word *thaec* originally meant 'the outer layer of roof'. So many structures were covered in this way that the word 'thatch' acquired its present restricted use of a covering of straw or reed. Patches of tiles, especially round inflammable areas near chimneys, might well be combined with thatch. Shingles, tiles made of oak boards, are frequently mentioned in records. In 1259 at Woodstock we can infer that they were rectangular in shape because men were 'sawing blocks of wood (*gobones*) to make from them shingles (*cendulas*) for the covering of buildings'. They have also been found in excavations of Viking age date at Winchester and they figure on hogs back representations of Viking houses.

Tiles and slate were certainly being used more frequently in the thirteenth century. Tiles were rectangular, with one or two peg

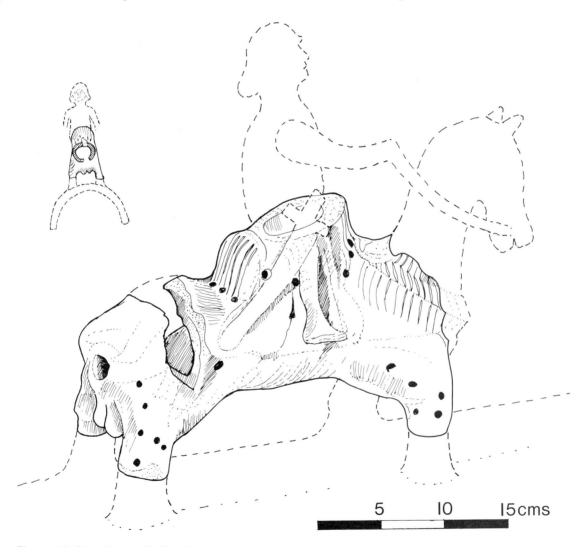

Figure 6.6: Ridgetile from Bedford Museum

holes, sometimes nibbed and occasionally painted with white slip. Medieval roofs were given a picturesque appearance by the presence of decorative ridgetiles, finials and louvres. Earlier types of ridgetiles had hand-moulded crests with low peaks or pyramids, later ones had elaborate coxcomb crestings cut by a knife. They could be covered with slip and coated with green glaze. Ceramic finials and ventilators were moulded into figures of kings, horsemen or animals (Figure 6.6).

Another form of roof covering which could be brought considerable distances was stone slates. Swithland slate, 9.7 km north-east of Leicester in the Charnwood area, was the source of most of the roofing material found at the Austin Friars, Leicester. They were basically rectangular in shape but also long, noticeably narrow slates and fish scale-shaped slates were found. The famous quarries of Collyweston in Northamptonshire were already providing 'sclatestone' in quantity in the fourteenth century; 9,500 stone slates for Rockingham Castle in 1375 at 85s per thousand. There was also a flourishing coastal trade in blue schist slates from Devon and Cornwall. They were usually less than 6 mm thick compared with the 1.25 – 2.54 cm of Cotswold slates. Excavated examples have been found at Corfe and Sherborne Castles (Dorset), Winchester, Southampton, Porchester Castle and Netley Abbey (Hampshire). They were widely used in Sussex. They are usually rectangular about 17.8 x 9 or 10 cm. They have a hole for fixing; a thirteenth-century example excavated at Totnes had a pine peg still attached.

9. Heating, Lighting and Flooring

The great hall, as we have seen, was often heated by a central hearth, but this method was gradually replaced by the wall fireplace which had already appeared in the Norman keeps of Colchester (Essex) (c. 1090 plus), Rochester (Kent) (1126-39) and King John's Palace, Southampton (Hants.) (c. 1150). The hearth was set back into the wall with a funnel or hood to collect the smoke. These Norman fireplaces were often headed with a semi-circular or segmental arch – and might be set in a slight projection, the walls being thickened by an external buttress. At the end of the twelfth century fireplaces with the hood projecting into the room were developed. They became the predominant type in thirteenth-century houses and castles, with pyramidal hoods, joggled lintels and corbels. Hoods or mantels of plaster were often used, and their shape can be detected in the form of a recess and holes for attachment. Angle brackets and moulded shelves, which served as stands for lights, were a feature of the second half of the fourteenth century. In the fifteenth century a plainer fireplace was favoured. Here the great oblong hood and lintel were combined and supported on curved corbels. The most popular shape however was the four-centred arch; the square frame invited carved decoration, often heraldic, in the spandrels.

The flue outlets or shafts connecting the fireplaces to the outside air at roof level received varied treatment in medieval houses.[18] Oblong vents in shallow buttresses were the earliest types of Norman chimneys and are found in the keeps of Castle Hedingham (Essex), Rochester (Kent), London and Colchester (Essex). At Canterbury (Kent), the domed chimney, on the first floor, vents horizontally through flues like small loops at the corners of the buttresses. By the mid-twelfth century the cylindrical chimney had appeared in castles such as at Framlingham (Suffolk) and the hall at Christchurch (Hants). They are found in pairs on the roof of Stokesay Castle. They were of two types – open topped, and with side vents and conical capping. In the thirteenth century chimneys of polygonal plan became common with vents in each facet of wall. The lantern form went out of fashion in the fourteenth century and was replaced by a crenellated top and often with the increase of fireplaces double chimneys appear. In the meantime lead-covered timber louvres or 'funerells', were used too as smoke ventilators, over the central hearths of medieval halls (Figures 8.2, 8.3). Octagonal shafts, long and slender, without side vents and open from the start became the familiar type of fifteenth-century chimney (Plate 6.4). The final development was the brick chimney, highly decorated with spirals and other ornaments, by the time of Henry VIII's reign (1509-47).

Plate 6.3: Constable's House, Christchurch, Hampshire. A twelfth-century first-floor hall house 20.4 x 7 m, built of rough Purbeck marble blocks. A basement and a main floor heated by a fireplace with a circular chimney-stack and lit by two-light semi-circular windows (Photo: J.M. Steane)

Figure 6.7: Artificial Lighting. 1. A pricket-type candlestick in which the end of the candle was impaled on an upright spike. 2. Candlestick containing a loop which gripped the body of the candle, fifteenth century. 3. Pricket-type iron candlestick with elaborate tripod-base. 4. Candlesticks of this type were usually reserved for the houses of the wealthy or for ecclesiastical use. 5. Multiple cresset lamp with small perforations for wicks. 6. Glass lamp found with small perforations for wicks. 6. Glass lamp found with thirteenth-century pottery. Would contain oil with a floating wick and would be suspended from the ceiling. 7. Small pottery cresset lamp, twelfth century. 8. Stone cresset lamp with handle. 1, 4, 5-8 Winchester Museum; 2,3 Museum of London

Plate 6.4: Wells, Somerset: Vicars' Close. Built for stand-ins for absent prebendaries by Bishop Ralph of Shrewsbury in 1348 – a mid-fourteenth-century planned street. Note subtle perspective effect of street which gradually decreases from north (foreground) to south. Also, this is an early experiment in an urban terrace design (Photo: J.M. Steane)

Plate 6.5: Wells, Somerset: No 22 Vicars' Close. The house is virtually intact. Note narrow flat chimney with pierced octagonal top. 'Hall' to bottom right with 'chamber' window above. To left, front door and two further slit windows. Wall gardens were added by Bishop Bubwith *c.* 1410-20) (Photo: J.M. Steane)

Artificial light was provided in medieval houses with difficulty and the traces of such attempts rarely survive. It seems that iron rings to support flares were the earliest method; these were replaced by moulded and traceried brackets with iron spikes on which candles were once fixed. Wooden beams with prickets 'on which the wax tapers should be placed' were ordered to be repaired in the king's chapel at Winchester Castle in Henry III's reign.

Candles were of several types; the best were made of wax and were highly prized. Civil servants were paid in robes, firing and candles. They were used for churches and great houses. The more common type were of tallow, made from melted-down animal fat. A third type were rushlights, made by dipping the pith of a reed in grease.

Medieval candlesticks (Figure 6.7) were either of the pricket type, in which the candle end is impaled on a vertical spike or made with a loop gripping the candle. The pricket type is usually on a tripod base. A magnificent example made of gilded copper alloy, with heraldic devices on the legs decorated with champlevé enamel in white, red and blue, was found in excavations at Grove Priory (Beds.).[19] The socketed form was more suited to the cheaper candles. Rushlight holders are quite commonly preserved in folk museums.

Other kinds of artificial lighting were the cresset lamp and lanterns. Cressets (from Old French *craisse* and ultimately from Latin *crassus* – animal fat) were bowls filled with fat or oil and a floating wick (Figure 6.7). Pottery cressets had pointed bases which fitted into wall brackets or even into earth floors. Stone cressets could have multiple circular recesses for the oil and were fitted with stone pedestals so they would stand on a shelf or table. A glass funnel-shaped cresset found at Winchester was probably suspended as is seen in medieval illustrations. Finally, iron lanterns were used with horn windows. Niches and brackets for such lamps are seen on stairways (as at Winchester College, Hants.) or at the side of doorways (at Porchester Castle, Hants.).

Our knowledge of floors in medieval domestic buildings is largely derived from excavated buildings or from documents. Very rarely do extant houses retain medieval floors;

generations of owners regarded the floors of their predecessors with distaste – fit only to be covered over. The stone floor of Boothby Pagnell Manor House (Lincs.) is an exception, which seems to be original. Otherwise earth floors were in widespread use, and surprisingly, beaten earth was sometimes used on top of wooden flooring. In 1260 Henry III instructed his bailiff 'to well earth the flooring (*planchicium*) at Havering'. In 1453 at New College, Oxford, 'a cartload of red earth for earthing (*terand*) the flore', was used on a chamber which had been boarded first. Occasionally plaster was used for floors and in 1269 Henry III instructed the sheriff 'to plaster the floor (*area*) of the queen's chamber' at Winchester Castle.

Most frequently, however, clay or gravel was used and here the custom in greater houses did not materially differ from that in peasant dwellings. The kitchen building at the Manor of the More at Rickmansworth *c.* 1300-50 was floored in successive layers of clay on yellow clay and gravel. Wharram Percy Manor House of the twelfth century had an undercroft floor of chalk, while the Manor House of Penhallam (Cornwall) had floors of clay and earth. In the hall here the dais was raised and retained by stones. Such earthen floors were covered with rushes to keep down the dust. They were the subject of Erasmus' strictures when visiting England, 'the floors are commonly of clay, strewed with rushes; under lies unmolested an ancient collection of beer, grease, fragments, bones, spittle, excrements of dogs and cats, and everything that is nasty'.

Glazed and decorated earthenware paving tiles were used from the thirteenth century onwards.[20] The idea was introduced from the continent and was used first at the Royal Palace of Clarendon *c.* 1240 (Figure 1.5). To begin with, such pavements were highly expensive but by the late thirteenth century they were being widely produced; floors were covered with them in merchants' houses in such places as Winchester and King's Lynn. Clifton House, King's Lynn, for instance, has early fourteenth-century tiled pavements covering the chamber and the hall; the tiles have been cut specially to fit round the central hearth. The Muniment Tower at New College, Oxford, has complete floors of tiles which were probably made at the Penn tileries, Buckinghamshire. Some of the same design were used to pave areas at Northolt Manor House (Middlesex). A splendid pavement, made of tiles from the Severn Valley in the second half of the fifteenth century, was found in the house built by the Bristol merchant William Canynges, and is now in the British Museum. Such pavements, however, were confined to the houses of the more prosperous upper crust of society. It is significant that in the pottery and tile-making settlement at Lyveden (Northants.), none of the buildings excavated had tiled floors. Only one had a tiled hearth; only a single fragment of incised tile was found. It seems that the tiles produced there were 'for export only'.

Wall surfaces and roof beams were also treated decoratively. They were finished off with a layer of plaster, whitewashed and then painted decorations were added. When the inserted sixteenth-century floor in the thirteenth-century hall at Cogges Manor Farm (Oxon.) was being reboarded, portions of the thick yellow plaster originally covering the wall was found. Under the floorboards one of the beams was revealed brilliantly painted in orange and yellow, picking out a floral pattern; it is likely to have come from a former screen. When the roof of Ducklington Rectory (Oxon.) was being restored, a series of reused fifteenth-century beams with painted heraldic decoration was found.[21] The heraldry suggested that they probably originated in Minster Lovell Manor House, several kilometres to the north. The paint had apparently been applied to the beams without any prior preparation of the surface except where blue paint had been laid over a white ground comprising a mixture of chalk and lead white. The range of the pigments was limited; white was a manufactured lead carbonate; black was pure carbon black, probably a ground wood charcoal. Blue was a blue dyestuff with no metallic constituent; the source was either indigo or woad. The orange-red used showed all the characterisation of red-lead. The medium was wax.

10. Furniture and Fittings

Furniture during the Middle Ages served the fundamental human needs of eating, working and repose (tables, seating and beds), and of storage (boards or shelves, chests and cupboards). A recent brilliant survey of extant medieval furniture in England, France and the Netherlands, correlated with other forms of contemporary evidence has been published.[22] Eames shows that one reason for the scarcity of surviving movable furniture is that built-in components were frequently supplied. Lockers and seats, actually attached to the fabric of the building, were particularly convenient in a mobile medieval higher society since they obviated the necessity of moving large quantities of furniture and protected property from thieves in periodically unoccupied dwellings. She adds that the style of furnishing reflected the 'estate' of the owner, his or her position in the social hierarchy. 'Estate' in fact was maintained and strengthened by such tangible and visual means. An array of silver plate on a stepped buffet, for instance, even if only temporarily displayed on a rich piece of brocade, was a vital piece of stage property to set off a lordly banquet. Similarly beds of state reflected in their relative magnificence the public position of their owners. Even the cradle of the heirs of the Dukes of Burgundy, covered in gold leaf and painted with arms and devices was designed for the display of the noble infant; a simpler lower cradle, the night cradle, was the one normally used by the baby. At the other end of the social spectrum, a peasant might occupy a chair before his own fireside in the company of his wife and children because in this context he was lord and master. The same man, however, would be allotted a form or a stool at a table below the dais in the hall of his seignorial lord.

Furniture for storage might take a fixed or movable form. Lockers were built into structures for the safe keeping of robes, plate and archives (Figure 6.9). Although very few have survived (one is in the Zouche Chapel of York Minster and another is part of the 'watching loft' of St Alban's Cathedral), it is thought that they were once common. Freestanding *armoires*, with drawers and shelves, are more frequently found; some have multiple tiers of

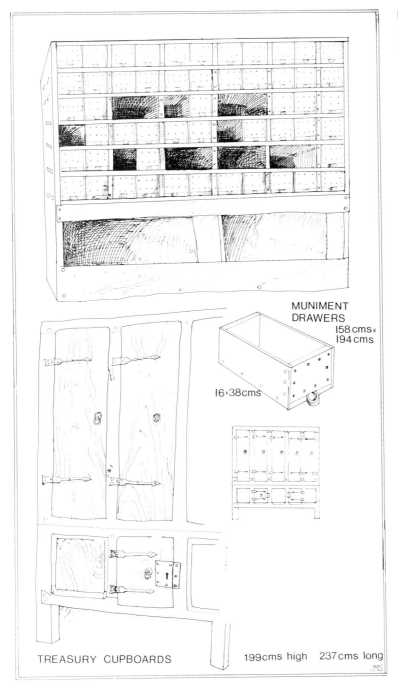

Figure 6.8: Medieval furniture from Vicars' Close, Wells, Somerset: Muniment Drawers and Treasury Cupboard

MUNIMENT DRAWERS
158 cms × 194 cms

16 × 38 cms

TREASURY CUPBOARDS   199 cms high   237 cms long

boxes like modern card-index files in which rolls were stored to permit speedy consultation. Winchester College, the Vicars' Close, Wells and St George's, Windsor have good examples, all late medieval (Figure 6.8). The *buffets, dressoirs and cupboards* were used in the hall or chamber for the display of plate or as a form of sideboard for serving wine or drink to important guests. *Chests* were of two main types: those that are fitted with flat lids and

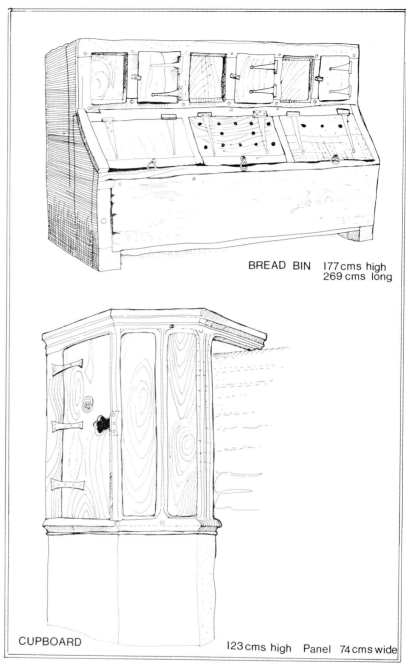

Figure 6.9: Medieval furniture from Vicars' Close, Wells, Somerset: Bread Bin and Cupboard

BREAD BIN   177 cms high
269 cms long

CUPBOARD   123 cms high   Panel 74 cms wide

those resting on the ground with lids that are domed. The former raised their contents from damp ground but were unsuitable for travelling purposes. Here the simple box form was safest: a canted or domed roof protected the innards from the weather. Many chests have survived partly due to the forgetful habits of people who left their possessions in them to institutions for safe keeping and partly due to the innate conservatism of churches, colleges and guilds.

The symbolic role of the seat or armchair was widely recognised in the Middle Ages: kings, judges or bishops were accorded special seats which denoted their power. The individual in control of a committee is still referred to as the 'chairman'. There are several royal and episcopal seats which have survived owing to their magnificence and the aura of ancient authority they gave the user. Such are the late twelfth-century turned chair in Hereford Cathedral, the St Edward's chair in Westminster Abbey (see p. 2) and the fourteenth-century bishops' throne at Exeter with its soaring pinnacled woodwork. Manuscript illuminations which tended to record only ceremonial events have given a mistaken impression that chairs were rare. They could in fact be possessed by peasants. The Worcestershire Thomas atte Frythe used 'a chayere' in his dwelling in 1409 while a record of 1529 shows another peasant owning four chairs. A peasant warming himself before a fireplace, carved on a misericord at Screveton church, (Notts.), is shown seated on an elaborately carved chair. Benches, forms and stools, however, were the commonest methods of seating. While they might well be fixed to window recesses, movable furniture in halls was more convenient since it allowed for greater flexibility of activities.

Fixed tables were very common during the Middle Ages. A group has survived in Winchester College hall with pedestal supports fixed to wooden floor boards; the pedestals and table boards are linked by heavy arched braces. Undoubtedly temporary ones with trestles were used too. An enormous circular table top, measuring 5.5 m in diameter, hangs on the wall of Winchester Castle. Although it is painted with Tudor insignia it has been claimed to be as old as the reign of Henry III.

No beds have come down to us earlier than the fifteenth century. Earlier seignorial beds – by the thirteenth century – already consisted of three parts. Above the bedstead was suspended a canopy or 'celour'; behind the head was the tester or 'dossier'. Towards the end of the Middle Ages interest centred round the rich textiles with which beds were hung. These beds in the houses of the nobility had to be displayed although they might never be intended to be slept in!

11. The Problems of Urban Archaeology

The clearances caused by war damage and more recently by the pressures of central town redevelopment have given archaeologists exceptional opportunities for recovering detailed information about English urban landscapes of the Middle Ages. The emphasis of the work in the period before 1200 AD has been to concentrate on the below-ground remains. After 1200 it is possible to marry the archaeological record with the architectural and documentary. Each approach is problematical.

Early urban excavations were frequently hamstrung by the small size of sites available, the expense of removing concrete and brick overburden, the necessity of speed and the (often justified) suspicions of developers. This keyhole approach was counterproductive revealing little more than scraps of walls leading under massive baulks in areas riddled with pits and cellars. Gradually the strategy was changed and in York, King's Lynn, Lincoln, Norwich, Oxford, Northampton and Southampton excavations were undertaken on carefully selected sites which covered several complete properties or units of occupation. The houses, shops and subsidiary buildings were now to be seen in their context of backyards, gardens, alleys, street frontages and the wider faunal and floral environment.

Certain circumstances favour urban archaeologists in their attempt to trace the evolution of town housing. Particularly helpful are sites such as urban castles which often contained sealed sequences of earlier occupation with well-defined chronological termini. Similarly, destructive events such as fires, which periodically swept through medieval towns, paradoxically provide a bonus. A conflagration spread through Norwich on April 25 1507; it destroyed 40 per cent of all the houses in the city.[23] A row in Pottergate had cellars below them and the burning embers, household goods and all, fell into these cellars. They were never cleared out and were covered with the clay floors of new buildings, thus preserving a marvellous cache of firmly dated items. Another advantage is that property boundaries in towns tend to remain constant. In York, for instance, the divisions between urban holdings have lasted over a thousand years. Economic prosperity or recession may lead to the subdivision or combination of urban plot boundaries but they can still be traced in towns like Stratford-on-Avon or Totnes which were not subject to intense redevelopment in the nineteenth or twentieth centuries. On the other hand, urban housing was subject to renewal. Carter reckoned that in Norwich there was a cycle of redevelopment every 150 to 200 years when either buildings wore out, or fashion dictated rebuilding.[24] All the houses in an area might tend to reach the end of the useful life at the same time. This resulted in the systematic destruction of earlier phases. Space was at a premium in towns and the exigencies of rubbish disposal created a nightmare of overlapping pits.

The standing buildings which have survived from the medieval period in towns are often atypical. They are likely to be the houses of wealthy burgesses, the so-called 'office holders', the elite of the 1 per cent which dominated the political and economic life of the towns. They survive because they were better built and their owners were in a better position to mobilise help when there was a fire threat.

The study of below-ground and upstanding remains would remain largely unintelligible unless it was consolidated by documentary research. In Norwich, for example, where documents covering more than 1,500 shelf feet are calendared and indexed, it is possible to follow the changes of ownership and the functions of individual properties within a street and thus to tie in the archaeological remains with the actual people who lived there.

We will now trace the evolution of medieval town housing by looking at the results of a series of recent excavations.

12. Anglo-Scandinavian Housing in York

York provides firm information about Anglo-Scandinavian housing of the tenth to eleventh centuries. Here the Danes shifted the centre of economic gravity to the south-east of the Roman fortress. Recent excavations in the 1970s have investigated the waterlogged deposits lying up to 3 or 4.6 m below the present street level at Pavement and a parallel thoroughfare known as Coppergate (from the Coopers – makers of barrels).[25]

Waterlogged conditions have preserved the timber and brushwood which was used for the building of platforms and fences and for the lining of refuse pits. The types of trees can be easily identified from their bark: major rafts and piles were made from oak or birch trees; alder, beech, hazel and birch branches were used for lesser fencing and brushwood flooring. There were two main Danish building techniques.

In the first, withies were woven round upright timbers of varying size and shape, and then plastered with a coat of mud and straw (daub). The other type involved the use of horizontally laid planks supported by the uprights; floors were made either of mortar or were timber or brushwood rafts. The plans of the buildings were either parallel or at right angles to the present line of Pavement; as has been noticed, the property boundaries along these streets did not change from Danish times until the eighteenth century. The tenement plots were long and narrow, each about 5.5 m in width.

The conditions of Danish York were not very pleasant. We can picture the town densely built over by long, narrow, rotting wooden houses with earth floors covered with decaying vegetation, surrounded by streets and yards filled with even fouler organic waste. Beetles, houseflies and other insects swarmed, attracted by the compost. This is a lurid picture but is based firmly on the systematic recording and analysis of insect remains. It must be admitted, however, that there is no evidence that people *lived* on these ground floors. They may well have worked there, but lived above. It is possible that while conditions within the Anglo-Scandinavian buildings at 6-8 Pavement were unsavoury by modern standards they 'may have been tolerable, even cosy, by the standards of the time.[26]

One observation is overwhelming – that organic material, both plant and animal, formed the basis of almost every aspect of life in tenth/eleventh-century York. A number of wood-destroying beetles of which *Anobium punctatum* (Deg), the woodworm, is the most abundant, have been found, together with the regular occurrence of the 'powder post beetle' *Lyctus linearis* (Gz). But more important than the damage inflicted by these beetles was wet rot of timbers where they entered the ground.

The multiplicity of floor layers was related to successive rebuildings, each with floors and occupation build up, each cycle taking only a few decades at most.

13. Danish and Early Medieval Houses in Lincoln and Southampton

Eighty kilometres to the south of York stands Lincoln where a similar sequence of Roman fortress followed by an early ecclesiastical centre is found. Here again the Danes exploited its potential as a route centre and recent excavations in the area of the old Roman *colonia* have provided an insight into their housing.[27]

The Roman defences left an imprint on the city but the gridiron street pattern was in decay. Several diagonal streets provided short cuts between the gates *c.* 400-900 AD. Two new streets also were laid out on the hillside, Flaxengate in the late ninth century, and Grantham Street at right angles, no later than the tenth century.

Flaxengate was surfaced with tightly--packed cobbles and soon afterwards was provided with a wooden drain (Plate 4.6). The late ninth-century buildings, constructed gable-end onto it, were plank-built with upright posts earth fast. They were heated by internal hearths of clay and tile. The plans of later phases of timber buildings were cut about by subsequent pits and only fragments were recovered, but evidently, by the eleventh century, a different building technique was being used whereby posts were usually set into sill beams. These were laid directly onto the ground surface, leaving only minimal traces. The floors were detectable, however, from areas of beaten clay or at times organic remains, suggesting they were covered with straw or rushes.[28]

There was a clear change in building materials from timber to stone in Lincoln in the late twelfth century. The same phenomenon has been noticed at Southampton, Canterbury and York. Several stone houses of the twelfth/thirteenth centuries also have survived from Stamford, at Moyse's Hall, Bury St Edmunds (Plate 6.6) and at the Music House at Norwich. The factors which may

have dictated this change are not clearly understood. It coincided with the more stable atmosphere of Henry II's reign which followed the unrest of Stephen's reign. More elaborate building is likely to have been an index of the economic prosperity arising from the revival of urban trade and industry. Town traders had more to lose now and were increasingly aware of the need for adequate fire protections. The 1189 London building assize encouraged the construction of party walls. In Lincoln stone houses have been attributed to Jews who were unpopular elements, and frequently the victims of mob violence, and it is true that the so-called Jew's House in Strait was owned by Belaset of Wallingford. The Music House, Norwich, was also originally in Jewish hands. 'Aaron the Jews House', Lincoln had no connection, however, with the famous money lender and merchant. Ready availability of nearby sources of stone was an obvious reason for the number of Lincoln's buildings, but in Southampton stone had to be imported by sea from Purbeck, the Isle of Wight, and even Caen.

Some of the best preserved examples of early medieval town houses which have survived are to be found in Southampton.[29] There had been an important Anglo-Saxon town at Hamwih on the eastern side of the peninsula between the Rivers Test and Itchen, but this had declined by the tenth century, and the medieval town of Southampton was re-sited along a gravel ridge, its long High Street running parallel to the shore. Earliest evidence for occupation in the eleventh century was found in All Saints parish north and west of Bargate, but from the twelfth century onwards, as the borough developed, the rich and wealthy are found concentrated in the south and central parishes. The Anglo-French community occupied the south-west quarter of the town; French Street, and the churches dedicated to St Michael, patron saint of Normandy, and St John recall this.

The earliest houses in Southampton, as in Lincoln, York and Northampton, were built of timber, but at the end of the twelfth century there was a major changeover to stone construction. The first stone houses were the properties of wealthy burgesses. They were of great size: the Norman House in Cuckoo

Plate 6.6: Bury St Edmunds, Suffolk: Moyse's Hall. The oldest domestic building in this monastic planned town. A Norman two-storey house built of flint and stone; probably not by a Jew. The hall and solar were on the upper floor. Two original windows face onto the Cornhill. Date *c.* 1180. Curious features such as clock and louvre added ineptly in late nineteenth century (Photo: J.M. Steane)

Plate 6.7: Southampton, Hampshire: 'King John's Palace'. An unusually complete large twelfth-century town house, two-storeyed, facing onto Blue Anchor Lane. This interior view of the north wall shows the upper floor providing accommodation and the lower devoted to warehouse use. The large square doorway (for bringing in bulky goods) opens from the street and descends by five steps to the present ground floor. A single small Norman window is to the right. Above is the hall, well lit, well heated, and provided with fitted wall cupboards (aumbries). The chimney breast to the right projects down to ground-floor level and contains a semicircular fire back (Photo: National Monuments Record)

Lane was 17.37 m wide by 32.3 m deep. It was probably matched by house 4, on High Street once the property of Walter Le Fleming, the greatest merchant capitalist of the thirteenth-century town. 'King John's Palace' was two-storied, standing on the quayside with its western wall incorporated into the town wall (Plate 6.7). Here the entire ground floor was turned over to warehousing and sales. The hall and chamber in these houses would have been placed on the first floor perhaps approached by an outer stair. Such houses had impressive two-light semicircular windows such as have also survived at Lincoln.

The long narrow plot characteristic of the English medieval town was the most import-ant determinant of the plans of houses placed upon it. These plots in Southampton were 91.4 m long running from the High Street to the town wall on the east and only 5.8 m wide. Obviously the High Street frontage was valued at a commercial premium and most houses of the thirteenth and fourteenth centur-ies were likely to be fronted by shops. These would be set over a vault which might be used as another shop or kept for storage. The house was gable-ended onto the street and contained a central hall which extended to the full height of the building. In addition there might be two chambers, one above the other, with a kitchen, latrine and other outbuildings in the yard at the rear. A fine example is preserved at 58 French Street, Southampton and the plan continued to be used at the end of the Middle Ages, as can be seen at the Duke of Wellington on Bridge Street and the Red Lion on the High Street.

These last two are timber built. There were obvious constructional advantages of timber, which enabled the practice of jettying★ and the increase of the height of buildings in the late medieval town. Improved fire control may have influenced this. Already in the early medieval town roof-tiles had replaced thatch; also slate began to enter the town from Devonshire from the 1170s and became the standard roofing material. In the London regulations, imitated in other towns, provision was made for the proper construction of

★The projecting part of a timber-framed building, especially the overhanging storey.

chimneys in stone; ovens and hearths were required to be sited well away from timber partitions; householders were to equip them-selves with adequate fire-fighting equipment.

Excavation in Southampton has uncovered plenty of evidence of good-class burgess housing, but little else. There is little evidence for the speculative building, in terraced blocks which was certainly being run up in the fourteenth and fifteenth centuries in London, York and Canterbury. In fact we know very little about the housing of the artisan class and the poor in Southampton. They probably failed to find sufficient accommodation within the walls and populated the suburban areas to the north and along East Street to the ancient church of St Mary. We have to turn to Winchester, York and Northampton for an appreciation of the housing of the lower orders of society.

14. Working-class Housing in Winchester, York and Northampton

Winchester, a Roman city, had emerged as the capital of the Anglo-Saxon kingdom of Wessex. It continued to be the seat of the treasury after 1066 and acquired a larger and better cathedral on an adjacent site to the Saxon Old Minster. It developed into an important industrial centre in the medieval period. Brook Street was mainly given over to cloth working in the fourteenth century and in particular the processes of dyeing and fulling. The dirtier process of tanning was carried out further downstream. There were two fortu-nate circumstances which account for the very full information uncovered by Martin Biddle's excavations here in the late 1960s. The area was low lying and had a rising water table. There was consequently no temptation to remove floors to level the site: in fact floors were laid one on top of the other to combat the damp. Also during the economic recession in the Late Middle Ages, Winchester declined, and the area was largely abandoned and became gardens. Rows of cottages were laid out across the site in the nineteenth century but these did not disturb it unduly because they did not have cellars. Brook Street there-fore retained, in buried form, excellent

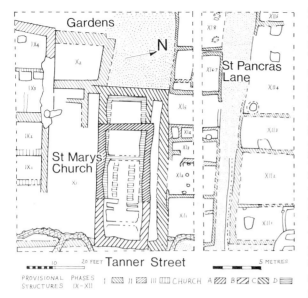

Figure 6.10: Ground Plan of Lower Brook Street, Winchester (after Biddle, 1967)

examples of the mixture of workshops, middle– and lower-class housing which jostled one another in this part of the town (Figure 6.10).[30]

Fronting Brook Street were workrooms and shops with specially chalk-lined water channels bringing water in and under the front walls. Behind were the domestic quarters or storerooms, or they might be on the floor above. Houses IX/X are particularly interesting because documents tell us that they belonged to Richard Bosynton at the beginning of the fifteenth century, a leading fuller who was also engaged in dyeing. When in 1407 he retired from business he split the property and a deed survives giving an exact description of the house. In the front was a narrow shop with running water particularly useful for his craft; above it was the solar, the living quarters – a warning to archaeologists who are mesmerised by ground-floor plans. This vital part of the house has of course vanished. Behind was a kitchen and at the rear was a small building facing onto a courtyard where the rack (*tentorium*) was situated. Here the cloths were stretched out to dry in the fulling process.

North of the church of St Mary was a row of four cottages fronting onto St Pancras Lane.

Such cottages were probably occupied by manual workers, engaged for wages in the cloth finishing activity of the Brooks area. They were perhaps a speculative development of the Priors of Frary and Kalendar, a religious fraternity who acquired the property sometime before the mid-fourteenth century. The cottages formed a unitary structure of four bays; the three western bays were nearly identical in plan but the eastern bay in the angle of Tanner Street and St Pancras Street probably formed a shop. In each of bays 2-4 the original layout was identical. One entered from St Pancras Lane by a door in the north-west corner. This was screened from the inside and in the angle was a hearth. In the opposite corner was a partitioned-off sleeping room. The building materials included walls of cob clay, with chalk admixture, and there were internal partitions of reddish brown cob, stiffened with stakes, and rendered with creamy plaster. Floors were made of rammed pebble chalk with small broken flints.

Careful though the excavation was at Winchester, it cannot rival the effect on the imagination of the survival of rows of fourteenth-century workers' homes in York.[31] The earliest of the rows was at 64-72 Goodramgate, situated in the churchyard of Holy Trinity and known as Lady Row. The fourteenth century saw an increase in the economic prosperity and the population of York, which caused a greater demand for housing. Several York parishes built houses in their churchyards with the intention that the rent should support the fashionable chantries. The row was probably built in 1316 and consisted of a two-storeyed development of small two-roomed houses. They were half-timbered and the row is in a line under a single continuous roof with the eaves parallel in the street. The upper storey is jettied towards the front. Eight trusses split the row into seven bays marked by simple brackets. Each cross wall apart from the gables was shared by two houses. There was thus a maximum use of a minimum of material. The tenants were identified with persons, whose trade is described as 'laborarius', i.e. a journeyman or some other wage earner.

Another row, 54-60 Stonegate, is a storey higher than the row in Goodramgate. There were five or six dwellings and each bay was a separate house. These would have had three rooms, a shop, a hall and a chamber. By the end of the fourteenth century it apparently housed people of middling status, like tailors, goldsmiths and chandlers. They formed the lowest layer of the city council, known as the forty-eight whereas the two upper layers, the twelve and the twenty-four were dominated by the mercers.

We turn now for a final example of medieval urban housing to Northampton.[32] Here on a sandstone bluff, above the crossing of the River Nene, a town grew up in the late Saxon period. It was an important route centre and roads radiated out across the Midlands; in particular the route from Southampton, northwards through Oxford, crossed the River Nene here on its way to Stamford. The first documentary reference to the place occurs in the Anglo-Saxon Chronicle under the year 913 AD – 'the army from Northampton . . . rode out'. An early defensive perimeter enclosing the main north-south (Horsemarket, Horse Shoe Street) and east-west streets (Marefair and Gold Street) has been reconstructed on topographical grounds. Markets grew up at the gates at the Mayorhold and All Saints. The Normans built a strong castle overlying the western part of the Anglo-Saxon town and established (as at Nottingham) a *novus burgus* of French settlers in the east, which they surrounded with defences. Excavations in the south-west quarter of the town along both sides of St Peter's Street have revealed an interesting sequence of urban housing.

To begin with, there were clusters of grubenhäuser (sunken-floored buildings) and halls laid down in a non-street related pattern. In the late Saxon period a street was constructed and rectangular timber buildings, respecting the line of the street, were erected along the frontages to the north and south. Since only post-holes, 'pier bases' and slots were found, it is difficult to say what the sizes of the houses were, but it does seem that they had their long sides facing the street. In the late thirteenth century these timber buildings were replaced by stone houses. House 4, for instance, measured 12 m x 5.75 m set with its gable-end onto the street. It is not unreasonable to assume that it was a two-storey

structure with the upper storey in timber. There was a walled yard area containing an oven to the east of the house. House 3 was smaller, 8 m x 6 m, and its long side lay to the street. It is possible that for a time timber buildings continued side by side with stone structures. In *c.* 1400 the whole of the street was reconstructed in a single action typical of the cyclical pattern within medieval urban development (Plate 6.8). House 1 was constructed of stone for the first time; houses 2 and 3 were rebuilt both with rear lines further north; house 4 was converted to an L-shaped plan. The basic plan was that of a rectangular box, 8-12 m long and 6 m broad.

The foundations of these dwellings were reasonably massive and would have supported a substantial superstructure. Only sparse finds of mortar suggest that they were supported by dwarf walls and timber superstructures. The lack of evidence for chimneys suggests that there were open fires placed in 'halls', open to the eaves with 'solars' at one end. St Peter's Street provides another example of the integration of industry within a residential area. Pits connected with tanning, a clay-lined trough and the presence of horn cores, all suggest industrial functions. In general the houses in St Peter's Street probably represent artisans' dwellings; they do not aspire to being merchants' houses but they are more substantial than the cottages Biddle excavated at St Pancras Lane, Winchester.

15. Medieval Gardens

Gardens were an important feature of both countryside and town in the Middle Ages; they were valued by all classes of society from rulers and ecclesiastics, with their extensive manorial and monastic garden and orchard complexes, to humble peasants with their half acres or less.[33] Sources of information about them are derived from place-names, from accounts of monastic houses, from conveyances of property and other rights, literature such as poems and romances, illustrations in tapestries and paintings, and finally in the material remains of the gardens and their products themselves.

Field names or place-names sometimes en-

able the sites of medieval gardens to be located. Middle English *erber*, 'garden', old Northern French *gardin*, 'garden' and O.E. *búr*, one meaning of which is an enclosed garden, are all found. Sometimes the names refer to vegetables or fruits grown.[34] Chaucer's Grisildis in the 'Clerk's Tale' was reduced to living off –

> Wortes cabbages or other herbs times oft,
> The which she shred and seeth [boiled] for
> her living.[35]

The O.E *wyrt* (vegetable) occurs for instance in Sowerby township, Yorkshire West Riding. Leeks were so popular with the Anglo-Saxons that they called kitchen gardens leek-garths (*leac-tun*) and the town name Leyton is derived from this.

It is clear that there were, at the top of the social scale, elaborate and ornamental gardens, primarily intended for pleasure, relaxation and entertainment. Such was no doubt one purpose behind the gardens laid out by Henry de Bray, a royal official to Edward I, at Harlestone (Northants.) in the 1290s. He built a hall and north chamber for £12. In 1292 he added a new grange and then a garden called 'The New Yerde'. In the next year he had some fishponds dug in the courtyard below. He put gates and doors in the garden and estate walls and in 1297 created a new walled herb garden. A tower was built next, and a mound which is likely to have been part of an arbour or 'privy playing place'. Finally Henry added a new kitchen with a fountain near it and built a dove house at the corner of the herb garden. Doubtless dove dung was handy manure for the garden. The emphasis here is on walling, fencing, hedging and palisading, and there is little doubt that in the violent thirteenth century the *hortus conclusus* had to be built and defended before it could be cultivated. The other characteristic is the piecemeal nature of garden layout; there is no grand design here – only a series of impulsive additions.[36]

At the other end of the scale were the gardens of ordinary tenants. They are seen in aerial photographs of deserted settlements, big rectangles with linear mounds lying at the bottom of the tofts, the yards surrounding the peasant houses.[37] Such boundaries are mentioned by Chaucer in his description of the widow's yard in the 'Nun's Priests' Tale'.

A yeerd she hadde, enclosed al aboute,
with stikkes, and a drye dych withoute.

Within these enclosures were grown a wide range of vegetables, fruits, herbs and even cereals. A Yorkshire tenant from Newhall in Bowling township grew leeks, herbs, flax and hemp in 1355.[38] Evidence for such garden produce is occasionally recovered as environmental samples during excavations although naturally it is impossible to distinguish it from produce bought from the local market. The barrel-latrine from a garden in central Worcester produced a wide variety of fruits and herbs.[39] Plenty of space for gardens was allowed for in medieval towns such as Winchester.[40] It seems that some larger gardens were run rather like allotments. At a Bradford court (Yorkshire, West Riding) in 1342 for instance, a jury found that Adam Notebroun, by enclosing his hedge, had caused the loss of Thomas Harper's herbs and peas. In 1355, however, the fact that Robert Dikson had *not* enclosed his garden at Bradford led to pigs consuming the herbs, leeks and grass belonging to Hugh Thomson. The fact that many men adopted the craft name 'le Gardener' shows that they were probably employed by the manor or by wealthy freemen in their gardens and orchards.

Monastic gardens are well documented.

They appear in plans such as that of St Gall, a projected ideal monastery of the ninth century, where there are three: one of medicinal herbs adjoining the house of the physician; a kitchen garden appropriately beside the Poultry yard; the monks' cemetery was shown as an ornamental orchard.[41] Many of the major office holders had their own gardens and Abingdon Abbey (Oxon.), had a gardener among the obedientiaries. These monastic gardens varied in scale from noble to minute. The Abbot of Westminster had five turfed alleyways and walks, a willow plantation (used for providing twigs to tie up the vines) and a vegetable patch containing flax, hemp and peas. The gardens provided for each inmate of the Carthusian Priory at Mount Grace, Yorkshire, were tiny.[42] Around a great cloister were cells enclosed in individual gardens, 15 m square. A wooden pentice ran along the wall of each garden, doubtless a necessity if one of these secluded and contemplative monks were to take the air daily in the fogs and rains of Yorkshire. A few of these monastic gardens have lasted down to the present day. The Hospitallers' garden at Hampton is now part of the garden of Hampton Court Palace. The Thames-side garden of the twelfth-century Templars has become the garden of the Inner and Middle Temples. Monasteries sometimes had pleasure gardens belonging to the whole community. They were known popularly as Paradises and were enclosed and often circular in shape. Here significantly the inmates told their rosaries. The sites of monastic gardens in both Oxford and Cambridge are pinpointed by Paradise Streets.

More surprisingly, it is possible that the plants themselves have survived the passage of time. When T.A. Dorrien-Smith took over Tresco Abbey estates in the Isles of Scilly in 1872 he chose two types of daffodil for commercial production which he found growing in the abbey ruins. They became known as 'Scilly White' and 'Soleil d'Or'; their origin is probably north African, but it is likely that they were introduced by monks. Birthwort, used in midwifery, and a standard herb in monastic gardens, is found in the ruins of Godstow Nunnery near Oxford. On the walls of Beaulieu Abbey are found winter savory, ploughmans spikenard, marjoram and clove pink. What has been hailed as 'the most remarkable collection of monastic survivors', is on the island of Steep Holm in the Bristol Channel.[43] These include a number of plants of southern European origin, all of them medicinal herbs, from the garden created by the Augustinian canons who lived here 1166-1266.

We rely for our visual picture of medieval gardens on illuminated manuscripts which indicate (at any rate in the manorial complexes) such features as enclosures, arbours, raised stone or brick flower beds, stone seats and ornamental ponds and fountains. However, it is quite uncertain whether these are derived from Roman sources (like for instance a good deal of medieval illustrations of costume), the vivid imagination of the scribes, or whether they had an underlying reality. We know from documents also that there were minor structures, tool sheds, fruit and fish houses but they have not so far been found by archaeology. Roman examples demonstrate that such garden remains *can* survive. At Fishbourne (Sussex), for instance, Cunliffe found the bedding trenches of fruit and flowers. At Pompeii excavation of the vine roots in a Roman vineyard have indicated the type of stock grown. Gravel paths and rows of artificial holes dug for orchard trees have been recognised from the air in the post-medieval gardens at Lyveden in Northamptonshire. The very considerable earthwork sites of abandoned formal gardens have been mapped by the Royal Commission in their recent work in Midland England.[44] What is needed is a greater realisation that garden layouts associated with houses, deserted in the Middle Ages and subsequently abandoned, can be recognised on the surface.

A final note on horticultural tools. There were two distinct forms of pottery watering pots found·in some quantities in London and elsewhere. Implements for working the ground included iron shod spades, socketed forks with three prongs, turf cutters, hoes, rakes, weed hooks, sickles and scythes, in fact many of the range used in agriculture. Perhaps the greatest single technological advance in gardening was the invention of the wheelbarrow, first heard of in England *c.* 1170 and 1209.

References

1. A valuable bibliography of the massive data connected with the thirty seasons of excavations of this site is in *Wharram Data Sheets*, Department of Archaeology, University of York, 1981.
2. The techniques used here were discussed by Hurst, J.G., 'Deserted medieval villages and the excavations at Wharram Percy, Yorkshire' in Bruce-Mitford, R.L.S., *Recent Archaeological Excavations in Britain*, London, 1956, 251-73.
3. Beresford, G., 'Three deserted medieval settlements on Dartmoor: a report on the late E. Marie Winter's excavations', *Med. Arch.*, XXIII, 1979, 98-158.
4. Hurst, J.G. and Beresford, M.W., *Deserted Medieval Villages*, London, 1971.
5. *Med. Arch.*, X, 1966, 214-16, XI, 1967, 312, 314; XII, 1968, 203-5; XIII, 1969, 281-3.
6. Beresford, G., *The Medieval Clay-Land Village: Excavations at Goltho and Barton Blount*, Soc. for Med. Arch., Monograph series 6, London, 1975.
7. *Med. Arch.*, XI, 1967, 307-8.
8. Steane, J.M. and Bryant, G.F., 'Excavations at the deserted medieval settlement at Lyveden', *Journal 12* of Northampton Museum and Art Gallery, 1975, 24-31.
9. Alcock, N. (ed.), *Cruck Construction*, Council for British Archaeology Research Report No. 42, 1981.
10. Field, R.K., 'Worcestershire peasant buildings, household goods and farming equipment in the later Middle Ages', *Med. Arch*, IX, 1965, 107–45.
11. Beresford, *The Medieval Clay-Land Village*, 13, 16, 18.
12. Smith, J.T., 'The evolution of the English peasant house to the late seventeenth century: The evidence of buildings', *J.B.A.A.*, 3rd ser., 33, 1970, 122-47.
13. The classic exposition of English medieval domestic architecture is Wood, M., *The English Medieval House*, London, 1965.
14. *Current Archaeology*, 56, April, 1977, 262-70.
15. See Wood, *The English Medieval House*, Chapters 2, 3, 4.
16. Faulkner, P.A., 'Domestic planning from the twelfth to the fourteenth centuries', *Arch J.*, CXV, 1958, 150-84.
17. Mercer, E., *English Vernacular Houses*, London, 1975, 79-95. The most important recent account is in Hewett, C.A., *English Historic Carpentry*, Chichester, 1980, strong on technical but weak on historical aspects.
18. Dunning, G.C., 'Medieval chimney pots', Chapter 5 in Jope, E.M. (ed.), *Studies in Building History*, London, 1961.
19. Baker, E., 'The Grove candlestick', *Council for*

British Archaeology, Group IX, Newsletter 11, 1981, 7-11.

20. Eames, E.S., *Medieval Tiles. A Handbook*, British Museum, London, 1968.

21. *Council for British Archaeology, Group IX, Newsletter*, 1981, 82-3.

22. Eames, P., 'Furniture in England, France and the Netherlands from the twelfth to the fifteenth century', *Furniture History Society Journal*, XIII, 1977. Also Hoffman, M., 'Beds and bedclothes in medieval Norway' in Harte, N.B. and Ponting, K.G., *Cloth and Clothing in Medieval Europe*, London, 1983, 351–67.

23. *Current Archaeology*, 48, January 1975, 12-13.

24. Carter, A., Roberts, J.P. and Sutermeister, H., 'The Norwich Survey, third interim report', *Norfolk Arch.*, XXXVI, 39-72.

25. Hall, R.A., 'The topography of Anglo-Scandinavian York' in Hall, R.A. (ed.), *Viking Age York and the North*, CBA Research Report No. 27, 1978, 31–6.

26. Kenward, H.K. *et al.*, 'The environment of Anglo-Scandinavian York' in Hall (ed.), ibid., 65–6.

27. Colyer, C., *Lincoln, the Archaeology of an Historic City*, Lincoln, 1975.

28. Jones, R.H., 'Medieval houses at Flaxengate, Lincoln', *The Archaeology of Lincoln*, XI-I, 1980.

29. Faulkner, P.A., 'The surviving medieval buildings' in Platt, C. and Coleman-Smith, R., *Excavations in Medieval Southampton, 1953-1969*, Leicester, 1975, 78-124.

30. Biddle, M., 'Excavations at Winchester, 1967, sixth interim report', *Antiqs J.*, XLVIII, 250-85.

31. Short, P., 'The fourteenth century rows of York', *Arch. J.*, 137, 1980, 86-137.

32. Williams, J.H., *St Peter's Street Northampton, Excavations 1973–6*, Northampton, 1979.

33. Four valuable studies of medieval gardens are McClean, T., *Medieval English Gardens*, London, 1981; Harvey, J., *Medieval Gardens*, London, 1981; Moorhouse, S.A., *The Rural Medieval Landscape in West Yorkshire: an Archaeological Survey to AD 1500*, vol. 3, Wakefield, 1981, 822-31; and Taylor, C.C., *The Archaeology of Gardens*, Princess Risborough, 1983.

34. Moorhouse, ibid., 822.

35. McClean, *Medieval English Gardens*, 197.

36. Willis, D. (ed.), *Estate Book of Henry Bray*, Camden Soc., 3rd ser., xxvii, London, 1916.

37. Beresford, M.W. and St Joseph, J.K., *Medieval England. An Aerial Survey*, Cambridge, 2nd edn, 1979, 130, 132.

38. For these examples from Yorkshire see Moorhouse, *The Rural Medieval Landscape in West Yorkshire*, 825.

39. Greig, J., 'The investigation of a medieval barrel-latrine from Worcester', *Journal of Arch. Science*, 1981, 8, 265–82.

40. Biddle, M. (ed.), *Winchester in the Early Middle Ages*, Oxford, 1976, 5-7, 494.

41. Harvey, *Medieval Gardens*, 32-3.

42. McClean, *Medieval English Gardens*, 107-8, 48-53.

43. Mabey, R. and Evans, T., *The Flowering of Britain*, London, 1980.

44. Royal Commission on Historical Monuments (England), *County of Northampton, Archaeological Sites*, vols. I-IV, London 1975-82. For garden remains at Lyveden vol. 1, *Archaeological Sites in North-East Northamptonshire*, London, 1975, 6, Figure 18.

7

MEDIEVAL INDUSTRIES AND CRAFTS

1. Reasons for Lack of Study

The industrial remains of medieval England have not been studied so extensively as the churches or houses. For one thing, they are less easy to recognise, being less monumental in construction, and at the same time being more vulnerable to technological change. Just as today, industrial processes in the iron and steel or textile industries rapidly become obsolescent and are swept away, so medieval industries often had quite a short life. This means that they are less likely to have left standing buildings behind. Churches and houses, to a lesser extent, were not so liable to destruction. They could be added to or adapted for new purposes to a far greater degree than industrial premises, and so are more likely to survive to the present day. Secondly, the interest in industrial archaeology is comparatively novel and has tended to concentrate on the beginnings of the modern period, the age of canals, railway and industrial inventions. Churches and houses, on the other hand, have been intensively studied since the mid-Victorian period and there is a huge body of accurate information about their styles, building construction and functions, which is being continually added to. Thirdly, although both great churches and large houses of the Middle Ages are well served with building accounts and other records, much of medieval industry is poorly documented. We know very little from records about the pottery industry, for example. The archaeologist is not able to seek out the material remains to illustrate the documents; rather he needs to use the remains themselves as the primary source of information because these are all that are left.

2. The Ironworking Industry

Of the extractive industries one of the most significant in the medieval economy was the mining, smelting and working of iron. The marks left by these processes on the landscape include abandoned iron ore mines.[1] At Bentley Grange, Emley (Yorks.) there was an outpost of Byland Abbey. Here fields bearing the corrugations of ridge-and-furrow have been overlain by a series of mounds which look from the air like a series of soggy puddings. Each is a heap of debris disposed around the openings of shallow shafts leading down to the iron-ore bed. Each hollow represents a collapsed shaft within which is a bush or tree.

The two main regions of medieval iron working were the Weald of Kent and Sussex, and the Forest of Dean.[2] Doubtless one reason for this was the heavily wooded nature of these areas. The iron industry required large quantities of charcoal which was made from the loppings of coppice wood and from upper and side branches of trees. In the twelfth century Dean was the main centre but from the thirteenth century the Weald began to overhaul it. It is clear that the demands of war forced the pace. In 1254, 30,000 horseshoes and 60,000 nails were purchased in the Weald. By the fifteenth century the Wealden forges were producing cannon for the French wars. In fact, Kent and Sussex for a time became heavily industrialised. In a survey, made in 1574, 38 forges and 32 furnaces were located in Sussex.

Walking among the Wealden woods, one comes across heaps of slag, relics of the more ancient process of smelting, which lasted until the fifteenth century. This process has been elucidated by a series of recent excavations at Minepit Wood (Sussex).[3] Here a number of shallow open-cast diggings were made to extract the ore. This was roasted in a horseshoe-shaped furnace made of sandstone. The calcined ore was then crushed and smelted by putting alternating layers of ore and charcoal in a stone and clay smelting furnace, enclosed and roofed by a timber-framed building. Hand or foot bellows were inserted through fired clay tubes called tuyères. The unrefined iron in the form of 'blooms' was then taken out of the furnace and brought to red heat before being beaten by hammers weighing from 523 to 1,134 kg. This drove out impurities and produced metallic iron which could then be wrought by the smith into many shapes.

Two changes in the technology of iron production occurred in the late fifteenth century: these were the introduction of the blast furnace and the use of water power. Layers of roasted ore and charcoal were loaded into the top of more or less permanent structures with the necessary blast provided by bellows powered by water. Water power was also used to drive the great hammers in the forges.

These developments caused further changes in the landscape which are still detectable today.[4] In Kent and Sussex there are minor streams with strings of artificial ponds (called 'furnace' or 'hammer ponds') held back by great dams which provided the necessary head of water for these purposes. A typical example of such a site is on the River Bewl, a feeder for the Teese, itself a tributary of the Medway, on the Kent/Sussex border. The furnace site stood at the foot of a wood where the valley is narrow and steep sided, allowing a short dam. It was found by noticing scatters of charcoal and forge cinders in overgrown coppice-woodland. The remains of the water-powered mechanism, providing the furnace blast, included a wheel-base built of oak timbers with associated material, suggesting a date of c. 1300. Fragments of the water wheel and its gearing of worn oak pegs were found. Such technological improvements prepared the way for the manufacture of heavy war material such as cannons and cannon balls in Tudor times.

Once the 'bloomsmith' had finished smelting the iron it was worked up in the string hearth to standard bars.[5] Some have survived; we have a gad (the billet or piece) of iron from Winchester weighing 1.28 kg and a bar from Chingley weighing 15 kg. Wrought iron by itself would not provide a long-lasting cutting edge. Steel had to be introduced; this was an expensive additional material and was imported during the Middle Ages from Sweden, Russia and Spain. Around 1300 it cost about £3 per ton compared with the cost of wrought iron at only 12s per ton.

The 'blacksmith' now took over (Plates 7.1, 7.2).[6] He was responsible for the manufacture of all iron and steel artefacts needed for peace and war in medieval society. His equipment included hammers, pincers, anvils and wedges. The smithing hearth could either be at ground level (as at Goltho, Lincs.) or at waist level (as at Alsted, Netherne Wood, Surrey). Basically it was a pile of burning coal or charcoal with a tuyère to provide protection for the bellows. With this the smith was able to achieve temperatures of the order of 1200°C. Most of the early work in shaping a tool is done hot–the heat treatment of steel requires temperatures in the range of 700-950°C. Near at hand was a water-cooling device called a 'bosh' where the smith cooled his tools rather than the products. Excavations of smithies have revealed two unmistakable signs, the presence of hammer scale, and furnace bottoms, a vitrified mass of fuel ash and hammer scale.

How was iron used in the Middle Ages? It had multifarious functions, including the making of tools, equipment and the strengthening of structures, but because it was expensive (it is suggested that it was ten times more costly to produce than today) it was used sparingly. The sharp working edges of spades or other implements were protected by pieces of forged iron; plough shares were also tipped with iron (Figure 5.4).

Even more costly steel was imported to reinforce workmen's iron tools. There were a number of ways for making steel which gave a good cutting-edge. One method involved having a layer of steel, covered with two plates of iron, so that when the tool is sharpened the steel projects at the thinned cutting edge. A second, and less effective method, was to weld a steel strip to the edge of a piece of iron; here

◁ **Plate 7.1:** Oxford: St Thomas the Martyr. South door of chancel consisting of battens with two strap hinges with scrolled ends and ornamental foliage scrolls, with a Scandinavian 'feel'. Thirteenth century (Photo: Oxfordshire County Council Department of Museum Services)

△ **Plate 7.2:** Eaton Bray, Bedfordshire. South door of church with more sophisticated and elaborate scrolled iron work including three straps, foliage and stamped rosette-ends (Photo: J.M. Steane)

sharpening soon wore away the steel edge. Further methods involved piling the material with alternate layers of iron and steel.

Society depended partly on oxen, but increasingly more on the horse for power and traction, and iron was used for harness bits and buckles, stirrups and spurs, for tyres fitted to wagon-wheels and for horseshoes. These last were produced in huge quantities. Richard I ordered 50,000 from the 60 or so forges set up in the Forest of Dean. Early medieval horse-shoes were wavy edged. Later they were larger and plainer in outline and by the fifteenth century the calkins were very marked and some shoes were fullered, i.e. round the edge runs a groove into which the nails fitted. Iron production was naturally stimulated by war. When Bedford Castle was being besieged in 1224, 15,000 crossbow quarrels and bolts were summoned up from Corfe Castle. Again there is a clear typological evolution of arrow-shape (see Figure 2.2). They began by being made

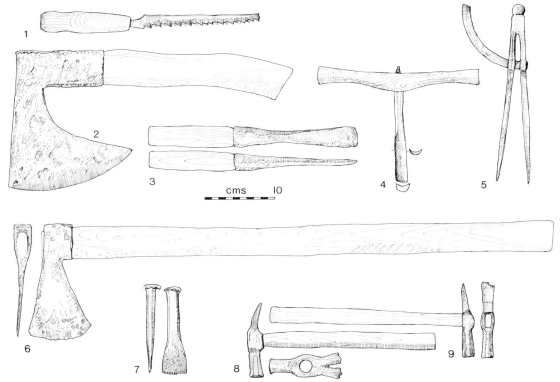

Figure 7.1: Tools from Museum of London. 1. Saw. 2. Woodworking axe. 3. Chisel. 4. Auger. 5. Calipers. 6. Felling axe. 7. Iron bolsters (for mason's work). 8/9 Hammers handles are restored

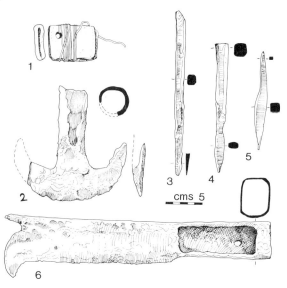

Figure 7.2: Tools from Weoley Castle, Birmingham. 1. Mason's plumb bob. 2. Turf cutter. 3,4,5. Chisels. 6. Billhook

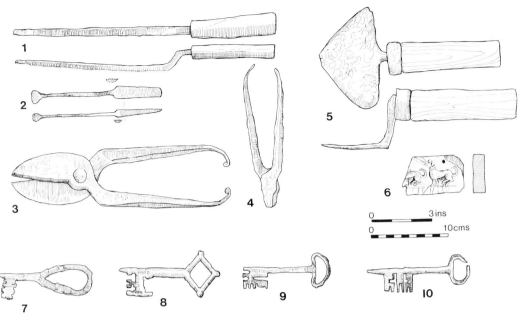

Figure 7.3: Tools from Museum of London. 1. Large file. 2. Small files. 3. Shears. 4. Pliers. 5. Mason's trowel. 6. Mould with figures of hounds. 7.-10. Keys from twelfth to fifteenth centuries, Northampton Museum

broad and triangular, but as they encountered an increase in defensive armour they became more bullet-shaped for armour-piercing. Hunting arrows were larger and were barbed to help them to stick into the quarry and bring it down.

Iron was, moreover, used occasionally in building-construction and extensively in the fittings of buildings.[7] Iron reinforcements had been used in the arcades at Sens Cathedral dating from *c.* 1140. When William of Sens obtained the contract for Canterbury Cathedral choir he employed similar techniques of using iron ties. After his crippling fall from the scaffolding his successors carried on in the same way. When the octagonal chapter-house of Westminster Abbey was built, 1245-55, the architect constructed an umbrella-like frame consisting of iron bars linked to hooks embedded in the slender central stone column. It did not prove sufficient to control the thrust, and flying buttresses had to be added to shore up the building. Iron ties, however, were also used in the chapels around the chevet★ of the abbey. Further structural uses of iron included

★The apsidal termination of the east end of a church.

the strengthening of doors, chests and windows by hinges and bars of iron. A wealth of information, for instance, was derived recently from a meticulous survey of the ironwork on the door of the Norman church at Stillingfleet, North Yorkshire.[8] The door was hinged on two C-shaped hinges each decorated with dragon terminals. The upper quarter was decorated with Adam and Eve figures, an interlocked cross and a Viking-type ship, all elaborate examples of smiths' work dating from the twelfth century. The location of missing nails and other portions which had originally been covered by iron were found by studying the differential weathering of the wooden components of the intricately carpentered door.

Finally, an examination of building accounts shows that nails, called by an inventive variety of names, helped to hold up medieval structures. A list bought for use at York Castle in 1327 included 220 braggenayl, 100 knopnayl, 3,260 doublenail, 1,200 greater spyking, 3,250 thaknail (presumably for nailing lathes), 1,800 lednail, 7,760 stotnayl, 300 tyngilnayl and 18,600 brodd. Excavation reports are full of rather arid lists of nails. More care should be taken with recording the exact position where nails were found. Clearly they were not just thrown about, they were hammered into objects which may have decayed away leaving only the nails. At the deserted settlement of Lyveden (Northants.), for instance, a large group found scattered in a doorway were likely to be derived from a decayed door while a linear distribution was plausibly interpreted as the remains of a collapsed fence.

Practically every medieval excavation yields iron objects. They are often exceedingly corroded with rust, difficult to identify and, unless they are rapidly conserved, they fall apart. Much valuable metallurgical analysis is now done to recover information about iron technology. Also X-ray photographs frequently indicate the original form of the tool or weapon under the corrosion deposits, and non-ferrous plating and inlays are shown up using this technique.

3. Charcoal Burning

The most important fuel used in connection with ironworking until the invention of coke in the early eighteenth century was charcoal.[9] Consequently charcoal burners are found working in close proximity to ironsmiths in the Middle Ages. The craft was an itinerant occupation practised by one man and his family who moved round the woodland areas searching for a plentiful supply of wood which they then negotiated the right to burn. Such workers were known as 'colliers', 'colemen' or 'ashburners' and the distribution of such names in the Middle Ages corresponds with known areas of ironworking.

The techniques followed by the charcoal burner, though simple, required considerable skill. First, he had to arrange with the woodland owner for the right to take dead wood or loppings. Such a grant was made to the monks of Byland Abbey in the twelfth century to mine iron at their grange at Bentley in Emley, which included for charcoal burning 'all dead wood which is without fruit or leaves lying or standing throughout the territory of the vill of Emley'. Such rights were closely hedged round to protect woodland. William

Le Spen obtained a licence for one week at Wakefield in 1324 to have a saw and a hatchet 'for felling, splitting and burning charcoal from old alders and hollow beeches'. This implied that he did not have the means to strip the natural woodland. During the later Middle Ages, however, grants were made involving total clearance rather than limited coppicing and lopping. The timber was dragged to the working site where the cords of wood were prepared. A saw-horse or even a saw-pit might be expected to be seen here. The sawn wood would be stacked in rows and held in place by vertical pegs.

Next the kiln would be built, initially by constructing a central vertical shaft of sawn wood down which the fire would eventually be introduced. The cords would be stacked vertically round the shaft and the whole mound covered with a layer of leaves and soil. The latter materials were used to seal the stack while still allowing in sufficient oxygen to feed a slow-burning fire. The stack was ignited and its contents gradually burned through to the outside emitting clouds of smoke and steam. Hurdle frames might be erected to protect the smouldering stack from the wind. When it had burned through, water was applied to quench the embers and the outer layer, now sunk down, was carefully peeled off, to expose the brittle black sticks of charcoal.

The archaeological remains of charcoal burning are somewhat elusive. The shelters of the charcoal burners were slight constructions, circular, sunken-floored and conical shaped, resembling prehistoric Bronze Age huts. The signs of kilns are large circular shallow banks about 6-13 m in diameter. In woodland on Blorenge mountain in Gwent, the charcoal burners' activities are visible as bright green stripes of vegetation, the effect of rich potash deposits on ledges on the slopes up the hillside. But the principal evidence left behind by the charcoal burners are 'black patches', which have often been reported by field workers in areas of former woodland. A recent survey of charcoal burning in Northamptonshire, using aerial photographs, has shown dense concentrations of black patches in former areas of medieval woodland in Rockingham Forest and Whittlewood.[10] It is noteworthy that these coincide with those areas where smiths and ironworking are mentioned in Domesday Book. There are curious blanks in other known forested areas such as Brixworth and Bromswold. Possibly the answer is that there were no suitable iron ores for smelting in these areas and consequently a reduced demand for charcoal.

4. Lead Working

One of the reasons for Roman interest in Britain was the potential it afforded for the exploitation of non-ferrous metals, in particular, lead, tin and copper. Within ten years of their conquest they are found mining lead in North Wales and the Mendips. Lead mines in Derbyshire were leased by the Abbess of Repton in 835 AD, and by the time of Domesday Book they were of considerable value. In the early Middle Ages the lead miners seem to have acquired considerable rights; by mining law they had the right to prospect anywhere except in churchyards, gardens, orchards and highways.[11] They also had the right of access to the nearest high road, even if this meant going through standing corn, and were privileged to take timber from the neighbouring woods to use in the mines.

By c. 1130-70 ample supplies of lead were available for the major construction sites of England.[12] There were complex systems of tunnels and shafts used to exploit the deep silver-lead workings. The wares of 'Carlisle Mine' dominated all markets except the Severn Valley where the lead from Llanymynech held sway. This situation changed radically following the Scottish incursions of 1172-3. The northern English argentiferous mining industry collapsed and prices doubled in all markets save the south-west. The way was open to a development of the lead industry in Mendip, Yorkshire, Flint, Durham and Derbyshire using non silver-bearing ores.[13] Simple trenches (grova) were cut into the outcropping veins of lead (rakes), ownership rights were then delineated and individual miners scooped out the ore (galena) from within the bounds of their meers.* Groups of these workings in the Derbyshire moors produced the raw material

*A measure of land, in Derbyshire, containing lead ore.

for 'boles' or smelting sites. They are not usually identifiable on the ground, having been obliterated by later deeper excavations.

The ore, once extracted, was graded and concentrated in preparation for smelting. This was done by initial hammering when the larger pieces (called the bing) were set aside. The ore was then crushed by 'buckers' (large iron pieces with curved undersides) on 'knocker stones', and washed in troughs. The unutilisable riddlings were sieved out and the resultant deposit was ready for 'boling'. These processes have left little trace but much evidence for the next stage, smelting, lies scattered in the landscape. Excavation of a 'bole' or lead smelting hearth near Beeley in Derbyshire has shown that the lead worker first hollowed out a hearth and loaded it with carefully mixed layers of brushwood and ore, weaving the former into a dense mesh to prevent the heavy ore falling into the fire before it had oxidised. When fired the 'galena' was converted into oxide, sulphur dioxide was dispersed into the air, and molten lead accumulated in the base of the furnace to be ladled out through the taphole.

During the next 400 years the raw materials were depleted (in Blanchard's phrase!) 'at a pace conditioned by the existence of exogenously determined demand cycles'. The industry shifted its focus from worked-out mines in Derbyshire to Mendip in the fourteenth century, and other deposits were opened up in Yorkshire, Flint and Durham. Here technological improvements such as the introduction of the 'turnbole', the 'blackwash oven' and the 'Durham system' enabled failing enterprises to save fuel and to make use of slags left over from primary 'boling'. The turnbole, a hearth which was 1.52 m high and could be turned like a windmill, has not left any discernible archaeological traces, but the black glassy slags and the circular stone structures of the improved ovens are to be found on the Derbyshire moors and the slopes of Weardale.

William I had shown an immediate and intelligent interest in the lead mines of Derbyshire. He entrusted the custody of the Peak Forest to William Peverel who built a castle in a dramatically dominant position.[14] From its bailey a wide sweep of bare hills can be seen criss-crossed with the now grassed-over lead workings. The Crown profited by, but did not control, the production of lead. It customarily took the thirteenth dish of ore in Derbyshire and the ninth dish of ore in Alston Moor (where there were other mines, on the borders of Cumberland, Yorkshire and Northumberland). In the 1530s lead was one of the main items of booty from the Dissolution of the monasteries. A flood of lead from the roofs of 800 religious houses swamped the market and forced prices down. Hastily constructed furnaces, such as the one found brutally cut into the floor of the Greyfriars church at Northampton, were used to smelt the lead.[15] Four ingots, stamped with the Tudor Rose and Crown, were retrieved from the floor at Rievaulx Abbey, doubtless loot from the roofs of the church.[16]

Lead was valuable in the Middle Ages as now: its ductility and low melting point meant that it was easily worked and versatile in use. Plumbers (from the Latin word for lead, *plumbum*) prepared their sheet lead from 'pigs', which were cast slabs, the shape of long loaves.[17] The lead was melted over a charcoal brazier and poured onto a level bed of sand making sheets about 1 m wide and 4 mm thick. The sheets were nailed to the roof – each sheet overlapping the top edge of the one further down. The valleys and gutters required careful shaping with shears tapped into position by wooden dressing mallets. Because lead tends to 'creep' when hot sun causes it to expand, roofs were made shallower pitched during the Later Middle Ages. Lead could also be cast into many shapes, including myriads of pilgrim badges (see p. 81).

5. Tin Mining

The south-western promontory of Devon and Cornwall has been exploited for tin since prehistoric times.[18] Cornish tin is said to have been carried over to France in the seventh century and during the Middle Ages it was a prized export, English tin mines being among the richest in Europe. Tin, like lead and copper, exists in veins or lodes embedded in rocks at various levels. When these veins outcrop on the banks of a stream, the tin-bearing ore is worn away by water action, and carried down the valley. The tin sinks because of its heavy specific gravity, forming a deposit in the gravel which can be up to 6.1 m thick. This alluvial tin was worked in prehistoric and early medieval times by digging away surface gravel and then directing water onto it.

The water was brought by artificial leats and this process of tin streaming leaves curving ridges of gravel waste behind. Later, shallow shafts were sunk as miners followed the lodes into the ground and this, of course, produced problems of drainage. To begin with baling was sufficient, but soon adits were driven into hillsides below workings and connected with them. In this way water was drained out and away. As in lead mining it was necessary to crush the ore and wash it before smelting it. The large ingots were cast in blocks with specially prolonged sides designed for ease of carriage by packhorse. For retail purposes the tin was recast in 'strakes' or rectangular lattices from which pieces were easily broken off for customers wishing to purchase small quantities.

The material was so valuable that strict laws were made for its regulation and the miners had to take their product to one of a small group of stannary towns (those in Cornwall were Lostwithiel, Launceston, Truro and Helston).[19] Here it was weighed and assayed (tested) so that the correct duty might be levied. There is a grim tower at Lydford in Devon built in 1195 as a prison for those convicted in the Devon stannary courts.[20] It seems that Devon produced more tin than Cornwall in the Early Middle Ages but by the fourteenth century it was outstripped by the Cornish tinners. Between 1450 and 1495 Devon tin production doubled but it still only reached the level of one-quarter of the Cornish output. It is said that the noble tower of the church at Widecombe-in-the-Moor, built in the early years of the sixteenth century, was financed by contributions of the local tinners.

6. Bronze Working

One reason for the importance of tin is that it was used in the production of bronze. The medieval bronzesmith worked with an assortment of alloys, but the principal ingredient was copper, mixed with small proportions of tin, zinc and lead. Medieval England had no large workable deposits of copper and had to import this material. Sheets of brass, a yellow alloy of copper and zinc, with a small quantity of lead and tin to assist fluidity when molten, were imported from the continent. Most towns had bronze craftsmen adept at turning out the large numbers of small goods which are found, well preserved, in almost every excavation of medieval levels.[21]

The evidence so far found at Oxford, York and London suggests that bronze working was on a domestic rather than an industrial scale. It takes the form of small pieces of slag, spillage, scrap metal, offcuts and crucibles (tiny ceramic containers for molten metal). Stone moulds for casting buckles, brooches, buttons and dagger pommels have come from Rochester, York and Hereford. Clay-mould fragments relating to the casting of bells have been found in or around churches but so far the tools used for working the metal have proved elusive.

The techniques for working bronze involve the casting of molten metal and the cold working of sheet metal and wire. Simple objects were cast in open or two-piece moulds: hollow wares required more complex moulds which had a central core and needed to be broken to release the casting. Sheet metal was hammered into shape and riveted to produce vessels like cauldrons. Wire might be made into pins or chain links. Pewter, an alloy largely of lead and tin, might be spun on a lathe. Decoration could be added during casting, or incised lines could be made by repeated pecking, using a punch and hammer. A final embellishment might be given by gilding, using gold leaf, or by painting or enamelling. Niello, a sulphide of iron, was applied to white metal or bronze to fill an incised decorative pattern with a contrasting black paste. Enamel inlay provided a brilliantly coloured vitreous paste which filled heraldic shields in a bronze piece, like the folding candlestick recently excavated at Grove Priory (Beds.).[22]

Bronze was the ideal material for small articles of dress such as buckles and strap fittings which were attached to mens' or womens' girdles, held up their hose, fastened knights' armour, and buckled on spurs or horse harness. The typology of buckles is well understood and provides an approximate dating technique. Belts were often decorated with small reinforcing mounts which take the form of circular studs, rosettes or bows. Dress was also held together by laces and strings strengthened with rolled cylinders of sheet bronze called points threaded through eyelet holes.[23] Horse harness similarly was embellished with articles in bronze like roundels, heraldic pendants and small rumbler bells made from two pieces of sheet metal enclosing an iron pea. Needleworking tools were a further useful product of the bronze worker's repertoire. Pins were manufactured at Coventry often with elaborate heads. Tweezers were made from folded sheets of strip metal and might have expanded rectangular ends which could have been used for opening a book or handling gold leaf. A manicure set, found at the deserted settlement at Lyveden, combined tweezers with other toilet instruments.

Bronze was also used for objects connected with trade and commerce. Seal matrices were owned by monasteries and every self-respecting merchant; by the thirteenth century peasants were even aspiring to the possession of a seal (see p. 32). Money changers, shop keepers and druggists all had a use for small balances; larger weights had a copper alloy shell and were filled with lead. Richard Earl of Cornwall and Poitou was elected King of the Romans 1257-72 and in 1260 he obtained a charter, for the Hansa merchants of London. He had the royal arms, those of the earldom of Cornwall and the double eagle of the Empire, cast onto these steelyard weights: they have been found on or near land and water routes associated with the wool trade. Medieval profits were kept in purses made of bronze frames to which were stitched fabric or leather bags (Figure 8.6).

Among the most valuable household movables were cast metal pots and jugs; they were handed down from one generation to the next and surviving whole vessels are rare. Fragments of bag-shaped cauldrons with three legs and skillets, together with manuscript illustrations, enable us to reconstruct them. The internal surfaces of skillets were tinned to prevent acids from attacking the copper body. Perforated spoons with socketed handles were used to skim the fat from the surface of stew in the cauldron (see Figure 8.3b). Jugs and ewers occur in the later medieval periods and are associated with higher standards of cleanliness and politesse. With aquamaniles (ewers in the shape of knights on horseback) they were used for washing hands and serving wine. It is thought that bronze cooking vessels gradually replaced pottery in some more prosperous households in the fourteenth and fifteenth centuries. Their advantage was that they could be repaired by riveting patches, and ultimately melted down when past repair. Their shapes were often copied by potters in their less durable material.

Among the largest objects made of bronze during the Middle Ages were church bells. The bell founder could hardly have made his living from this once-and-for all process, he would also have cast buckles, belt fittings or pots and be known as a girdler, a potter or bell founder. Between Milford Street and Guilder Lane in Salisbury a bronze foundry site was excavated, it included a bell founding pit with some fragments of cope★ in the pit bearing impressions of bell surfaces as well as pieces of moulds for the production of domestic vessels including tripod skillets. It was evidently the workshop of John Barber, brazier, who died in 1404.[24] More often, however, bell foundry pits and the hearths for smelting the metal are found under or near church towers as at Hadstock (Essex). The reason is that bells were so heavy that their movement was difficult and it was as well to make them as near as possible to where they were to be suspended. At Winchester, the bell pits for the Norman cathedral were found a few yards away from the bell foundry of the Saxon cathedral. Here fragments of the copes were seen to be made of dung which incorporated remains of straw, thus throwing incidental light on the nature of the cereal crops of the time.[25]

7. Quarrying and Building

Each medieval stone church tower, bridge, abbey, manor-house, castle, town wall or palace presupposes a quarry. It is evident that

★The outer portion or case of a mould.

by the late Saxon period stone was being transported over large distances in eastern and southern England.[26] The most prized building stones occurred in the band or ridge of Jurassic limestone which is found running diagonally across England from Yorkshire to Somerset. These oolitic freestones were carried 112.7 km east into Hampshire, and into the lower Thames Valley, over East Anglia and along the eastern coasts, 80.5 km west into Devon and the Welsh borderland. Carts and wagons were used to transport the stone and large blocks up to 508 kg are found (as in the Anglo-Saxon church at Breamore in Hampshire) 112.7 km from their source near Bath. Waterways, in particular the network in the Fenland, were used to transport stone from the Barnack quarries all over eastern England. Moreover, Caen stone was brought in from Normandy after the Conquest to provide for the great Norman drive in monastic and cathedral building on a grand scale.

Nearly 5 km south-east of Stamford near Barnack village and its Anglo-Saxon towered church lies a 24.3 ha– field known as 'the hills and holes'.[27] It is pockmarked with abandoned quarry pits now grassed over and filled with scrub. The small scale and multiple ownership of the individual undertakings is implied by the many workings. A number of abbeys had concessions and leases of strips of land at Barnack quarries. From here came the stone from which the great churches at Ramsey, Crowland, Sawtry, Bury St Edmunds and Peterborough were built. It was taken to a wharf by the River Nene still marked by two stones standing in a field called 'Robin Hood and Little John'. Sawtry Abbey had a special canal still called the Monks' Lode which went through Whittlesea Mere to bring in the Barnack stone. Blocks have been found on the bed of the mere with destination marks cut into them. Transported by water the stone furnished Norwich Cathedral and many of the Cambridge colleges; it even reached Lavenham in Suffolk, 96.6 km away.

Before beginning any architectural work it was necessary for the patron, whether he was king, noble or ecclesiastic, to have a clear idea of what the completed building was to be like. The *Liberate* and *Close* Rolls of Henry III are full of specific instructions for the alterations and additions to the royal palaces and castles.[28] This room is to be decorated with sculpture, painting and stained glass, that building is to be enlarged by so many feet, and so on. In many cases, where the contract specifying the work has survived, it is made clear that the design is to follow or to rival some existing building. The chapel at Windsor Castle in 1243 was to have a high wooden roof 'made after the manner of the roof of the new work at Lichfield, so that the stone work may be seen'. Henry VI, when founding his college at Eton, specified the principal measurements for the choir of the chapel, 'and so the seid Qwere schall be lenger than the qwere of the Newe College at Oxford bi xlvii fote brodder by viii fote. And the walles heyer by xxti fote. And also heyer than the walles of seynt Stephenes Chapell at Westmonstre.'[29] There is clearly in the Eton instructions an element of keeping up with the Joneses! In 1487-8 the steeple of Helmingham Church, Suffolk was to be built and a contract was made with the mason of Copham in Norfolk. It was to be 18.3 m high and of the breadth, width and thickness of the steeple at Framsden, with the same number of string courses, faced with split flint showing black 'so that it be after the facyon of the stepyll of Bramston.[30] The practice of copying a neighbouring building such as this led to the emergence of local styles. The spires of Northamptonshire and the towers of Somerset are cases in point. As groups they are closely related in design.[31]

Medieval architectural drawings have very rarely survived in England. This was probably due to a lack of any contemporary feeling that such plans should be preserved rather than the inability of builders to make or use them. It may well be that on the site itself the actual laying out of the building on the ground took the place of a drawn plan. We know from references to 'tracing houses' that drawings of various features were supplied. William of Sens who was the 'most skilled craftsman in wood and stone' was given the job of rebuilding Canterbury Cathedral after it had been burnt out in 1174. He conceived and carried out the design, providing the workmen with models for mouldings; the result is that the arcades at Canterbury are exactly like those which William had built across the Channel at Sens.[32] Later we know that plans were drawn on wood or canvas. When Sir William Sinclair built Roslyn chapel in Scotland 'he first caused the draughts to be drawn upon Eastland boards [i.e. those imported from the Baltic] and made the carpenters to carve them, according to the draughts thereon, and then gave them for patterns to the masons that they might cut the like in stone'.[33]

Sometimes stone surfaces in masons' sheds were used instead of notebooks, parchment or boards. Such is the sketch of an early geometrical style window inscribed on a block of clunch from the site of the hospital of St John the Evangelist at Cambridge.[34]

The first stage of building was the laying of foundations. In this process the Normans seem to have been singularly deficient.[35] Despite their famed massiveness of construction, they were content with excessively shallow foundations, with the results that a great number of their towers fell – with disastrous effects to the rest of the building – especially if they were centrally placed. At times when the ground needed to be made more solid it was reinforced with wooden piles. Piles of beech, for instance, were granted to the Friars Minor of Winchester for the foundations of their church in 1239. Winchester Cathedral was founded on such boggy ground that a diver was employed for 20 years when restoration works were going on in this century; his job was to bolster up the watery foundations.

Timber was often used intramurally by medieval builders.[36] At Castle Acre Castle (Norfolk) a bank of made earth, threatened with slumping, endangered a wall which had been built upon it. It was strengthened with timber; the empty chases are left today where the timber has rotted. At Lincoln Castle the curtain wall was built on a rough framework of longitudinal baulks crossed by transverse timbers at intervals. Foundations could also be reinforced by timber. At the Old Minster, Winchester, the tenth-century apsidal-end was strengthened at ground level by timbers and a similar technique was found by Peers in the rubble foundations under the choir of York Minster dated to c. 1080.

The walls of major Norman buildings were usually faced with ashlar (rectangular blocks of dressed stone) and filled with rubble. This

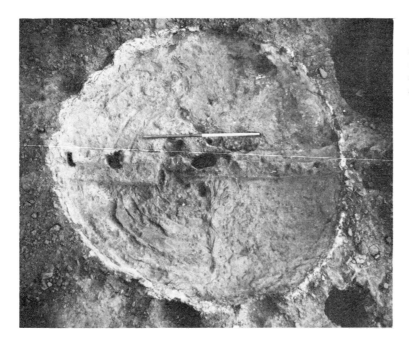

Plate 7.3: Late Saxon Mortar Mixer, St Peters Street, Northampton. Scale in half metres. Excavation in 1973 (Photo: Northampton Development Corporation)

Plate 7.4: Bedford Castle. Lime kiln associated with the rebuilding and refortification of the castle, 1216-24. The lime kiln was 5.80 m in diameter at the top: reducing to an oval shape 4.10 x 4.50 m at the base. It was 2.80 m in depth with four quadrant shaped platforms and opposed stoke holes. Such a setting implies a 'flare' kiln in which material is calcined by radiant heat. The fuel supply is likely to have been timber or charcoal (Photo: Bedfordshire County Council)

might take the form of mortar, flints, broken tiles and unshaped stone. Mortar naturally had to be mixed on the site. At Northampton, three Anglo-Saxon mortar mixers were built on a site near the present St Peter's Church, dating from the ninth century.[37] Circular bowls, 2 m and 3 m in diameter, had been cut into the natural ironstone and lined with wattlework. There were central postholes which were for pivots, probably supporting beams from which paddles were suspended, the whole being capstan driven; layers of concrete and mortar had built up within two of the bowls. One of the constituents used in making mortar was lime, another interesting element in the archaeology of building. At Bedford, a large lime kiln, 5.80 m in diameter at the top and 2.80 in depth was excavated in 1973. It was loaded and emptied from the top.[38] Charcoal and other fuel was introduced through the stokeholes at the bottom and heat penetrated through channels in the base of the kiln which permitted a through draught. The burned lime was probably used in the making of mortar for bonding the castle stonework when it was refortified between 1216 and 1224.

As the walls went up higher, wooden scaffolding had to be provided, steel tubular scaffolding being a modern invention. During the Middle Ages builders had to make do with saplings or firs, tied together by withies with shorter logs as horizontal crosspieces, such as are still used in the southern Mediterranean and Middle Eastern countries today.[39] This horizontal scaffolding was fitted into slots in the wall known as 'putlog' holes. These can be traced on the outside of ancient buildings; when blocked up a different shade of mortar betrays their former presence. Sometimes, as at Walberswick Church, Suffolk, the sawn-off ends of the scaffolding can be seen in these slots. Platforms were provided by means of hurdles.

The raising of stone blocks and timber baulks to the great heights sometimes reached by gothic buildings was done with the help of windlasses. 'Great wheels' have survived in seven places including Durham, Tewkesbury, Peterborough and Salisbury (Figure 7.5). Their principle was simply to wind the hoisting rope round the prolonged axis of the wheel with power provided by the operator who could either walk inside the treadwheel or climb rungs attached to the outside rim. The earlier versions are so called 'compass-arm wheels' where the spokes (arms) were driven right through the shaft on which the wheel was mounted. The later type (from the mid-sixteenth century) had spokes that were chords to the wheel's circle, the shaft fitting into the square opening which the spokes formed near the centre. Hooks were attached to blocks of stone by means of the 'lewis', an invention of the Greeks also known to medieval builders (Figure 7.4).

The 124 m of Salisbury Cathedral tower and spire challenged the resourcefulness of the fourteenth-century carpenters who left behind their windlass as well as the extraordinarily intricate but strong web of scaffolding which is built into the cone of the spire in nine receding stages (Plate 7.5).

The masons who were responsible for raising medieval buildings were divided into two broad overlapping classes.[40] There were the so-called 'rough masons' who hewed stones with axes or hammers and laid them, and the 'freemasons', who worked with axes, chisels and mallets on the finer freestone carvings, mouldings and traceries. The dressing of blocks and cutting of mouldings was done on a bench by a 'banker mason'. He might work on the stone inside the building or, perhaps more likely, in a temporary shed outside known as the *lodge*. The foundations of two such masons' workshops were found to the south of Bishop Stillington's chantry chapel at Wells Cathedral. Here as the masons worked they generated over a metre of waste, chippings and dust which was trampled into the ground and formed a 'working floor'. '*Freestone*' was any fine grained sandstone or limestone which can be freely worked in any direction. It is ideal for the carving of leaves and flowers, for decorating capitals and cornices: it can be sawn for mouldings and cut for tracery. It can be carved for gargoyles or images. *Setting out floors* have also survived at Wells and York. Above the north porch of the nave of Wells Cathedral is an upper room, accessible only from the triforium, which is floored in smooth plaster-of-Paris. Upon this is a maze of incised lines forming architectural settings-out.[41] The master mason used it as a draughting surface; templates could be made from the designs which then provided guidelines for the stone cutters. In fact the freemasons not only had to be adept with cutting and carving, they had to be experts in the art of setting out; with the final cementing of the stones in place the slightest slip or carelessness of too much or too little mortar might spoil the symmetry of a delicate design such as a rose window or an intricate piece of fan-vaulting.

The so-called 'masons' lodges' were the schools where rough masons might gradually

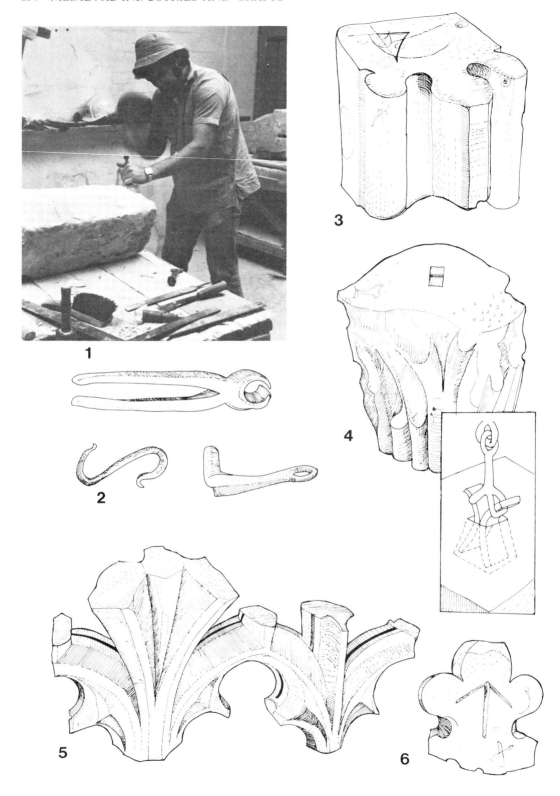

1

2

3

4

5

6

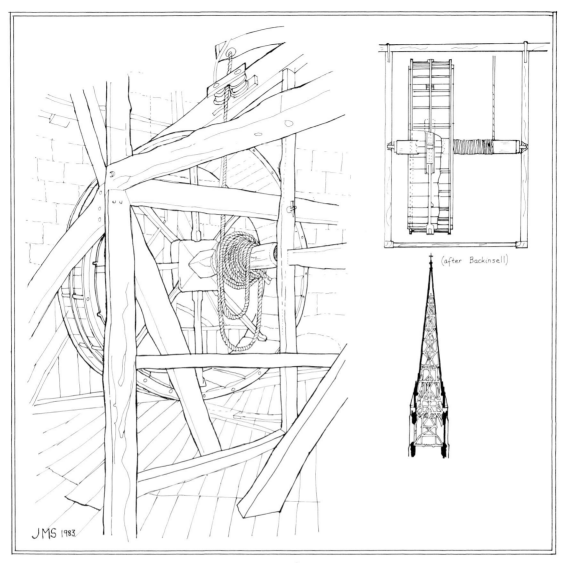

(after Backinsell)

JMS 1983

Figure 7.4: Modern Mason at Work. Tools and Architectural Fragments from Hailes Abbey, Gloucestershire. 1. Pincers. 2. S-shaped link and half a lewis. 3. Vault rib with a network of scribed lines on the top surface, probably masons' signatures, meant to show which mason was responsible for the cutting or the dressing. Also an indicator of the quality of a novice-mason's work. 4. Arch springer from aisle vault with slot in upper surface cut to receive *lewis clamp*. Inset shows a lewis clamp when fitted, linking the stone to the rope leaving the sides and base clear. Using this the mason can check the alignment of the stone as it is lowered into place. 5. Section of cloister window tracery illustrating the complexity of the mason's task in shaping and piecing together carved stone. 6. Grooves cut in dressed and shaped stone to give the mortar a better key or grip

△ **Figure 7.5:** Windlass in Salisbury Cathedral at Top of Central Tower under Spire. Inset section of spire showing nine stages of original scaffolding still in place

Plate 7.5: Salisbury Cathedral. The web of scaffolding built into the cone of the fourteenth-century spire. (Photo: J.M. Steane)

move on to freestone carving or where the apprentice might learn his craft. The scattered nature of the work meant that a mason's life was a thoroughly nomadic one. For one thing, they were frequently 'impressed' for the king's works. Sheriffs were commanded by the Crown to find so many masons for the large-scale operations of a royal house or castle and they scoured the country, forcing skilled men to leave home. But masons also moved around from job to job in the normal course of their working life. Robert Spillesby, for instance, worked at Eton as a freemason; he is also found at York Minster as master mason from 1466-72. Henry Jannings again was apprentice mason at Eton 1453-4, and by 1476 had apparently been promoted to master mason at St George's Chapel, Windsor. Masons left their distinctive marks, mostly geometrical designs incised into worked blocks of stone,[42] and by mapping their distribution, the journeyings of individual masons can be followed. This of course had the effect of spreading new styles in building. The 'Perpendicular' diffused throughout Cornish churches in this way.[43]

Craftsmen were sought at a distance and far off buildings were specified as models. The Somerset style appears for this reason in some Cornish towers and screens; also the roof-truss construction involving square-set purlins which derived ultimately from the aisled hall spread in this way over the south-west.

Life was transient for the medieval masons.

It could also be short. Stone cutting within the confined space of a lodge or workshop doubtless brought on silicosis caused by the intake into their lungs of grit and stone dust. The archetypal mason, attracted to the stoneyards of Oxford, Jude the Obscure, perished of consumption.

When the walls had been built and the roof put on, most internal wall surfaces were plastered and then whitewashed or painted. The strange habit of Victorian church restorers of stripping walls down to the masonry which they then pointed with unsuitably hard and dark cement, would have surprised medieval builders. A final finish in fact was often provided in churches by painting walls with sacred, historiated or moralistic subjects. In houses legendary and allegorical scenes were sometimes chosen. Patterns stencilled with lines to imitate marble or masonry were common.

8. Purbeck Marble and Alabaster

Two types of stone worked in medieval England were valued for artistic rather than utilitarian reasons. These were marble and alabaster. Purbeck marble, found on the Isle of Purbeck in Dorset, is a freshwater deposit composed mainly of the fossilised shells of small snails.[44] When freshly quarried the rough mass looks like grey porridge; it is capable, however, of taking a high polish and makes a very handsome material contrasting with lighter limestone. The biographer of St Hugh at Lincoln praised it: 'this stone disdains to be tamed with steel until it have first been subdued by art, for its surface must first be softened by long grinding with sand and its hardness relaxed with vinegar . . . of this are formed those slender columns which stand round the great piers, even as a bevy of maidens stand marshalled for a dance.' It was first used for effigies and monuments in the twelfth century, but later formed contrasting shafts and bands favoured by thirteenth-century builders. It was used in quantity in Salisbury and Lincoln Cathedrals and at Westminster Abbey. Indeed nearly every English church of any importance built between 1170 and 1350 made use of the polished pillars, the capitals, bases and string courses. There are two good archaeological reasons for thinking that Purbeck marble was delivered not only in the block but as finished sculpture.[45] Along West Street of the village of Corfe (Plate 4.7), the centre of the trade, were layers of marble fragments, 3-3.7 m thick, in which pieces of moulding and leaf carving were common. They are also still found among tumbled heaps of debris at Downshay Farm and Afflington, the very site of the medieval quarries. Moreover, the Purbeck marble capitals of the nave at Chichester Cathedral are carved with foliage, in size and shape all alike; in many cases these are distinct misfits in regard to the Caen stone with which they are walled. We know that in 1279 the sheriff of Dorset bought 300 columns of marble and 200 capitals for the Countess of Arundel for her nunnery at Markham. It is clear from this that Purbeck marble was sculptured where it was quarried and customarily delivered as prefabricated units.

The same material was favoured for tombs and effigies. The famous figures of knights in mail armour, flowing surcoats, and bearing shields and swords, in the Temple Church, London, display with their gleaming solemnity and noble calm the prowess of Purbeck marblers. Monumental effigies of Purbeck marble are rare after c. 1280-1300. They went out of fashion about the time of the Black Death, and were then replaced by bronze or alabaster, but the architectural features of tombs continued to be made of this material.

Alabaster is not marble but gypsum, a sulphate of lime, which appears in abundance, in a massive or rock form in great detached blocks and in rocky strata, in Nottinghamshire, Derbyshire and Staffordshire.[46] It was quarried in the late Middle Ages from the ridge south-west of Tutbury in Staffordshire and from Chellaston Hill about 6.4 km southeast of Derby. This slightly translucent stone was much prized by medieval sculptors; it was transported in small blocks necessary for panels and free-standing figures to workshops in Nottingham, York, Lincoln, Burton-on-Trent and London. It was soft and easily cut when first quarried; when carved it hardens somewhat, is amenable to colouring and gilding, and polishes like marble. Thomas Prentys at Chellaston owned an integrated firm of quarry and workshop. He was the main quarry-owner there, to whom French customers travelled to buy blocks of alabaster. Elaborate alabaster tombs were turned out by his workmen for patrons all over England. Exact portraiture was not required, simply visible evidence of the patron's social position and family connections. Sometimes as in church buildings copies were demanded. Sir Walter Manny, one of the foremost soldiers of his day, and founder of the London Charterhouse, stipulated in his will in 1371 for 'a tomb of alabaster, made as a knight in armour such as was made for Sir John de Beauchamp in St. Pauls in London'. Even more impressive were the great carved reredoses, screens covering church walls behind altars made of carved alabaster panels framed in wood (Figure 3.5). One of the finest and largest was brought from Peter Mason of Nottingham for £200 – an enormous sum of money – for the high altar of St George's Windsor. The 17-day journey from Nottingham to Windsor involved ten carts each with eight horses. An elaborate tomb with an effigy such as that of Ralph Greene of Lowick in Northamptonshire cost £40. Smaller stock scenes such as St John's head on a plate, the Five Joys of the Virgin and the Passion of Christ, which were turned out in their hundreds, were crude in execution and cheap; but they looked rich with their gilded knobs and picked out in red, green and blue paint.[47] English alabaster panels were exported all over Europe. Gradually the supplies of white alabaster declined and iron-stained material began to be used in the sixteenth century. It was the Reformation, however, that killed the industry. It is said that following the Edwardian iconoclastic legislation of the 1540s and 1550s whole shiploads packed with second-hand alabaster sculptures left the country for the continent. Some 3,000 are to be found in the churches of France, Italy and Spain; they even made their way to Poland and Iceland. It is paradoxical that more are to be found on the continent than in their country of origin. Those left in England were hurriedly buried or were smashed into little pieces.

9. Timber and Wood: Carpentry and Woodworking Crafts

Before stone came into more general use for churches and important structures in the late Saxon period the universal building material was timber. Forty years ago practically our sole source of knowledge of Saxon timber building techniques was to be found at the church of Greenstead-juxta-Ongar, Essex.[48] Here, miraculously, the greater part of the north and south walls, together with part of the west gable survived. They are all built of logs of oak which are split into halves and reared, with their curved surfaces outwards, upon a sill and fitting into a grooved top plate. This has now been supplemented by new information from three directions. Improvements in excavation techniques, particularly in the recognition of post-holes and posts in trenches enable us to trace the remains of timber structures that have rotted away. The excavators of the Anglo-Saxon palaces of Yeavering, Cheddar, and now Northampton, have been able to plan these complexes of buildings with assurance. Secondly, the discovery of waterlogged deposits in considerable areas of towns such as York and Dublin has revealed the lower parts of timber structures preserved *in situ*. Further, our understanding of carpentry has also been enlarged by experiments in reconstructing Saxon buildings, as at West Stow, Suffolk.[49]

The Saxon or medieval carpenter, when

selecting the tree in the wood to be cut down, was guided by the condition of the bark. Splits showed the presence of straight or spiral fissures; damage to the tree underneath caused by boughs falling away could also be detected. The tree was converted into usable timber in the woodland itself. The green unseasoned wood was split with wedges of seasoned wood into halves, quarters, eighths, sixteenths and even thirty-seconds without using a saw. It is possible to check the methods used by the medieval carpenter in preparing his timber by examining the original and often very weathered ends of the joists sticking out from under a jettied storey.[50] The age of the timber when felled can be calculated, also the method of cutting up the baulk by the nicks left by the wedges; the adze marks with their rippling waves contrast with the corrugations left by the pit-saw (Plates 7.6, 7.7).

The basic woodworking tool was, however, the axe, which came in a multiplicity of shapes each determined by its special function – felling, smoothing, cutting mortises, and so on: during the thirteenth or fourteenth centuries some important tools were added to the woodworker's kit including the brace, using the crank principle for speedy boring by continuous rotation, improved augers, requiring little pressure to draw themselves into the wood, and the twybill, which eased the cutting of joints in large timbers. Thirteenth-century sculptures and fifteenth-century manuscript drawings of Noah show him surrounded with a rich armoury of woodworking tools (see Plate 7.8).[51]

A further dimension has been added to the known methods of the medieval carpenter by the close and informed examination of surviving timber structures, particularly roofs, floors, window frames or doors, pioneered by Cecil Hewitt. In the church at Hadstock (Essex) an Anglo-Saxon door made of four oak planks has been recognised. The planks are ingeniously and economically assembled with splayed rebated edge-joints tied together with D-sectioned ledges transfixed by iron clenches and roves. In the same church the double-splayed windows high up in the nave walls have frames, expertly carpentered of four separate timbers, double-pegged at each joint.[52]

The Chantry House, Henley-on-Thames, Oxon., *c.* 1425. Two examples of the 'signatures' left by carpenters' tools on timber. **Plate 7.6** (above), evidence for pit-sawing; **Plate 7.7** (below), evidence for adzing. Both are on the moulded bressumer on the 'important' side of the building (Photo: J.M. Steane)

Plate 7.8: Wells Cathedral, West Front. Noah at work building the ark. He is using a broad bladed shipwright's axe and is smoothing a plank resting on two trestles. Further tools, an axe and a hammer? lie beneath. The ark itself appears to be carvel built. *c.* 1250 (Photo: J.M. Steane)

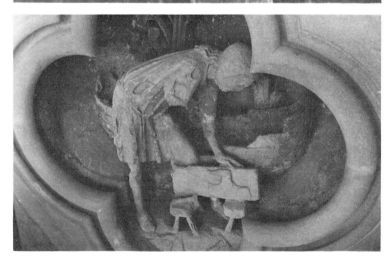

Plate 7.9: Blackfriars, Gloucester. The late thirteenth-century oaken roof, trussed coupled rafters with scissors bracing. The scale of the great preaching space can be appreciated from this building recently restored by the Department of the Environment (Photo: J.M. Steane)

PRN 3436

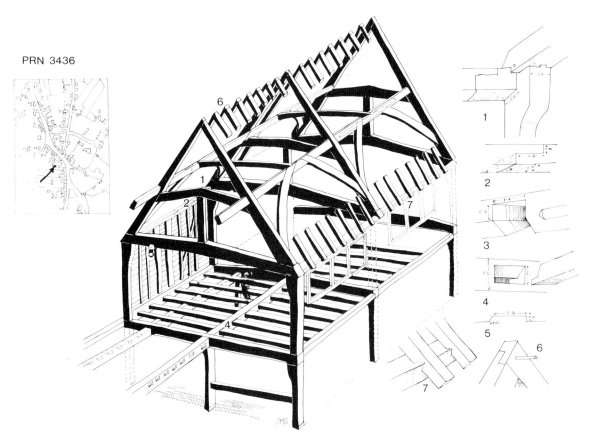

Figure 7.6: The George Inn (now an hotel), Dorchester-on-Thames, Oxfordshire. Perspective of timber framing and carpentry details 1. Tie beam, principal and wall-plate. 2. Scarf joint. 3. Dove-tailed joint. 4. Spur soffit tenons at end of joist. 5. Slot to take wall plate for gallery. 6. Common rafters halved and pegged. 7. Rafters notched on wall plate

It has been by a meticulous examination of hundreds of such joints that Hewitt has been able to build up a typology of carpentry practice which now can take its place alongside other chronological aids in the study of medieval buildings. These rapid developments in carpentry skills took place at different times at different places. Occasionally, however, it is possible to place parts of buildings, and consequently the joints used in them, in chronological sequence. A good example is at Wells Cathedral,[53] where in the high timber roof above the nave vault (Plate 7.10), there is a clear break in the building connected with a political event, the Interdict (1209-13). The transverse design of the rafter couples continued after the break, but the joint type changed with the introduction of the so-called secret form of the notched lap. The nave roof of Wells Cathedral also illustrates how a severe structural problem was overcome by boldness and ingenuity on the part of the carpenters. The original pitch of the late twelfth-century roof was steep, but the roofing material was lead sheeting which was unusually cheap because of the proximity of the Mendip mines. The steep pitch caused the heavy metal to creep and produced problems of maintenance. The answer of the Wells' carpenters was daringly to shear off the rafters at the eaves to produce space for building up the wall to form a parapet. In the meantime they shored up the

truncated rafters. These temporary timbers are still in place (Plate 7.10). Access to the roof was now an easy matter by ladders propped on the parapet rather than springing from ground level.

Because so few wooden objects have come down to us from the Middle Ages it is sometimes forgotten that thousands of expendable household articles such as trenchers, bowls and dishes, spoons, barrels and buckets were made of wood. The processing of these objects leaves behind identifiable waste which has been preserved in the black, waterlogged workshop sites of the woodturners of Anglo-Scandinavian York (Figure 7.7).[54] The wooden bowls, their main product, have rarely survived but the cores, discs and pieces of end-waste have been found discarded in their hundreds. Experiments using pole-lathes of a design that produces identical duplicates of the waste found in eleventh/twelfth-century deposits makes us confident that we have properly deduced the processes involved.

10. Brick and Tile-making

The Romans had used tiles extensively in building, both for bonding courses in walls and for roofing. There is a possibility that the tiles in Brixworth Church (Northants.) are mid-Saxon in date but the industry was re-

Plate 7.10: Wells Cathedral, Somerset. A view taken in the upper stages of the church showing the nave roof of *c.* 1209 with temporary shoring inserted to carry the weight of the rafters truncated to provide space for the insertion of parapet walks (Photo: J.M. Steane)

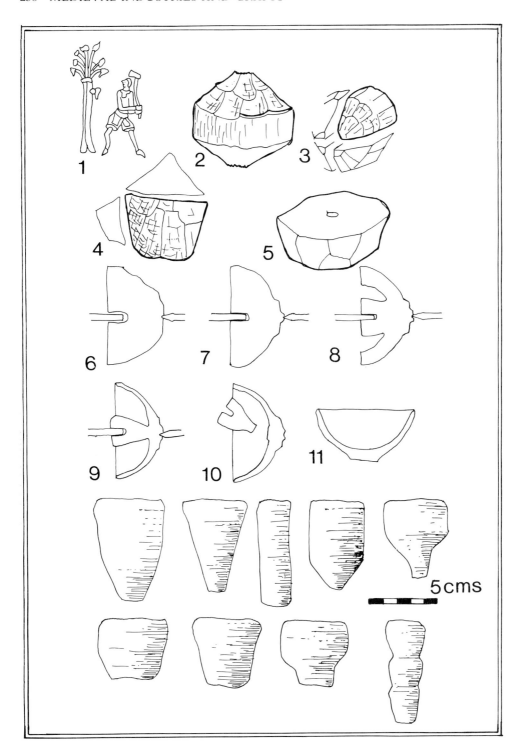

Figure 7.7: Late Saxon Woodturning. 1. Chopping down tree. 2-5. Production of blocks of wood. 6-8. Turning the bowl. 9-11 Waste cores (after Morris, 1982)

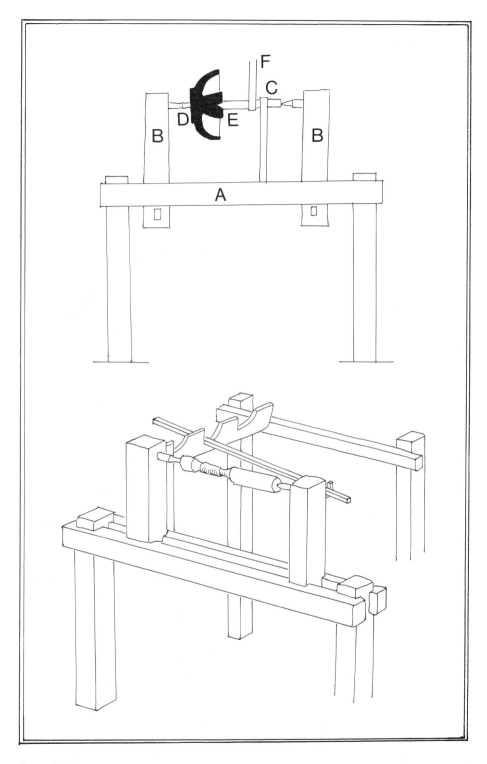

Figure 7.8: Reconstruction of a Late Saxon Pole Lathe (after Morris, 1982)

started in earnest in the thirteenth century. The frequency of disastrous fires in towns led to the use of tiles for roofing purposes and in London it became compulsory from 1212 onwards to roof buildings in this material. The technique of medieval brick and tile-making is well documented thanks to the survival of full accounts of the brickyard owned by the medieval corporation of Hull.[55] During the autumn and winter the tilers dug and tempered the clay, repaired their tools, and prepared their 'hacksteads'. These were areas of ground where the bricks and tiles were laid out to dry under straw or hay or sometimes covered with 'nattes', cloth equivalents to tarpaulins. Open-sided buildings were used for the drying of the 'green' tiles. Fuel at Hull included coal, wood and turf, and this was collected and stored. During the summer the kilns were cleaned out and repaired.

Several medieval brickworks and tileries have been recently excavated.[56] A tilery at the deserted medieval village of Lyveden in Northamptonshire preserved a number of features which illustrate the technology of the industry.[57] A massive limestone-slabbed platform covered by a thick layer of clean clay was the tiler's clay dump. Its position alongside a road indicates that he was bringing in clay by cart from a clay pit some distance away. The moulding and drying of the tiles were carried out in the long building found to the north of the clay dump. When the tiles were dried they were loaded through a side door into the kiln. This consisted of an open-topped rectangular structure made of well masoned limestone blocks cut into the ground and banked up by clay. The furnace chamber underneath was built of tile and consisted of two long arched flues with a stoke-hole in front of the façade.

The load of green tiles was stacked on edge (there are impressions on their sides which demonstrated this) on top of the spine walls of the furnace, and covered with a layer of broken tiles, earth, clay and turves. The fire was lit in the flues and was raked out frequently into the stoke-pit in front of the kiln. The hot air and gases percolated through the gaps between the furnace arches and were carried by an updraught into the body of the kiln and out at the top, heating the load of tiles on the way. Assuming it was stacked high the

capacity of the Lyveden kiln would have been 5.4 cu m and the oven would have held some 2,950 tiles. This particular tilery was making roof and undecorated floor tiles.

More impressive were decorated medieval paving tiles.[58] A polychrome (many-coloured) effect in a pavement was obtained by the use of different coloured tiles and a polychrome pattern on a tile was obtained by the use of different coloured body clays. The decoration was added to the surface of the tile in three ways. In the earlier period (thirteenth/fourteenth centuries) it was impressed by means of a wooden stamp. The inlay of white clay was then pressed into the decorated impression. In the fifteenth-century cheaper decorated tiles were made by dipping the stamp into white clay before it was pressed into the tile. The glaze was then applied and the tile fired. Five colours were obtainable. The lead glaze might be applied direct to the red earthenware body, producing brown. Yellow could be obtained by applying a lead glaze over an inlay or slip (thin clay wash) coating of white-firing clay. Light green was produced by adding copper to the lead glaze over a white slip; dark green by adding copper to the lead glaze directly over the red body. Near black was obtained, either by adding more copper or by over-firing.

Various schools of tile makers have been postulated. At Salisbury, for instance, the cathedral, dedicated in 1258, was paved with the tiles inlaid with the same designs as those used at the nearby Clarendon Royal Palace in the early 1250s (Figure 1.5). The use spread to other buildings in Salisbury and thence into the surrounding districts. What probably happened is that craftsmen moved from site to site, taking their blocks and patterns with them. They used the local clays and set up their workshops and kilns near the place where the tiles were to be laid.

Some tiles were inlaid with most complex designs. Those from Chertsey Abbey are the most famous. They were decorated with pictorial subjects of two sequences, the romance of Tristran and Isolde and a series connected with Richard Coeur-de-Lion. It is possible that they were based on manuscript illuminations and they were made between 1250 and 1290. Similar designs have been

Plate 7.11: Warden Abbey, Old Warden, Bedfordshire. Pavement of mosaic tiles. The glaze slip and line-impressed decoration give 'a glimpse of the vibrancy of fluctuating colour that was a principal characteristic of medieval pavements' (Baker). Excavation in 1974 (Photo: Bedfordshire County Council)

a

b

Plate 7.12: Warden Abbey, Old Warden, Bedfordshire. Two mosaic tiles from pavement 2 inscribed with symbols, numbers and words which acted as laying instructions *c.* 1300. (a) The edge of a tile shaped like a leg inscribed with *tibia* (leg) and a carpenter's mark. (b) The edge of a tile shaped like a shoe inscribed with *pes* (foot) and a carpenter's mark (Photos: Bedfordshire County Council)

noticed at Hailes Abbey in Gloucestershire and at Halesowen Abbey in Worcestershire. Many of these tiles were of most irregular shape (Plates 7.11, 7.12).[59] Complicated rectilinear shapes and all curvilinear shapes had to be drawn individually on a clay slab and then cut out, before they were glazed and fired. They had to be slowly and carefully loaded into kilns with special shelving. Such processes required skill and expense and this did not lend itself to mass production and such mosaic pavements were rarely made after the end of the thirteenth century. That tile makers were not always illiterate and low-status workers seems to be indicated by an interesting series of fourteenth century tiles dug up recently at Warden Abbey, Bedfordshire. Here there were several pictures in mosaic tiles, including a horse and a man in armour, and Samson grappling with a lion. The backs and sides of the majority of the 200 tiles displayed a quantity of graffiti, a complicated series of symbols, numbers and words which acted as laying instructions. These included Arabic numerals (introduced into England in the twelfth century) and Latin inscriptions such as *pes* (meaning foot), *stola* (an ecclesiastical garment) and *sub equo* (under the horse), clearly giving directions as to what the tile was representing or where in the picture the tile should go (Plates 7.12a, b).

11. Pottery Making

Medieval pottery has attracted much study during the last 30 years. For one reason it is the most commonly found artifact on medieval occupation sites. Evidently large quantities were used, broken and thrown away. Many of the materials from which we make containers today such as cardboard, plastic, tin and steel were not available to medieval societies, who had to make do with leather, wood and pottery. This accounts for the great variety of forms of medieval pottery including strange vessels such as costrels (drinking bottles) (Figure 8.4), fish dishes and chafing dishes (hollow receptacles for charcoal which heated other dishes which were placed on them); even watering cans were made out of pottery. If it can be dated accurately it could provide the key to understanding many sites.

Unfortunately the dating of medieval pottery is full of difficulties.[60] There are several methods, and each has shortcomings. Sometimes coins are found in association with pottery. We can tell when coins are minted easily enough but not how long they were in circulation before they were lost. If a coin was found dropped into a pit full of pottery and the whole lot sealed with earth we should only know that the pottery had been deposited after the coin was made but not how long after. It is clear from the worn condition of medieval silver pennies that they were worth a great deal more to their owners than small denomination coins are to us: if they were lost they would have been searched for assiduously. They are not therefore very valuable as dating evidence. Clearly what is true of coins is equally true of trying to date pottery by association with small finds. These are difficult themselves to put into chronological sequence since, although some were highly susceptible to fashion, many lasted a long time. Judging

from numerous repairs made to buckles and other metal objects they had a very long life in a poverty-stricken medieval village. It is equally hazardous to date medieval pottery by trying to put it into a typological sequence by studying technique, fabric or decoration. The trouble with this is that pottery produced in one part of the country such as East Anglia began to decline in quality in the Early Middle Ages, so that the later pottery is inferior in quality to earlier. Although this does not run counter to the idea of seriation, it sometimes confuses the issue.

In other areas, however, the later material showed a distinct advance on the late Saxon wares. In fact, fabric, decoration and design changed and waxed and waned in quality in different parts of the country at the same time. A more hopeful way of building up information about the dating of medieval pottery is to excavate sites which have a very short life, well dated by documents, like a castle which is known to have been built at a certain time, and then abandoned and destroyed. The pottery found in this sort of site will be well dated and by comparing it with other similar material found in undocumented sites a useful start will have been made in dating them.

A method which holds some promise for dating burned clay features from industrial sites is known as thermo-remanent magnetic dating (also sometimes referred to as archaeomagnetic dating). The principle behind this relies on the fact that the earth's magnetic field is constantly changing both in direction and intensity. Clay contains the magnetic material, iron, and is often used for lining kilns and furnaces, being thus subject to high temperatures. After cooling it retains the magnetic field which existed at the last time of firing. Provided that it remains undisturbed in an archaeological deposit it is possible to measure it and compare it with values for other sites of comparable age where the date is known. In this way it is possible to build up curves plotting certain values associated with the magnetic field for sites of known age and to read off the date of sites of unknown age.[61]

Obviously we would know more about this problem if potters figured more in the documentary record.[62] Unfortunately it seems that the medieval potter and his products were held in low esteem. Hardly any illustrations of potters are found in manuscript sources. Where he is mentioned in records it is often difficult to distinguish him from makers of metal pots. While the terms *crocker* and *figulus* usually refer to the clay potter, the more frequently occurring words *pottarius, ollarius* or *ollator* are applied equally to the makers of clay or metal vessels. In the poll tax records of the fourteenth century, potters were assessed at the lowest rate for man and wife, the four-pence paid by the mass of the peasantry, rather than the sixpenny rate paid by most craftsmen. His status in fact by comparison with other craftsmen was a lowly one. The country potter was usually a cottager with between 0.6 ha and 2.0 ha. Gradually in certain places there grew up communities of full-time potters who mass-produced their wares; the craft was on the way to becoming an industry. Great quantities of coarse cooking pots, storage jars and baggy jugs were made and distributed over a 32 or a 48 km radius from the kilns. Despite this the industry never improved either working methods or techniques throughout the Middle Ages. It seems likely that the market for medieval pottery was a low-class one; nobles are seldom shown in manuscript illuminations using articles at table which could with much certainty be described as pottery. The highly ornate wares such as knight jugs, made at Nottingham or puzzle jugs (trick jugs which would shoot wine or water over the unwary victim!) were probably made for rich tradesmen rather than a lordly clientele. These men tended to spend their money on glassware, bronze or pewter or foreign imported pottery in the Later Middle Ages. The English potters lost heart and increasingly churned out spiritless and un-decorated uniform pots which though tech-nically efficient, lacked much artistic flair.

A great deal is now known about the technology of the medieval pottery industry owing to the fact that a complex of work-shops, yards, claypits, storesheds and kilns has been excavated at a rural site, Lyveden in Northamptonshire.[63] Here in the middle of the royal Forest of Rockingham, and on the edge of five parishes, a small community of farmers began clearance in the late Saxon period. To begin with they brought their everyday pot-tery from Stamford 24 km to the north. There was some industrial working from the start as iron smelting furnaces and quantities of metal working slag show.

About the beginning of the thirteenth century the inhabitants of Lyveden turned to pottery making and by 1285 they were so well known that the village was referred to as Potter's Lyveden. The three necessities, clay and tempering, timber and brushwood, and water, were all present on the site. Soon the tofts on the stream bank were riddled with

Plate 7.13: Lyveden, Northamp-tonshire. Thirteenth/fourteenth-century potter's complex. On right side of photo are stone-lined pudd-ling pits set in yard surface. In centre is workshop with limestone wall footings, opposed entrances, stone puddling pit in right side, cut by diagonal feature which is a modern field drain. Claystore in outshut (lean-to) at rear. On left side is a multi-flued kiln cut by another modern drain. Note the well-made path leading from workshop to kiln. Scale in feet (Photo: H. Atkinson FRPS)

Plate 7.14: Lyveden, Northamptonshire. Late medieval potter's tools. These are placed next to potsherds which demonstrate various uses. (a) Antler burnisher for smoothing pottery. (b) Knife for slashing handles and paring down vessels. (c) (d) Antler points for perforating spigots and curfew handles. (e) Bone and tooth fragments for incising patterns. Scale in inches (Photo: H. Atkinson FRPS)

clay pits which were systematically filled with rubbish as the clay was worked out. Water was easily available through a number of stone-lined cisterns and wells which were cut down to the water table (Plates 8.1, 8.2). From analysis of charcoal it seems as though oak, hazel, ash, blackthorn and field maple were used as fuel.

From studying the remains of the buildings and the small objects of stone, bone and metal found trampled into their floors and into yard surfaces it is possible to reconstruct the techniques used by the potters (Plate 7.14). It is likely that the clay was left to weather in dumps after it had been dug. Remains of heaps were found in the corners of some of the buildings. It was then mixed with water and ground-up limestone which was used as a tempering agent to 'open up' the clay and make it much less likely to crack when it was fired in the kiln. This process was carried out in stone-lined clay puddling pits which were found, usually in pairs, in a number of the potters' tofts (or yards). The clay was now ready for shaping (Plate 7.13).

This took place in the potters' workshop which was a rectangular building with clay dumps in an outshut or lean-to at the back. From a close study of thousands of potsherds and a number of complete vessels it seems that many of them were coil-built. The potter built them up by using long sausage-shaped strips.

He finished the vessel off by revolving it on a slow wheel paring the sides of a thick vessel down with a knife. Later on in the fourteenth and fifteenth centuries the pottery at Lyveden had a more sandy and smoother fabric and was made on a rapidly revolving wheel. Decoration was added in a number of ways. Strips and hatched pads could be applied, finger pressing to dimple the clay, rouletting (a little toothed wheel run over the surface) and knife slashing (particularly for handles) were all used. The vessel could be painted on. Lead glaze was used with jugs and on the insides of vessels which needed to be waterproofed, such as bowls or fish dishes. Copper could be added to give the impression of light green, dark green or black. The tools used in all these processes were found at Lyveden. They included iron knives, honestones for sharpening them, pivot stones for the pottery wheel, bone tools for smoothing the sides of the pots, or piercing holes in their sides to take jug handles, or acting as templates for the rim forms (Plate 7.14).

When the pots had been made they needed to be dried until they were the consistency of leather. This was done by stacking them on hacksteads (shelves) in an airy place. An open sided store-shed was found near the workshop in one of the potters' tofts. They needed drying because if they were fired immediately in the kiln, the water in the clay would expand

Plate 7.15: Lyveden, Northamptonshire. Thirteenth/fourteenth-century double-flued pottery kiln with apsidal- ended oven pit and central pedestal supporting oven pit floor. Scale in feet (Photo: H. Atkinson FRPS)

Plate 7.16: Lyveden, Northamptonshire. Single-flued ridgetile kiln with central pedestal, oven pit and stoke hole to south (in front of photo). The right-hand cheek of the flue has been robbed-out. Excavation in 1968/9 (Photo: H. Atkinson FRPS)

into steam thus cracking and bursting the pot.

Medieval pottery kilns were of a number of types (Plates 7.15 and 7.16).[64] The early ones consisted simply of an oven-pit and a stoking-pit, the two joined together by a stoke-pit arch. At times this type had a raised oven floor which might be supported either on a pedestal or on a series of kiln bricks. The second type consisted of an oven on the same level as two stoking-pits, one on either side of it. Both stoke-pits had fires in them.

In the oven might be a raised floor,

supported on a spine wall or a pedestal. The load of pots was stacked on the pedestal. The third type had at least three flues and might have as many as five or six. The pots were stacked on the oven floors, and sometimes the large size of the kiln meant that it was possible to have a walk-in entrance and a permanent dome. A fourth type had flues arranged parallel side by side and particularly good examples of these occurred at Lyveden (Plate 7.15). The substructure was made of limestone which had frequently been relined as it was destroyed by burning and raking out the ashes. The superstructure is never found in excavated examples and it used to be thought that it must have consisted of a clay dome. Experiments in firing medieval type kilns, however, show that open-topped structures with only a temporary cover of wasters, turves or straw would fire perfectly well.[65] The vessels were stacked upside down. Often the glaze ran down as it melted and fused the jugs together. The shape of the rim of the one above was thus impressed on the one below.

Once a kiln was loaded the firing would have taken approximately 24 hours, half this time would have been spent in stepping up the temperature from cold to the peak of 1000°C. Once the load was fired it would need to be left to cool off slowly for several days before the pottery was extracted and the wasters discarded. About thirty forms of pottery were made in a fifteenth-century pottery establishment.[66] They included, first, vessels used for the preparation and serving of food. These comprised (most frequently) cooking pots, cauldrons, skillets (a vessel with three or four feet and a long handle), pipkins (a small pot used in cooking), handled ladles, dishes and bowls. Most plates would appear to have been made of wood. The second category were vessels used in the bulk storage and transfer of foodstuffs and liquids. They included amphorae and storage jars. These were large capacity vessels and were frequently strengthened with applied strips, also useful for ease of handling. Small capacity liquid containers (up to 22.8 litres) and drinking vessels included jugs, pitchers, aquamaniles, costrels, bottles and ring vases. Pottery was also used for miscellaneous vessels for household use such as lamps (cresset lamps were simply

cone-shaped and carried oil and a floating wick), lids, money boxes, curfews (large pie-shaped vessels with handles and holes, put over fires at night to damp them down – their name comes from the French *couvre feu* – meaning fire-covers), urinals, mortars and bee-hive bases.

Moreover, all kinds of roof furniture were produced in a pottery – these included ridge-tiles, hip tiles, flat roof tiles, finials (ornaments placed on the apex of a roof), louvres (decorative pierced openings to act as smoke vents and ventilators), chimney pots, water pipes, floor tiles and bricks. Finally, industrial vessels such as crucibles and vessels like alembics used in distilling were made of pottery (see Figure 3.8).

12. Salt Making

Salt was a vital commodity in the medieval economy. It was used in the absence of refrigeration for the preservation of meat and fish, essential if animal protein was to be available all the year round.[67] There were two means of obtaining it. The first was by making use of the salt residues of ancient seas buried in the Keuper Marl beds of the Triassic system. These inland centres of production in Worcestershire and Cheshire involved brine pits (*putei*) and salt pans (*salinae*), especially around Droitwich. The brine was boiled down using leaden pans or vats (*plumbi*) and furnaces (*furni*). More frequently exploited, however, was the evaporation of sea water in shallow artificial lakes or 'pans'. The procedure was to rake up the silty mud after each spring tide and store it under cover, whence it would be taken as needed and the brine separated from the silt by either settling or filtering. Settling ponds were used – these were shallow clay-lined pits known as *floors*: in good weather these could equally have been used for sun evaporation. The concentrated brine was then fully evaporated over heat by boiling in shallow lead or latten or iron pans. Charcoal and turves were used as fuel. The creeks and marshes of the Lincolnshire and Essex coasts were used for salt making since prehistoric times.[68] When looking for the signs of the medieval salt industry in the landscape there are two kinds of evidence. The collecting channels and the heaps of debris, chiefly burnt clay and ash, burnt and unburnt peat and mounds of silt from the earthworks of 'salterns', lie scattered over the reclaimed marsh and fen. In some of these mounds the circular clay-lined hollows of the pans can be seen. When ploughed the signs of salterns are a scatter of pottery, burned clay, and slag and charcoal.[69] Farmers find that these patches of discoloured soil, the so-called 'red hills' or 'hot beds', are sterile and crops do not grow well.

When the distribution of the mounds are plotted on a map it is noticeable that they occur in a series of rows more or less parallel with the coast. What has happened is that the salt makers were driven farther and farther eastwards towards the sea as their labours produced an accumulation of mud and silt. This helped to reclaim land. The oldest of the mounds are furthest inland; they became grassed over and sheep now graze where salt had formerly been extracted.

The second sign of the salt trade in the landscape is the frequent street or trackway name 'Salt' or 'Salters Way'. These plus Salters Corner and Salford are all found on Ordnance Survey maps of today.[70] There was a regular system of packhorse routes both from the area around Droitwich in the Cheshire salt field and from the coasts. A map, published by Darby, shows that the trade spread into many other counties as is evidenced by the tolls levied on the salt traders.[71] Salt was also imported from Bourgeneuf Bay on the southern coastline of Brittany. This produced a coarse and heavily polluted salt which was sometimes black in colour, sometimes gray, or even green. Great convoys of ships travelled backwards and forwards to the bay in the last months of winter to collect salt for the summer herring season in the North and Baltic Seas.

How was the salt used? There were two methods of salting food.[72] The first was dry-salting in which the meat or fish was buried in a granular bed of salt. The lumps had to be crushed by grinding in a mortar for this process. The second was brine curing; here a strong solution of salt and water was prepared and the meat or fish immersed in it. It was particularly important in the fish trade. Monastic communities stocked up each year with quantities of salted herrings which they purchased in the markets of Stourbridge (near Cambridge) or St Ives. Fish was eaten universally on Fridays throughout the year and during Lent, the 40 day fast which preceded Easter. Fresh fish was scarce inland, despite the considerable production from rural fish ponds and so salt fish, notably Baltic herrings, were consumed. This was one of the staples of the German Hanseatic traders during the fourteenth and the fifteenth centuries. Salt had to be taken to sea because the herring, though plentiful, is a fatty fish whose oils turn rancid very rapidly: if it was to be salted the process had to be begun within 24 hours of the catch.

13. Leather-working

The importance of leather to medieval society can only be understood if it is remembered that there was no rubber, no plastic, no cardboard. The toughness and waterproof qualities of leather made it a suitable material for use in containers, covering and clothing. The body of Henry I was wrapped in a bull skin on its peregrination to the grave! When suitably hardened, leather was universally used for footwear and sometimes for armour. Complete hides were sometimes used for tarpaulins. The process of leather manufacture is known as tanning. This converts the decaying skin of the animal into a relatively strong, flexible membrane which is resistant to rotting.

The technique of the tanner has to take into consideration the fact that the skin is formed of three layers, the outer layer or epidermis, the middle layer or corium, and the under layer or flesh. Only the corium is useful. It is a fine network of intermeshing fibres which give the leather its unique qualities. The other two have to be removed in the preliminary stages. After initial cleaning the hides of ox, cows and calves were soaked in pits containing solutions of lime and water in ever increasing strength. This destroyed the epidermal layer and loosened surface hair. After several days or weeks the skins were 'fleshed' by being scraped on a beam to remove the flesh and hair. They were then 'bated' or 'pured' by immersing in a mixture of bird droppings and cold water or dog dung and warm water. This had the effect of making the skins soft and porous and thus ready to receive the effects of tanning. They were then immersed in a decoction of crushed oak-bark and water. The skins were moved from pit to pit of increasing strength of this astringent liquid solution. The best leather took up to a year to prepare; the hides were supposed to lie in the 'wooses' (ooze or liquor) for this period and strict regulations were issued to prevent the hastening of the process which would have resulted in a low quality product. After tanning the leather would be dressed by the curer; he stretched, shaved and made it supple by the application of greases.

Another technique, altogether known as 'tawing', was used to prepare leather from the skins of deer, sheep and horses. This was not such a lengthy process and involved dipping the skins in a solution of alum, and oiling them.

When looking for the material remains of the tanning industry in medieval towns it is as well to remember that leather dressers settled 'where they may have water in brooks and rivers to dress their leather [for], without great store of running water they cannot dress the same'. Complaints of fouling the town water supplies by leather-workers were frequent. Soon after 1300 it was said that they were polluting the River Fleet in London. At York, Tanners Row was near the River Ouse to facilitate the soaking of skins by attaching them to poles in the river, presumably downstream from the places where drinking water was collected.[73] This proximity to water has had the good effect at times of preserving large quantities of leather. The vats themselves are sometimes found. Again at York, a series of tan pits was found covered with lime, sand and clay. The pits were large enough to stack the cattle skins without folding them, and were shallow enough to facilitate emptying. Those at Coppergate, York, date from the ninth century. A similar series of eight clay-lined pits dating from the mid-sixteenth century was excavated at St Peters Street, Northampton. They were probably the remains of a tawing rather than a tanning establishment.[74]

Many museums preserve items of medieval leatherwork (Figure 8.8). A sample list taken from the earliest freemens' rolls of the City of York (1272-8) shows how many crafts were represented in the leather trade. Tanner (*tannatour*), skinner (*pelliparius*), dresser (*alutarius*), glover (*cirotecarius*), girdler (*zonarius*), harness maker and cobbler (*sutor*). They used five main techniques in decorating and embellishing the leather.[75] When damped it could be engraved with a blunt tool. When soaked in wax or oil, the leather became supple and easy to work. After drying, it reverted to its previous stiffness ensuring that the shape and decoration of the so-called *cuir bouilli* (not boiled!) remained permanent. Other techniques involved the use of metal stamps, usually heraldic in subject, e.g. fleurs-de-lys, lions passant, eagles displayed, etc. Embossing was done more rarely; here the leather was stretched over a carved design from the back. Incision using a sharp knife was used in the Late Middle Ages to outline lettering.

The kind of objects made of leather and often surviving are sheaths for knives or daggers, belts and straps, saddles and reins, book covers and gloves. At times leather took the place of pottery, portable bottles or costrels, and large jugs for beer, later called black-jacks. Leather was also used to cover inkwells and pencases. The most human items found in medieval excavations are shoes (Figure 8.9).

14. The Wool and Cloth Trades

In many parts of medieval England the sheep and not the plough tended to be the dominant interest among farmers. But whereas we breed our sheep for mutton or lamb, in the Middle Ages meat was the last resort to which sheep not good enough for wool were put. They had other important uses. Ewes' milk was made into cheese. Sheep skins were made into parchment and we can gain a good idea of their comparative size from the wide membranes used for the folios of great Bibles or the Pipe Rolls which came from the backs of large sheep. The rolls, on which the records of the courts of justice were kept, came from the skins of smaller sheep. Arable fields were also used as folds for sheep, so that their dung and urine fertilised the fallow acres.

Archaeology can provide us with two sorts of information about the appearance of medieval sheep.[76] The skeletal remains from excavations are often rather fragmentary but the discovery of a large number of sheep bones at Baynard's Castle, London, provided eleven horned and 19 polled fragments of skulls, 15 split medially from the infill of the dock basin adjacent to the castle *c.* 1499-1500. This evidence of horned sheep is backed up by another source, from representations of sheep found on the monumental brasses of wool merchants (Figure 5.5). From these it is evident that in general they had long slender necks and fine boned limbs. The skeletal material confirms that they were inferior in size to modern sheep. The brasses also show that a number were long-woolled. These were the famous Cotswold and Lincoln breeds, which produced comparatively large sheep with long wool. Contrasting with these were the smaller, more active, short-woolled sheep, which lived on the upland pastures of the Pennines, Wales, Shropshire, Herefordshire and Cornwall.

Documentary sources show that both lay and ecclesiastical landowners were increasing their flocks of sheep through the twelfth and thirteenth centuries with an eye on the export of wool abroad. There were some 29,000 sheep on the Bishop of Winchester's estates in 1259. In 1303 Henry de Lacy, Earl of Lincoln, had 13,400 sheep (half in Yorkshire and Lincolnshire and the rest in the south). The Cistercian abbeys of the north grew steadily richer on the produce of the sheep runs. Villagers shared in these profits and their flocks often outnumbered those of their lords! In 1225 the villagers of South Domerham in Wiltshire had 3,760 sheep as against 570 belonging to the demesne farm of their lord, Glastonbury Abbey.[77]

How did wool produced in sheep farms all over England reach the hands of merchants, exporting from a limited number of ports? Wholesale contracts between growers and exporters looked after the large-scale production of the great estates. Middlemen dealt with small producers and under the name of 'woolmen' they emerged in the fifteenth century as wealthy as the export merchants themselves. The greatest woolmen were those of the Cotswolds; at Northleach, a village in the middle of this bare upland country, criss-crossed with stone walls, lived families of wool dealers, the Forteys, the Midwinters, the Busshes. They rebuilt the towering and fretted Northleach Church in the Perpendicular style. Seven of them are commemorated in monumental brasses; their feet are found planted squarely on woolpacks, or at times one foot rests on a woolpack and the other on a sheep (see Figure 5.5.).[78] They lie there in their long civilian gowns, their eyes narrowly calculating, surrounded by their merchants' marks, displayed as proudly as any coat of arms. In Chipping Campden High Street is the fourteenth-century stone house of William Grevil, 'the flower of the wool merchants of all England'.[79] At Fairford, in the church which he rebuilt, and furnished with such glorious stained-glass, lies John Tame. Other woolmens' brasses are found in the Cotswold churches of Cirencester, Sevenhampton and Lechlade.

The Middlemen collected the wool together. The export trade, however, was in the hands of the Flemings for the first two centuries after the Norman Conquest when they were superseded by the Italians. The Crown, during the reign of Edward I, intervened to tax the wool trade in order to finance expensive wars in Wales, Scotland and France. There are a series of finely engraved seals which were used by royal officials responsible for taxing wool and hides (Figure 7.9). They had the arms of England on one side on a shield and on the other without a shield. The wool was stored at the ports in warehouses like the one which has survived at Southampton. This is a capacious two-storey structure with a fine open medieval roof, standing end-on to the south or town quay. It dates from *c.* 1400.[80]

During the fourteenth century control of the English wool trade fell into the hands of a small monopolistic company of English merchants; they channelled all wool exports through the *staple*, that is a fixed place through which the export of wool was compulsorily directed. This was sited in the Low Countries to begin with and subsequently in Calais. The system enabled the staplers to shoulder enormous export taxes and to make

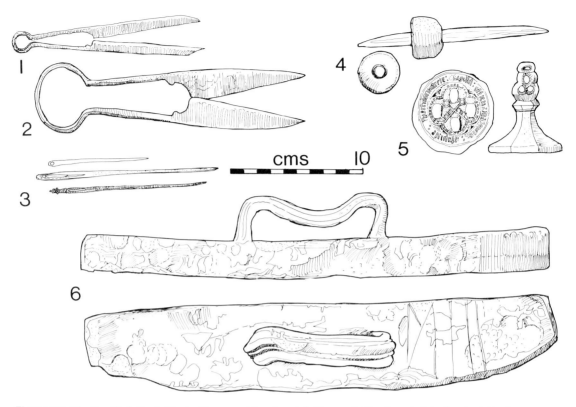

Figure 7.9: Woollen Cloth Trade Tools, Museum of London. 1,2. Shears. 3. Needles. 4. Spindle whorl. 5. Seal. 6. Lead 'iron' for pressing cloth

the king his war-loans; in return the staple secured for them low prices in England and high prices abroad. A curious dual effect of the staple was the decline of the English wool trade from 35,000 sacks in the early years of the fourteenth century to 8,000 sacks in the middle of the fifteenth century. As this trade began to fail, the English cloth industry gained strength.[81]

Archaeological evidence for the making of cloth goes back into the prehistoric period. The practice of spinning in the pre-Roman Iron Age is attested by spindle whorls; weaving, by the presence of post-holes, supposed to be used for the support of upright looms; and by doughnut-shaped objects interpreted as loom weights.

By the Early Middle Ages the trade was well organised and begins to enter the documentary record. It involved a large number of processes, some of which have left traces of a tangible kind. The first was the sorting of wool. The better quality was used for ordinary cloths and the worst was made up into coarse cloth known sometimes as cog-ware and alternatively as Kendal cloth.

The dyer then in order next doth stand with sweating brow and a laborious hand.

At Winchester, in Lower Brook Street, the complete layout of a dyer's workshop was found,[82] dating from the thirteenth/fourteenth centuries, supplied by water along chalk-lined water channels (Figure 6.10). Dyeing involved two mediums, the colouring matter, and the mordant which fixes the dye to the wool. The most common dyestuff was the blue woad (*Isatis tinctoria*) which can still be found growing wild, particularly in the West Country. It was imported in the Middle Ages from Picardy and Toulouse into England via the port of Southampton. The supply which was harvested in midsummer, was normally exhausted from January to May when it was replaced by russet reds derived from madder. Further shades of brown and red were provided by several species of lichens. Textiles from archaeological contexts in Southampton have also yielded traces of yellow weld which was mixed with woad to produce green.[83]

The next process was carding and combing, both essentially home-based industries. St Blaise, who was martyred by being combed to death, was the patron saint of wool combers.[84] His image is found carved in the rood screen at Lavenham in Suffolk. Long stapled wools were prepared for spinning with keckles or combs. These survive usually as individual iron teeth. They were set in a rectangular wooden block with a handle. A mass of wool was transferred from one comb to another and back until long parallel fibres remained. Carding combs were wooden boards with handles and rows of inclined wire teeth; they were used in pairs again to disentangle wool and bind the fibres together.[85]

Spinning was traditionally a female occupation. The distaff was used, evidence being provided by spindle whorls. These could be made of ceramic, stone or lead, and were mounted on spindles to act as flywheels and to conserve the spinning momentum generated by the spinner's hand. It is possible that the heavier stone discs were used when plying two or more yarns.

The most important process was weaving which was done (apart from tapestries) on the horizontal loom, from the eleventh century onwards. Naturally the wooden framework does not normally survive. Iron weaving combs were used to beat in the weft. Bands of tinning are found along the toothed edge; presumably to combat corrosion which might have discoloured the cloth. Bone thread pickers or pin beaters, which have a straight stem, pointed or specially shaped at both ends, are also associated with weaving. They are usually highly polished.

After weaving there were still further processes, summed up well by Langland.

Cloth that cometh from the weaving is not
        comely to war.

Till it be fulled under foot or in fulling
        stocks
Washen well with water, and with teasels
        cratched
Towked and taynted and under tailors
        hands.

The newly woven cloth was hung over a rail or spread on a table and extraneous matter was removed by iron forceps with fine tips.

When the raw cloth was fulled it was scoured, cleansed and thickened, by beating it in water. This was done originally by men trampling or 'walking' upon the cloth in a trough (a fuller was called a 'walker', hence the common surname). The fulling agent most commonly used was a natural finely divided hydrated aluminium silicate which takes up fats, known as Fuller's earth. From the thirteenth century onwards the cloth was beaten with hammers while immersed in a suspension of Fuller's earth in water. It has been suggested that this invention caused a veritable industrial revolution as the cloth industry spread from the older and more restrictive urban centres to the countryside attracted by the water power which drove the fulling mills.[86] This is not to say that these industries abandoned the towns. In Lower Brook Street, Winchester, in addition to the dyers were fullers and in house IX the layout of a cloth finishing workshop was found (Figure 6.10).[87]

The newly fulled cloth was now stretched on tenters to dry. References to tenter grounds are common in medieval records. At Lavenham there is still a 'tenters close'. Tenters were frames, consisting of two horizontal wooden rails, supported by vertical posts. Each rail had a row of iron tenter hooks set along them; the cloth was attached to the hooks and tension was applied by adjusting the housing in the posts. The cloth finally passed into the hands of the rowers who used teasels, the dried heads of the 'fullers thistle' (*Dypsacus fullonum*), to draw up all the loose fibres from the surface of the cloth. The cloth was then attached by pairs of barbicks on to the cropping board for the shearman to cut the loose fibres and give the cloth a finer and softer finish. The tools used in these last two processes, the teasel-frame and the clothier's shears, are used as decorative motifs in the celebrated chapel of John Lane (d.

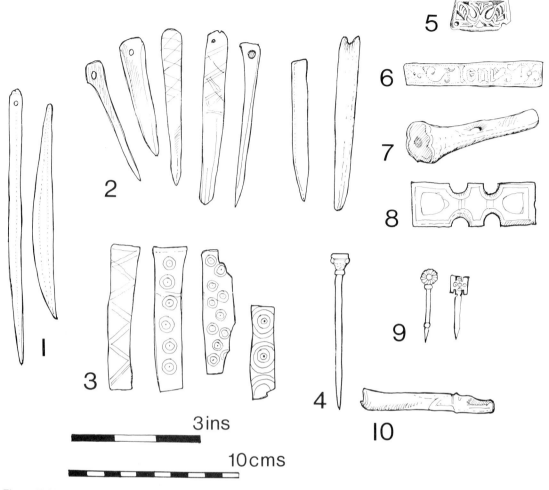

Figure 7.10: Bone Objects from Museum of Oxford including: 1-2. Needles and awls. 3. Plaques decorated with ring and dot decoration. 4. Pin. 5. Decorative panel. 6. Plaque with devotional inscription. 7. Bone whistle. 8. Plaque. 9. Decorative pins. 10. Animal motif on end of bone tube

1526) in Cullompton Church, Devon.[88]

An immense number of people were employed in the cloth industry. The aulnagers, who were inspectors employed to maintain standards, recorded in their accounts for Suffolk for the year 1395 that 733 broadcloths were made by 120 persons and 300 makers turned out 9,200 narrow cloths. There were whole villages where every process of cloth-making was carried on, often in conjunction with farming. The French herald stated this in 1549: 'Your clothiers dwell in great farms abroad in the country where as well they make cloth and keep husbandry as doe graze and feed sheep and cattle'. Such places were Lavenham, Long Melford and Kersey in Suffolk.[89]

Lavenham, in the fifteenth century, experienced general prosperity from the fame of its blue broadcloth which resulted in the almost total rebuilding of the village in a single architectural style. Nowhere in England can one experience so profoundly the feeling of walking through a late medieval working and living place. The winding streets are lined with closely set half-timbered clothiers' houses, tradesmen's shops, inns, cloth halls and rows of weavers' dwellings. Some of the plastered fronts of the houses have impressions of the fleur-de-lys, the local wool mark of the aulnagers. The crowning glory is the flint towered church, a joint effort on the part of the De Vere Lords of the Manor, and the prosperous merchant clothiers led by Thomas Spring. The base of the tower displays the coats of arms of the De Veres, mingling with the merchants' marks of the Springs. By the time the parapet had been built the Springs had been granted arms themselves; these are emblazoned round it. This is archaeological evidence for the great wealth of Thomas Spring III who died owning 16 Suffolk and seven Norfolk manors, together with property in 97 villages in the two counties.

Lavenham has survived in virtually a fossilised state for the simple reason that the industry left it in the sixteenth century for other centres. As happens today, conditions favouring conservation flourished in an atmosphere of economic recession.

15. The Glass Industry

The English managed to master most of the technical processes in the industries – so far described – and even to excel in them during the Middle Ages. They found the greatest difficulty, however, in adapting to the manufacture of glass and most of the work that took place in this country appears to have been carried out by foreigners. There are two main product types each with their own techniques, typologies and histories – vessels and windows.[90]

Anglo-Saxon glass was a fusion of a silica composition (sand) and an alkali – derived from the ash of sea plants. The glass produced in pre-Conquest sites such as Monkwearmouth and Jarrow, Repton St Wystan and Winchester was 'finely cut, precisely grozed, and produced in a shower of colours and shapes'. It is also very well preserved. Unfortunately, a major technological change took place around the end of the first millenium AD which resulted in a glass composition much more prone to weathering and decay. This was the substitution of ash from bracken and woodland sources in place of marine ash. Beechwood was the critical component and

also the main fuel. Glassmakers tended to prosper in those wooded areas where these resources were available – the Wealden sands and forests of Surrey and Sussex. But the glass produced by these methods had one fatal flaw, its high potassium content led to a rapid iridescent flaking and decomposition.

The first of these Surrey glassmakers known by name was Lawrence *Vitrearius* who came from Normandy, a well-known centre of glass production, and was established at Pickhurst in Surrey in 1226. Henry III obtained glass for the east end of Westminster Abbey from him and his work was also found at Salisbury Cathedral. The quality of Wealden glass was however suspect, particularly with regard to coloured glass, and this was in the main imported into England from Burgundy, Flanders, Lorraine and Normany.

The archaeology of the Wealden glass industry is difficult to study. Glassmakers were nomadic and their movements can be traced in the Weald by the complaints of local inhabitants deploring the loss of wood. Since coppicing was widely practised it is unlikely that the supplies ran out. Also since the area is largely stoneless the sites are heavily robbed and the resulting remains are somewhat slight. Winbolt, who studied the industry 50 years ago, identified 27 sites; these have been increased to 42 by Kenyon.

The best example of these is at Blundens Wood, Hambleden (Surrey).[91] The site was first seen as a mound about 5 m across with a smaller mound near it; these mounds proved to be furnaces. The larger of the two was a through-draught type with a central flue and a hearth at each end; on each side of the middle portion was a shelf or siege, a built-up platform making a bench on which the crucibles for melting the glass were stood. On each of the sieges was a pair of hollows in which the crucibles stood; glass scum overflowing them had covered the sieges and collected in the flue. Around the siege-structure was an outer cavity which was perhaps left for insulation. The furnace may have been covered by a barrel-shaped roof of stones and clay. The other two small furnaces were probably used for fritting★ and anneal-

★A calcined mixture of sand and fluxes, ready to be melted in a crucible.

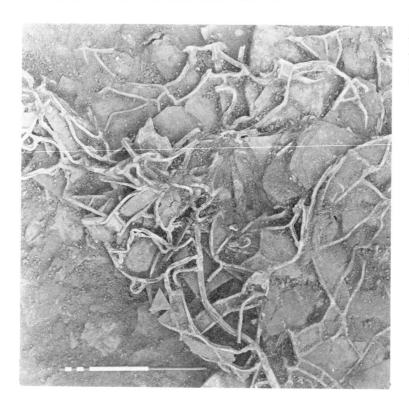

Plate 7.17: Medieval Glass and Twisted Lead Cames from Bradwell Abbey, Buckinghamshire (Photo: Milton Keynes Development Corporation)

ing. Fragments of crucibles were found in large numbers, a common size being about 26–30 cm in diameter. The glass found among the furnace-waste of these Wealden furnaces showed signs of painting or leading marks, and was in all probability imported as cullet.* The main product was doubtless plain window glass and the crown production** was the only method used.

These products of English medieval glass furnaces in Surrey pale into insignificance beside the superb quality glass beakers found during 1982 in a cesspit in Foster Lane, City of London.[92] About 50 fragments of so-called 'Syro-Frankish' ware were recovered. They were of a very thin, clear glass, decorated with brilliantly coloured enamels. One beaker showed a rampant lion in red, yellow and blue foliage, and a white shield, containing a wolf in blue standing over a red crown. An inscription recording that a 'Magister Bartolomeus' made them provides a link with

the beginnings of decorated glassmaking in Venice. A certain Bartolomeo of Zara is known to have painted glass in Venice between 1290 and 1325.

The production of stained-glass windows was a complex business involving several processes. The quality and colour of the glass was the first requirement. Coloured glass was imported from abroad but the pigments of the painted pattern were applied in the glazier's shop.[93] For instance, we know that in 1350 a brazen mortar with an iron pestle was purchased at Westminster Palace for grinding 'geet' (black lead glass), and other paints for colouring glass. Also an iron plate with an iron grinder was bought for grinding silver filings, 'geet' and gum arabic for painting glass. The designs were fired and often the firing changed the colour of the glass. Theophilus, a tenth-century author of a handbook for decorators and builders of churches, pointed out that glass of a tawny flesh-like colour after being heated for two hours would become a light purple, while after six hours heating it became reddish-purple. The glass was cut not with a

*Broken or refuse glass for re-smelting.
**Window glass made in circular sheets.

diamond point but the sheets were cracked by being touched with a hot soldering iron and by dropping cold water on them. A grozing iron then could nibble them into shape. Lead cames★ of H-section, cast in moulds of stone and wood, were used when assembling the glass into panels. Finally a blacksmith might be brought in to make the iron framework to which the panels were secured rigidly in the windows. To assess the proportion of ancient glass which has survived in a window it is necessary to walk round outside the building; the differential weathering will immediately indicate the older material, it will have acquired the texture of granular porridge; the restored portions of the design will stand out as smooth and shiny. At Bradwell Abbey in 1982 a stained-glass panel, complete with iron bar and crumpled lead framework, was excavated producing a rare opportunity to study simultaneously all the techniques of the medieval glazier (Plate 7.17).[94]

★Small grooved bars of lead used for framing glass.

References

1. Beresford, M.W. and St Joseph, J.K., *Medieval England. An Aerial Survey*, Cambridge, 2nd edn, 1979, 256.
2. Straker, E., *Wealden Iron*, London, 1931 (reprinted 1967), and Beresford and St Joseph, ibid., 258-9.
3. Money, J.H., 'Medieval ironworkings in Minepit Wood, Rotherfield, Sussex', *Med. Arch.*, XV, 1971, 86-111.
4. Straker, *Wealden Iron*, 69-74.
5. Tylecote, R.F., 'The Medieval smith and his methods' in Crossley, D.W.(ed.), *Medieval Industry*, CBA Research Report 40, 1981, 42-50.
6. Goodall, I.H., 'The medieval blacksmith and his products' in Crossley (ed.), ibid., 51-62.
7. Wilcox, R.P., *Timber and Iron Reinforcement in early Buildings*, Society of Antiquaries, London, 1981, 103-4.
8. Addyman, P.V. and Goodall, I.H., 'The Norman church and door of Stillingfleet, North Yorkshire', *Archaeologia*, CVI, 1979, 75-105.
9. Moorhouse, S.A., 'The rural medieval landscape' in Faull, M.L. and Moorhouse, S.A. (eds.), *West Yorkshire: an Archaeological Survey to AD 1500*, Wakefield, 1981, 3, 783-5.

10. Foard, G., 'Charcoal burning and iron production in Northamptonshire: soil mark evidence', *Council for British Archaeology Group 9 Newsletter*, 12, 1982, 28-31.
11. Salzman, L.F., *English Industries of the Middle Ages*, Oxford, 1923, 41-68.
12. Blanchard, I.S.W., 'Lead mining and smelting in medieval England and Wales' in Crossley, D.W. (ed.), *Medieval Industry*, CBA Research Report 1981, 72-84.
13. Beresford and St Joseph, *Medieval England. An Aerial Survey*, 259-60.
14. St J. O'Neil, B.H., *Peveril Castle*, HMSO Guide, 1979, 2.
15. Williams, J.H., 'Excavations at Greyfriars, Northampton, 1972', *Northamptonshire Archaeology*, 13, 1978, 107.
16. Dunning, G.C., 'A lead ingot at Rievaulx Abbey', *Antiq. J.*, XXXII, 1952, 199-202.
17. Watson, P., *Building the Medieval Cathedrals*, Cambridge, 1980, 29.
18. Hamilton Jenkins, A.K., *The Cornish Miner*, London, 1927, 28.
19. Salzman, *English Industries of the Middle Ages*, 77.
20. Saunders, A.D., 'Lydford Castle, Devon', *Med. Arch.*, XXIV, 1980, 123-86.
21. *London Museum Medieval Catalogue*, London, 1954 (reprinted 1967), 199-207, 264-290. Also Baart, J. *et al.*, *Opgravingen in Amsterdam: 20 jaar stadskernonderzoek*, Amsterdam, 1977; Goodall, A.R., 'The medieval bronzesmith and his products' in Crossley, D.W. (ed.), *Medieval Industry*, CBA Research Report 40, 1981, 63-72.
22. Baker, E., 'The medieval travelling candlestick from Grove Priory, Bedfordshire', *Antiq. J.*, LXI, 1981, 336-8.
23. Steane, J.M. and Bryant, G.F.,'Excavations at the deserted medieval settlement at Lyveden', *Journal 12* of Northampton Museum and Art Gallery, 1975, 107-18.
24. *Med. Arch.*, XVII, 1973, 185-7.
25. *Med. Arch.*, X, 1966, 171.
26. Jope, E.M., 'The Saxon building-stone industry in Southern and Midland England', *Med. Arch.*, VIII, 1964, 91-118.
27. Steane, J.M., *The Northamptonshire Landscape*, London, 1974, 80, 136-7, Plate 11.
28. Salzman, L.F., *Building in England down to 1540*, Oxford, 1952, 384-6.
29. Ibid., 527.
30. Platt, C., *Medieval England, London*,1978, 141-3.
31. Atkinson, T.D., *Local Style in English Architecture*, London, 1947, 90, 96.
32. Parker, J.H. 'On the English Origin of Gothic Architecture', *Archaeologia*, XLIII, 1871, 80-1.
33. Salzman, *English Industries of the Middle Ages*, 122.

34. Biddle, M., 'A thirteenth century architectural sketch from the Hospital of St. John the Evangelist, Cambridge', *Cambridge Antiq. Soc.*, LIV, 1961, 99-108.

35. Clapham, A.W., *English Romanesque Architecture after the Conquest*, Oxford, 1934, 117.

36. Wilcox, R.P., *Timber and Iron Reinforcement in Early Buildings*, Soc. of Antiquaries, London, 1981, 13.

37. Williams, J.H., *Excavations at St. Peter's Street, Northampton, 1973-6*, Northampton, 1979, 118-33.

38. Baker, D. *et al.*, 'Excavations in Bedford 1967-77', *Bedfordshire Arch. J.*, 13, 1979, 46-50.

39. Scaffolding is often depicted in MSS illuminations, e.g. building of the Temple with scaffolding. Bodleian Library MS Douce 112 f 11, Book of Hours, Flemish, *c.* 1500.

40. Knoop, D. and Jones, G.P., *The Medieval Mason*, Manchester, 1967, 66-97.

41. Colchester, L.S. and Harvey, J.H.,'Wells Cathedral', *Arch. J.*, 131, 1974, 214 and Figure 2. I am grateful to Mr Colchester for showing me this.

42. Spring, R.O.C., *The Masons' Marks of Salisbury Cathedral*, Salisbury, 1980.

43. Jope, E.M., 'Cornish houses 1400-1700' in Jope, E.M. (ed.), *Studies in Building History*, London, 1961, 195.

44. Clifton-Taylor, A., *The Pattern of English Building*, London, 1972, 179-83.

45. Drury, G.D., 'The use of Purbeck Marble in medieval times', *Proc. of Dorset Natural History and Archaeological Society*, 70, 1948, 74-98.

46. Cheetham, F.W., *Medieval English Alabaster Carvings in the Castle Museum, Nottingham*, Nottingham, 1973.

47. Hildburgh, W.L., 'English alabaster carvings as records of the medieval religious drama', *Archaeologia*, XCIII, 1949, 51-101.

48. Hewitt, C.A., *English Historic Carpentry*, Chichester, 1980, 5-13.

49. Darrah, R., 'Working unseasoned wood' in McGrail, S. (ed.), *Woodworking Techniques before AD 1500*, British Archaeological Reports International Series 129, 1982, 219-31.

50. Steane, J.M. and Gibson, R., *The Chantry House Henley-on-Thames*, Henley, 1982.

51. *Bodleian Library, Barlow, M.S., 53 (R)*.

52. Hewett, C.A., 'Anglo-Saxon carpentry' in Clemoes, P. (ed.), *Anglo-Saxon England*, 7, Cambridge, 1978, 205-29.

53. Hewitt, C.A., *English Historic Carpentry*, 69. My thanks to L.S. Colchester for showing me the high roofs of Wells Cathedral.

54. Morris, C.A., 'Aspects of Anglo-Saxon and Anglo-Scandinavian lathe-turning' in McGrail

(ed.), *Woodworking Techniques before AD 1500*, British Archaeological Reports International Series 129, 1982, 245-61.

55. Brooks, F.W., 'A Medieval brickyard at Hull', *J. Brit. Archaeol. Assoc.*, 3rd ser., IV, 1939, 151-74. For Brixworth tiles, see *J. Brit. Archaeol. Assoc.*, 130, 1977, 99-100.

56. Drury, P.J., 'The production of brick and tile in Medieval England' in Crossley, D.W. (ed.), *Medieval Industry*, CBA Research Report 40, 1981, 126-42.

57. Steane and Bryant, 'Excavations at the deserted medieval settlement at Lyveden, Northants', 33-8.

58. Eames, E.S., *Catalogue of Medieval Lead-glazed Earthenware Tiles in the British Museum*, London, 1980.

59. Eames, E.S., 'A thirteenth-century tile kiln site at North Grange, Meaux, Beverley, Yorkshire', *Med. Arch.*, V, 1961, 137-68.

60. Hurst, J.G., 'White Castle and the dating of medieval pottery', *Med. Arch.*, VI-VII, 1962-3, 135-55.

61. Aitken, M.J. and Weaver, G.H.,'Magnetic dating: some archaeomagnetic measurements in Britain', *Archaeometry*, 5, 1962, 4-24. Its preliminary applications to pottery of the medieval period are surveyed in Hurst, J.G., 'Post Roman archaeological dating and its correlation with archaeomagnetic results', *Archaeometry*, 5, 1962, 25-7.

62. Le Patourel, H.E.J., 'Documentary evidence and the medieval pottery industry', *Med. Arch.*, XII, 1968, 101-26.

63. Steane and Bryant, 'Excavations at the deserted medieval settlement at Lyveden, Northants', *Journal* of Northampton Museum and Art Gallery, 2 (1967), 5 (1969), 9 (1971), 12 (1975).

64. Musty, J., 'Medieval pottery kilns' in Evison, V.I., Hodges, H. and Hurst, J.G., *Medieval Pottery from Excavations*, London, 1974, 41-65.

65. Bryant, G.F., 'Experimental kiln firings at Barton-on-Humber, S. Humberside, 1971', *Med. Arch.*, XXI, 1977,106-23.

66. Musty, 'Medieval pottery kilns', 60-1.

67. Tannahill, R., *Food in History*, London, 1973, 212-14. A saltworks has been discovered at Wood St Nantwich, Cheshire, *Med. Arch.*, XXV, 1981, 227.

68. Darby, H.C., *Medieval Fenland*, Newton Abbot, 1974, 37-42.

69. De Brisay, K., 'Excavation of a redhill at Peldon, Essex, with notes on some other sites', *Antiq. J.*, LVIII, 1978, 31-60.

70. Houghton, F.T.S., 'Saltways, *Trans. Birmingham Arch. Soc.*, LIV, 1929-30, 1-18; Whitley, Rev. D₁, 'Saltways of Droitwich district', *Trans.*

Birmingham Arch. Soc., XLIV, 1923, 1-16.

71. Darby, H.C. (ed.), *A New Historical Geography of England before 1600*, Cambridge, 1980, 66.

72. Tannahill, *Food in History*, 210-12.

73. Radley, J., 'Economic aspects of Anglo-Danish York', *Med. Arch.*, XV, 1971, 50-1.

74. Williams, J.H., *Excavations at St. Peters St., Northampton, 1973-6*, Northampton, 1979, 98-102.

75. *London Museum Medieval Catalogue*, London, 1967, 185-90.

76. Armitage, P.L. and Goodall, J.A., 'Medieval horned and polled sheep: the archaeological and iconographic evidence', *Antiq. J.*, LVII, 1977, 73-90.

77. Power, E., *The Wool Trade in English Medieval History*, Oxford, 1941, 31, 35.

78. Anderson, M.D., *Looking for History in British Churches*, London, 1951, 220.

79. Finberg, H.P.R., *The Gloucestershire Landscape*, London, 1975, 89.

80. Platt, C. and Coleman-Smith, R., *Excavations in Medieval Southampton, 1953-1969*, Leicester, 1975, 72-5. It has to be admitted that this building is only traditionally connected with the wool trade. There is no proof of it.

81. Power, *The Wool Trade in English Medieval History*, 102-3.

82. Biddle, M., 'Excavations at Winchester, 1970: Ninth interim report', *Antiq. J.*, LII, 1972, 107-10.

83. Platt and Coleman-Smith, *Excavations in Medieval Southampton*, I, 35; II, 19,335, 336, 338, 339.

84. Bond, F., *Dedications and Patron Saints of English Churches*, Oxford, 1914, 119-20.

85. Goodall, I., 'Ironwork in medieval Britain. An archaeological study', unpublished PhD thesis for University of Cardiff, 1980.

86. Carus-Wilson, E.M., 'An Industrial Revolution of the Thirteenth Century', *Econ. Hist. Rev.*, XI, 1941, 39-60.

87. Biddle, 'Excavations at Winchester, 1970', 110.

88. Carus-Wilson, E., 'The significance of the secular sculptures in the Lane Chapel, Cullompton', *Med. Arch.*, 1, 1957, 104–17.

89. Scarfe, N., *The Suffolk Landscape*, London, 1972, 187-9.

90. Hunter, J.R., 'The medieval glass industry' in Crossley (ed.), *Medieval Industry*, CBA Research Report 40, 1981, 143-50.

91. Wood, E.S. 'A medieval glasshouse at Blundens Wood, Hambleden, Surrey', *Surrey Archaeol. Collect*, 62, 1965, 54-79.

92. 'Superb medieval glass found in city', *The Times*, 4 Dec. 1982.

93. Woodforde, C., '*The Norwich School of Glass Painting in the Fifteenth Century*', Oxford, 1950.

94. My thanks are due to Robert Croft of Milton Keynes Archaeological Unit for showing me this.

8

THE ARCHAEOLOGY
OF THE NECESSITIES
OF LIFE

This chapter summarises the recent archaeological evidence in England and Wales for medieval food, drink, clothing and footwear.

1. Food: The Limiting Factors of the Evidence

Food was vital to the population of medieval England in two obvious basic respects. An adequate food intake was necessary to produce sufficient energy to survive; it was necessary to build up strength to maintain an optimum working capacity. The converse was also true; an inadequate or unbalanced diet let to the retardation of growth in children and young people; malnutrition was responsible for chronic ill health and exposed society to high mortality. Traditional sources of information about food include artistic representations in manuscripts or carvings; these are notoriously difficult to interpret owing to the large element of convention involved rather than a scrupulous observation of contemporary practice. Literary sources again are of uncertain reliability although household accounts can be valuable for the food of the rich. The direct material remains of food found on living floors, refuse pits, middens and habitation sites offer the most hopeful way to an understanding of the medieval diet of all classes.

There are, however, numerous limiting factors in considering the archaeological evidence for food.[1] Some remains have a much better survival rate than others. Animal bones, the main evidence for the meat component, are found in great quantities. The skeletal remains of oxen, being more robust, last much better than pig. Fish bones have often been overlooked since they can only be recovered in

quantity by sieving. Cereals, despite the fact that they were of far greater importance in the medieval diet, are more elusive, often only surviving as grain impressions on pottery or in carbonised form. The context, too, provides problems. Food remains may come from closed structures such as pits or wells in which case there will be deposits of limited date-range. On the other hand it is unlikely that we will know how often such features were cleared out, or how much of the accumulated rubbish was deposited on fields or stored in middens. Clearly the stratification of such middens will have to be extremely carefully looked at. Refuse found over floors may be evidence of squalor or simply the result of an understandable failure to clear up on departure! The main imponderable is to ascertain how representative is the excavated evidence of the total refuse of the community. Another difficulty is to tie a particular body of evidence with a specific social group. The diet of different strata of medieval townspeople is particularly problematical because of the geographical contiguity of the diverse social groupings within the town. Lastly, food remains have, until recently, been given short shrift by archaeologists compared with the pains lavished on artifactual evidence.

2. Meat

What, then, can be learned from studying the bones from medieval excavations? The most obvious is the recognition of species – of wild and domestic animals, providing meat. Bone specialists still disagree as to the best ways of analysing the data. Some count the bone fragments which can be identified as coming from different species; others calculate the meat weight which such bones may have supported. Others scorn both these techniques and substitute informed guesses on 'the least number of animals' represented by the bones. We can tell the age of killing from an analysis of several factors, the most important of which are tooth eruption and replacement, the extent of epiphysial fusion, the closure of cranial sutures, tooth wear and antler development. The second is of particular value. During longitudinal growth the ends of the bone (known as epiphyses) are separated from the shaft by a pad of cartilage. When growth ceases, this ossifies, uniting the ephiphysis with the shaft. The sequence of fusion and the age at which it occurs is known by studying the long bones which often survive. We can work out from this the slaughtering times in husbandry practice. From close study of chopping and saw cuts much can be learned of butchery practice. When the edges of the bones are sharp it seems that roasting rather than stewing was the main culinary technique. The pathology of bones contains clues about the physical condition of animals. Malnutrition can be detected in bone formation; some disorders are provoked by diets deficient in calcium or phosphorus. Castration of young males is indicated by a greater length of long bones and by less rugged skeletal frames. Arthritis lipping and lesions can also be diagnosed.

As interest grows in the total medieval environment it should be possible to compare the bone material derived from a number of sites of differing dates, geographical situations and social complexions. At present, however, such excavated evidence is still so sparse that the sites tend to choose themselves. A valuable start has been made at Southampton.[2] Here the bones from the Saxon town of Hamwih have been compared with those from the medieval town of Southampton. The Hamwih material produced nearly 50,000 identifiable fragments from the five Melbourne Street sites; it seems that the great bulk of the animal bone was thrown away and buried in the town itself. The town apparently was homogeneous in its meat-eating habits; there was no marked differentiation of diet or class. Southampton's medieval bone sample was smaller: 10,000 fragments were recovered by eye and 5,000 examples, mostly of fish, were rescued by fine sieving. The material covers a wider span of time and, while relatively homogeneous in the early period, showed a considerable differentiation in the later. There was a pronounced social bias in favour of the more affluent. The poorer neighbourhoods have not so far been looked at.

At Hamwih it seems that the food supply came from 'a good sufficiency of sizeable cattle'. The fragment count shows cattle with a lead (53 per cent) followed by sheep (32 per cent) and pig (15 per cent). The bone weight produces the same ranking but the cattle lead is greater (72 per cent), sheep (15 per cent) and pig (2 per cent). These cattle apparently had a mean shoulder height of 115 cm. The sheep were small with a shoulder height of 62 cm; they were probably not kept primarily for food but for the industrial value of their wool. The pigs were killed young, a recognition of their prolific breeding habits, rapid turnover and quick rise to sexual maturity. Hamwih, in sum, seems to have been amply provisioned and the human population well nourished. This is reflected in the style of butchery where many of the chopped pieces can be reassembled with crisp bone fits suggesting that they had been roasted rather than stewed, a sign of high living standards. The lack of bone material from wild animals, such as deer, contrasted with another Saxon site at Ramsbury (Wilts.) where red deer and roe deer mingled in great abundance with beaver, badger and fox.

At Southampton sheep bones accounted for 40 per cent among the main domestic species; they were mostly old and tough, all of them small and it seems likely that they continued to be thought of mainly as wool producers. A second observation is that pig had begun to supplement cattle to a greater extent, doubtless because they were easier and less demanding to breed than cattle. Only after the Black Death did the desertion of many villages give the bigger animals a better chance and cattle showed a recovery. The Southampton sheep, however, continued to become ever more diminutive – with a ludicrously miniature height of less than 50 cm for an adult sheep at its shoulders.

It could be that they stayed under-nourished and therefore small; the smaller the animal, the greater the heat loss and therefore small sheep had a greater natural stimulus to grow a thick protective coat of wool! Butchery techniques showed a tendency towards finer sawing, more precise dismemberment, and more careful jointing in place of the early rough and ready chops. A greater proportion of the younger and more tender animals were chosen for roasting, this selection implying a measure of extravagance and taste. The fact that all parts of the animals were found in both Hamwih and Southampton suggests that butchering was carried out in the town. This was paralleled in Anglo-Scandinavian York where it centred by an early date on the Shambles (*Flesshamelles* – flesh shambles or flesh benches) first recorded in Domesday Book.

When we turn to rural sites the quantities of bone drop markedly as one would expect from much smaller (and thinner?) populations. At Wythemail, a single farm enclosure on the Northamptonshire uplands, dating from the thirteenth/fourteenth centuries, the bone material would fit only five cattle and five sheep.[3] Bone measurements suggest weight ratios of 10:1 in favour of cattle. It was noted at Wythemail that the majority of sheep bones were from fully mature animals. Doubtless they were killed when their careers as wool gatherers came to an end at seven years. The younger animals represented may well have died from natural causes: in some protein-starved areas of the world today the eating of dead as opposed to killed meat is one of the facts of life.

Wharram Percy provides another upland site, this time on the chalk wolds of Yorkshire.[4] Here sheep outnumbered cattle (60 per cent sheep, 30 per cent ox, 8 per cent pig and 2 per cent deer) as has been noticed by Beresford and Hurst on other village sites. Moreover, the culling pattern was different. The largest number of both cattle and sheep was killed at a little over two years and the evidence does not support the contention that sheep were kept to a relatively great age to obtain from them as many clips of wool as possible.

Some interesting comparisons can be made if we now move up the social scale and investigate the diet of monastic households.

The bones from Kirkstall Abbey, a Cistercian house, and Pontefract Priory, a Cluniac house, have received some attention.[5] At Kirkstall a large dump of bones 22.9 m x 36.6 m and 45 cm to 90 cm in thickness, representing the remains of 5,000 animals consumed from *c.* 1450-1530, was found associated with the meat kitchen. Nearly all the larger bones had been chopped; the ends had frequently been chopped a second time which suggests that they had been stewed. Meat stew had apparently taken over from vegetable stew as a traditional item in Cistercian diet as monastic standards lapsed! Most of the Kirkstall bones came from domestic animals, represented by 90 per cent ox, 5 per cent sheep, 3 per cent pig and 2 per cent deer. This provides a useful reminder that despite the fame of Cistercian wool, these monasteries were even more noted for raising beef and dairy cattle. Fountains Abbey at the Dissolution, for instance, had 2,356 horned cattle but only 326 sheep.

The majority of the Kirkstall bones were from mature animals, two to three years old; it seems that the monks were able to keep most of their stock through the winter. The cattle were hornless and compared well in size with modern stock. The great age of some and the large size of the cannon bones indicated draught oxen. Doubtless they found their way to the pot when they were too old to pull the plough!

The Cistercian sheep were smaller than those of the present day. They were both of the horned and unhorned breeds; it is thought that the horned were the short-woolled sheep and the hornless the long-woolled valley sheep. Despite the fame of Cistercian wool, it is cattle which figure widely both in the *Valor Ecclesiasticus*, 1535, and in the archaeological record.

One would expect that these wealthy monastic sites would display a greater variety of food remains including more from wild animals and birds, than the more normal urban and rural households. It is true that rabbit and hare, red and fallow deer and wild fowl bones were found at Kirkstall and Pontefract. Also molluscs, including oysters and edible land snails, were identified. Only when we move upwards in the social scale, however, this time to analyse the debris from the kitchen or the table of the lord of a northern castle, can we appreciate the extraordinary variety of foods available to an aristocratic household of the fifteenth century.

The contents of a blocked-up drain at Castle Barnard, Durham, demonstrates that the natural environment was being exploited fully, to produce a more exotic supplement to the normal medieval diet for the lords of this northern castle.[6] As well as goose and dove the bird remains included grouse, partridge, waders, red shank, moorhen, song thrush, redwing, blue tit and thrush. These were doubtless caught using nets, snares, bird lime, traps and whistle lures. They remind one of a medieval method of roasting miscellaneous birds which started with the smallest bird being stuffed inside a slightly larger species, ending up with the whole bundle being encased in a swan or a peacock! Moreover, the spoils of the hunt reached the table. A shaft of a femur from a red deer showed that a haunch and shank of venison had been cooked. Roe deer, rabbit, hare and fallow deer bones were also found. The fallow deer are likely to have been caught in one of the 20 parks said to have been kept by the Bishops of Durham at the time. The rabbit may have come from one of the many coney garths or warrens. Ox, pig and sheep were all present, also suckling pig and lamb.

3. Fish

Fish, too, was a major component at Castle Barnard, where 121 g of fish bone were found. When we compare the fish remains found in late Saxon and late medieval contexts considerable developments have clearly taken place. At Hamwih the people were not very adventurous fishermen; their plaice, flounder and eels were available in the immediate estuary. At Southampton, however, fishbones were found in greater quantities; perhaps their chance of survival was greater in accumulated garderobe deposits. The plaice and flounder now outnumber the eel. Evidently there was a greater readiness to fish the deeper waters in the twelfth/thirteenth centuries. At Castle Barnard, however, no less than twelve different types of fish were found. These ranged from

fragments of cartilagenous fish (a group which includes sharks, rays and dogfish), trout, pike, carp, eel, conger eel, whiting, cod, haddock, ling, gurnard and flatfish. Some of these, such as whiting, live in the North Sea in depths of between 30 and 100 m. Cod are abundant in the North Sea both in inshore and offshore waters. Haddock are seldom caught at less than 60 m depth and ling inhabit waters 100-400 m deep. Clearly these medieval fishermen off the north-east coast were venturing out into deep waters. They were probably taking most of their fish using hooks and lines. Eels and trout could have been fished from the rivers nearby.

Herring (*Clupea harengus*) was also recovered from the sieved material at Castle Barnard. This is a pelagic marine fish which formerly occurred in immense shoals in the North Sea. Prior to the introduction of the mid water trawl it was caught in a drift or seine net. Judging from the quantity found, 415 vertebral bones, it was one of the more important fish consumed on the site. The herring had been exploited in bulk at least since the late Anglo-Saxon period. A remarkable layer of the remains of between 1,000 and 2,000 small herrings was found on the site of St Mary Bishophill Junior at York.[7] The site seems to have been used for commercial fish processing. Brother John Anlaby, kitchener of Selby Abbey, purchased large quantities of red and white herrings in 1415-16. They included 30,000 red herrings from William Muston at 12s 10d per (long) thousand. His other purchases show that preserved fish were already travelling quite long distances in the fifteenth century. Thirty salt fish called lobbes (pollack) were bought at Scarborough, seven salt fish called ling were bought from John Knight, shipman, and 120 stockfish (*piscibus duris*) were bought at Hull from Robert Percy at 3d each. This widespread trade in preserved fish is born out by finds at Northampton, 96.6 km from the sea.[8] Here herring was the only main species present in the period 900-1100 AD. Cod, ling and flatfish were brought in between 1100-1400. In the production of stockfish, such as large cod and ling, the inedible head and entrails are removed, and the carcass divided into manageable sections. Hence all that was found in the Northampton material were the vertebral centra without the head bones. A similar observation was made among fish bones from King's Lynn and Great Yarmouth where there were large quantities of ling vertebrae but few head bones. Some of the large cod from Northampton were imported barrelled up whole and we have seen evidence for the trade from the Wash and North Sea when discussing roads (p. 105).

4. Cereals

Plant remains from medieval England can be identified in various forms. These vary from complete preservation in peat layers of water-logged deposits, where the anaerobic environment prevents decay, to carbonisation resulting from accidental fire or overparching which leads to some distortion but often leaves the seed or stalk recognisable. Pollen samples may yield information about the environment but in practice they are difficult to interpret since it is always doubtful how much pollen is local and how much is derived from the wider area. A further source is found in casts of grain imprints on pottery.

It seems that wheat and barley were staple crops in different areas of southern England from the Neolithic to the Iron Age and beyond. Oats appear in several Iron Age and Roman sites, more as an 'accidental contaminant than a cereal independently cultivated'. Godwin goes on to suggest that the cultivated cereal (*Avena sativa*) was introduced by the Anglo-Saxons, familiar with it in their own homeland.[9] It is certainly found as the pre-dominant grain in the Anglo-Scandinavian levels at 6-8 Pavement, York.

Further south wheat and barley undoubtedly were the bulk grain crops. At Northampton a sample from a drying oven in house 1, St Peters Street, yielded 70 charred grains of which 78 per cent were wheat (*Triticum spp.*), 14 per cent barley (*Hordeum vulgare* L.) and 8 per cent oats (*Avena* spp. including *Avena fatva* L. wild oats). Analysis carried out on samples from pit 101, High Street B site, Southampton produced seven damaged grains resembling *Triticum* (wheat) type, one resembling *Hordeum* (barley) type and one *Secale* (rye) type. There was also an unusually high

representation of cereal pollen in the sample tested, reflecting the enclosed urban situation of the pit, for in a typical rural environment the pollen of trees and wild grasses usually outweighs the cereal pollen. The Barnard Castle drain produced oat grains, and wheat grains of bread type, smaller grained than modern varieties, which it is thought could have been used as 'bulk' in medieval dishes such as pottage and frumenty. Judging from the frequent occurrence of seeds of weeds of cultivation such as hairy tare (*Vicia hirsuta*), stinking mayweed (*Anthemis cotula* L) and white charlock, medieval cereals were rarely clean. Oats, on the other hand, had problems peculiar to their own, being more likely to ferment and overheat in the stack than other cereals. Care had to be taken to dry the crops properly by artificial means in corn-drying ovens, three of which were found at Hound Tor (Devon).

Charred grains of oats were found among the ash samples collected from the corn-drying kiln in Barn 3 of Hound Tor village.[10] Oats, in this Highland Zone context, are useful for two purposes. They produce a reasonable quantity of grain despite poor acid soils, rainy districts and low summer temperatures. Also they supply a straw which is more palatable and nutritious than that of other cereals and can be used in place of hay for winter fodder.

Obviously corn-drying kilns should be investigated for possible grain samples. They have been found all over the Highland Zone but they are also known from Midland England as the climatic deterioration set in. Brixworth and Faxton in Northamptonshire and Stamford Castle in Lincolnshire have produced such structures recently. They are shaped rather like ovens with stoke-hole, well constructed flues and a circular or rectangular firing chamber. After the grain was dried, parched and stored, there were still two further processes before it could be converted into food. It had to be milled and the resultant flour or meal was then baked. We have already looked at the structural remains of mills; bakehouses will be briefly considered in the section on kitchens.

5. Brewing

At Penhallam Manor (Cornwall), the kitchen was provided with bake oven and facilities for brewing including a malting kiln raised on a platform and heated by a straight-sided flue over 1 m long and 50 cm wide.[11] This reminds us that bread was not the only food made from cereals. It was washed down with ale prepared from malt, which in turn was derived from barley.

The barley was steeped in water until the grain became swollen and soft. The sodden grain was then piled into a heap to encourage the development of heat by the absorption of oxygen from the air. As the barley began to sprout, diastase developed which converted starch into dextrin and subsequently into grape sugar. The grain was now kiln-roasted which halted the entire chemical development. Querns were used to crush the malt which was then acted on by water in the next process of turning it into ale.

Beer and ale are distinguished in Anglo-Saxon Leech books and glossaries and their flavourings come under the general term *gruit* and perhaps *wyrt*. These flavourings included heather, various herbs and hops. Hops are of two kinds – the so-called '*hege-hymele*' (found growing wild in hedges) and the cultivated version. The use of hops to make beer bitter and to improve its keeping properties has been attributed to the Dutch who were thought to have brought them to England *c.* 1400 AD. The late Saxon boat found in the Graveney marshes and dated to the tenth century was apparently carrying a cargo of hops when it foundered and this has been claimed as the first solid evidence in England for the use of hops in brewing.[12] Medieval brewing is sometimes considered to have been traditionally women's business; certainly the most celebrated brewstress of the fifteenth century was the mystic from King's Lynn, Margery Kempe. In Midland peasant society, however, the ratio between male and female brewers fluctuated.[13] Sometimes stiff competition was engendered as when in 1420 Juliana Bryd of Oldbury broke into John Skyner's house and 'out of badness' cut down his alestake!

Home-brewing was associated with a particular type of pottery vessel during the fifteenth century.[14] These were large, tall pots with a bung-hole near the base, referred to as 'cisterns', 'alepots' or 'stands'. The 'spiggots', 'ducels' or 'forcets' were taps used to control the flow of liquid by being inserted in the bung-holes. They were made of wood, as we know from their being frequently purchased from turners. A very large vessel, in fact the largest pot in Oxfordshire County Museum, which came from Churchill, is an example of such a cistern.[15]

To sum up it seems that alcohol in one form or another 'was an essential narcotic which helped to anaesthetise men against the strains of contemporary life'.[16] Thomas quotes a fifteenth-century heretic who was of the opinion that there was more good in a cask of ale than in the four Gospels; malt, he thought, did more than the Bible to justify God's ways to man!

6. Vegetables and Fruit

When we try to assess the extent to which vegetables figure in the medieval diet we are forced to rely more heavily on literary and documentary sources because vegetables tend to leave even less trace in the archaeological record than cereals. One reason is that they were eaten before they seeded and only the seed is likely to survive. A recent study on medieval gardens states: 'our medieval ancestors did not think much of vegetables. The ones that interested them were either starchy ones or ones that gave a good strong taste to starch.'[17]

The starchiest vegetables were the pulses, peas and beans. The bean was a version of our broad bean, *Faba vulgaris*, and was particularly suited to the damp English climate. Medieval cookery books regarded beans as a basic ingredient. 'The beans are to be taken out of their "hulls" dried in the oven, and made into broth which was to be eaten with bacon'; or made into bean and onion pottage. Because the seeds of leguminous crops decay rapidly they are seldom preserved unless they are accidentally charred. There are records in York of pollen attributable to *Vicia* or its close relatives. This could represent the field bean (*Vicia faba* L.), the pea (*Pisum sativum*) or wild vetch species. Charred seeds of *Vicia faba* (the field bean) were found in Anglo-Scandinavian levels at 6/8 Pavement, York. Insects infesting crops occasionally afford a clue about the crops themselves. A type of bean beetle, *Bruchus rufimanus*, which attacks growing crops of broad beans and house beans and overwinters in stored beans, inhabited a late Saxon pit at St Peter's Street, Northampton. The pea similarly flourished in the rainy English countryside; the white pea grew in the fields and made the best thick pottage or was fed to the pigs, while the green pea (*Pisum sativum*) was used for green pottage. Beans were so basic and commonplace that they gave rise to proverbs such as 'I don't give a bean' or 'I haven't got a bean'. It may have been the protein-rich contribution of peas and beans that contributed towards the startling expansion of population and growth of urban life in the Middle Ages.[18]

Those vegetables which provided the most flavour to medieval meals were the pungent, hardy, easy-to-grow and above all strong tasting members of the Allium family. The most important were the leek (*Allium porrum*), the onion (*Allium cep*) and garlic (*Allium sativum*). As previously mentioned, leeks were so popular with the Anglo-Saxons that their word for a kitchen garden was leek garth (*leac-tun*); their word for a gardener was leek-keeper (*leac-ward*).

Garden accounts of Thomas Keynsham, who was in charge of a number of Glastonbury Abbey gardens at Mells, Pilton, Marksbury and Batcombe, show that the gardens contained beans, leeks, onions, garlic, hemp, flax, madder and herbs.[19] The eight gardens had 23 beds of leeks between them and in 1333 were full of garlic, having no less than 11,000 cloves of which 3,000 were kept for planting, 2,000 sent to the abbot's kitchen and 6,000 to the abbey larder. One shudders to think of the odour generated until one recalls a writer of the fourteenth century 'the stench of garlic voids the stench of dunghills'.

The only other vegetable which was in universal use was the cabbage. John the Gardener devoted a section of his treatise to 'the sowing and setting of Wurtys'. The cabbage, 'wortes', or kale (as it was called) appeared on the tables of all classes from the labouring poor, who were glad to eat fresh

greens in winter when they were tired of living off dried peas and salted bacon, to the nobility and even royalty. The cabbage, in fact, was one of the ingredients of 'compost', a composition always to have at hand, which appears as number 100 in Richard II's collection of royal recipes, *The Form of Cury*.[20] Compost was a typically medieval soggy concoction of parsley and onion roots, pared cabbages and rapes, pea pottage and salt, profusely spiced with Greek wine and clarified honey, mustard, raisins and currants.

Fruit remains have a greater survival prospect than vegetables. The contents of a fifteenth-century barrel-latrine from central Worcester[21] included a number of macrofossils from edible plants such as mustard, linseed, grape, bramble, strawberry, sloe, damson, cherry, apple, gooseberry, coriander, fennel, fig, hazlenut, bilberry and oat. The smaller pips are usually swallowed whole with fruit such as those of strawberry, apple and grape and in such a context a likely source was from food voided after it had passed through the human digestive tract. The other fruit stones were probably debris from meals. Latrine deposits often yield such a characteristic 'medieval fruit salad' group of plant remains.

Some were probably imports from the continent. Worcester is on the River Severn and the grapes (or raisins) and figs might well have come from Europe. Others were locally grown. It is curious that the plum was absent but its place was taken by the semi-cultivated damson (*P. Spinosa Spp. insititia*) and by the wild sloe (*P. spinosa*)[22] A number of other seeds were present including *Foeniculum vulgare* (fennel) and *Coriandrum sativum* (coriander) which were probably used for flavouring food. Umbelliferous seeds were used in the past for their powers of preventing flatulence as well as their flavour.

Occasionally, plant remains are found which suggest the presence of drugs. At Worcester again the seeds of *Atropa belladonna* (deadly nightshade) and *Hyoscyamus niger* (henbane) were present; both these contain alkaloids and could act as drugs if consumed. Another sample of medieval plant remains, this time from a pit in the Goldsmith House site, Goss Street, Chester, produced some very curious components which would have had serious after effects if they had passed through a human digestive system.[23] They included the seeds of *Agrostemma githago*, the corncockle, which is poisonous to man and beast. So many were found (the crushed remains of well over 160 seeds), that 'we are left with the possibility that they were intentionally collected and exploited for their drug or poison content'.

Chronic poisoning results from consuming *Agrostemma* seeds; it is also thought that the saponin content increases one's susceptibility to leprosy, a disease endemic in Britain in the Middle Ages. Alternatively it can be used for medicinal purposes because 'it stayeth the flux of the belly and the overmuch flowing of womens termes . . . stoppeth the laske (diarrhoea)'. Several other species present in the pit including *Pteridium aquilinum* (bracken) and *Brassica nigra* (black mustard) could also have been used medicinally. Altogether one can only speculate on the motives of the person who gathered together this potentially poisonous crop of plants!

7. *Kitchens and Cooking*

The kitchen was usually a detached building not only in the greater establishments of the Middle Ages but in quite humble homes. In 1292 the widow, Margery de la Strete, agreed with her son that he should take over her house but she was to continue to have access for brewing and other necessary things 'in that house (*domo*) which is called the kitchen'.[24] The use of the word '*domus*' rather than '*camera*' is revealing because it implies a separate building. Doubtless the main reason for keeping the kitchen separate was fear of fire, a very real danger in view of the flimsy material of early kitchens. Such buildings have been quite often found in excavations. At Weoley Castle, Birmingham, a thirteenth-century detached kitchen (12.6 m x 6.9 m) with a great hearth was found.[25] It had a reed-thatched roof and a pentice gave access to a stone hall which was burned down *c.* 1260. At Northolt Manor, a kitchen of *c.* 1300-50 was a detached timber-framed building, 27.9 m square with a central hearth and a post-hole for a spit or a firehood. Most of the cooking here seems to have been done outside in an extensive pebbled area with

many hearths. The detached kitchen at the royal hunting lodge at Writtle had a similar outside annexe where there was a great bakeoven and two further ovens set in the external wall (Figure 1.3).[26] Kitchens could also be octagonal and stone-vaulted as at Durham and Glastonbury. Towards the end of the Middle Ages kitchens tend to have been square or oblong and many were integrated into the main building (Figures 8.1, 8.2). At New College, Oxford the kitchen was part of the original fourteenth-century work and is the eastern one-storey portion of an oblong block containing first-floor hall and buttery. The tradition of the detached kitchen persisted as late as the 1470s when a magnificent tower-kitchen, 23.2 m square with squinch arches supporting an octagonal timber roof was raised at Stanton Harcourt (Oxon.). The one universal characteristic of these kitchens is the creation of a large uncluttered space – with plenty of ventilation to get rid of smoke and smells. The final development in plan occurred in the early sixteenth century when the kitchen was often placed in an extension of the butteries at right angles to the hall block. Corpus Christi College, Oxford has this arrangement with access from the screens passage at the back of the hall.

The most obvious fittings which survive in medieval kitchens are the fireplaces and ovens. Early timber kitchens had central hearths and these were probably retained for stand-by purposes even when the kitchen was updated with chimneyed fireplaces. At Glastonbury the abbot's kitchen is square externally with segmental headed fireplaces built across each angle, making it internally octagonal. The smoke and smell were dispersed through a cunningly contrived louvre at the top of the space which rises to the full height of the building. There were four lateral fireplaces in the monastic kitchen at Durham, plus a kiln for smoking bacon. Both Durham and Glastonbury are provided with superb fireproof roofs of stone. The size of the fireplaces in noble and in royal kitchens was large enough to roast whole oxen. For these long spits were required, together with boys who kept them turning; only feeble attempts were made to mechanise this process in the Middle Ages.

A typical medieval kitchen had at least one

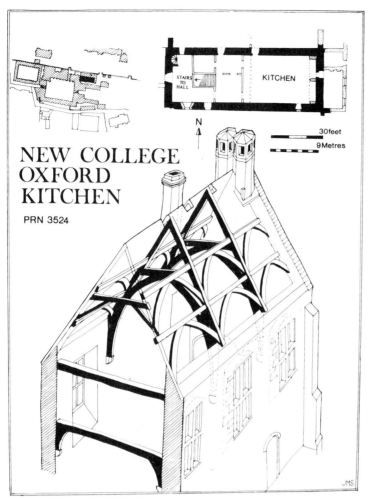

NEW COLLEGE
OXFORD
KITCHEN

PRN 3524

STAIRS TO HALL

KITCHEN

N

30feet
9 Metres

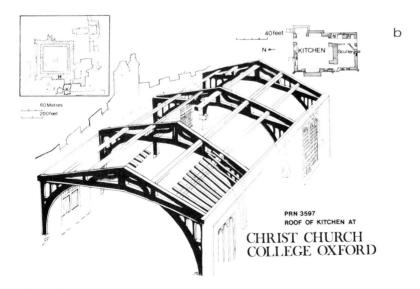

40feet

N

KITCHEN   Scullery

60 Metres
200feet

PRN 3597
ROOF OF KITCHEN AT

CHRIST CHURCH
COLLEGE OXFORD

Figure 8.1: Kitchens: (a) New College, Oxford; (b) Christ Church College, Oxford

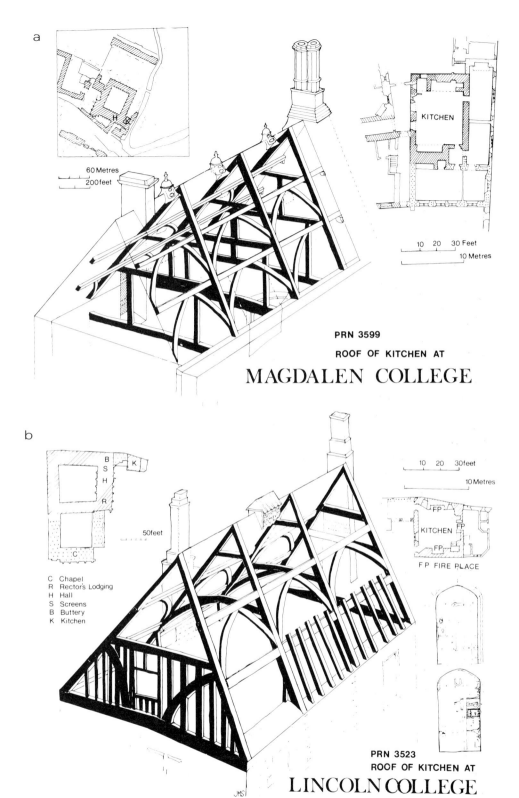

a

60 Metres
200 feet

KITCHEN

10 20 30 Feet
10 Metres

PRN 3599
ROOF OF KITCHEN AT
MAGDALEN COLLEGE

b

B
S
H
R
K
C

10 20 30 feet
10 Metres

FP
KITCHEN FP
FP
FP FIRE PLACE

C Chapel
R Rector's Lodging
H Hall
S Screens
B Buttery
K Kitchen

50 feet

PRN 3523
ROOF OF KITCHEN AT
LINCOLN COLLEGE

JMS

Figure 8.2: Kitchens: (a) Magdalen College, Oxford; (b) Lincoln College, Oxford

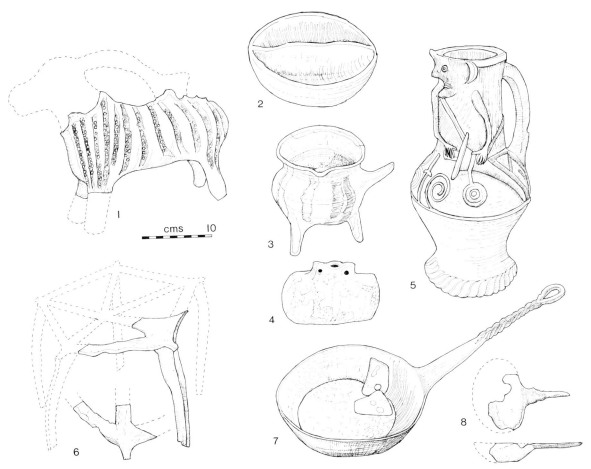

Figure 8.3(a): Cooking Utensils from Winchester. 1. Aquamanile, a ceramic vessel in the shape of an animal used for carrying water for washing hands at table. 2. Salt cellar. 3. Three-legged skillet, a copy of a metal form of vessel. 4. Costrel with lug perforated for suspension. 5. Facejug. 6. Brandreth, platform for supporting vessels over a fire. 7. Much repaired frying pan. 8. Ladle

large oven for baking various breads, custards, pies and pastries. This would be oval-shaped and built into the thickness of the kitchen wall.[27] At the Knights Templars' preceptory at South Witham (Lincs.) there were five ovens built into the walls of the kitchen. In the fifteenth-century settlement at Lyveden in Northamptonshire circular ovens were built in the yard outside the long-house.[28] A bundle of faggots would have been placed inside the oven and lighted; an iron door was closed in front. The faggots burned fast and heated both the air and the masonry surrounding the oven. When the ashes were swept out the bread and pastries were placed inside using a spade-like instrument known as a peel and the 'bake metes' were cooked as the oven slowly cooled.

The kitchen, otherwise, contained little real furniture. A large chopping block (seen in the fourteenth-century Luttrell Psalter) 'for cutting meat into pecys or into gobettys' was essential. There is still such a block in the kitchen of Magdalen College, Oxford though modern legislation unreasonably demands its removal (1982). Enormous mortars and pestles were in constant use, for pounding meats and pulverising spices. Again the Luttrell Psalter shows a boy using a pestle twice his own height. There might be a large vat for storing freshly caught fish, a locked spice cabinet and a dressoir or

Figure 8.3(b): Cooking Utensils from Museum of London. 1-4. Knives. Note cutler's marks and bone handles. 5-7. Spoons. Pear-shaped bowls, slender stems, decorative knops. 8-9. Flesh hooks. 10. Skimmer. 11. Skillet of bronze. 12. Bowl or small cauldron with ring for suspension. 13. Large skillet

long massive plank where food received its final embellishment before presentation at the feast.

Many medieval culinary techniques were similar to our own and are summed up in Chaucer's description of the cook in *The Canterbury Tales* who knew how to 'roost and seeth and boille and frye'. Judging from menus, roasting was one of the most popular methods for preparing feast-foods, a possible reason being that it required comparatively little expert attention. Spits were kept turning as whole oxen, haunches of venison, heads of boar and game birds were roasted. At times such roasting flesh was covered with a paste of saffron, egg yolks and flour to give it a gilded appearance (known as *endoring*).[29]

Other techniques involved 'parboyling, stewing, scaldying, broyling and tostying', the first being suitable for softening salted meat. Massive iron or bronze cauldrons, large enough to reach to men's waists, (if manuscript illustrations can be believed) were stood on three legs directly over the flames. The recipes order 'seeth it standying' or 'cook it thick'. Three-pronged flesh hooks were used for drawing pieces of meat out of the cauldrons.[30] Sometimes smaller amounts of food were placed in earthenware jars with watertight lids. These were set on a shelf pierced with holes within the cauldron and immersed in boiling water.

Pottery from medieval kitchen deposits can tell us a great deal about culinary techniques.[31] Evidence, in the form of sooting, wear-marks and residues, can provide clues as to the uses to which the pots were put. Many of the pots from Sandal Castle revealed sooting or burning on one part of the base and body only, implying that they were placed on the edge and not over the fire. Some jugs were partially sooted but clean inside suggesting a liquid had been heated; January in Chaucer's 'The Merchant's Tale' quaffed 'a cordial for the fire, that claret laced with spice can lend desire'. A number were sooted only on the outside of the rim and these may have been used as the inner vessel into which food or herbs were put and suspended over a fire in boiling water in a larger container. There was a possibility at Sandal that the external vessel was a metal cauldron but in southern England large pottery cooking pots are the norm. Fire was usually transported in pots which would show internal sooting. Large pie-shaped pots pierced with vents were used as curfews to cover the embers last thing at night. Piles were allegedly treated by putting hot charcoal and herbs in a pot which was then placed under a siege or stool with a hole in the seat on which the sufferer sat!

Many recipes order the cook 'to frye it uppe in gode grece'. Butter or *whyte grece* (lard) was melted in frying pans like the late Saxon one excavated at Winchester (Figure 8.3). This has a slightly oval bowl with sloping sides. Its looped handle is nicely designed so that it can be stored by hanging on the wall. It would have been difficult to cook solid dishes like omelettes or cereal cakes which require an even temperature all over because of the thin rounded base and patches. It could well have been used for frying fish. The fact that the bowl has been repaired in three places shows that it was much prized by its owner-cook. Favourite fried foods included apple *fritours* or parsnip slices which were dipped in a batter of ale, eggs and flour before being fried. *Skymours* (slotted spatulas) were used to skim off grease and to remove fried foods from the pan (Figure 8.3a). Iron ladles with long handles so that cooks could stand a safe distance from the flames were also essential equipment. When not in use, these utensils were hung on hooks or stored on shelves along kitchen walls.

After reading a medieval cookery book like *A Form of Cury* it is obvious that Charlemagne spoke the truth when he said that herbs were 'the friend of physicians and the praise of cooks'. For making a simple salad, for instance, it was recommended that the cook 'take parsel, sawge, garlec, chibollas, oynons,

leek, borage, myntes, porrectes, fenel, and ton tressis (watercress), rew, rosemarye, purslayne, lave and waisshe hem clene. Pike hem, pluk hem small with thyn hond and myng (mix) hem wel with rawe oile. Lay on vynegar and salt and serve it forth.'[32] All the colouring agents used in medieval cooking were organic. The favourite one was saffron, used to transform the colour of food to gold. It was extremely expensive because it takes the stigmas of 75,000 crocus flowers to produce 1 lb (453 g) of saffron. It was grown in fields round Saffron Waldron, Suffolk.

Spices were also considered an 'essential luxury' imported from the Orient. They came to Europe often via Italian merchants who weighed them by the heavy beam, the *peso grosso*. The guild members of the spice merchants were known as *grossarii* from which we derive the name grocer. Spices were pulverised with mortars and pestles. Fragments of such mortars, often made of Purbeck marble, are frequently found on medieval kitchen sites: they have protruding ears or lugs and fit snugly on the ground. Within them spices were ground to *pouders* mentioned in the recipes. White powder was ginger or a combination of ginger blended with cinnamon and mace. It was thought to 'quychen the remembraunce'. Pepper was another highly prized spice which had a strong reputation for its digestive qualities. Sugar, because it was rare and imported from the east, was classified as a spice. It was generally sold in the loaf. Honey was the ubiquitous sweetener but medieval bees are only found in ones and twos in below-ground excavation. Presumably they avoided expiring in water-logged deposits!

8. Water

One of the major factors influencing the location of settlement was the availability of water. Springs and wells were more desirable than rivers partly because they were less likely to become polluted and partly because water from those sources was more controllable. The importance of water supply is reflected in many place-names. To take a few examples at random from Northamptonshire there is Maidwell (the maiden's well), Rothwell (the

Plate 8.1: Lyveden, Northamptonshire. Cistern from pottery-making site. The sides have been cut back to reveal extent of well-pit and lining of dry stone (Photo: H. Atkinson FRPS)

Plate 8.2: Lyveden, Northamptonshire. Thirteenth/fourteenth century. Stone-lined well or cistern. The limestone indicates the extent of the well-pit. The well itself is lined with dry stone walling and was filled at this stage with pottery wasters. Scale in inches (Photo: H. Atkinson FRPS)

red well, red because of the iron stone), Barnwell (warrior's spring), Pipewell (Pippa's Spring), Weldon (hill with spring), Twywell (double spring).

Most rural settlements, when excavated, produce examples of water pits, wells and cisterns. At Caldecote (Herts.), there was a sequence of water pits followed by wells in the late fourteenth or early fifteenth centuries. The wells varied in depth from 3 to 3.90 m and had been constructed with considerable care; two were unlined and the sides of a third had been built of clunch ashlar. At Lyveden (Northants.), one of the wells found in this industrial settlement was built in a massive circular well pit about 3 m in diameter (Plate 8.1).[33] The pit had been dug into the yellow clay subsoil with iron shod wooden spades, the remains of two of which were found in the fill. The well was

bottle-shaped and was of drystone limestone construction. At the top it was 30 cm in diameter but gradually bellied out to become 75 cm at the base. It was dated to the thirteenth/fourteenth centuries. Doubtless water was fetched into the house from these wells by means of pottery and leather containers. We know that such water pots were made at Lyveden. Three tenants were recorded in a manor court held in 1403 as holding 1.2 ha of land 'for digging clay for the making of water pots'.

Town sites are riddled with wells. In the Saxon town of Hamwih (Southampton), the wells normally had a woven wicker lining to stabilise the surrounding gravels, but at one site a more unusual method of construction had been used.[34] A large cone had been excavated 1.70 m in diameter and 1.40 m deep.

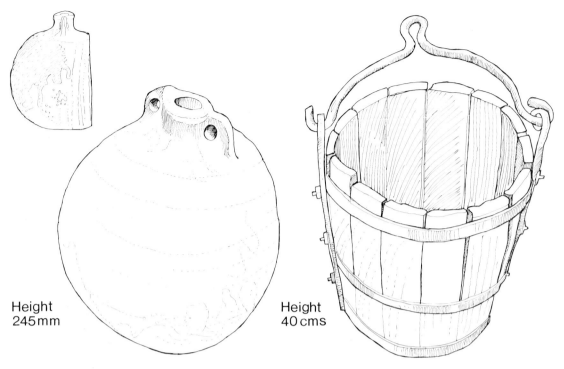

Height
245mm

Height
40 cms

Figure 8.4: Costrel and Well Bucket from Weoley Castle, Birmingham

A circular shaft had then been sunk to water level and was shored with a wooden barrel.

Wells in later medieval Southampton were stone-lined and in one house in High Street, dating from the thirteenth century, there was a specially built stone well chamber.[35] Pollution of wells from cess pits must always have been a danger in cramped towns. In 1420 John Beret, recently mayor, acquired and repaired the friary conduit and this brought fresh water for the first time within reach of every householder in Southampton.

The bottoms of wells, although difficult to excavate, often contain finds of great interest (Figure 8.4). They may well include pottery vessels which have been dropped in and have survived the fall unbroken. Waterlogging also means that timber, shoes, leather offcuts, fruit stones and seeds and other organic waste have an excellent chance of survival (Plate 8.3). Occasionally in more important buildings we are given some inkling of the methods used to bring water to the surface. At the royal palace of King's Langley (Herts.), for instance, there was a large well which had a huge weathering cone at the top,[36] 11.50 m in diameter. It is likely that the well in this case was over 50 m deep, and the weight of a chain of this length and a bucket and its contents would have been too heavy for a conventional windlass. Probably a treadmill, such as existed at Clarendon Palace and is still worked at Carisbrooke Castle (Isle of Wight), was used. At least there was known to be a well house over the head. At Lydford Castle (Devon), in the filling of the well, were found several interesting items such as a single-arm pickaxe, the binding of a shovel, the remains of a wooden bucket, and a number of timbers which may have been part of the lifting mechanism.[37] The cost of digging a large well was considerable. At King's Langley in 1279 'and in the wages of divers diggers in the great well for the same period £18 1s 7d'.

For more sophisticated schemes of water supply we must turn to the church. Roman Britain had of course known the use of long-distance aqueducts and pipes at such places as Dorchester (Dorset) and Lincoln.[38] Roman forts and villas were supplied with lead water

Plate 8.3: Mid-Saxon Well, Odell, Bedfordshire. Set in a circular construction pit the well comprised a platform of timbers (foreground) with a wattle lining (beyond) in which a reused basket was suspended as a filter (Photo: Bedfordshire County Council)

pipes and cisterns and it is clear that such systems worked by gravity. The church, as the inheritor of so much that was Roman, was foremost in the revival of good drainage systems which could compare with those of the Romans. Abbot Aethelwold of Abingdon (Oxon.), is said to have provided his abbey with notable improvements in water supply including a 'watercourse which runs under the dormitory to the stream which is called Okke' and was probably aimed at flushing the convent's drain.[39]

At Christchurch Cathedral Priory, Canterbury, there are two drawings in the same hand, dating from *c.* 1165, which show a complex system.[40] A number of ancient wells were retained to act as a reserve in case the new hydraulic system failed or had to be repaired. The source was outside the city and was collected in a conduit house; it then passed through a pipe by way of five reservoirs or settling tanks. On entering the monastery it was distributed to different places by filling tanks and cisterns each of which was at a lower level than the preceding. Water was drawn off by plugs and spigots or cocks, and thus made its way to the great laver in the infirmary cloister where the monks performed their ablutions. Other pipes led it through to lavers in front of the refectory and thence it was led underground to the great fishpond, to the various offices in the monastery, and the waste ended up in the great sewer.

Another early and ambitious conduit was built before 1166 to provide the cathedral close at Lichfield with a water supply.[41] The source of water was at a place called Pipe (which means 'water pipe', or 'water course'), 2.3 km to the west of Lichfield. The conduit head still stands in Pipe Park: it is cut into steeply sloping land and is a gabled building with a roof of huge corbelled stones supported internally by a fine pointed arch. It is thirteenth century in date. There were no settling tanks along the line of the pipe, but there were a number of outlets sited where the pipe ran close to a stream making a convenient place for the water to escape when repairs were needed. The supply to the close, despite occasional shortages due to leaks, worked well for 800 years until it was discontinued in 1969.

At Mount Grace Priory, a Carthusian community sited in remote North Yorkshire, there was an efficient and ingenious system.[42] Here there was a spring on the hillside to the east of the priory, which was enclosed in a small rectangular building of fine ashlar with a gabled roof of stone and an arched opening in its west wall. A stone-built aqueduct led from it carrying the fresh water supply to the charterhouse. It led to cell No 4 and then crossed the great cloister diagonally to the site of a distributing conduit. From there drains led the surplus water to fishponds to the west of the charterhouse. The water for flushing the drains was drawn from a separate spring further north.

Royal castles also had efficient systems of water supply. The engineer Maurice, who built the keeps at Dover and Newcastle for Henry II, apparently understood how to distribute water from the central source, the castle well.[43] At Dover natural springs flow out of chalk cliffs into the sea at the mean tide level, 122 m below the foot of the castle. The well in an angle turret in the keep taps this water. Details of the circulation system were found in 1931 and included double lead pipes laid in a conduit for protection. These were 8.9 cm in diameter which provided water to various mural chambers below the level of the well-head. At Newcastle, completed in 1177, there is a well 30.2 m deep connected to a bowl and lead pipe which carried water to the rooms below. Some found its way to a tank over the outer stairs whence it supplied the kitchens and the ground-floor chamber.

Towards the end of the Middle Ages there was a greater understanding of the mechanics of water evidenced by frequent changes in drainage systems in some of the greater houses. At the Manor of the More, Rickmansworth (Herts.), the fourth period house (1426+) had a water supply from a source on the hillside.[44] The water was carried in a wooden pipe from the gateway and across the moat. A brick and tile conduit replaced this, carrying the water now in lead pipes, the plumbers 'forcing of the pipes across the moat'. Trenches remain for the lead pipes which converged on what must have been the conduit head in the courtyard. These works may well have been carried out by George Neville, Archbishop of York (1465-76).

It is hardly surprising that the most impressive remains of a medieval conduit system should have come from a royal palace near the capital (Figure 8.5). The Palace of Westminster was supplied with fresh water by a system of leaden pipes and cisterns; the source may have been in the area of Hyde Park.[45] The first mention of a conduit occurs in 1169-70 and by this means water was conveyed to a 'lavatory in the king's hall'. A new lavatory or washbasin was made in 1287-8, incorporating marble columns, and the water issued from five heads of gilded copper. Constant repairs were required and in 1347-8 the whole water system in the palace was overhauled.

The first mention of a conduit head in New Palace Yard is recorded in 1399 when it was refurbished for Henry IV's coronation. The construction of an underground car park below the yard on the north side of Westminster Hall revealed the foundations of a Great Conduit. Examination showed it to be octagonal and it lay on the axis of Westminster Hall midway between the hall and the clock tower on the north side of the yard. The fifteenth-century foundation measured 8 m across; there were inlet and outlet channels lined in stone and brick and a central basin of Reigate stone. The foundations straddled an earlier stone culvert and fragmentary remains of a superb polished Purbeck marble basin dating from the twelfth century were found. This was originally a central basin of twelve lobes richly decorated set within and above an encircling balustrade. Between the basin and balustrade water flowed in a trough and out through

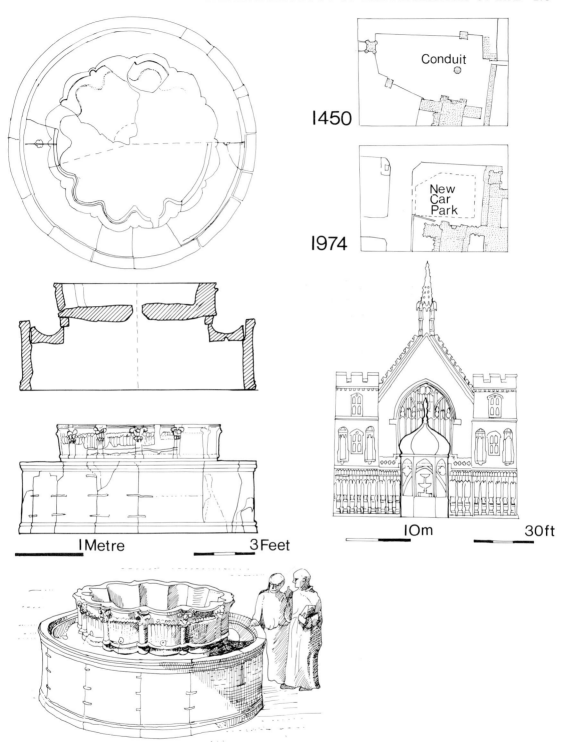

Figure 8.5: New Palace Yard, Westminster: Twelfth-century Fountain and Fifteenth-century Conduit (after Davison, 1974)

outlets in the sides. This basin had been used as hard-core for the fifteenth century rebuilt conduit head which itself was an impressive element in a piece of medieval formal planning.

9. Wine

The Romans made valiant, if largely unsuccessful, attempts to grow vines in the province of Britain. In excavations as long ago as 1851 it seems that vine plants were found near the villa at Boxmoor (Herts.).[46] Grape pips came from Roman sites at Southwark and Silchester but these may have been imported fruit or raisins. Such uncertain local vintages can only have been in the nature of a supplement to the major imports of Spanish wine. Subsequently, large quantities were brought into Roman Britain from Bordeaux and the Moselle valley. This wine trade did not cease immediately with the Anglo-Saxon migrations. Celtic Britain still went on importing its wine, oil and dried fruit in containers (known as class B amphorae) in the fifth and sixth centuries.[47] There was of course a demand for communion wine from the newly converted English. Bede states that there were vineyards 'in some places', but it is probable that these remained few until the climate began to warm up in the eighth and ninth centuries. By 1100-1200 the climate was more like that of northern France today with summer temperatures generally about 1°C higher than now (see p. 174). Domesday Book records the existence of 55 vineyards of all sizes in England.

Vitis vinifera, the oldest cultivated species of vine, descended from the wild wood vine (*Vitis silvestris*), needs a long maturation period to produce good grapes. It is evident that the Norman abbots provided a great boost to viticulture. Monasteries were stable societies in which vines flourished. William of Malmesbury in the twelfth century describes the Vale of Gloucester as the principal wine-growing district in England. Here in Gloucestershire, Worcestershire and Herefordshire were light clay and sandy soils, south facing slopes and warm summers, and vines grew well. The sites of monastic vineyards at Tewkesbury, Hereford and Ledbury were all located a few

decades ago. 'A waterlogged pit at Gloucester containing the skins and pips of grapes . . . evidently the refuse from wine pressing has now been recognised to be medieval in date'.[48] There are also ample records for the cultivation of the vine from the Archbishop of Canterbury's vineyards at Teynsham and Northfleet in Kent from the twelfth century[49] and from the Fenland monasteries of Ramsey and Thorney. The quantities of wine consumed in some monasteries was heroic. The *Caritas*★ at Battle Abbey of a gallon of wine per monk per week seems to have been comparatively moderate.[50] It is probable, however, that the more usual end-product of English vineyards was verjuice, the much prized grape vinegar, frequently used in cooking. Wine was only produced in a few regions and in good years by people unable to afford French wine.

Wine in the late Saxon and early Norman period was the common drink in great secular households as well as religious establishments. It was bought by kings, bishops and the middle and upper ranks of society, being transported across the Channel and the North Sea from the Seine basin, from Burgundy and the Rhineland. The large wine vessel, or cask, called the tun, became a unit used in measuring the carrying capacity of a ship. This trade in wine, ill documented in the early medieval period, is confirmed by archaeology.[51] Pottery vessels, of continental origin, thought to have been used as wine-jugs, provide information about the marketing areas. Sherds of the Pingsdorf ware of the Rhineland have been found in parts of the south coast as far west as Southampton and along the east coast as far north as York. With the Norman Conquest the pattern of trade tended to shift down Channel and Norman wine came across with the invaders. This was associated with distinctive red painted jugs from Normandy and Rouen which are found in profusion in ports and other parts of southern England.

The collapse of English power in Normandy in John's reign led to a major change in the shape of the wine trade. The Gascon wines had captured the English market by the early

★The allowance of food to be eaten in a monastery.

thirteenth century. The trade is documented in great detail.[52] Royal, great noble and religious households often bought their wine overseas, shipping it themselves, and thus avoiding paying customs duties if it was not for resale. Others acquired their wine from merchants at ports of entry. London, Hull, Southampton and Bristol were all major distribution centres. We find, for instance, the royal butler in the fourteenth century buying in bulk at Hull and distributing the wine throughout a wide range of royal manors, castles and religious houses by means of a network of waterways radiating from the Humber. In Bristol the wine was shipped to the port and stored in the cellars of the city burgesses and in those of the Gascon traders who frequented the port. At Southampton, similarly, royal officers would visit the cellars of the wine merchants and select the best wines in anticipation of royal visits to Winchester, Salisbury, Oxford or Odiham. The retail distribution was primarily the work of taverners who sold wine in a common tavern by the gallon, pottle, quart or pint. There were 354 taverns in London as early as 1309. Such taverners were subject to many regulations: small transactions, for instance, had to be open and public and no cloth might be hung before the cellar door to prevent the consumer seeing the wine drawn from the cask.

The tangible evidence for the medieval wine trade is both structural and artifactual. Merchants' houses were adapted for storing the bulky wine casks. Masonry undercrofts are found in merchants' houses at Southampton: here they are mostly barrel-vaulted.[53] At Winchelsea, where access into some houses was from steps leading down from the street, ribbed vaults were common, while at Chester the usual form was the quadripartite groined vault. Doubtless timber accessories were added such as those required in 1236 for constructing a gantry and making slides for unloading barrels of royal wine at Windsor.

Parts of an actual medieval wine barrel were found in a Norman pit at Pevensey Castle.[54] The capacity was 8.27 gallons or 37.6 litres. A cask of this capacity and its contents would have weighed about 41-45 kg and could have been carried on a man's shoulder. The Bayeux Tapestry shows one being loaded in this way

by a man provisioning William's fleet.

The wine trade carried to Britain considerable quantities of the pottery of the Saintonge region (near Bordeaux).[55] This ware is extremely distinctive; fine and white, smooth to the touch. The jugs moreover have marked characteristics; large bridge spouts, plain strap handles and flat bases. The polychrome ware with its delicate green and yellow painted decorations and scrolls, birds and shields, outlined in dark brown or black and covered with clear glaze, is the finest class of pottery. It can, moreover, be dated with unusual accuracy since it has been found in some of Edward I's castle sites which gives it a date-range of c. 1280-1310. Geographically the distribution of the ware is widespread. It has been found at the large ports of southern England such as London, Stonar, Southampton and Bristol. It has also come from towns, castles and ecclesiastical sites, emphasising that here were the heavy consumers of French wine. The occurrences in Wales, Scotland and Ireland demonstrate the far flung extent of the Gascon wine trade.

It has been claimed that the success of the Gascon vineyards spelt doom for the home production of wine in England.[56] It is true that there are many references to the decay of English viticulture in the thirteenth and fourteenth centuries – to land 'where vines once grew'. The real reason, however, is the unfavourable climatic conditions which developed in the fourteenth century.[57] Vines require freedom from late spring frosts especially during and after flowering. They also demand sunshine and warmth in summer, not too much rain, warmth and sunshine during the autumn to raise the sugar content, and a dormant winter season in which frosts are seldom seen. Unfortunately, only rarely were these conditions satisfied in the Later Middle Ages; consequently producers could seldom hope for the ripening of grapes to full maturity.

10. Clothing and Shoes

It is significant that most studies of medieval garments have appeared in histories of 'costume' rather than of 'clothing'. Our knowledge is biased heavily in favour of costumes worn by the upper classes since it is mainly based on literature, funeral brasses, memorial effigies, stained glass and illuminated manuscripts. The few garments which have survived relatively intact from the Middle Ages are again likely to be ceremonial robes worn by rulers, or vestments, treasured by churches through the ages.[58] For ordinary clothing of the working people we have again had to rely on the generalised and frequently idealised versions of manuscript drawings. In this field it might be hoped that archaeology could furnish fresh evidence.

Unfortunately, there are several reasons why this remains an unsatisfactory situation. The conversion to Christianity led to the practice of burying bodies without grave goods so that the chief place where we might expect to look for preserved clothing, the damp grave areas, yield only skeletons, accompanied by shrouds or the occasional hair shirt.[59] A few pins is not much from which to reconstruct the costume of a vanished society. A second reason why there is a paucity of information is that people used and reused their clothing in medieval times, inheriting pieces of earlier cloth and leather to refashion and pass on to their children. 'A dress was a major investment to be handed down from mother to daughter to servant and to be retrimmed through the years and as it passed from person to person'.[60] Very little was lost, only buttons, belt buckles, hooks and eyes, and other such unreliable fastenings which gave way as they do today. The principal reason for the scarcity of evidence, however, is that textile almost invariably decomposes away. Occasionally tiny fragments are preserved in contact with bronze such as on the backs of brooches. But in general we are left only with small pieces of cloth buried with coin hoards or tailors' offcuts dropped into wells, cesspits and latrines.

Such remains are unpromising for the information they give about garments but they tell us a lot about cloth. A medieval barrel-latrine at Worcester produced several cloth remains.[61] Some of the fibres were extremely deteriorated, having almost no strength or substance and were inseparable from their muddy support. An examination of them showed that they were all of wool and their colours ranged from a rich dark brown, medium and reddish brown, to blue with some white fibres. None had selvedges or starting borders and one sample seemed to have been napped. The cloth in this latrine was not the result of casual rubbish dumping but rather because it filled the role of lavatory paper or it may have been used for feminine hygiene.

These discoloured fragments of textiles from excavations require very careful handling if they are to be made to yield interesting data. The cloth pieces found in the tomb at the London Charterhouse Chapel, which was thought to be that of Sir Walter de Manny, the founder (d. 1372), were cleaned by washing out the mud in several changes of warm saponin water, allowing them to dry and then scratching them carefully with a razor blade to reveal details of weaving.[62] Such treatment showed that two different fabrics were represented. Most of the material related to the cerecloth, a plain tabby★ woven textile, and the remaining fabric formed a braid with brown and blue warps, a brown weft, the material being a coarse linen made of flax.

Work on medieval textiles indicates the very considerable variety in quality of cloths produced by the weavers. The famous cloth known as *haberget*, which was a speciality of Stamford in the thirteenth century, was a double-width cloth woven in pieces up to 30 m long.[63] It was used for ordinary lay clothing of the period for tunics, super tunics and cloaks, sometimes for complete suits or 'robes' and the demand came from all classes from royalty downwards. It was made in different colours, green (*virid'*), peacock (*de pounaz*), dark brown (*in burneto*), and in grain (*in grein* or scarlet) and was sold in different qualities. It could be obtained for almost the lowest price any cloth sold at, while the top quality *habergets* were put into the luxury class. Carus-Wilson plausibly argues that it took its curious name from the fact that it looked like *hauberks* which are represented in art with a diamond pattern of crisscross lines. She illustrates a number of pieces of cloth which have a

★A general term for silk taffeta – originally striped – but afterwards applied to silks of a uniform colour.

'broken diamond' or 'broken lozenge twill'.[64] Her conclusions are that these diamond twills were all made of unfulled worsted yarn and all have a prominent diamond pattern which is not obliterated by shrinking and felting.

Habergets die out in the thirteenth century and it has been suggested that this was connected with the replacement of the warp-weighted vertical loom by the horizontal treadle loom. This had important repercussions on the nature of the cloth produced. Finishing techniques such as fulling, raising and shearing now became all important; they combined to obliterate the pattern of the weave in the cloths which became notable for their soft 'handle' and smooth, almost silky, finish. These processes set up similar developments in the spinning side of the industry: the weft could be more loosely spun for this type of cloth and as a result the spinning wheel came to be used for it. The warp for greater strength still continued to be spun on the distaff. The effect of this on clothing was that cloth became more efficient in keeping people warm; less layers were needed despite the climatic deterioration of the Later Middle Ages.

Recent textile finds at Southampton, Lincoln and York included fragments of exotic imports from the east. They illustrate the extravagance of costume sported by the burgher class of these prosperous northern and southern ports and trading centres as well as their long-range trading contracts.[65] Among the fragments from Southampton was a piece of weft-face compound silk twill, in poor condition, hardly showing the colours it once had, since it had faded to a uniform golden tan; infra-red photography suggested stems or leaf veins of a formal floral design. It has been identified with the samite worn by the nobility in the early medieval period, with a possibly

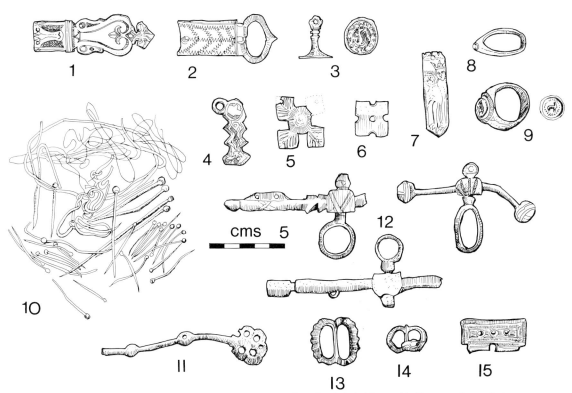

Figure 8.6: Bronze Objects from Museum of Oxford. 1. Belt chape. 2. Strap end and buckle. 3. Personal seal. 4-6. Belt mounts. 7. Strap end with devotional scene inscribed. 8-9. Rings. 10. Bronze wire and pins. 11. Bronze mount. 12. Purse frames. 13-14. Double buckles. 15. Belt fitting

Byzantine origin. Also from Southampton there was a piece of silk with a tabby weave which is similar to the silk used for the turquoise blue facing of a Christian bishop's travelling cloak buried in 1372 at Qast Ibrim in Nubia. It was possibly dyed with madder and weld.

Another archaeological approach to a reconstruction of medieval clothing is by way of personal fittings, the tiny pieces of bronze, iron and bone. These remain rather like the numbers in a child's puzzle, connected by dotted lines from which we are expected to draw the remaining costume. This can only be done with the help of the documentary and pictorial evidence.

Buckles and strap fittings are among the commonest finds on medieval excavations (Figure 8.6);[66] they may come from men's belts or women's girdles, hose suspenders, shoes, armour, spurs or horse harness. Buckle frames are most frequently made of cast bronze while the pin may be cast or cut from sheet or wire. The buckle is attached to the end of the strap by means of a buckle-plate. The other end of the strap is often protected by a strap-end or pendant. They fit into a fairly consistent typology. Earlier ones of the thirteenth century have heavily moulded frames and often decorated plates, sometimes with large heads to the rivets. Lyre-shaped buckles and strap-ends date from the fourteenth century. Another characteristic type is double-hooped, usually of circular or rectangular form or figure-of-eight shaped. One fascinating feature emerged from a study of the dozens of bronze dress fittings found at the deserted village of Lyveden (Northants.).[67] Many of them had obviously been repaired again and again. Belt buckles had been provided with new plates which had been in their turn derived from other articles. Fittings in fact, like garments, were probably handed down and such providence may reflect a very poor rural society: a contemporary parallel is the use put to petrol tins as building materials in African villages.

Clothing was held together in the late medieval period by brooches, by lacing, ornamental ribbons and points tied onto the costume. The archaeological evidence for this takes the form of numerous cylindrical lace or tag-ends of rolled sheet bronze similar to those still used in shoes. Sometimes they retain the end of the ribbon cord or leather thong. The fifteenth century chamberlain was advised when dressing his lord:

> Then drawe on his sokkis and hosyn by the fure
> his shon faced or bokelid draw them on sure
> strike his hosyn upwarde his legge ye endure
> then trusse them up strayte to his pleasure
> then lace his dublett every hoole.

These points were also used to fasten stockings. A silken garment used in Chaucer's time was known as the *paltok*,★ and striped hose made in two parts and bound to the *paltoks* with laces called harlottes, was considered an indecent fashion.[68]

Dress fittings by and large had a mainly functional use; they held garments together. The wearing of jewellery on the other hand had more complicated motives (Figure 8.7).[69] It might be simply to show off acquired wealth. An aesthetic admiration for the craftsmanship of the goldsmith or silversmith was sometimes mixed with superstition because jewellery was thought to give amuletic protection. Other people wore jewels as badges to show where their political loyalties or amorous devotions lay. There were jewels designed to express love, betrothal and mourning. The find spots of hoards of medieval jewellery such as the Thame hoard (Oxon.) or the Fishpool hoard (Notts.) suggest that jewellery was considered to be a convenient method of storing wealth, something easily carried and hidden. Occasionally jewels were kept simply because they had been owned by someone famous: an example is the magnificent founder's jewel of William of Wykeham which is in the Treasury at New College, Oxford. The conversion to Christianity meant that people were not buried with grave goods after the seventh century but exceptions were the finger rings (with which bishops, archbishops and abbots had been consecrated in the heyday of their power) and crosiers which were interred

★A short coat or sleeved doublet.

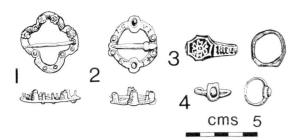

Figure 8.7: Jewellery. 1-2 Ring brooches with multiple stones in high settings. 3. Finger ring with inscription, fifteenth century, from Dorchester Museum. 4. Bronze finger ring with glass bezel from Lyveden, Northants

with their dead owners.

The materials used in medieval jewellery included gold, silver, bronze, pewter and tin. Gemstones included diamonds which appear in Western Europe from the fourteenth century onwards. Rubies are more commonly used, most being cabochons, with rounded tops and flat bottoms and did not need to be cut. Sapphires were attributed with magical powers and were often set in churchmen's rings. The types of jewel which have most frequently survived are finger-rings and brooches. Bishops' rings had to be of pure gold and set with gems which had not been engraved.[70] They were blessed by the Pope and acquired the name 'pontifical'. They were worn on the fourth finger of the right hand and were exceptionally large in size being worn over the glove. A splendid ring which had a large central stone surrounded by a series of spokes, each with a gem, was found in Archbishop Walter de Grey's tomb at York Minster.[71] At the other end of the spectrum were the two bronze rings, probably lost by peasants, found at the deserted settlement at Lyveden (Northants.);[72] one, from a well-filling, had a setting for a blue glass stone. We can tell how finger-rings and other jewellery were worn by studying the hands, necks and waists sculptured on alabaster effigies; paintings like the Wilton Diptych are also guides to fashions in royal jewellery.

Rings were largely symbolic in function, brooches, on the other hand, began in the eleventh and twelfth centuries to be worn with the practical reason to hold garments like heavy cloaks, tunics and kirtles together. Only later did they develop largely as display goods.

The design of early medieval examples continued the Anglo-Saxon disc brooch tradition. Ring brooches became more popular in the thirteenth century. They were simple circular shapes of cast metal with a swivelling pin and were held in place by the pull of the material through which they were pushed. More elaborate brooches had ornamental bosses cast with the ring or soldered onto it with settings for paste or enamel. One such was found at Sydling St Thomas in Dorset and is now in the Dorchester Museum. What is perhaps the finest medieval brooch, the Dunstable swan jewel, of gold and white enamel may have been used as a superior kind of livery badge and was lost *c.* 1460 at the time of the collapse of the Lancastrian dynasty.[73] Similarly the exquisite heart-shaped gold brooch with bands of white and blue enamel from the Fishpool, Nottinghamshire hoard may be a Lancastrian livery badge.[74]

Purses were metal-framed in the Later Middle Ages. They consisted of one or two bags of fabric or leather slung between a rigid bar and hinged hoops (Figure 8.6). A swivel loop enabled the purse to be suspended from the belt. Belts were also at times decorated with small bells. These were also attached to the collars of pet dogs and hawks.

It must be confessed that all these are mere scraps and, in sum, archaeology has not so far produced a body of evidence about medieval clothing as fruitful as that provided by contemporary illuminated MSS. The opposite is true when we consider footwear (Figure 8.9). The saintly and regal personages portrayed in early medieval manuscript drawings are represented (perhaps rather unrealistically) as barefoot, or dressed in flowing robes covering all but the tip of the foot. Excavations have been much more informative. Good collections of Anglo-Scandinavian footwear have come from York.[75] The leather has been well-preserved because it has been waterlogged and in a number of cases complete shoes have been recovered. 'Typical shoes are made on the turnshoe principle with whole-cut (one piece) uppers, side-seamed at the instep and blind-stitched to a single-thickness sole: some have triangular reinforcings at the heel.' They were apparently simply slipped over the foot and did not need fastenings. Ankle boots were also

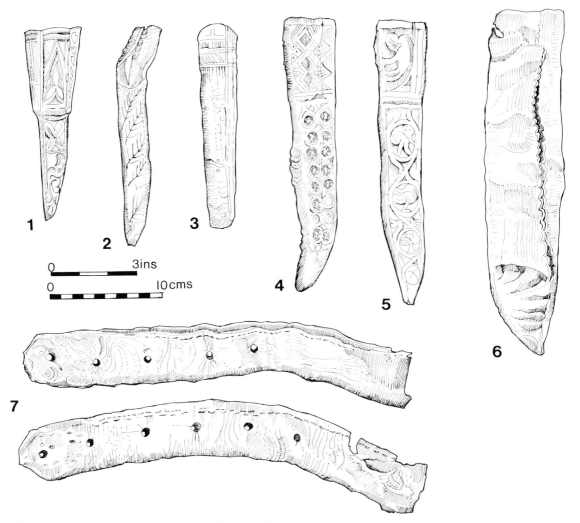

Figure 8.8: Leather Sheaths and Belts from Museum of Oxford. 1,2,3. Decorated knife sheaths. 4,5,6. Dagger sheaths. 7. Leather belt

worn; they were made with whole-uppers and instep seams and had a flap which was fastened over the instep by means of a toggle and loop. The sole was blind-stitched to the upper; the heel arrangement involved the sole being extended to a point instead of it following the outline of the foot at the heel. The stitching used was usually animal fibre (perhaps wool) or leather thonging.

Footwear was doubtless more variegated than has so far been suggested. In medieval levels at Amsterdam, house shoes, mules, clogs and boots have all been found[76] and they are mirrored in contemporary English illustra-

tions. Shoes recovered in later medieval excavations indicate that the extreme fashions illustrated in manuscripts were certainly not figments of the scribes' imagination. Southampton, for instance, has provided a number of thirteenth-century shoe soles which became increasingly pointed in design. Shoe fashions appear to have crossed national frontiers. A fine series of long, narrow soles with pointed toes, dating to the fourteenth century, has been recovered from Threave Castle, Galloway.[77] Similar examples were cited from Oakham Castle (Rutland) and Dover Castle (Kent). The toes of such shoes were piked and

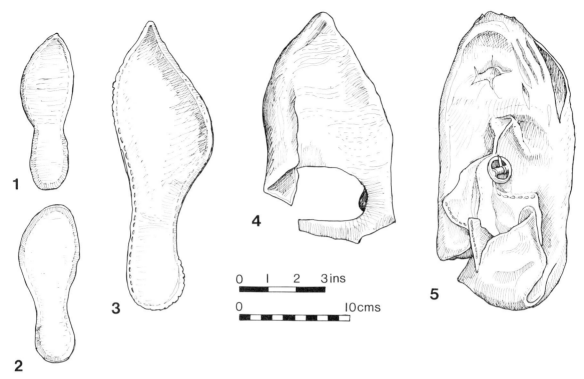

Figure 8.9: Leather Shoes from Museum of Oxford. 1-2. Children's shoe soles. 3. Pointed sole, fourteenth century. 4. Pointed upper. 5. Ankle boot with circular buckle

stuffed; when they had peaks as long as a man's finger they were called *crakowes*, and were thought to be more like demons' claws than mens' adornments. They were not, however, chained by their ends to the knees, a fabrication of a sixteenth-century chronicler. By the time of Henry VIII the toes of shoes had become blunted and the extremes of fashion dictated a bulbous profile with slashing of the tongue and upper. Archaeology confirms this as several examples in the Northampton Museum demonstrate.

We have noticed from time to time the hints of an economical use of medieval clothing. The same is true of footwear. The condition of many shoes found in excavations is extremely worn. One from the bottom of a well at the deserted settlement of Lyveden (Northants.) had the treads of the forepart and the heel worn into holes.[78] There is in fact a much greater likelihood of recovering cobbler's waste, offcuts and the weaver's throwouts than a pair of new shoes. 'Make do and mend' might well have been the motto of English medieval peasant society.

References

1. For the limiting factors of archaeological evidence see Chaplin, R.E., *The Study of Animal Bones from Archaeological Sites*, London and New York, 1971, 120–42.
2. Bourdillon, J., 'Town life and animal husbandry in the Southampton area as suggested by the excavated bones', *Proc. Hants Field Club and Archaeological Society*, 36, 1980, 181-91.
3. Hurst, D.G. and Hurst, J.G., 'Excavations at the medieval village of Wythemail', *Med. Arch.*, XIII, 1969, 201-3.
4. Ryder, M.L., 'Animal remains from Wharram Percy', *Yorkshire Arch. J.*, 46, 1974, 42-52.
5. Ryder, M.L., 'Livestock remains from four medieval sites in Yorkshire, *Agric. Hist. Rev.*, 9, 1961, 105–10.
6. Donaldson, A.M., Jones, A.K.G. and Rackham, D.J., 'A dinner in the Great Hall: Report on the contents of a fifteenth century drain', *J.B.A.A.*, CXXXIII, 1980, 86-96.
7. Kenward, H.K. *et al.*, 'The environment of Anglo-Scandinavian York' in Hall, R.A. (ed.), *Viking Age York and the North*, CBA Research Report No. 27, 1978, 65.

8. Williams, J.H., *St. Peter's Street Northampton Excavations 1973-6*, Northampton, 1979, 335-6.

9. Godwin, H., *The History of the British Flora*, Cambridge, 1975, 408-9.

10. Beresford, G., 'Three deserted medieval settlements on Dartmoor. A report on the late E. Marie Winter's excavations', *Med. Arch.*, XXIII, 1979, 143.

11. Beresford, G., 'The medieval manor of Penhallam, Cornwall', *Med. Arch.*, XVIII, 1974, 111-12.

12. Wilson, D.G., 'Plant remains from the Graveney boat and the early history of *Humulus Lupulus* L., in W. Europe', *New Phytolotist*, 1975, 75, 627-48.

13. Hilton, R.H., *The English Peasantry in the Later Middle Ages*, Oxford, 1975, 104.

14. Moorhouse, S., 'Documentary evidence for the uses of medieval pottery', *Medieval Ceramics*, 2, 1978, 3-21.

15. Hinton, D.A., *Medieval Pottery of the Oxford Region*, Ashmolean Museum, Oxford, 1973, 10.

16. Thomas, K., *Religion and the Decline of Magic*, Harmondsworth, 1982, 21-3.

17. McLean, T., *Medieval English Gardens*, London, 1981, 197.

18. White, L., *Medieval Technology & Social Change*, Oxford, 1962, 76.

19. Keil, I., 'The garden at Glastonbury Abbey 1333-41', *Somerset Arch. Soc.*, 104, 1958-61, 96-101.

20. Sass, L., *'To the King's Taste', Richard II's Book of Feasts and Recipes*, London, 1976, provides an entertaining selection of medieval recipes. I owe this reference to J. Blair.

21. Greig, J., 'The investigation of a medieval barrel-latrine from Worcester', *Journal of Arch. Science*, 8, 1981, 265-82.

22. Williams, J.T., 'Plant remains in the 15th century cloisters of the college of Vicars Choral, Hereford', *Med. Arch.*, XV, 1971, 117-18, claims to have a medieval plum stone.

23. Wilson, D. Gay, 'Plant foods and poisons from medieval Chester', *Journal of Chester Arch Soc.*, 58, 1975, 55-67.

24. Wood, M., *The English Medieval House*, London, 1965, 247-55.

25. Oswald, A., 'Excavation of a thirteenth century wooden building at Weoley Castle, Birmingham 1960-1', *Med. Arch.*, VI-VII, 1962-3, 118-20.

26. Rahtz, P.A., 'Excavations at King John's Hunting Lodge, Writtle, Essex', 1955-7, *Society for Med. Arch. Monograph Series 3*, London, 1969, 38-51.

27. At Grove Priory (Beds.), a large central oven has been found in the kitchen (1982).

28. Steane, J.M. and Bryant, G.F., 'Excavations at the deserted medieval settlement at Lyveden, Northants', *Journal 12* of Northampton Museum and Art Gallery, 12, 1975, 28-9.

29. Sass, *'To the King's Taste'*, 82-3.

30. For flesh hooks see *London Museum Medieval Catalogue*, London, 1967, 125 and for cauldrons, 201-7.

31. Moorhouse S., 'The medieval pottery' in Mayes, P. and Butler, L., *Sandal Castle Excavations 1964-73*, Wakefield, 1983, 182.

32. Sass, *'To the King's Taste'*, 80.

33. Steane and Bryant, 'Excavations at the deserted medieval settlement at Lyveden, Northants', 20.

34. Holdsworth, P., 'Saxon Southampton', *Med. Arch.*, XX, 1976, 43.

35. Platt, C. and Coleman-Smith, R., *Excavations in Medieval Southampton, 1953-69*, Leicester, 1975, i, 240, 241, 249, 267.

36. Neal, D.S., 'The Palace of King's Langley', *Med. Arch.*, XXI, 1977, 137-8.

37. Saunders, A.D., 'Lydford Castle, Devon', *Med. Arch.*, XXIV, 1980, 137-8.

38. Frere, S.S. *Britannia*, London, 1967, 244-5.

39. Stevenson, J. (ed.), *Chronicon Monasterii de Abingdon*, Rolls Series, 1858, ii, 278.

40. Willis, R., 'The architectural history of the conventual buildings of the monastery of Christchurch in Canterbury', *Arch. Cantiana*, VII, 1868, 158-83.

41. Gould, J., 'The twelfth century water-supply to Lichfield Close', *Antiqs. J.*, LVI, 1976, 73-9.

42. *Med. Arch.*, VI-VII, 1962-3, 317.

43. Macpherson, E.R., 'The Norman waterworks in the keep of Dover Castle', *Arch. Cant.*, XLIII, 1931, 167-72.

44. Biddle, M., Barfield, L. and Millard, A., 'The excavation of the Manor of the More, Rickmansworth, Hertfordshire', *Arch. J.*, CXVI, 1959, 154.

45. *Med. Arch.*, XVII, 1973, 174. I am grateful to the excavator B.K. Davison for supplying me with additional information and illustrations of this work.

46. Frere, *Britannia*, 293.

47. Thomas, C., *The Early Christian Archaeology of North Britain*, London, 1971, 24–5.

48. Hurst, H., 'Viticulture at Gloucester', *Antiq. J.*, LVIII, 1978, 162.

49. Sutcliffe, D., 'The vineyards of Northfleet and Teynham in the thirteenth century', *Arch. Cantiana*, XLVI, 1934, 140-9.

50. Knowles, Dom. D., *The Monastic Order in England*, Cambridge, 1950, 717.

51. Dunning, G.C., 'The trade in medieval pottery around the North Sea', *Rotterdam Papers*, Rotterdam, 1968, 35-58.

52. James, M.K., *Studies in the Medieval Wine Trade*,

Oxford, 1971, 176.

53. Faulkner, P.A., 'The surviving medieval buildings' in Platt, C. and Coleman-Smith, R., *Excavations in Medieval Southampton, 1953–69*, Leicester, 1975, 78–124.

54. Dunning, G.C., 'A Norman pit at Pevensey Castle and its contents', *Antiqs. J.*, XXXVIII, 1958, 205-17.

55. Dunning, 'The trade in medieval pottery', 45-7.

56. Carus Wilson, E.M., 'The effects of the acquisition and of the loss of Gascony on the English wine trade', *Bulletin of the Institute of Historical Research*, XXI, 1946-8, 145-54.

57. Lamb, H.H., 'The early medieval warm epoch and its sequel', *Palaeogeography, Palaeoclimatology, Palaeoecology*, 1965, 13-37.

58. There is an altar frontal, now in Dorchester Museum (Dorset), made up from fifteenth- and sixteenth-century vestments in eight strips, with ten figures. *Royal Commission for Historical Monuments*, Dorset, vol. II, South East, I, Plate 31; II, part 2, 403.

59. The excavation of St Budoc's Church, Oxford, which was pulled down to construct Oxford castle's eastern barbican, revealed a stone coffin inside which was a skeleton partially wrapped in a hair shirt. Attached to the shirt were the pupae of a species of carnivorous fly. Hassall, T.G., *Oxford, the City Beneath Your Feet*, Oxford Archaeological Excavations Committee, 1972, 16.

60. Prior, M., 'The accounts of Thomas West of Wallingford, a sixteenth century trader on the Thames', *Oxoniensia*, XLVI, 1981, 74.

61. Greig, 'The investigation of a medieval barrel-latrine from Worcester', 265-82.

62. Knowles, M.D. and Grimes, W.F., *Charterhouse*, London, 1954.

63. Carus-Wilson, E., 'Haberget: a medieval textile conundrum', *Med. Arch.*, XIII, 1969, 148-66.

64. MacGregor, A., *Anglo Scandinavian Finds from Lloyds Bank, Pavement and other Sites*, Council for British Archaeology, for York Archaeological

Trust 1982, 102-36, provides prolific evidence for these early medieval textiles in the north.

65. Platt and Coleman-Smith, *Excavations in Medieval Southampton* vol. 2, 334-7; and MacGregor, ibid., 132-6.

66. Goodall, A.R., 'The medieval bronze smith and his products' in Crossley, D.W. (ed.), *Medieval Industry*, CBA Research Report No. 40, London, 1981, 63–71.

67. Steane and Bryant, 'Excavations at the deserted medieval settlement at Lyveden, Northants', 107.

68. Nevinson, J.L., 'Civil costume' in Poole, A.L. (ed.), *Medieval England*, Oxford, 1958, 1, 305.

69. Hinton, D., *Medieval Jewellery*, Shire Archaeology, Princes Risborough, 1982.

70. Oman, C., *British Rings, 800-1914*, London, 1974.

71. Ramm, H.G. *et al.*, 'The tombs of Archbishops Walter de Gray and Godfrey de Ludham in York Minster', *Archaeologia*, CIII, 1971, 101-47.

72. Steane and Bryant 'Excavations at the deserted medieval settlement at Lyveden, Northants', 113.

73. Cherry, J., 'The Dunstable swan jewel', *J. Brit. Arch. Assocn.*, 1969, 38-53.

74. Cherry, J., 'Medieval jewellery from the Fishpool, Nottinghamshire, hoard', *Archaeologia*, CIV, 1973, 314.

75. MacGregor, *Anglo Scandinavian Finds*, 138-43; MacGregor, A., 'Industry and commerce' in Hall, R.A. (ed.), *Viking Age York and the North*, CBA Research Report No. 27, London, 1978, 53.

76. Baart, J. *et al.*, *Opgravingen in Amsterdam*, Amsterdam, 1977, 69-91.

77. Good, G.L. and Tabraham, C.J., 'Excavations at Threave Castle, Galloway', *Med. Arch.*, XXV, 1981, 124.

78. Steane and Bryant, 'Excavations at the deserted medieval settlement at Lyveden, Northants', 151.

INDEX

horseshoes 109, 115, 217, 219

Hoskins, W.G. 117, 149; *The Making of the English Landscape* 149

hospices 78

hospitals 96-102, 115; Ewelme 101, 102; Harbledown 96, 97; lazar house 96; Leper 96; St Bartholomews, Bristol 100, 101; St Cross, Winchester 102; St Mary Magdalene, Glastonbury 101; St Mary Magdalene, Winchester 97; St Nicholas, Salisbury 101

Hound Tor 143, 144, 186, 262; Down 186

houses 7, 11, 14, 19, 25, 40, 53, 59, 101, 128; burgess housing 207; cottages 150, 190, 211; crofts 146, 150; cruck-framed 191, 192, 193; disease caused by 179; half-timbered 211, 252; highland 186-9; Hound Tor 186-7; jettying 210, 234; laithe houses 187; London bridge 110-12; long houses 186-93, 268; lowland housing 189-90; Lyveden 191; merchant housing 132, 210, 249; peasant housing 81, 175, 185, 186, 190-3; timber framed 193; tofts 149, 190, 214, 243, 244; tower houses 61; urban houses 206-13; *see also* manor houses

Houses of Parliament 4; House of Commons 7

Hull 125, 136, 137; Blackfriarsgate 136; brick and tile making 240; fish 261; Holy Trinity Church 30, 126, 136; market place 136; Mayor of 140; Myrtongate 136; port 135, 136; wine 277

Humber, river: docks 137; lighthouse 140, 177; pottery 130; shore 126; waterway 85, 135; wine trade 277

Hundehage 27

hundreds 26, 82

hunting 11, 122, 168; horn 166; scenes 166, 167

Huntingdon Castle 40

Huntingdonshire 19, 123, 174

huntsmen 167

Hurst Castle 50

Hustings Courts 22, 23

Hutholes 186

Iceland 138, 139, 234

Icknield Way 105

Idsworth 155

Iffley Church 90

Ightham Mote 30

Ilfracombe 139-40

illness 77-8; arthritis 78, 94, 95; cures 77-9, 97; dental caries 94; diet 258; gall stones 94; leprosy 96-7; monastic care 73; piles 270; plague 130, 178-9; rickets 93; syphilis 96; tuberculosis 96; von Recklinghausen's disease 96; *see also* Black Death

illuminated manuscripts 97, 137, 156, 206, 215, 243, 278, 281, 282

industry 217-55; brick 136; centre 210; revival 208; technological change 217; war stimulates 122, 219; *see* bronze working, cloth trade, ironworking, lead working, leather-working, mines, wood turning

Inkpen Hill 27

inns 28, 115-17, 252

insects 174, 178-9, 207, 264

Ipswich 25

Ireland 139, 169, 277

iron objects: cauldrons 269; forceps 251; irons 28; ladles 270; lanterns 202; salt pans 246; screens 70; spurs 30, 109, 115, 219; staples and rings 2; stirrups 109, 115; tyres 219; weaving combs 251; X-ray photographs of 222; *see also* horse harness, horseshoes, nails, plough, tools

iron-smelting 217, 218; blast furnace 171, 218; bloomsmith 218; furnace 77, 217, 218, 243; tuyères 218; water power 171, 218

ironworking 217-23

Isle of Ely 107, 174

Isle of Man 169

Isle of Portland 154

Isle of Purbeck 232

Isle of Wight 41, 50, 139, 140, 208, 272

Isles of Scilly 214

Italy 23, 36, 77, 133, 234, 249

Itchen, river 119, 132, 208

James of St George 46

Jannings, H. 232

Jarrow 253

jewellery 280-1; bishops' rings 30, 280-1; brooches 281; Dunstable swan jewel 281; fake 3; Fishpool hoard 280-1; necklet 95; rings 95, 279-81; Thame hoard 280; wardrobe 7, 8, 11; William of Wykeham's 280

John, King of England: Beaulieu 74; burial 2; Dunwich 176; forests 163; hunting lodge 13; loss of Normandy 131, 276; siege of Rochester Castle 43; travels 105; wolves 167

John of Gaunt 48

justice 25-8; legal records 11; trial 25, 26, 27; *see also* courts

Jutland 130

Kelsale 126

Kenilworth Castle 48

Kent: Canterbury Castle 53; chimneys 199; coast 176; coastal defence 50; Courtier House 30; denns 157; Eynsford Castle 40, 48; houses 193; ironworking 217-8; Pilgrims Way 78; Romney Marsh 177; shoes 282; vineyards 276

Kersey 252

Keynsham, Thomas 264

keys 191, 221

Kidlington, Draytonsmore 157

kilns: charcoal 222; clay lining 242; corn drying 50, 186, 262; lime 229; malt 73, 263; pottery 131, 243-6; tile 240, 241

Kilsby 104

King's Langley 272

King's Lynn 25, 125, 131, 133, 263; churches: St Margaret 125, 131, 132, St Nicholas 132, 139; fishbones 262; halls 25; harbour 132; markets: Saturday market place 131, Sunday market 125, Tuesday market 132; merchant houses 202; steelyard 132

King Street 108

Kingston 111

Kingswood 77

Kinver 11

Kirk, K.P. 78

Kirk Merrington 145

Kirkstall Abbey 65, 260

kitchens: floor 202; lower class 211; merchant houses 210; monastic 73, 173; octagonal 73, 265; sites and examples: Clarendon 25, Durham 265, Glastonbury 73, 265, Lincoln, bishop's palace 18, Northolt Manor 265, Oxford, Corpus Christi College, Christchurch College, Lincoln College, Magdalen College, New College 265-7, Wells, bishop's palace 21, Weoley 48, 49, 265, Writtle 12, 13, 265

kitchen utensils: aquamanile 246, 268; brandreth 268; cauldron 269, 270; chopping block 268; cooking pots 243, 246, 270; costrel 137, 242, 246, 248, 268; curfews 246, 270; face jugs 268; flesh hooks 269; frying pan 268, 270; jars 136, 243, 246, 269; jugs 97, 115, 243, 244, 246, 270; knives 269; ladle 268, 270; peel 268; pestle and mortar 268, 270; salt cellar 268; skillet 246, 268, 269; skimmer 269, 270; spoons 269; vat 268; *see also* pottery

kitchener 261

Knight, John 261

Knights Templar 105, 170, 172, 268

knives, weapons 38, 39

markets 25, 56, 104, 122-6; castle walls 122, 123; churches 125, 126; monastery gates 123, 124; places 64, 67, 117, 122, 123, 124-6, 127, 136; rural 126; street 119
Markham Nunnery 233
Marksbury 264
Marlborough 107, 108, 124
Marlow 111
marshes: causeways 107; coastal 176-8; draining 76, 132, 170; frozen 175; Graveney 137, 263; ridge-and-furrow 153; Romney 177, 178; salt 83, 178, 246; Welsh 172; *see also* fenland
Mason, Peter 233
masons 47, 123, 227, 232; apprentice mason, Henry Jannings 232; banker mason 229; free masons 46, 229, Robert Spillesby 232; John Flauner 47; lodges 229, 232; marks 94, 230, 232; master mason, Henry Jannings 232, Robert Spillesby 232; rough masons 46, 229; setting out floors 229; work 230
Matilda Empress 2
Maud, Queen 96
Maurice, royal engineer 274
Maxey 149
mayors 4, 22, 23, 76
meadow: common 158; land 159; water 64
Meare 191, 192
meat 65, 73, 167, 169, 192, 258-61, 263-4, 268, 269
Meaux Abbey 76, 135, 137
medicine 97; *see also* herbs
Medina, river 50
Mediterranean 139, 170
Medway 32, 113, 218
Melbury Sampford Church 31
Mells 264
Melton Mowbray 26
Menai Straits 45
Mendips 47, 223, 237
merchants: Caynges, William 203; clothiers 252; companies 22; German 130, 132, 225; houses 202, 203, 210; Le Fleming, Walter 210; spice 270; Spring, Thomas 253; wine 277; wool 249
Mercia 35, 119, 126
mercury 3, 72
Mersey Estuary 47, 65
Merthyrgeryn Grange 76
Middlesex 195, 203
Middleton 146, 147
Middleton Stoney 82
Midwinters, woollen traders 249
Mileham 40
mills, water 67, 76, 122, 169-70, 175; fulling 76, 169, 171, 251; laundering 171; operating bellows 171,

218; pond 67, 169; rats 179; sawing 171; stones 25, 169, 170; tanning 171; tidal 170; wheel 76, 218
Milton Keynes 152
Minepit Wood 218
mines: iron ore 77, 217, open cast 218; lead 223, 224; silver-lead 223; tin 224
Minster Lovell 203
Minter, Mrs 186
mints 8, 11
miracles 77, 78, 97
moats 58-61; Bishop's Waltham 16; bridges 48; drainage 175; enclosures 168; preserving timber 47; Wells 19, 21, 68; Weoley Castle 49-50; Westminster 7
molluscs 260
monasteries: Aberconwy 65, 76; alien 122; Basingwerk 76; Bristol 77; Canterbury 63, 71, 100; Christchurch 100; Hadstock 91; Kingswood 77; Malmesbury 77; Picardy 139; Rochester 63; Stanlaw 65; Strata Florida 76; Vale Royal 74; Valle Crucis 65; Worcester 63; *see also* priories
monastic buildings and life: accommodation 22, 72; chapter house 8, 66, 71-2, 78, 181, 221; church 64, 68-71; construction 90; diet 260; dormitories 66, 70-1, 78, 97, 100; finance 73-4, 76, 107; fishponds 65, 171; granges 65, 67, 76-7, 107, 217; infirmary 66, 72-3, 100; kitchens 13, 73, 173; lavatory 72; markets by gates 123-4; outer court 67-8; refectory 71, 72, 73; rere-dorter 65, 71-2; ruins 81; seals 32; slype 72; surveys 161; warming house 72; water supply; *see also* cloisters
Moneyers 122
monkey 133
Monkwearmouth 253
Monmouth 112
Monmouthshire 43
Montacute William 26
Montfichet Castle 8
Montgomery Castle 38
Montgomeryshire 154
Moor Grange 65, 76
moors 143, 172, 186; Dartmoor 186; North Yorkshire 146
moots 26
morningstar 96
Moulton Park 168
Mount Grace Priory 101, 214, 274

nails 109, 217; coffin 70, 95; door 222; types 221
Nassaborough 26
Neath Abbey 76, 176
Neath, river 76

needles 50
Nene, river 74, 105, 107, 212, 226
Netley Abbey 72, 74, 199
Netley Castle 50
Nether Alderley 169
Netheravon Church 90
Nether Chalford 150
Netherlands 25, 203
Netherne Wood 218
Nettlebed 108, 162
Newark 107
Newark Castle 19
Newbridge 112
Newcastle 56, 70, 107, 274
Newcastle-under-Lyne 107
Newcastle-upon-Tyne 157
New Forest 11, 163
Newmarket 78
New Shoreham 138
niello 225
Norden, J. 122, 172
Norfolk: Broads 172-4; castles 40-2, 227; churches 83; clothier 253; coast 176, 178; fens 157, 178; masons 227; villages 143, 145, 149
Normandy 36, 131, 133, 253, 276
Northampton 104, 107, 110, 122, 131; Castle 40, 212; churches: All Saints 125, 212, Greyfriars 224, St Peters 228; fair 179; fish bones 261-2; houses 212, timber housing 208; market 125, 212; museum 39, 221, 283; palace 234; streets: Gold Street 212, Horsemarket 212, Horseshoe Street 212, Marefair Street 212, Mayorhold 212, St Peters Street 212, 228, 248, 262, 264
Northamptonshire: alabaster carving 233; castles 35, 36, 41; cattle 260; charcoal burning 222; churches 90, 237; clothing 280; Eleanor crosses 108; field walking 155; fish ponds 172; gardens 213; hundred meeting places 26; ironwork 222; jewellery 281; long house 189; markets 124; ovens 268; parks 168-9; potteries 115, 243-5; quarries 199; roads 104, 109, 151; shoes 283; spires 227; stone 226; tilery 240; uplands 145; villages 143, 147; water 270, 271; windmills 170
Northfleet 276
Northleach 88, 158, 249
North Leigh 145
Northolt Manor House 203, 265
North Sea: fishing 247, 261; land lost 175; shipping 138-9; storms 137, 177; trade 130, 132, 276
Northumberland 46, 143, 174, 224
Norton Priory 65, 70
Norway 138
Norwich 56, 78, 159; Cathedral 63,